ALASTAIR SAWDAY'S
SPECIAL PLACES

PUBS & INNS
OF ENGLAND & WALES

Design: Caroline King

Maps & Mapping: Bartholomew Mapping, a division of HarperCollins, Glasgow

Printing: Pims, Somerset, UK

US Distribution: The Globe Pequot Press, Guilford, Connecticut

Published in 2004

Alastair Sawday Publishing Co. Ltd
The Home Farm Stables, Barrow Gurney, Bristol BS48 3RW
Tel: +44 (0)1275 464891 Fax: +44 (0)1275 464887
E-mail: info@specialplacestostay.com Web: www.specialplacestostay.com

The Globe Pequot Press
P.O. Box 480, Guilford, Connecticut 06437, USA
Tel: +1 203 458 4500 Fax: +1 203 458 4601
E-mail: info@globe-pequot.com Web: www.GlobePequot.com

First edition

ISBN 1-901970-43-4 in the UK
ISBN 0-7627-3599-6 in the US

Printed in UK

A WORD FROM ALASTAIR SAWDAY

I hardly ever go to pubs. I am awaiting this book before I get back into the habit.

My last attempt to get back into pub-going met with disaster. It was in North Devon and Cornwall and I was faced, night after night, with the sort of food and mood that shrivel the soul. I gave up.

But then – a miracle. I was dragged – twice – to a pub, a great local favourite. We were entertained by a pub-crawling group of Morris dancers; they took over the car park and I was transfixed. On my next visit there was a Big Band playing in the chaotic garden. It was dotty, unexpected, joyous. So I went back, taking as my guest a rather grand Nigerian friend who was maybe looking forward to something smarter. Offered a choice of cheese and onion rolls or onion and cheese rolls, she melted – and the locals made her feel like a queen.

Emboldened, I tried another, and so began to untangle the knot of old prejudices. It is in a small house, with few obvious signs of being a pub – except for the two blazing hearths, each in the dividing wall between rooms and thus serving both, the hop-rich local beers, the deep bowls of home-made soup and the genial chatter. Not an inch of pretension in sight. So I am converted... pubs can be as special as B&Bs and hotels. And we have found an editor, David Hancock, who seems to know every single decent pub in Britain.

We set out on the vast task of finding the most special places – for that is what we do – with our usual creative mix of prejudice, inspiration and grit. We have dug out pubs with style and great food; pubs with modest food but heaps of atmosphere; pubs with brilliant company; pubs that make you feel warm inside; pubs with fires to toast your backside after a wet walk; the engagingly odd ones, the breathtakingly inventive, the downright eccentric and pubs where you can nourish the fantasy that the world has not changed. Banished are the seamy, sticky-carpeted dives, the chained-and-themed horrors, the ear-splitting hell-holes inhabited by louts. Here are the places that have survived the grim commerce of our century. We salute them.

Alastair Sawday

ACKNOWLEDGEMENTS

Paul Crossthwaite kicked the book off with methodical research and sound advice. Toby Sawday was poised to pitch in when we met David Hancock and realised that he was 'Mr Pub' – he just knows them all. So we handed him the task and he tackled it with massive skill and a blazing commitment. This book is really 'his'. He has never flagged, never complained.

He has worked with a fine team of researchers: Elizabeth Carter, Colin Cheyne, Martin Greaves, Rebecca Harris, Alex Owen and Allen Stidwell. They have been brilliant and easy and the book owes vast amounts to them. Jo Boissevain worked her way through every word in pursuit of style and error – bless her. Our entire Production team got involved in the compilation too, under the eagle eye of Julia Richardson; Rachel Coe and Beth Thomas tirelessly chased for details and images – the latter were then tweaked to their best advantage by Paul Groom. Others have urged the beast along: Roanne Finch and Danielle Williams – in fact nobody here has been untouched by this book.

The exercise has been ably coordinated to its close by Jackie King, our Managing Editor. It was a bold decision to enter this crowded market place, but I felt we had something special to offer. Having seen the results of so much hard work I know that we were right.

Alastair Sawday

Series Editor:	Alastair Sawday
Editor:	David Hancock
Editorial Director:	Annie Shillito
Editorial:	Jackie King, Sarah Bolton, Roanne Finch, Danielle Williams
Copy Editor:	Jo Boissevain
Production:	Julia Richardson, Rachel Coe, Paul Groom, Beth Thomas
Web & IT:	Russell Wilkinson, Matt Kenefick
Sales & Marketing & PR:	Siobhan Flynn, Paula Brown, Sarah Bolton
Writing:	Jo Boissevain, Elizabeth Carter, Colin Cheyne, Paul Crossthwaite, Martin Greaves, Rebecca Harris, David Hancock, Alex Owen, Toby Sawday, Allen Stidwell
Features:	Elizabeth Carter, Rebecca Harris
Inspections:	Elizabeth Carter, Colin Cheyne, Paul Crossthwaite, Martin Greaves, Rebecca Harris, Alex Owen, Toby Sawday, Allen Stidwell

Martin Greaves - Our Man in Wales
Martin, my good friend and colleague, died suddenly on March 28th 2004. He began his pub/hotel inspecting career over 25 years ago and his knowledge of the 'pub scene' was invaluable in compiling this guide. His death is a great personal loss and a loss to those guides to which he regularly contributed. *David Hancock*

WHAT'S IN THE BOOK?

- **Introduction**
  General map
  Map pages

Pubs & Inns of England & Wales

Features:
At the sign of the four seasons - between entries 172 & 173
An evening in the life of - between entries 289 & 290
Real Ale Festival - between entries 406 & 407

- **Back of the book**
  Best for Real Ale • Best Breweries on site • Best unspoilt pubs •
  Best for Locally sourced/Organic produce • Best for Fish • Best for
  Cheese • Best Waterside pubs • Best Pubs with views • Best
  Winter pubs • Best Summer pubs

  Quick reference indices:
  50% or more of local produce used & a significant percentage
  organic • Pub & loo access for wheelchair users • Dogs welcome
  in some areas of pub • No piped music • Live music •
  Family room

  Index by pub name
  Index by town
  How to use this book
  Explanation of symbols

CONTENTS

england

CONTENTS

england

CONTENTS

wales

INTRODUCTION

What makes a Sawday pub or inn 'special'?

There are over 60,000 pubs in Britain and here are 545 of the very best in England and Wales, inspected and chosen because we liked them and think you will too.

What makes this particular collection of pubs and inns so different and special? Alastair Sawday's guides are all about individuality – we went in search of the quirky, the unusual, the hidden gems and the little-known. We looked for a genuine welcome from hands-on publicans, good local food, keen staff and individual charm and character – and the 'wow' factor that would draw you back time and again, be it for wonderful food and wine, cosy drinks beside blazing log fires or a glorious riverside garden for summer. The result is an eclectic selection of hugely individual pubs and inns that stand out from the crowd.

What is real ale?

Keg or cask ale – what's the difference? One's a living organism, the other isn't. After the brewing process, cask-conditioned green beer ('real ale') is put into barrels to allow a secondary fermentation, producing a unique flavour and bubbles that are natural. Keg beer is beer that has been filtered and sterilised and, like lager, it's dead – until the gas is pumped back to give the distinguishing bubbles. Stored in sealed containers it tastes more like bottled beers – also put through the same process. Their advantage? They have a longer shelf life, and are easier to dispense.

In the 1960s and early 1970s the big breweries flooded the market with keg beers and lager. Then, in 1971, CAMRA (The Campaign for Real Ale) was founded. Their success in inspiring the real ale revival has been a dramatic example of a consumer group in action, forcing the brewing industry to rethink its stategy and produce real ales.

The new century has seen a flowering of craft breweries across the country, with beer being brewed on farms, on industrial estates and in sheds behind pubs. The Progressive Beer Duty was introduced in 2002 to give micro-brewers a further boost; now there are over 400 independent breweries in Britain.

Gastropubs

A term born in London and growing in Lancashire. In London, basic back-street boozers are being transformed into thriving food/gastronomy pubs where restaurant-quality food is served in informal, good-looking surroundings. The ripple-effect out of the capital has been impressive.

INTRODUCTION

Changing lifestyles, drink-driving laws and high rents have seen many village locals threatened with closure as few can survive on beer sales alone. Food is the key to the survival of the country pub and the trend for young entrepreneurs and talented chefs to buy failing pubs and reinvent them as restaurant-pubs is growing.

What is modern British food?

In restaurants in the 60s and 70s, 'haute cuisine' was the thing. In the 80s it was 'nouvelle': that's haute without the cream. And pub food meant scampi in a basket.

The essence of the new British style is a freshness of approach (let the ingredients do the talking) combined with two things: the re-invention of dishes like steak and kidney pie, and the re-discovery of British produce – 'local' and 'seasonal', of course. So you have Cumbrian ham in Cumbria, fish from the nearest coast, asparagus in season and partridge from the local shoot – roasted, perhaps, with red cabbage and quince. 'Mod-Brit' may also mean a nod to the Mediterranean and oriental shores – as in tagliatelle with roasted peppers, or squid with chilli.

Country dining pubs

Passion, enthusiasm, home-cooking, locally sourced ingredients, micro-brewery ales, character, flair, individuality and attention to detail were the buzz words and phrases drummed into our inspectors. England and Wales are awash with tired country locals, all swirly carpets, traditional furnishings and laminated menus listing deep-frozen foods. Hearts would soar when we found a rustic, well-loved pub with a big welcome and a crackling fire and the landlord's personality etched into the fabric of the building. Equally, chalkboard menus promoting local seasonal produce, farm meats, village-baked bread and local brewery ale lifted the spirits and rubber-stamped the required 'wow' factor. As did glorious gardens, waterside settingsand pubs with wonderful views – perfect pubs for summer eating and drinking, in or out.

Inns and pubs with rooms

As food quality in pubs improves so does the standard of bedrooms. Our top pubs are luring foodies away from formal and expensive restaurants – and pubs that have good bedrooms have an even more winning combination. True, some are almost hotels, but a lively bar, real beer and superb bar food firmly place them in the classic 'inn' category. Others are more humble village pubs where enthusiasm to get things just right in the bar reaches upstairs into simple, but comfortable, bedrooms.

INTRODUCTION

Timeless gems

Often family-owned for generations, locked in a time-warp and hidden away in remote villages or city backstreets, these belong to Britain's diminishing breed of traditional pubs. They are often in historic or unusual buildings and the hub of the community; we have unearthed an interesting crop. Expect few frills and modern-day intrusions, but lively banter, ale tapped from the cask and, if you're lucky, soup and sandwiches – wonderful!

How we go about it

We have visited all these pubs and inns. Without a visit there can be no proper evaluation of friendliness, atmosphere, authenticity and style of food. We needed the sort of detail that cannot be gleaned over the phone or via an internet site. And we do the writing ourselves because we want a lively, vibrant book that avoids brochure-speak and tired cliché. If it's in, it's special, and the write-up should tell you if it's your sort of special. Please let us know if a place isn't what we led you to expect. Things change rapidly in the pub world, and we'd appreciate your feedback.

Most places have a half-page entry. We have chosen 48 pubs and inns for a full-page entry. Our "Best For..." choices stand out for being the best of their type. Among them there are fabulous food pubs, a rural local with owners passionate about everything organic, a city pub with great beer and atmosphere, and a seaside inn specialising in seafood, with stunning saltmarsh views and stylishly simple rooms. These places are really 'special'.

The Worth a Visit section includes those pubs that didn't make a full entry this time but are still well worth seeking out. In this section, too, you will find top-flight pubs that have recently changed hands and food pubs that we believe are on the up. For all, we would appreciate your comments and feedback.

The changing pub scene

Local food

We have already touched on the fact that rural pubs have had to change, improve and even diversify (sometimes into part-post office/shop) in order to meet social changes and the demands of today's pub-goer. Gone are the regular days of drinking in a country local; healthier lifestyles, drink-driving laws and financial constraints have rung their death knell. Pubs are now often seen as places to go to eat, with the increasing fondness for healthier eating and appreciation of the merits of local food, more and more people expect food that is fresh and vital, not tired and frozen.

INTRODUCTION

In our feature 'At the Sign of the Four Seasons' – between Gloucester and Hampshire – Elizabeth Carter explores the steadily growing trend for pub kitchens to source produce from local suppliers in the aftermath of the foot and mouth crisis and other food scares. But she asks one important question – do our current crop of young chefs and licensees understand what seasonal food really is about?

Stay at an inn

With the trend for weekending away at a country inn – or pulling off the motorway to find a friendly pub to stay in rather than a formulaic Travel Inn and neighbouring Little Chef – our second feature 'An Evening in the Life of' (between Mersyside and Norfolk) goes behind the scenes to profile one of England's top all-round inns, the Griffin at Fletching, East Sussex. Rebecca Harris takes a light-hearted look at the daily tasks involved in running this well-oiled pub.

Brilliant beer

Our final feature (between Suffolk and Surrey) describes the beer festival atmosphere at one of London's great ale pubs, the White Horse in Parsons Green. Landlord Mark Dorber is passionate about beer, not just the six wonderful brews he dispenses on handpump, but unusual Belgian Trappist beers and over 50 foreign bottled beers. His quarterly beer festivals champion regional breweries and are extremely popular.

His enthusiasm for beer has recently seen him initiate Britain's first Beer Education Trust or Beer Academy. Introductory one-day and three-day courses will be aimed at broadening people's knowledge of beer, from the history of brewing, the brewing process and beer styles of the world to learning about flavours, hops and pairing beer with food through tutored tastings.

Finding the right place for you

At the back of the book we highlight pubs that stand out for a special reason. There you'll find lists for the best:

- Pubs for real ale
- Pubs that brew their own beer
- Unspoilt pubs
- Pubs for locally-sourced/organic food
- Pubs for fish
- Pubs for cheese

INTRODUCTION

- Waterside pubs
- Pubs with views
- Winter pubs
- Summer pubs

Quick reference indices

At the back of the book we also list those pubs with:

- wheelchair facilities
- a family room
- no piped music
- live music
- a welcome for your dog
- local and/organic produce

How to use this book

Opening times

We asked owners to give the days/sessions their pub is closed. Nearly half the pubs and inns tell us they are open all day, so their entries do not have 'Closed' details. Other pubs are most usually open from noon until 2.30pm-3pm and, then, from 6pm-7pm until 11pm, but do check before setting out, especially in winter.

Meals and meal prices

We give the times meals are served and the approximate cost of main courses – in bar or restaurant – and set menus, where they exist. But, things can change, so check when booking.

Map and directions

The map pages at the front of the book show the position, with an entry number, for each of our special pubs and inns. Our maps are for guidance only; use a detailed road map or you may get lost! The map and entry numbers are given at the foot of the separate guide entries. The directions given are, again, for guidance.

Bedrooms, bathrooms and breakfasts

Unlike the other titles in our series this is not a guide to places to stay. We have given general bedroom details and, where our inspectors saw (and liked) them, mentioned the rooms in the write-ups.

If you're thinking of staying the night in a simple pub or inn do bear in mind that an early night might not be possible if folk are

INTRODUCTION

carousing below. Many bedrooms have ensuite bathrooms –
if this is important to you, check before booking. Breakfasts are
generally included in the room price; again, check. Most places
serve breakfast between 8am and 10am.

Bedroom prices

Prices are per room for two people sharing. If a price range is
given, then the lowest price is usually for the least expensive
double room in low season and the highest for the most expensive
room in high season. These may change during the year. The
single room rate (or the single occupancy of a double room)
generally follows. Occasionally, prices are for half board, i.e.
they include dinner, bed and breakfast.

Symbols

On the inside back cover we explain our symbols. Use them as
a guide, not as a statement of fact, and double-check anything
that is particularly important to you.

Real Ale Tankard The symbol identifies those pubs with a real
passion for beer. It is given to pubs serving four or more real
ales, including local micro-brewery beers.

Wine Glass As food improves in pubs so does the wine quality
and the selection of wines available by the glass. In many top
food pubs wine sales far exceed beer sales. We give this symbol
to pubs that serve eight or more wines by the glass.

Children The symbol is given to places that accept children of
any age. That doesn't necessarily mean that they can go everywhere
in the pub, or that highchairs and special menus are provided.
Nor does it mean that children should be anything less than
closely monitored! Some pubs do offer early suppers for children
staying overnight. Please call to check details such as separate
family room, toys, menus and play equipment in the garden.

Dogs The dog symbol is given to places where your dog can go
into some part of the pub – generally the bar only. It is unlikely
to include restaurant areas and many pubs don't allow dogs in
the bedrooms.

Payment All our pubs and inns take cash and cheques with a
cheque card. If they also take credit cards, we have given them
the appropriate symbol. Check that your credit card is acceptable.
Visa and MasterCard are generally fine. American Express is

INTRODUCTION

sometimes accepted; Diners Club hardly ever. Debit cards are widely accepted.

Smoking Most separate dining areas will either be smoke-free or have smoking restrictions. Most bedrooms are also non-smoking.

Wheelchair We use this symbol when those in wheelchairs can access the bar and loos.

Walking This symbol shows that the pub is in, or very close to, a popular walking area and there's a good network of footpaths in the area.

Practical matters   Bookings

Most pubs and inns will ask for a credit card number and a contact phone number when you telephone to book a room. At weekends, top gastropubs and country food pubs are often full and it is best to book a table well in advance. At other times, only tables in the dining rooms can be reserved, while tables in the bar often operate on a first come, first served basis.

Tipping

It is not obligatory but it is appreciated, particularly in pubs with restaurants.

Environment   We have a challenging environmental policy, driven by an annual environmental audit and a Green Team. We try to reduce our ecological 'footprint' by:

- Planting trees. We are officially Carbon Neutral. The emissions directly related to our office, paper production and printing of this book have been neutralised ('sequestered') through the planting of indigenous trees in Devon with Future Forests.

- Using part-recycled, or low-energy, paper for our books.

- Re-using paper, recycling stationery, tins, bottles, ink cartridges, plastic.

- Encouraging staff use of bicycles (they are loaned free) and car-sharing. We have two modest company cars, one running on LPG and the other on recycled cooking oils.

- Planning to turn our offices into a model of eco-office development.

- Switching to a green electricity supplier.

INTRODUCTION

- Banking with Triodos, the ethical bank in Bristol.
- Celebrating the use of organic, home-grown and locally-produced food through our Fine Breakfast Scheme.
- Using organic food for all our company events and meals.
- Publishing books that support, in however small a way, the rural economy and small-scale businesses.
- Setting up our own Trust to support local and other initiatives.
- Working to establish an organic standard for B&Bs with the Soil Association (preliminary meetings have taken place).
- Publishing *The Little Earth Book*, a best-selling collection of essays on environmental issues, *The Little Food Book*, a hard-hitting analysis of the food industry, and *The Little Money Book*, a stimulating new look at the way money works. See our web site www.fragile-earth.com for details.

Web site   Our web site www.specialplacestostay.com has online pages for all the places featured here and from all our other books – around 4,000 Special Places in total. There's a searchable database, a taster of the write-ups and colour photos. For more details see the back of the book.

Disclaimer   You should know that we do not check such things as fire alarms, kitchen hygiene or any other regulation with which owners of properties in this guide should comply, for that is their responsibility.

We make no claims to pure objectivity in choosing our Special Places. They are here because we like them. Our opinions and tastes are ours alone and this book is a statement of them; we hope that you will share them. We have done our utmost to get our facts right but apologise unreservedly for any mistakes that may have crept in. Feedback from you is invaluable. With your help and our own inspections we can maintain our reputation for dependability.

David Hancock

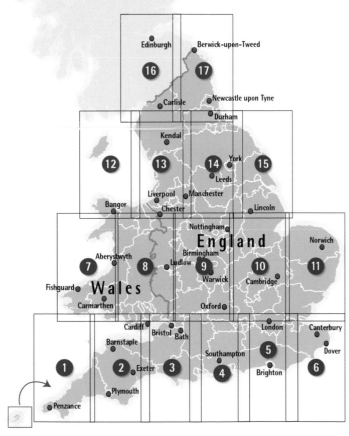

Edinburgh **16** Berwick-upon-Tweed **17**

Carlisle Newcastle upon Tyne
Durham

Kendal

12 **13** **14** York **15**
Leeds

Liverpool Manchester
Bangor Chester

Nottingham

England

Aberystwyth Birmingham Norwich
7 **8** Ludlow **9** **10** **11**
Warwick Cambridge
Fishguard **Wales**
Carmarthen Oxford

Cardiff London Canterbury
Bristol Bath Dover
Barnstaple **5**
1 **2** **3** Southampton **6**
Exeter **4** Brighton
Plymouth

Penzance

©Bartholomew Ltd, 2004

A guide to our map numbers

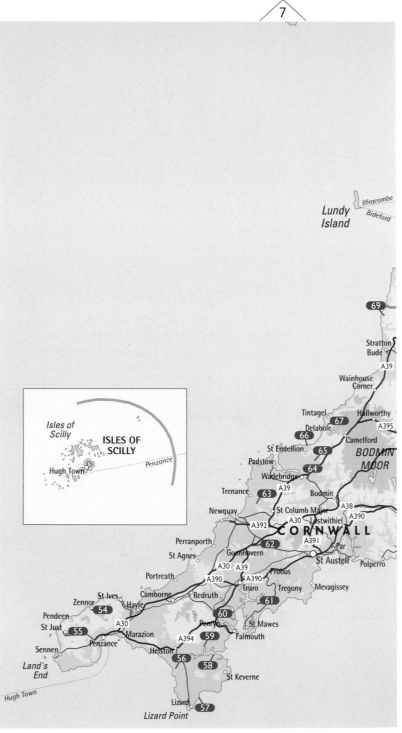

©Bartholomew Ltd, 2004

Map 1

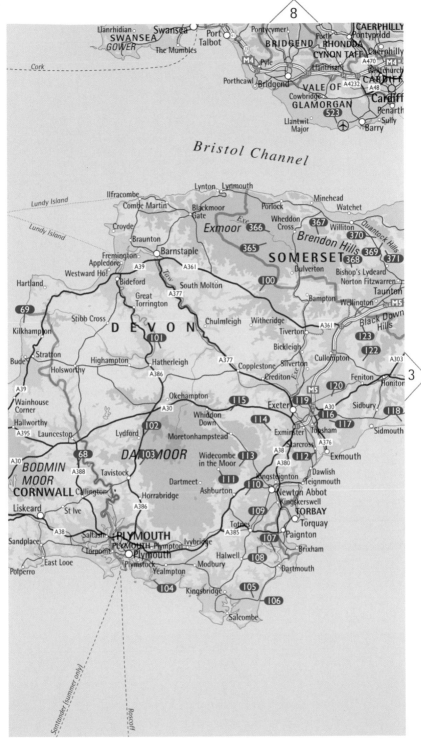

Map 2

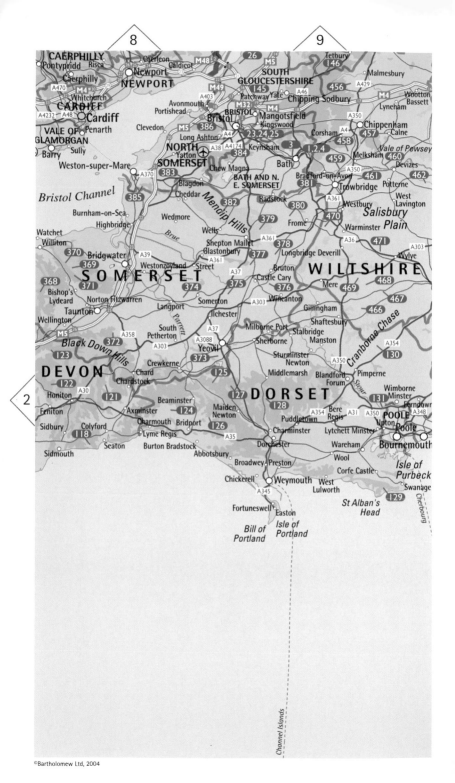

Map 3

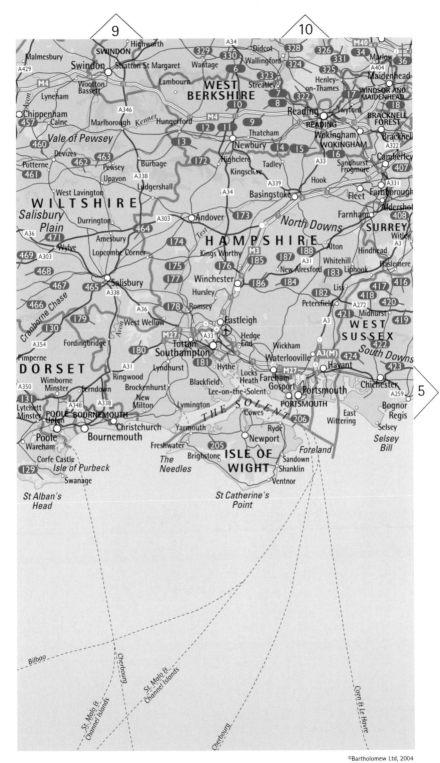

Map 4

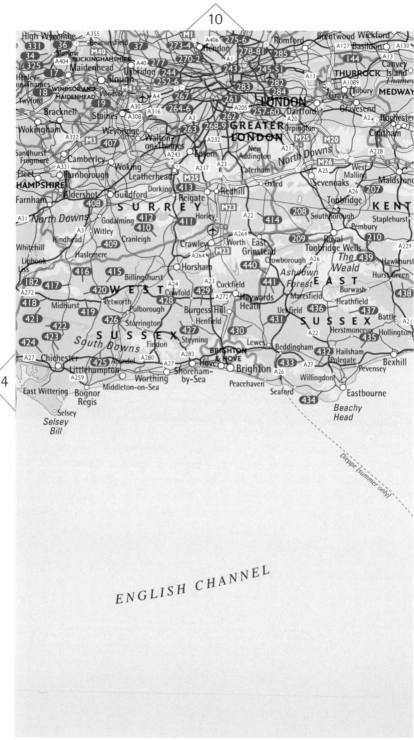

Map 5

©Bartholomew Ltd, 2004

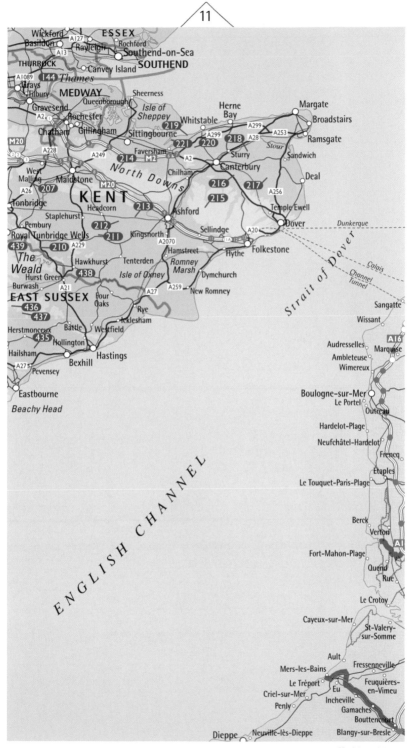

Map 6

©Bartholomew Ltd, 2004

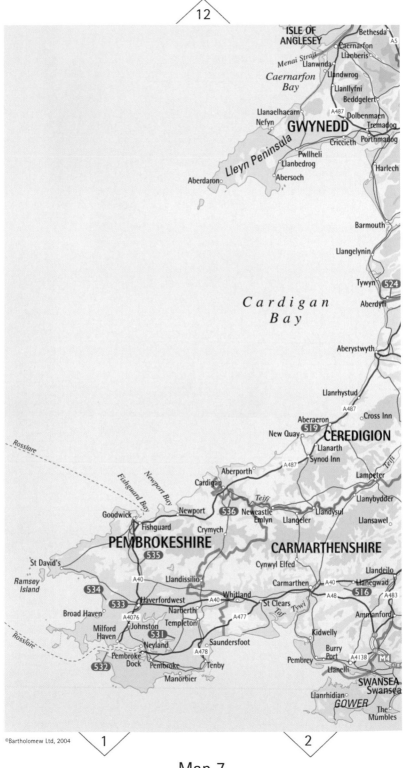

ISLE OF
ANGLESEY
Bethesda
A5
Caernarfon
Llanberis
Menai Strait
Llanwnda
Llandwrog
Caernarfon
Bay
Llanllyfni
Beddgelert
Llanaelhaearn
A487
Dolbenmaen
Nefyn
GWYNEDD
Tremadog
Criccieth
Porthmadog
Lleyn Peninsula
Pwllheli
Llanbedrog
Harlech
Aberdaron
Abersoch

Barmouth

Llangelynin

Tywyn
524

Cardigan
Bay
Aberdyfi

Aberystwyth

Llanrhystud
A487
Aberaeron
Cross Inn
Rosslare
New Quay
519
CEREDIGION
Llanarth
Synod Inn
Aberporth
A487
Lampeter
Fishguard Bay
Cardigan
Teifi
Llanybydder
Newport Bay
Newport
536
Newcastle
Llandysul
Llansawel
Goodwick
Emlyn
Llangeler
Fishguard
Crymych
PEMBROKESHIRE
CARMARTHENSHIRE
535
Cynwyl Elfed
Llandeilo
St David's
Llandissilio
Carmarthen
A40
Llanegwad
Ramsey
A40
Whitland
A48
516
Island
534
Haverfordwest
A40
St Clears
A483
533
Narberth
Taf
Twi
Ammanford
Broad Haven
Templeton
A477
A4076
Milford
Johnston
531
Kidwelly
M4
Haven
Saundersfoot
Neyland
A478
Burry
Pembrey
Pembroke
532
Port
A4138
Dock
Pembroke
Tenby
Llanelli
Rosslare
Manorbier
SWANSEA
Swansea
Llanrhidian
GOWER
The
Mumbles

©Bartholomew Ltd, 2004

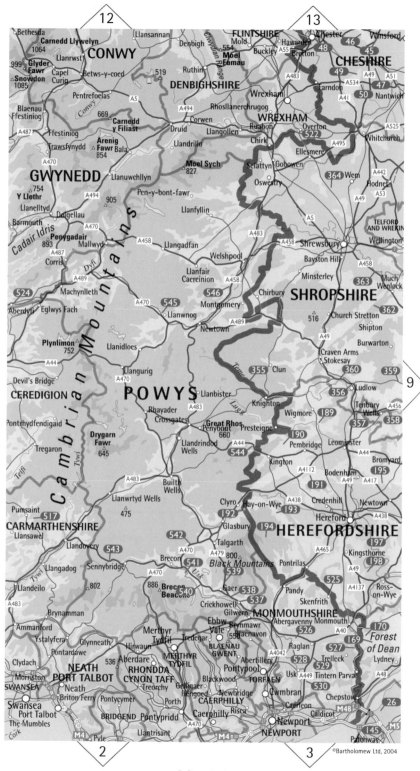

Map 8

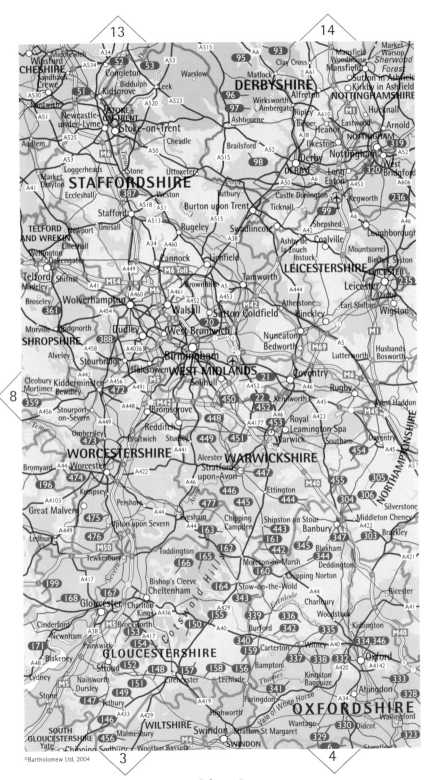

Map 9

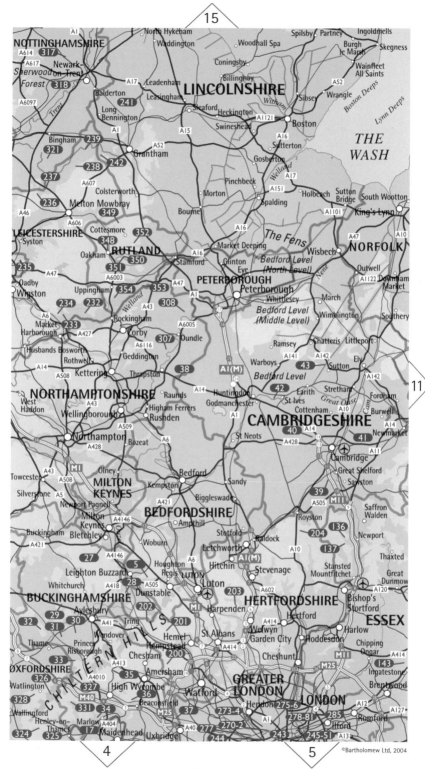

Map 10

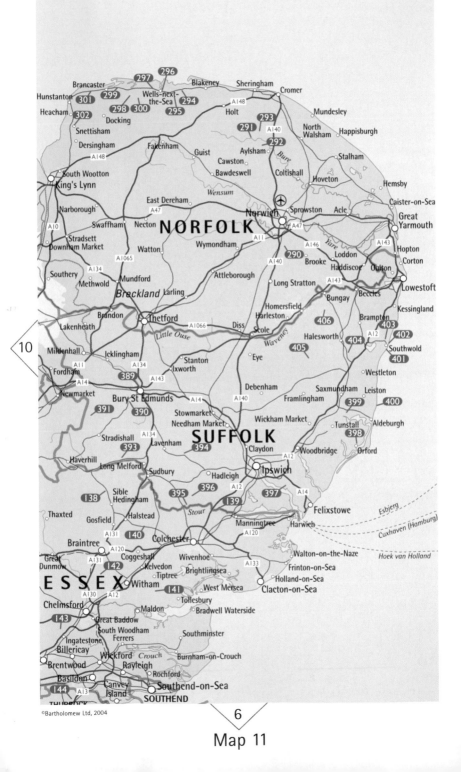

©Bartholomew Ltd, 2004

Map 11

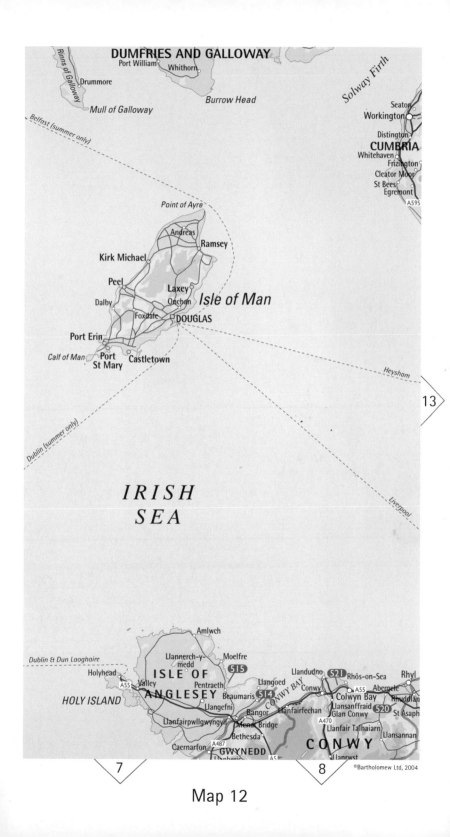

Map 12

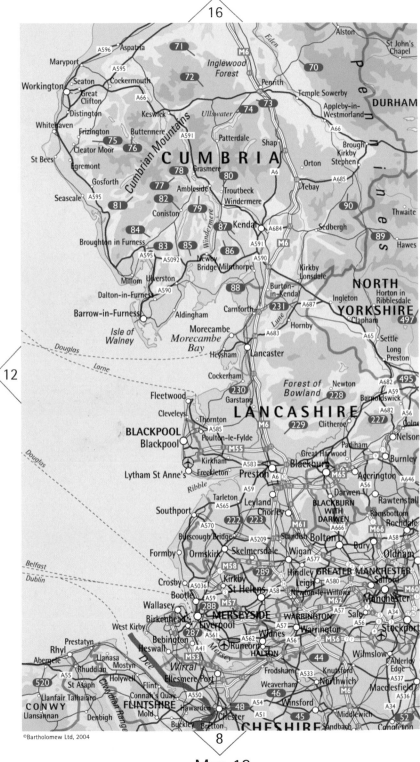

Map 13

©Bartholomew Ltd, 2004

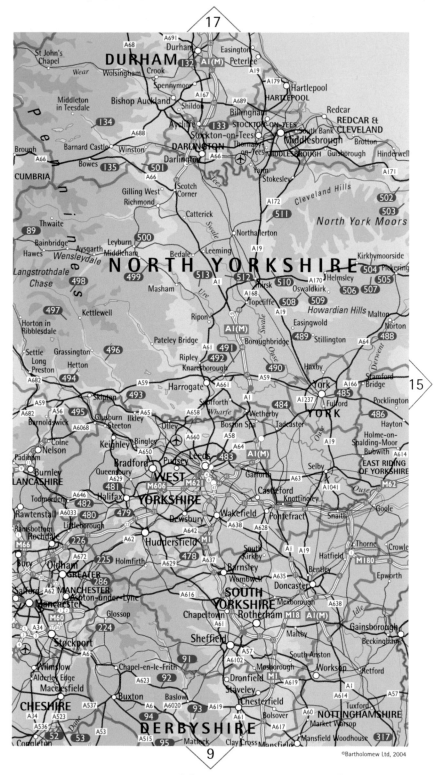

Map 14

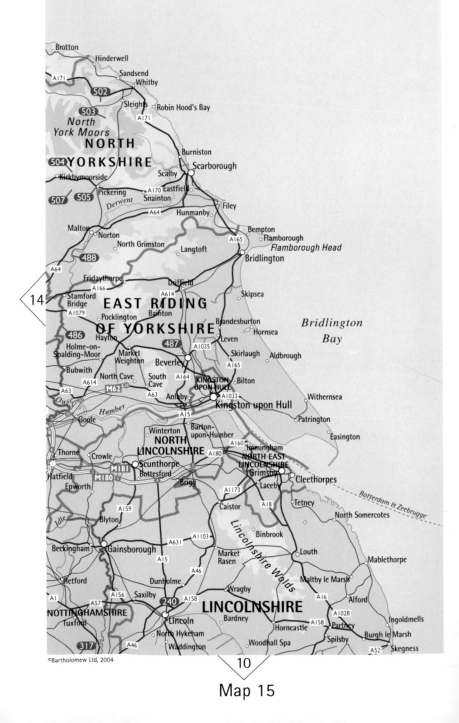

Map 15

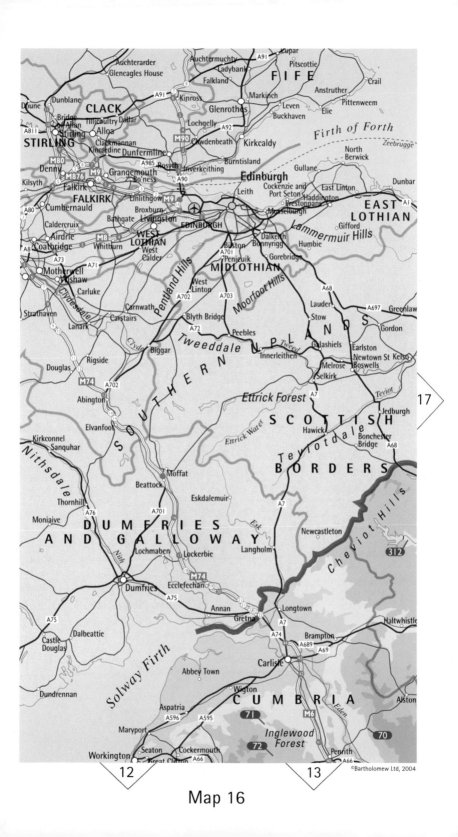

Map 16

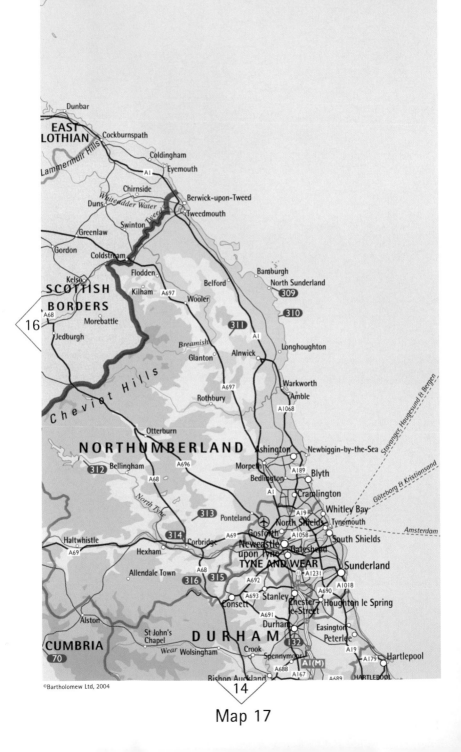

Map 17

HOW TO USE THIS BOOK

explanations

❶ directions
Use as a guide; the owner can give more details.

❷ meals
Approx. cost of a main course in restaurant or bar.

❸ room price
Room for two sharing + single occ. rate when it applies.

❹ closed
Assume normal pub hours (12pm-3pm; 6pm-11pm) unless stated otherwise.

❺ symbols
see the last page of the book for fuller explanation:

    wheelchair access to pub and toilets

    children of all ages welcome

   no smoking areas

   credit cards accepted

   dogs welcome

   4 or more handpumped ales

   8 or more wines by the glass

    good walks

❻ Map & entry numbers
Map number; entry number.

sample entry

Suffolk

The George
Cavendish

Take an ancient inn on a perfect Suffolk green, decorate in neutral colours, add a dash of modern art, five delightful bedrooms and a talented chef and you have somewhere 'worth a detour'. The timbered, 600-year-old frame was rescued from near-collapse by Jonathan and Charlotte, who have brought cosmopolitan chic to a village pub. The ground floor has a smart country-restaurant feel, with every table laid for eating, but there are plenty of quiet corners in which to enjoy a pint of Woodforde's Wherry or Nethergate's Augustinian. The bar area leads onto a terrace with heated canopies and more dining tables: people come for the food. Jonathan (once head chef at Conran's Bluebird in Chelsea) and his team can be seen in the open kitchen whipping up modern dishes from colourful mediterranean – tortellini of lobster and truffle, Moroccan spiced lamb rump with stuffed piminto – to age-old favourites like game pudding with port wine gravy or roast pork with parsnip mash and sage jus. Service is charming, the wine list soars above most pub efforts, and the bedrooms have bright wool carpets and pretty views.

❶ directions   On A1092 between Haverhill & Long Melford.
❷ meals   12pm-3pm; 6pm-10pm; 6.30pm-9.30pm Sundays. Main courses £4.75-£19.85; set menus £13, £16.50 & £20.
❸ rooms   5 doubles £70-£110. Singles £48.
❹ closed   Mondays January-April.

Jonathan & Charlotte Nicholson
The George,
The Green, Cavendish,
Suffolk CO10 8BA
tel   01787 280248
web   www.georgecavendish.co.uk

map: 11 entry: 393

❺
❻

england

The Salamander
Bath

The main bar, like a Victorian apothecary, is stacked with bottles on a Welsh dresser, hand pumps gleam under the glass fluted lights, and looking up is a hoppy heaven. The narrow room stretches its wooden self from the Parisian café-style front window to the moody orange recesses of the back. Bath Ales dominate, though the bottled beer list is eclectic (Leffe and Erdinger, for example), and there are the usual oddities such as an old beer tap collection; Malcolm Follain has turned The Salamander round into one the most popular pubs in Bath. Up a set of creaky stairs hides the 'dining room', a light, chic restaurant space with trompe-l'oeil panels, bentwood chairs and an open kitchen where chefs prepare such dishes as Gressingham duck with griottine cherry sauce. There's good bar-food and a sophisticated restaurant menu. A fine pub without the spittle.

directions	Behind Jollys in Bath city centre, off Milsom Street.
meals	12pm-2.30pm (3pm Sundays); 6.30pm-9.30pm. No food Monday evenings. Main courses £8.95-£14.95.

Malcom Follain
The Salamander,
3 John Street, Bath,
Bath & N.E. Somerset BA1 2JL
tel 01225 428889
web www.bathales.co.uk

map: 3 entry: 1

The Old Green Tree
Bath

Right in Bath city centre, the tiny dark pub, fanatical about ale (at least five guest beers are chalked up on the board outside) is humming with life even before midday. Deep in conversation, old regulars clutch pint jars to their chests as you squeeze through the narrow wooden-floored bar into the cabin-like non-smoking room. Undecorated since the panelling was installed in 1928, the pub is part of our heritage and has no intention of changing – Tim and Nick refuse any form of modernisation. In three little, low-ceilinged rooms, old dog-eared banknotes from across the world and a mosaic of foreign coins are stuck up with yellowing sellotape behind the bar – along with artists' work in spring and summer. The menu is far from traditional, however, with adventurous twists on old English dishes. They clearly have a devoted following, both young and old, and drinkers are not limited to beer: there are malts, wines, Pimms, hot toddies and good coffee. Easily a place to fall into idle chat with a stranger.

directions	Green Street, off Milson Street
meals	12pm-2.45pm. Main courses £4-£6.50

Tim Bethune & Nick Luke
The Old Green Tree,
12 Green Street,
Bath,
Bath & N.E. Somerset BA1 2JZ
tel 01225 448259

map: 3 entry: 2

The Hop Pole
Bath

That clever bunch over at Bath Ales have waved their magic wand over the Hop Pole, creating a space that banishes much of the usual stuffy pub masculinity while not forgetting where the roots of the real pub lie – in its ales. If you're pedalling your thirsty selves along the Bristol-to-Bath cycle path, you'd do well to meander very slightly off course and come here. Just out of the main throb of town, this gently sophisticated boozer has a wonderful summer courtyard – a verdant riot in the hotter months, with pergolas and vines – and a polished feel that suggests that more thought has gone into it than most spittle and chips pubs. Moody oranges, dark wood and a smattering of pub 'antiques' are made more contemporary by the extra space. It's a surprise to find, down a set of steps, the long, beamed dining room with its classy wooden boathouse finish and tantalising menu, for this is primarily a pub – good ales, settles, wooden floorboards – and a fine cup of coffee.

The Star Inn
Bath

Now this really is a historic pub. Listed on the National Inventory of Historic Pubs and the subject of a hearty local Save our Pub campaign, it's serious boozer and museum piece wrapped into one. A pub since 1760, refitted in the 19th century, The Star is partitioned off into numbered rooms, each with its panelled walls and opaque toplights. A real coal fire pumps out the heat in one room and you can still get a free pinch of snuff from the tins on the ledge above the wall. In short, it reeks of history. You can almost imagine the wrinkled Victorian regulars pressing their lips to their pewter tankards. To this day Bass is served in four-pint jugs which you can take away for a small deposit. There are no meals, just the odd bap from a basket on the bar – no fuss. What counts is the beer, so much so that Alan has started brewing his own Abbey Ales and has since scaled the heady heights of the real ale world to win several awards for his Bellringer tipple. A jewel.

directions	Near Royal Victoria park, a 10-minute walk from centre.
meals	12pm-2pm (3pm Sundays); 7pm-11pm. No food on Mondays. Main courses £8.95-£14.95

directions	On A4 (London Road) in Bath.
meals	Fresh rolls served all day, c. £1.60.
closed	2.30pm-5.30pm; 3pm-7pm Sundays.

Elaine Dennehy & Barry Wallace
The Hop Pole, 7 Albion Buildings,
Upper Bristol Road, Bath,
Bath & N.E. Somerset BA1 3AR
tel   01225 446327
web   www.bathales.co.uk

map: 3 entry: 3

Alan Morgan
The Star Inn,
23 Vineyards, The Paragon, Bath,
Bath & N.E. Somerset BA1 5NA
tel   01225 425072
web   www.star-inn-bath.co.uk

map: 3 entry: 4

Bedfordshire

The Five Bells
Stanbridge

This place is so popular that it starts to buzz from earliest evening. The bar is a warm room, where walls are painted a vibrant red, the ceiling is yellow and the beams have been shot-blasted back to their natural ochre. (One small problem: they are a little close to the ground, so if you are a six-footer, watch your head.) Prints line the walls, candles dot the tables, there's a crackling log fire at one end – with piles of logs stacked against the walls – and deep squashy sofas at the other. The bar would be pretty good on its own, but the Five Bells also has a restaurant. Painted in cool colours, it is light and airy with rustically chic furnishings and an elegant feel. The menu is imaginative modern British and lists such treats as pan-fried duck breast with wilted greens and chocolate vinaigrette, and medallions of pork fillet with carrot and ginger rösti and a light orange jus. Beers include well-kept Bass and Black Sheep and wines come by the glass.

Berkshire

Harrow Inn
West Ilsley

Inside the 600-year-old inn there are all the antique tables, country settles and Turkey rugs you could wish for. Add Victorian prints on dark terracotta walls and a log fire and you have somewhere that's smartly rustic and rather special, the sort of place where you'd expect to sample a good wine or an expertly-kept ale – quite possibly Morland Old Speckled Hen: Morland founded their brewery here in West Ilsley in 1711. And there's plenty of space inside and out, with a garden and a picnic-tabled front terrace overlooking the duck pond and the cricket. Sit out on a summer Sunday and catch the sound of leather on willow; expect to rub shoulders with the local racing fraternity and the foodies who come for Alan Berry's innovative and excellent dishes. There are lunchtime baguettes of pork and Dijon mustard, rabbit confit with vanilla risotto, Whitby cod roasted with garlic and rosemary and Angus steaks. Walkers fuel up here, too.

directions	2 miles off A5 in Stanbridge, just outside Leighton Buzzard.
meals	12pm-2.30pm; 7pm-9pm. Main courses £3.90-£9.50 (bar); £10-£18 (restaurant).

Andrew McKenzie & Emma Moffitt
The Five Bells, 1 Station Road,
Stanbridge, Leighton Buzzard,
Bedfordshire LU7 9JF
tel   01525 210224
web   www.traditional-freehouses.com

map: 10 entry: 5

directions	M4 junc 13; A34 for Oxford; 2nd turning on left to West Ilsley.
meals	12pm-2pm; 6pm-9pm. Main courses £10-£15.
closed	3pm-6pm (5pm Sundays). Open all day weekends in summer.

Alan Berry
Harrow Inn,
West Ilsley,
Newbury,
Berkshire RG20 7AR
tel   01635 281260

map: 4 entry: 6

Berkshire

The Bell Inn
Aldworth

Once a manor hall, now a no-frills pub, The Bell has the style of village pubs long gone and has been in the Macaulay family for 200 years. Plain benches, tables and chairs are not the most comfortable, a battered wood-burning stove stands in one small room – there's a more impressive hearth in the public bar – and early evening drinkers cluster around the glass hatch. But it's a joyfully unspoilt place to which people flock. Fifty years ago the regulars were all agricultural workers – which may explain why piped music and mobile phones are still so fiercely opposed. The food fits the image and they keep it simple: crusty rolls are filled with thick slices of home-baked ham, there's stilton and cheddar, and, in winter, hearty homemade soup. Drink prices are another draw: the real ales from the local West Berkshire Brewery and the house wines are very well priced.

directions	Off B4009, 3 miles W of Streatley.
meals	11am-2.30pm (12pm-2.45pm Sun); 6pm-10pm (7pm Sun). Filled rolls £1.90-£2.95.
closed	Christmas Day; Mondays except Bank Holidays.

H E Macaulay
The Bell Inn,
Aldworth,
Reading,
Berkshire RG8 9SE
tel 01635 578272

map: 4 entry: 7

Berkshire

Royal Oak
Yattendon

It comes brimful of surprises and a dash of class – everything you might expect of an English inn on the attractive square of an unspoiled village. French-born manageress Corinne MacRae oozes Gallic charm and professionalism, and, while the bar remains a popular haunt serving real ales and fine wines, today's inn is geared to a restaurant-with-rooms experience. Expect plump country sofas and chairs, big flowers and a crackling winter fire; the oak-beamed brasserie-bar comes decked in cottagey furniture and vibrant yellow. Two dining rooms sport crisp white napery, and there's a walled garden for fair-weather quaffing. But the action here revolves around Jason Gladwin's innovative, modern British repertoire, showcasing well-sourced local ingredients such as seared scallops with pancetta crisps, venison with chestnut puree, rum baba and poached fruit. Five classy bedrooms complete the upscale package.

directions	From Hermitage B4009; turn to Yattendon at Fox Inn.
meals	12pm-2.30pm; 6pm-10pm. Main courses £12-£18.
rooms	5 doubles £105-£140.
closed	New Year's Day.

Corinne Macrae
Royal Oak,
The Square,
Yattendon,
Berkshire RG18 0UG
tel 01635 201325

map: 4 entry: 8

Berkshire

The Pot Kiln
Frilsham

A remote and determinedly old-fashioned ale house on the tiny Yattendon to Bucklebury lane, particularly lovely in summer: sit back with a pint in the sheltered garden and look onto soothing vistas of fields and woodland. Old brick kilns (abandoned after the war) were sited here and the building is built of red bricks, hence the name. Also adopting a kiln-connected name is the fine ale, Brick Kiln Bitter, brewed by a micro-brewery in the outbuildings to the rear; there's Dr Hexters too. Inside is distinctly unspoilt, with three simply furnished bars leading off a small lobby bar. Bare boards, sturdy tables, cushioned wall benches and warming open fires create an unfussy, relaxing atmosphere, and a mix of chatty locals and passing ramblers fill the bars. Expect hearty country cooking and hot jam sponge – and, if you're in for a pint on a Sunday evening, some impromptu strumming of the folk guitar.

directions	In Yattendon turn opp. church for Frilsham. Cross m'way; on for Bucklebury. On right after 0.5 miles.
meals	12pm-2pm; 7pm-9.30pm. Main courses £7.10-£10.65. Rolls only, on Sundays.
closed	Tuesdays.

Philip Gent
The Pot Kiln,
Frilsham,
Yattendon,
Berkshire RG18 0XX
tel   01635 201366

map: 4 entry: 9

Berkshire

Crab at Chieveley
Chieveley

So much seafood in such horse-racing country – but this is no ordinary pub. You have a talking helicopter pad, bedrooms that mimic exotic hotel rooms from around the world, a nautical-meets-modern bistro, and menus to knock the socks off any seafood lover. There are a fish bar, a couple of ale handpumps and a small seating area with black leather sofas beside a vast inglenook. The wooden-floored dining areas are smart with black leather banquettes and fine modern furniture, while walls have colourful mediterranean prints, nautical paraphernalia and the odd fishing net. Though dauntingly long, the repertoire of Fish Bar and restaurant menus ebbs and flows with a sprinkling of classics and novel ideas, together with the odd concession to carnivores and a separate vegetarian menu. Open since August, the Crab has proved to be quite a catch.

directions	In Chieveley, left at Red Lion pub onto School Road; right at T-junc.; pub at top of hill.
meals	12pm-2.30pm; 6pm-10pm. Main courses £10-£32.
rooms	10 doubles £130. Singles £100.

David Barnard
Crab at Chieveley,
Wantage Road, Chieveley,
Newbury, Berkshire RG20 8UE
tel   01635 247550
web   www.crabatchieveley.com

map: 4 entry: 10

Berkshire

The Red House
Marsh Benham

Things have moved on since the old days when this was the Water Rat. Today's well-groomed hostelry has a different appeal. A cycle bell's throw from the towpath of the Kennet & Avon Canal, the Red House is a fine gastropub with a Frenchman at the helm. Xavier Le-Bellego has as polished a pedigree as his young chef: both have worked with Raymond Blanc. Warm red walls, a long dark wooden bar and blond floorboards lend a chic informality to the bistro-cum-bar, while the airier dining room, where antique bookcases are filled with real live books, strikes something of a library note. The kitchen delivers a modern British repertoire to match the surroundings: seared tuna in lime and ginger, braised duck with green peppercorn sauce, medallions of venison, zingy lemon tart. Wines are fantastic and ale drinkers are not forgotton – slake your thirst with a pint of Fuller's London Pride at smart teak tables on the front terrace.

directions	M4 junc. 13; A4 between Newbury & Hungerford (10 mins from M4).
meals	1pm-2.30pm; 7pm-10pm. Main courses c.£14.50.
closed	3pm-6pm; Sunday & Monday evenings.

Xavier Le-Bellego
The Red House,
Marsh Benham,
Newbury,
Berkshire RG20 8LY
tel   01635 582017

map: 4 entry: 11

Berkshire

Dundas Arms
Kintbury

The Dalzell-Pipers have run this delightfully old-fashioned inn since the 1960s. At the junction of river and canal, ducks and swans entertain diners while narrowboats glide by. No wonder the summer crowds flock. The food is good too, with both the carpeted small bar and the dining room a stage for David's traditional country cooking. Using fresh ingredients, notably estate game and prime meats from local dealers, the short, daily-changing menus highlight grilled downland lamb with leek and mint sauce and such staples as bread and butter pud. There's a great wine list, though ale drinkers are unlikely to be disappointed with West Berkshire's Good Old Boy on handpump. Revamped bedrooms are in a converted livery and stable block, where French windows open to a quiet riverside terrace.

directions	1 mile off A4 between Newbury & Hungerford.
meals	12pm-2pm; 7pm-9pm. No food Monday evenings. Main courses £7-£14.
rooms	5: 3 doubles, 2 twins £85. Singles £75.
closed	Sunday evenings.

David Dalzell-Piper
Dundas Arms,
53 Station Road, Kintbury,
Hungerford, Berkshire RG17 9UT
tel   01488 658263
web   www.dundasarms.co.uk

map: 4 entry: 12

Berkshire

Crown & Garter
Inkpen

Quiet lanes dip through fields and woodland, past cottages draped in honeysuckle – this is England at its most fairytale. The oldest part of the building is the bar area where an inglenook warms your cockles and deep pink ceilings are criss-crossed by ancient beams. Beers served are Arkells' Moonlight and the locals Good Old Boy and Mr Chubbs. Gill, ex-university lecturer, has had a complete lifestyle change to take over here, aided by her father and her son (as yet, too young to do much!). Delicious wild mushroom risotto, seafood and steaks can be eaten in the bar or restaurant – or in the garden under a huge oak. Save space for profiteroles, pear crumble or lemon posset. The bedrooms, newly built around a garden, have painted floorboards and blended voiles.

directions	M4 junc. 13; A4 for Speen & Winchester; left to Kintbury; there, left at village store; on left after 2 miles.
meals	12pm-2pm (2.30pm Sundays); 6.30pm-9.30pm (7pm Sundays). Main courses £7-£16.
rooms	8: 5 doubles, 3 twins, £70. Singles £50.
closed	Monday & Tuesday lunchtimes.

Gillian Hern
Crown & Garter,
Great Common, Inkpen,
Hungerford, Berkshire RG17 9QR
tel   01488 668325
web   www.crownandgarter.com

map: 4 entry: 13

Berkshire

The Angel
Woolhampton

A tropical paradise off the A4. From the outside, the large Victorian-era pub looks unprepossessing, save for a few exotic plants on the terrace, but inside it's eclectic and flamboyant enough to make the jaw drop. The ceiling by the bar is coated with wine bottles, there are dark parquet floors, huge palms and cacti, vibrant walls (deep green, burnt yellow, terracotta) and a glamorous silver coffee machine by the bar. In the dining room, walls are lined with posters, pictures and a large mural, and everywhere there's an unexpected touch: a bowl of exotic fruits on the bar, white lilies, a glowing candle on every table. Furniture is dark, wooden and comfortable, from the dining room chairs to the cushioned settles. Chef-patron Andrew Taylor's menus catch the mood and come dotted with luxurious touches – cream of artichoke with shaved black truffle, penne with chorizo, roast partridge, apple tarte tatin with iced praline parfait. The wine list is superb and offers 20 by the glass. 'Expect the unexpected' is the motto here.

directions	On A4 between Reading & Newbury.
meals	12pm-2.30pm; 6pm-9.45pm. Main courses £12.95-£29.50.
closed	Sunday evenings & Mondays.

Andrew Taylor
The Angel,
Bath Road, Woolhampton,
Reading, Berkshire RG7 5RT
tel   0118 971 3307
web   www.a4angel.com

map: 4 entry: 14

Berkshire

Elm Tree
Beech Hill

Bob and Debbie Walton's highly individual, quirky gem deserves its place on our pub map. The Elm Tree has not lost sight of its pubby roots yet there's a delightful blend of traditional and 'off-the-wall' here. One bar's green walls are covered in all manner of clocks – a riot of ticks and chimes – along with signed monochrome photographs of old Hollywood stars; cosiness comes from a wood-burning stove. The conservatory style dining area has a more orthodox look and furniture is cottagey and traditional. Being high on a hill, there are sweeping farmland views – best from the conservatory and the picnic benches under the veranda. In the barn-style restaurant, where children may eat, the menu is true to the spirit of the place, blending the traditional with the more adventurous: fresh pizzas, wok stir-fries, blackened salmon fillet on grilled vegetables, T-bone steak. A special's board displays local and organic dishes.

directions	M4 junc. 11, A33 for Basingstoke.; after 2 miles into Beech Hill Rd.
meals	12pm-3pm; 6.30pm-10pm. Main courses £5.50-£13.50.
closed	3pm-5pm Monday-Saturday.

Debra Walton
Elm Tree,
Beech Hill Road, Beech Hill,
Reading, Berkshire RG7 2AZ
tel   0118 988 3505
web   www.the-elmtree.com

map: 4 entry: 15

Berkshire

George & Dragon
Swallowfield

Anyone would slay a dragon to get to this inviting, unassuming old inn's door on a meandering lane someway out of the village. Though very much food-centred, it hasn't compromised its pubby roots and gives an open-hearted welcome to drinkers: Fuller's London Pride, Flowers IPA, good wines. There's oodles of character in flagstones, stripped beams and timbers, exposed brickwork and a winter fire in the big inglenook. Walls are warm terracotta strung with country prints, and over the bar is a collection of old woodworkers' planes and blue and white crockery. It's cosy and relaxed, with newspapers to browse, cottagey furniture in the bar, and a series of connecting rooms set up for the business of dining. An enterprising, thoroughly modern menu raids the globe for inspiration while respecting British classics, and is supplemented by daily blackboard specials; try pan-fried red snapper, five-cheese tortellini, treacle sponge. In summer, a pretty garden for you and your (well-behaved) children.

directions	M4 junc. 11; A33; turn for Swallowfield.
meals	12pm-2.30pm (3pm Sundays); 7pm-10pm (9pm Sundays). Main courses £10.95-£17.

Paul Dailey
George & Dragon,
Church Road,
Swallowfield, Reading,
Berkshire RG7 1TJ
tel   0118 988 4432

map: 4 entry: 16

Berkshire

The Horns
Crazies Hill

Inside the Tudor hunting lodge: beams and timbers, winter fires, solid scrubbed-wood tables and mediterranean-hued walls festooned with rugby and cricketing pictures and cartoons. There's a sweet little snug behind the bar to discover, a new bar that overlooks the landscaped garden (with play area) and a dining room that soars like a medieval hall. Once a barn, its exposed brickwork, beams and timbers are draped in hops, hunting pictures and horns, atmospherically lit by wrought-iron chandeliers. The whole place is welcoming, friendly, convivial, with an 'easy-like-Sunday-morning' feel and not a fruit machine in sight. The regular menu is supplemented by an appealing list of daily specials, the repertoire following a traditional route with the odd nod to far-reaching shores. Puddings play at home and are deeply comforting.

directions	Turn off A4 at Knowle Hill to Crazies Hill; 1 mile past bistro, left to Crazies Hill; left at bus shelter.
meals	12pm-2.30pm (4pm Sundays); 7pm-9.30pm (10pm Fri & Sat). Main courses £4.25-£15.95.
closed	3pm-6pm; Sunday evenings.

Andrew Hearn & Sarah Folley
The Horns,
Crazies Hill,
Wargrave,
Berkshire RG10 8LY
tel 0118 940 1416

map: 4 entry: 17

Berkshire

The Royal Oak
Paley Street

Modest at first glance, it has star quality inside. Nick Parkinson (son of showbiz dad Michael) may have given this small inn a contemporary and stylish lift, but he has cleverly managed to keep lots of the traditional character. There are scrubbed wooden floors and stripped beams, timbers and panelling, and a collection of cricketing mementos that enthralled our inspector... along with photographs of star personalities and Dad's interviewees: Mohamed Ali, Victoria Beckham, Sting. The bar is cosy and inviting, with solid wooden furniture, an open fire and a couple of armchairs. Beyond, dining tables are laid with white linen on gingham undercloths. Filled baguettes are available at lunchtime, while the dining room's food is modern and classy, with a very good choice of wines by the glass. The Royal Oak is friendly and well-run, opening its door to drinkers and diners with equal enthusiasm.

directions	On B3024 west of Paley Street, between A330 south of Maidenhead & Twyford.
meals	12pm-2.30pm; 6pm-10pm. Main courses £10.50-£14.75.
closed	3pm-6pm; Sundays.

Nick Parkinson
The Royal Oak,
Paley Street,
Maidenhead,
Berkshire SL6 3JN
tel 01628 620541

map: 5 entry: 18

Berkshire

Two Brewers
Windsor

A locals' secret revealed. In the royal town, next to the Home Park gates and the famous Long Walk, a dark, atmospheric gem. Small rooms meander around a tiny panelled bar and come quaintly decked with dark beams, wooden floors and scrubbed-wood tables. One room with big shared tables flourishes dark red walls and matching ceilings; the other two have more intimate seating areas. There are winter fires, magazines to dip into and walls crammed with interesting paraphernalia – posters, press-cuttings, pictures, mirrors. On a blackboard above the fire, anecdotes commemorating each day are chalked up in preference to the usual menu specials. But you won't go hungry: the compact menu follows a steady pub line, with two daily specials, roasts on Sundays and homely puddings. Beer, champagne, cigars... and a sprinkling of pavement tables to tempt you after the rigours of The Big Tour.

directions	Off High Street, next to Mews.
meals	12pm-2.30pm (4pm weekends); 6.30pm-10pm. Main courses £8-£13.50.

Robert Gillespie
Two Brewers,
34 Park Street,
Windsor,
Berkshire SL4 1LB

tel   01753 855426

map: 5 entry: 19

Birmingham

The Cock
Sutton Coldfield

The Cock was just an unremarkable, sleepy little village pub. Then along came the Belfry golf course. It's now used by a very wealthy crowd indeed. Recently revamped, it's still a surprise to walk from a typical pub car park (admittedly sprinkled with Ferraris) into something that is half traditional pub and half Manhattan cocktail lounge. If that makes the place sound over the top – it's not; it all works. The bar is dimly lit and modern with small alcoves, soft seating and a large dining area. A designer has been at work; vibrant colours on the walls, colour-washed beams, a display of pasta in a 'distressed' dresser and a cigar bar. There are six wines available by the glass as well as three ales on handpump. The cooking is modern European with a mediterranean bias and ranges from pizzas to steak via swordfish. The menu is limited but the ingredients are good – fresh and locally sourced as much as possible – and there is a 'specials' board with lots of fish.

directions	M42 junc. 9; follow signs to Wishaw (via Curdworth).
meals	12pm-2.30pm (4.30pm Sundays); 6pm-9pm. No food Sunday evenings. Main courses £5.50-£16.

Xavier Parker
The Cock,
Bulls Lane, Wishaw,
Sutton Coldfield,
Birmingham B76 9QL

tel   0121 313 3960

map: 9 entry: 20

Birmingham

The Malt Shovel
Barston

There's a touch of the Mediterranean about this pretty pub. Never mind that the nearest expanse of water is the Stratford-upon-Avon canal: it's painted in sunshiny yellows with green windows and shutters and it serves fish – lots of it. Eat in the bar, stylish and modern with mirrors and light wood, the airy barn-restaurant or the flowery garden in summer... wherever you are, you'll be treating yourself to some seriously good food. Hard to resist smoked haddock and goat's cheese on sun-dried tomatoes with rocket salad, sautéed calamari with linguini, garlic, parsley and flaked chilli, blackened swordfish on harissa-roasted courgettes and red pepper emulsion. Sunday lunches are particularly popular, when, again, you will be served with something different: venison with black pudding, maybe, or pork loin with herbed roast potatoes. The ales are good and so are the wines. No wonder this classy inn continues to pull in the crowds.

directions	Off A452; 1 mile beyond village.
meals	12pm-2.30pm; 6.30pm-9.30pm. No food Sunday evenings. Main courses £11-£14.

Anthony Day
The Malt Shovel,
Barston Lane,
Barston,
Birmingham B92 0JP
tel   01675 443223

map: 9 entry: 21

Birmingham

The Orange Tree
Chadwick End

The 'flagship' dining pub of the Classic Country Pubs group with a striking cream-painted timbered exterior. Inside are earthy colours, lime-washed low beams, open log fires, subdued lighting, deep sofas around low tables and chunky lightwood furnishings in airy eating rooms. A trendy Italian-style deli counter shows off superb breads, cheeses and vintage oils. This tastefully rustic, almost mediterranean décor is matched by the ambitious, Italian-inspired menu. Diners with deep pockets descend in their droves for authentic wood-fired pizzas, robust, full-flavoured meat dishes cooked on an in-view rotisserie spit, perhaps lamb rump with mediterranean vegetables and rosemary potatoes, or homemade pasta meals such as tagliatelle bolognaise, delicious warm salads and fishy specials. Great wines by the bottle or glass, Greene King ales and summer dining on a heated patio filled with stylish teak tables.

directions	On A4141 between Warwick & Solihull. On edge of village, 5 miles south of M42 junc. 5.
meals	12pm-2.30pm (4.30pm Sundays); 6pm-10pm. No food Sun evenings. Main courses £5.50-£13.50.

Paul Hales
The Orange Tree,
Warwick Road, Chadwick End,
Birmingham B93 0BN
tel   01564 785364
web   www.theorangetree.biz

map: 9 entry: 22

Bristol

Old Duke
Bristol

There's nothing else like it in Bristol. A shrine to jazz and blues – the bathrooms go by the names of Ella and Duke – where yellowing posters of jazz greats plaster the walls and a scuffed wooden stage jumps with the sounds of live swing, blues and jazz bands every night (and at lunchtime on Sundays). There's a New Orleans speakeasy-British-pub feel to this den, not far from the Bristol Old Vic, with etched windows, shallow wooden booths and Smiles by the hearty pint. It's not smart, it's not 'jazz pretentious' but music certainly dominates. On busier nights you can meet a wall of old and young, from the jazz-anorak scruffy to the post-theatre smart, tapping feet and chatting loudly. Don't come here for a quiet chinwag or a snazzy meal (there is the occasional curry or stew) but for hip-swingingly good music and a fantastic atmosphere that brings smiles to the glummest faces. See the web site for band listings. Weekend evenings are particularly busy.

directions	Central Bristol; on Welsh Back.
meals	12pm-6pm. No food at weekends. Main courses £3-£5.

Stuart Seydal
Old Duke,
45 King Street,
Bristol BS1 4ER

tel	0117 927 7137
web	www.theoldduke.com

map: 3 entry: 23

Bristol

Hope & Anchor
Bristol

If you're meandering through the madness that is central Bristol, with leaden legs and hungry belly, scan the horizon for Cabot Tower – a Victorian commemorative spike that pierces the skyline. Saunter up Brandon Hill towards said spike and over the other side. Where the park meets the road squats the Hope & Anchor, a welcome godsend on this featureless road. Utterly unpretentious and with a dedicated following – from arty youth to well-shod Cliftonites – this is everything the modern pub should be. Without even trying, the menu oozes confidence: stonkingly good grub without the garnished gastro-pomp. The ales change according to the landlord's whim, chosen from a list of 70 that come and go, and the interiors have that gentle wooden feel of settles and scuffed bare boards. In the summer, the steep 'Secret Garden' – not so secret – hums with life.

directions	A4 into Bristol along waterfront; left at roundabout up Jacob's Wells Road (B4466); half-way up on right.
meals	12pm-10pm (9.30pm Sundays). Main courses £5-£11.50.

Martin Hughes
Hope & Anchor,
38 Jacobs Wells Road,
Bristol BS8 1DR

tel	0117 929 2987

map: 3 entry: 24

Bristol

The Hare on the Hill
Kingsdown

Not much to encourage you from the outside, but step through the swing doors and you immediately feel that you're in a proper pub that knows its business. Bath Ales took on this down-at-heel street corner boozer in 1998 for complete renovation – yet it feels as if it's been like this for the past 100 years. Wooden floors, simple furniture and fuss-free décor lend a certain masculinity and the cosmopolitan/student crowd clearly appreciates the changes that have happened in the last five years and enjoy what the landlord, James, prides himself on: good beer and conversation. No piped music or games machines, and the TV in the corner provided for occasional sport, barely makes an impact. The place is full of nooks and crannies so you can easily find a quiet spot to enjoy a chat and a cracking pint of Bath Gem. Tasty, honest food is prepared and cooked on the spot, and it was CAMRA Pub of the Year the moment Bath Ales moved in.

directions	At top of Nine Tree Hill overlooking Stokes Croft.
meals	12pm-2pm (3pm Sundays); 6pm-9pm. Main courses £2.95-£5.95.
closed	2.30pm-5pm Mondays-Thursdays.

James Blackwell
The Hare on the Hill,
Dove Street, Kingsdown,
Bristol BS2 8LX
tel   0117 908 1982
web   www.bathales.co.uk

map: 3 entry: 25

Bristol

White Hart Inn
Littleton upon Severn

Park at the back, but go in at the front: it's worth it for the door alone. Step into a panelled vestibule with a wonderful turned staircase; settle in before huge fireplaces in large, ancient rooms. Tables, chairs and cushioned settles are scattered across the polished flag floors of this rambling 16th-century former farmhouse, where the beers are good and the menu inventive. Liz trained with Roux so you're in for a treat. There's a family room, a sheltered terrace, a splendid garden at the front for summer revels, and no music, just a vintage footie table in the back bar. Wharfe Wompers, famous Oggies and Harty Noggins are the stuff of local folklore, served with plenty of chips and plain salads – equally hearty are the soups, ploughmans, baguettes and nursery puds. The old barn has been converted to take four bedrooms overlooking the garden.

directions	From old Severn Bridge for Avonmouth, then Thornbury. 1st left at Elberton.
meals	12pm-2pm; 6pm-9.30pm. Main courses £3.95-£10.95.
rooms	4 doubles £55-£75. Singles £55.
closed	3pm-6pm Monday-Saturday; 4pm-7pm Sundays.

Howard & Liz Turner
White Hart Inn,
Littleton upon Severn,
Thornbury,
Bristol BS35 1NR
tel   01454 412275

map: 8 entry: 26

Buckinghamshire

The Crooked Billet
Newton Longville

The twin talents of former Sommelier of the Year John Gilchrist and head chef and wife Emma have put the 16th-century pub on the county's culinary map. With innovative menus and a 350-bin wine list (all, astonishingly, available by the glass), you may imagine it's more restaurant than pub. But the Billet is an exemplary local with a great bar, weekly-changing ales and a great pubby atmosphere. Munch sandwiches, salads or steak and chips in the beamed bar at lunch – or roast partridge with foie gras ravioli and puy lentil broth in the restaurant, which is inviting with its open fires, deep red walls, candles and country prints. Delicious cheeses come with fig and walnut cake and Emma's seasonal menus make full use of produce, including herbs, from a wide network of first-class suppliers, villagers included. You may have to book weeks in advance.

directions	From Milton Keynes A421 for Buckingham, left for N. Longville.
meals	12pm-2pm; 12.30pm-2.30pm Sundays; 7pm-9.30pm. No food Sunday evenings. Main courses £5-£13.
closed	Mondays.

John & Emma Gilchrist
The Crooked Billet, 2 Westbrook End,
Newton Longville, Milton Keynes,
Buckinghamshire MK17 0DF
tel 01908 373936
web www.thebillet.co.uk

map: 10 entry: 27

Buckinghamshire

The Stag Inn
Mentmore

Michael, once master chef at the Household Cavalry, is passionate about food and the best local produce; Jenny serves and surveys and deals with customers magnificently. The mellow stone building looks like a hunting lodge, its terrace facing Mentmore Towers, once home of the Rothschilds. Treat yourself to a champagne cocktail in the sloping garden in summer. In winter, when logs smoulder, the lounge bar is the place to be – small, bright and cosy with patterned sofas and carpeting, low tables and fresh flowers. Here are those excellent Charles Wells ales – Eagle and Bombardier – and good nosh, notably local sausages with mash and onion gravy. The low-lit, more formal restaurant is approached from the front of the building and has its own bar. On the à la carte menu are such treats as pan-roasted cod with samphire, or roasted loin of lamb with honey and mustard dressing on spicy couscous. A host of roasts on Sundays and a stunning array of wines by the bottle or the glass.

directions	Off A418, 5 miles NE of Aylesbury.
meals	12pm-2pm; 7pm-9.30pm. Main courses £6-£12.

Jenny & Mike Tuckwood
The Stag Inn, The Green, Mentmore,
Leighton Buzzard,
Buckinghamshire LU7 0QF
tel 01296 668423
web www.thestagmentmore.com

map: 10 entry: 28

Buckinghamshire

The Five Arrows
Waddesdon

Live like a lord at this inn-hotel, with its rug-strewn wooden floors, antique furnishings and unusual paintings from Lord Rothschild's collection. It is part of the model village built in 1887 by Baron Rothschild to go with his château, Waddesdon Manor, and its Versailles-like gardens. Julian Alexander-Worster runs it for the estate and creates an indulgent mood in perfect keeping with its lofty ceilings, wood panelling, parquet floors and open fires. On a cushioned settle in the bar, enjoy a pint of Fuller's London Pride or a glass of champagne and catch up on the news. In the dining room, savour carefully sourced produce subtly transformed into escalope of pork with cream and wild mushroom sauce, roasted sea bass with fennel and Parmesan crisps, honeycomb ice cream. The magnificent wine list focuses on Rothschild interests around the world. A sheltered garden, splendid bedrooms and, of course, impeccable service.

directions	6 miles west of Aylesbury on A41.
meals	12pm-2.30pm; 7pm-9.30pm; 7.30pm-8.30pm Sundays. Main courses £13.50-£19.
rooms	11: 7 doubles, 1 twin, 1 single, 2 suites £65-£150.

Julian Alexander-Worster
The Five Arrows,
Waddesdon, Aylesbury,
Buckinghamshire HP18 0JE
tel   01296 651727
web   www.waddesdon.org

map: 10 entry: 29

Buckinghamshire

The Dinton Hermit
Ford

With a bright fire, friendly proprietors, freshly-prepared food and four-poster beds — who wants to be a hermit! This pretty, low-ceilinged, newly renovated pub overlooking farmland on the edge of the village is named after one John Bigg who, after signing Charles II's death warrant, took to living in a cave. Quaff local Devil's Elbow, Whapweasel and Old Humbug in the cosy bar with its huge inglenook, then move into the stone-walled restaurant for some fabulous food. At lunch and dinner there's crispy duck with warm plum dressing, sea bass roasted in lemon and garlic with olive mash, chocolate rum pot. In 2003 John and Debbie Collinswood lengthened the old brick cottage and introduced modern, flower-themed bedrooms to the converted stable block, where there's lots of glorious contemporary colour.

directions	Off A418 between Thame & Aylesbury.
meals	12pm-2pm; 7pm-9pm. Main courses £10-£20.
rooms	13 doubles £80. Singles from £65.
closed	Sunday evenings; Mondays

John & Debbie Collinswood
The Dinton Hermit,
Water Lane, Ford Village, Aylesbury,
Buckinghamshire HP17 8XH
tel   01296 747473
web   www.dinton-hermit.com

map: 10 entry: 30

Buckinghamshire

Green Dragon
Haddenham

In what was once a manorial courthouse by Haddenham's pretty green, Paul Berry turns out some fabulous modern food. In the attractive, open-plan bar, kitted out with a laid-back medley of furniture and some appealing watercolours, relax over a pint of village-brewed Notley Ale from Vale Brewery, or one of several good wines by the glass. Menus here are imaginative and change daily. Graze on a decent lunchtime sandwich or a platter of British and Irish organic cheeses – or settle down to something more substantial such as coriander-crusted cod with spinach linguini and chilli tomato jam (they have 18 different ways with fish). The sweet-toothed will be happy with a pretty plateful of Tuscany orange cake or ambrosial raspberry sorbet. Families come for Sunday lunch and on warm days in the sheltered courtyard at the back you can go all continental and lunch outside.

directions	2 miles from Thame; follow signs for Haddenham & Thame Parkway station.
meals	12pm-2pm (3pm Sundays); 7pm-9.30pm. No food Sunday eve. Main courses £9.
closed	3pm-7pm.

Paul Berry
Green Dragon,
8 Churchway, Haddenham,
Buckinghamshire HP17 8AA
tel   01844 291403
web   www.eatatthedragon.co.uk

Buckinghamshire

The Mole & Chicken
Easington

With its stunning views from the immaculate garden but so far from the beaten track, this pub has become more seductive since it gained five stylishly simple bedrooms in the low-beamed cottage next door. Once the village store and beer-and-cider pub, the pretty building at the end of the terrace has come up in the world. Inside, rag-washed walls are decorated with hunting prints and candle sconces; a beamed ceiling and a hand-painted floor in Tuscan style are lit by two roaring log fires. This is a really cosy winter pub, so come on a damp Sunday and settle in for the day. Quirky blackboard menus list 'phishy food', 'belly warmers' and 'chicken feed' alongside old pub favourites and specials like slow-roasted lamb shank. There are; quench your thirst with a pint of local Vale Best Bitter, or delve into the 38-strong list of malts. Then retire next door for deep sleep.

directions	From Thame B4011 to Long Crendon. There, up Carters Lane opp. Chandos Arms; follow signs.
meals	12pm-3pm; 6pm-10pm. 12pm-9.30pm Sundays. Main courses £8.95-£15.95.
rooms	5 doubles £50-£65.
closed	3pm-6pm.

Shane Ellis
The Mole & Chicken,
Easington, Long Crendon,
Buckinghamshire HP18 9EY
tel   01844 208387
web   www.moleandchicken.co.uk

Buckinghamshire

Lions of Bledlow
Bledlow

Easily accessible from London, yet surrounded by beech woods – The Lions is popular with townies and ramblers alike. Mark McKeown has been here for years and has managed to keep the best of the old while ringing in the new. Ancient tiled floors, low black-beamed ceilings, several inglenooks (one huge), beautiful tables made from single sections of an elm tree, and Civil War memorabilia; the 400-year-old pub is hugely appealing and full of atmosphere. There's a big main bar, plus a games room, a restaurant, a side terrace for summer and tables at the front overlooking the pretty green. Upmarket pub food is the order of the day, great platefuls of it – plus children's portions, a decent choice of wines and a handful of pumped ales. Tuck in heartily, then stride off into the hills. Superb walks start from the door.

directions	From M40 junc. 6 B4009 for Princes Risborough. After Chinnor follow Bledlow brown tourist sign right.
meals	12pm-2.30pm; 7pm-9.30pm (9pm Sundays). Main courses £5.95-£10.95.

Mark McKeown
Lions of Bledlow,
Church End, Bledlow,
Princes Risborough,
Buckinghamshire HP27 9PE
tel   01844 343345

map: 10 entry: 33

Buckinghamshire

Royal Oak
Marlow

A mile yet a world away from Marlow's bustle, the old whitewashed cottage stands in a hamlet on the edge of Marlow Common. It's one of a thriving trio of dining pubs owned by David and Becky Salisbury (see Alford Arms in Hertfordshire and The Swan in Buckinghamshire) and from the moment you pull up outside you know you're in for a treat. Go past the rosemary-edged terrace and into a stylish, open-plan bar, warm with terracotta walls, rug-strewn boards, scrubbed tables, cushioned pews and crackling log fire; order a pint of local Rebellion ale or one of the 13 wines available by the glass, then find a corner from which to check out the daily chalkboard or printed menu. Innovative modern pub grub comes in the form of 'small plates' (warm monkfish tart with béarnaise) and main meals (honeyed roast duck on saffron and ginger couscous). Sprawling summer gardens are filled with fragrant herbs and flowers and there's a sunny terrace with teak tables and smart brollies.

directions	From Marlow A4155; right signed Bovingdon Green.
meals	12pm-2.30pm (3pm Sundays); 7pm-10pm. Main courses £9.75-£12.75.

Ms Trasna Rice-Giff
Royal Oak,
Frieth Road,
Bovingdon Green, Marlow,
Buckinghamshire SL7 2JF
tel   01628 488611

map: 10 entry: 34

Buckinghamshire

The Polecat Inn
Prestwood

A quirky place, fun and packed with character. Chintzy curtains, low lighting and beams, button-backed chairs, cosy corners, antique clocks, rugs and a fireplace stacked with logs make it feel more home than pub; with all the glass-cased furry creatures on display, the yellow-painted, 17th-century Polecat Inn could as easily be called The Badger or The Stoat. The unusual flint bar serves several real ales, including Morland Old Speckled Hen and Marston's Pedigree, and there is an impressive selection of malts, and 16 wines by the glass. Among ticking clocks and happy banter, diners tuck into tempting specials such as magret of duck with orange and cognac sauce, spiced chickpea fritters with ratatouille, or braised lamb shank with puy lentils, wine, herbs and garlic. A slab of the rich chocolate torte will probably finish you off. Take one of the walking maps thoughtfully provided by John, and work off any over-indulgence in the Chiltern Hills. It's a beautifully run place, and has a gorgeous garden.

directions	On A4128 between Great Missenden & High Wycombe.
meals	12pm-2.30pm; 6.30pm-9pm. Main courses £7.90-£12.70.
closed	Sunday evenings.

John Gamble
The Polecat Inn,
170 Wycombe Road,
Prestwood,
Buckinghamshire HP16 0HJ
tel   01494 862253

map: 10 entry: 35

Buckinghamshire

The Royal Standard of England
Forty Green

There's been a public house here for 900 years, possibly even longer – giving it a fair claim to be the oldest pub in the country (along with several other contenders). Some of the timbers are 11th century, some of the wattle and daub 13th – though to the untrained eye, with its small windows and stained-glass panels, the red-brick building looks merely Tudor. Inside, you find a good old traditional dining pub with roasts and pies on the menu and dining tables in the King Charles Bar (Charles II is rumoured to have sheltered here after the Battle of Worcester; in truth, he never came near Beaconsfield). Open fireplaces include one taken from Edmund Burke's country house just down the road. The beer is excellent – try a pint of the heady Marston's Owd Roger – and there's a modest wine selection. The Royal also claims to have the biggest pub car park in the country!

directions	M40 junc. 2; B474 for Hazlemere; turn for Forty Green.
meals	12pm-2.15pm (2.30pm Sundays); 6.30pm-9pm; 7pm-9.30pm Sun. Main courses £7-£14.
closed	3pm-5.30pm (7pm Sundays).

Cyril Cairn
The Royal Standard of England,
Forty Green,
Beaconsfield,
Buckinghamshire HP9 1XT
tel   01494 673382

map: 10 entry: 36

Buckinghamshire

The Swan
Denham

Swap the bland and everyday for the picture-book perfection of Denham village and the stylish Swan. Georgian, double-fronted, swathed in wisteria, the building has had a makeover by David and Becky Salisbury (of the Alford Arms and the Royal Oak). Like its more established siblings, the Swan has been transformed by rug-strewn boards, modishly chunky tables, cushioned settles, big mirrors, a log fire and a fabulous terrace and garden for outdoor meals. Food is modern British. If pressed for time, choose from the 'small plates' list — mussel and clam chowder or twice-baked dolcelatte soufflé with watercress salad. If you've nothing to rush for, linger over pot-roast pheasant in red wine with creamy mash, accompanied by a pint of Courage Best or one of 13 wines by the glass. The owners have thought of everything, including a play area for the kids.

directions	From A412 (M25 junc. 17 or M40 junc. 1) follow signs for Denham.
meals	12pm-2.30pm (3pm Sundays); 7pm-10pm. Main courses £9.75-£13.

David & Becky Salisbury
The Swan,
Village Road, Denham,
Buckinghamshire UB9 5BH
tel   01895 832085
web   www.swaninndenham.co.uk

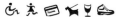

map: 10 entry: 37

Cambridgeshire

The Pheasant
Keyston

The Huntsbridge group is known for injecting urban chic into rural hideaways. The formula is simple enough: one remarkably self-assured chef (Martin Lee), a menu that looks to the mediterranean and points beyond, and a classic thatched exterior. Add an enterprising list of wines and well kept ales and you have The Pheasant to a T. The text-book country pub does beams, open fires and comfy sofas better than anyone, and the cooking is as restorative as the surroundings, with the likes of risotto with artichokes, wood-roast peppers and rosemary, roast suckling pig served with cavolo nero and soft Parmesan polenta, and baked custard tart with nutmeg ice cream. Folk come from miles around. If you don't want a full-blown meal, there's bar food and beautiful unpasteurised European cheeses. The Pheasant never forgets it's a pub and Adnams ales, together with two or three guest ales are always on handpump.

directions	Keyston off A14, halfway between Huntingdon & Kettering.
meals	12pm-2pm; 6.30pm-9.30pm. Main courses £8.50-£12.50.
closed	3pm-6pm.

John Hoskins
The Pheasant,
Village Loop Road, Keyston,
Cambridgeshire PE28 0RE
tel   01832 710340
web   www.huntsbridge.com

map: 10 entry: 38

Queen's Head
Newton

The unprepossessing exterior gives no hint of the charm that awaits inside. David and Juliet Short have run the Queen's Head for a quarter of a century, their commitment to traditional values drawing real-pub-lovers from far and wide. There's a timeless appeal in the bare, almost spartan, beamed main bar where clattering floorboards, plain wooden tables, benches, settles, old paintings and splendid winter fire are watched over by a fine old clock that keeps the beat. A tiny carpeted lounge with deep red walls, dark beams and well-worn, almost rickety furniture is a cosier alternative, especially in winter when the fire is blazing. The whole interior is unusual and utterly unspoilt, a proper background for shove-ha'penny and cribbage. And the food is just as simple and straightforward: magnificent rare roast beef sliced wafer thin, ham on the bone, a mug of rich brown soup, homemade bread, all dispensed with slow deliberation and great charm – quite perfect accompaniments to Adnams ales tapped from the cask. This is a place to treasure – and many do, returning time and time again.

directions	M11 junc. 11; A10 for Royston; left on B1368.
meals	11.30am-2.30pm; 7pm-9.30pm. Main courses £2.10-£4.80.
closed	Christmas Day; 2.30pm-6pm (7.00pm Sundays).

David & Juliet Short
Queen's Head,
Newton,
Cambridge,
Cambridgeshire CB2 5PG
tel   01223 870436

map: 10 entry: 39

Cambridgeshire

Three Horseshoes
Madingley

From the outside, the thatched pub looks old-worldy; push the door and you embrace the new century. Here is a simple, stylish, open feel in pale wooden floors and furniture, soft sage and cream paintwork, modern prints; there is space and light yet the familiar features of the old pub remain. The bar has local ales such as Cambridge Boathouse Bitter, a modern open log fire and a blackboard menu packed with Italian country dishes and imaginative combinations. Chef-patron Richard Stokes is part of John Hoskin's classy Huntsbridge Group (see entries for the Falcon Fotheringhay, and The Pheasant at Keyston), and he serves fabulous food – some of the best in the region. Excellent unpretentious service matches the laid-back atmosphere of the busy bar while formality and white linen come together in the conservatory dining room, popular with business lunchers. In either room the choice of wines is superb – pity the designated driver.

directions	Off A1303, 2 miles west of Cambridge.
meals	12pm-2pm (2.30pm Sundays); 6.30pm-9.30pm. Main courses £9.50-£20.
closed	Sunday evenings.

Richard Stokes
Three Horseshoes,
High Street,
Madingley,
Cambridgeshire CB3 8AB
tel   01954 210221

map: 10 entry: 40

Cambridgeshire

Crown & Punchbowl
Horningsea

The second of Oliver Thain and Richard Bradley's pubs (the other's The Cock, Hemingford Grey) combines the traditional with contemporary zing. But the large, homely set-up (two buildings, one 17th century, the other Victorian, backing onto the church and graveyard) is actually run as a restaurant. There is no bar as such – only one real ale is served – but the menu has many old-fashioned delights: homemade sausages with a choice of flavoured mash and sauces, and lots of fish, such as poached smoked haddock with poached egg and goat's cheese cream. The bedrooms, too, are excellent: light, spacious, cottage-style rooms, not grand, but simply, pleasantly decorated with good modern bathrooms. With manager Richard 'Ray' Day so charming and 'on the ball', it is hard not to like such a place.

directions	Off A14, 2 miles north west of Cambridge
meals	12pm-2.30pm; 6.30pm-9pm (9.30pm Fridays & Saturdays). Main courses £9.95-£14.95; set menu £12.95 & £15.95 (lunch).
rooms	5: 4 doubles, 1 twin £69.95. Singles £49.95.
closed	Sunday evenings.

Oliver Thain
Crown & Punchbowl, High Street,
Horningsea, Cambridge,
Cambridgeshire CB5 9JG
tel   01223 860643
web   www.cambscuisine.com

map: 10 entry: 41

The Cock
Hemingford Grey

Oliver Thain and Richard Bradley are members of that new breed of licensees: young, entrepreneurial, unafraid to experiment. Yet at this, the first of their pub ventures (their second being the Crown & Punchbowl, Horningsea, see left) they have gone back to basics, stripping the lovely 17th-century village pub right back to its original simplicity. Step directly from the street in to a bar warmed by a log burner. It's cosy and attractive with bare floorboards, a low-beamed ceiling and traditional benches and settles at which you sup award-winning East Anglian ales: Adnams, Woodfordes Wherry, Black Dog. For food, move into the airy, non-smoking restaurant where buttermilk walls and modern prints go beautifully with wooden floors and tables. The menu is strong on pub classics and the chef makes his own sausages, served with a choice of mash and stilton, perhaps, or spring onions, and wonderful sauces (green peppercorn, mustard). Fish and game dishes reveal a refreshing, modern view, with a seasonal choice chalked up on a changing menu. British and Irish farmhouse cheeses are another joy, as are the puddings – such as cardamom panna cotta with luscious summer fruits.

directions	From A14 south for Hemingford Grey; 2 miles S of Huntingdon.
meals	12pm-2.30pm; 6.45pm-9.30pm. No food on Sunday evenings. Main courses £8.95-£17.95; set menu £8.95 & £11.95 (lunch).
closed	3pm-6pm.

Oliver Thain
The Cock, 47 High Street,
Hemingford Grey, Huntingdon,
Cambridgeshire PE28 9BJ
tel 01480 463609
web www.cambscuisine.com

map: 10 entry: 42

Cambridgeshire

Anchor Inn
Sutton Gault

Wedged between the bridge and the raised dyke, the little inn was built in 1650 to bed and board the men conscripted to tame the vast watery tracts of swamp and scrub. Whether you sit under the huge Fenland sky on the terrace and take in the miles of peace and quiet, or blow in with the winter winds and hunker down in front of one of three open fires, you'll relish the experience of being a part of this excellent, independent country inn run with panache by the Moores. Rooms are understated and stylish and the cooking is a major draw – light, imaginative and surprising. The combination of flavours is artful – baked saddle of rabbit wrapped in Italian ham with a confit leg, soft cheesy polenta and cider sauce – and the results are consistent and successful. Good bedrooms, too.

directions	6 miles west of Ely, off B1381 in Sutton Gault.
meals	12pm-2pm (2.30pm Sundays); 7pm-9pm; 6.30pm-9.30pm Sat. Main courses £10.50-£15.50; set menu £19.95 (Sundays only).
rooms	2: 1 double, 1 twin £75-£99.50. Singles £50-£65.

Robin Moore
Anchor Inn,
Sutton Gault, Ely,
Cambridgeshire CB6 2BD
tel 01353 778537
web www.anchor-inn-restaurant.co.uk

map: 10 entry: 43

Cheshire

Chetwode Arms
Lower Whitley

The 400-year-old, Cheshire-brick roadside inn hides a rabbit warren of small rooms and passageways. There's the bar room itself, tiny, with an open coal fire, and four more: one, very snug, that can be used as a small private dining room, and the largest with TV, darts, and long scrubbed-pine tables. There are low ceilings, exposed brick and beams, fresh flowers and mirrors – oodles of atmosphere, and good food too. In the dining room – opening onto a terrace that overlooks the pub's own bowling green – you'll find contented diners eating roast rump of lamb with rich redcurrant gravy, hearty venison casserole, or roast and smoked salmon fishcakes with homemade chips. Or, simply, decent lunchtime sandwiches, salads and ploughman's. There are four ales on tap from Marston's, Tetley, Cains and Highgate Brewery's and over eight wines by the glass – and a huge landscaped garden, with a play area for children. The Chetwode is great for keen drinkers of beer, and a super dining pub for families.

directions	On A49 2 miles from M56 junc. 10.
meals	12pm-3pm; 6pm-9pm. Main courses £8.95-£19.95.

Derek Richardson
Chetwode Arms,
Street Lane,
Lower Whitley, Warrington,
Cheshire WA4 4EN
tel 01925 730203

map: 13 entry: 44

Cheshire

The Fox & Barrel
Cotebrook

The gardens are an attraction, even in winter, and the staff are attentive, be you here for a swift half or a slap-up meal. Inside, a comfortable mix of tables and chairs, snug corners, interesting ornaments and pictures and prints on bay-windowed walls, a large open brick fire stacked with logs, and quarry tiles covered with traditional patterned rugs. All is spotless and welcoming. There's also a large and pleasant candlelit dining room in cream and deep green; tables have flowers and the background music – Glen Miller, perhaps – is gentle on the ear. There are several cask ales and two guest beers, good wines and enjoyable food generously served: roast shank of lamb, stir-fry duck with egg noodles, soup of the day, all homemade, of course. Once a week live New Orleans jazz pulls in a lively crowd, and the service is exemplary.

directions	On A49 next to Oulton Park.
meals	12pm-2.30pm (3pm Sundays); 6.30pm-9.30pm (6pm Saturdays; 9pm Sundays). Main courses £8.50-£15.50.

Martin Cocking
The Fox & Barrel,
Forest Road, Cotebrook, Tarporley,
Cheshire CW6 9DZ

tel	01829 760529
web	www.thefoxandbarrel.com

map: 13 entry: 45

Cheshire

The Boot Inn
Boothsdale

Strewn with ivy and pyracantha, here is the archetypal country cottage turned pub. Set against wooded hills in the middle of fruit farming country ('Little Switzerland'), the village local looks west towards the Welsh Hills and south over the Cheshire plain. This is a gorgeous, sheltered, rural spot with good walks nearby – ask to see their booklet. The pub has been opened up inside with the bar at the hub, though you still get the flavour of individual rooms. Old quarry tiles, some wood panelling, characterful beams and a log-burning stove pull the customers in: walkers, talkers, drinkers. Children too; they have donkeys, dog and cats to keep them happy. The stone-flagged dining room opens onto a garden you can spill into on warm days and there's a log fire in winter. Popular food ranges from sandwiches at the bar to to leek and roasted pepper tart. Tetleys, Cains and Pedigree are available on draught and there are 15 wines, four by glass.

directions	From Chester A54 for Manchester; right for Oscroft & Willington. In 2 miles left at T-junc. for Boothsdale.
meals	11am-2.30pm; 6pm-9.30pm. Main courses £7.95-£16.95.

Mike Gollings
The Boot Inn,
Boothsdale,
Willington,
Tarporley, Cheshire CW6 0NH

tel	01829 751375

map: 13 entry: 46

The Dysart Arms
Bunbury

It is one of those rare places – all things to all people. With separate areas clustered round a central bar, it feels open and cosy at the same time. There's an inglenook packed with logs, a dining area in a library, the staff are lovely, the food is special, the beers and wines superb. Once a farm on the Dysart estate, this 18th-century brick building by the church protects a listed interior. The refreshingly airy rooms have scrubbed floorboards, yellow walls, good solid tables and chairs, pictures, prints and plants, and French windows opening to the terrace and garden. Two walls are lined with books. They're proud of their food here and rightly so: treat yourself to oatcakes filled with bacon and field mushrooms, chicken and red pepper kebabs, golden syrup sponge… the cheeses are taken as seriously as the cask ales (try the local Westwood Bitter), and the wines are thoughtfully chosen. Warm, intimate, friendly… the place appears to run on well-oiled wheels.

The Albion
Chester

It's an unprepossessing pub near the Chester almshouses, not far from the Roman wall… but wait until you get inside. Dedicated to the First World War, it has bucket-loads of memorabilia – sepia photographs, 'Your Country Needs You' posters, flocked wallpaper, soft glowing lamps, leather sofas and piano. Mike Mercer has been here for 32 years and insists on old-fashioned good behaviour; this is no place for yobs or noisy children! Standards are high on the refreshment front, too, with four cask ales, a flurry of malt whiskies and a decent selection of New World wines. 'Trench Rations' come in un-trench-like portions: lamb's liver with bacon and onions in a rich cider gravy, boiled gammon and pease pudding, Staffordshire oatcakes, cottage pie. There's even hot chocolate on the menu – Green & Black's organic. A nostalgic city pub with an eccentric streak.

directions	Off A49, 3.5 miles from Tarporley.
meals	12pm-2.15pm; 6pm-9.30pm (9pm Sundays). No food New Year's Eve. Main courses £6.95-£15.95.
closed	Christmas Day.

directions	Opposite city walls between The Newgate & River Dee.
meals	12pm-2pm; 5pm-8pm; 6pm-8.30pm Sat (7pm Sundays). Main courses £6.95.
rooms	2 doubles. Ask for prices.
closed	3pm-5.50pm (6pm Sat; 7pm Sun). Open all day Friday.

	Darren & Elizabeth Snell
	The Dysart Arms,
	Bowes Gate Road, Bunbury,
	Nantwich, Cheshire CW6 9PH
tel	01829 260183
web	www.dysartarms-bunbury.co.uk

map: 8 entry: 47

	Michael Mercer
	The Albion,
	Albion Street, Chester,
	Cheshire CH1 1RN
tel	01244 340343
web	www.albioninnchester.co.uk

map: 13 entry: 48

The Pheasant Inn
Higher Burwardsley

Come and stand before the largest fireplace in Cheshire with a pint of Weetwood Old Dog in your hand after a breezy hike along the Sandstone Trail. Or sit out on the terrace and gaze across the Cheshire Plain to North Wales. Gloriously positioned up in the Peckforton Hills, the Pheasant has been stylishly re-done. The old laid-back feel has survived the smartening up of the beamed and wooden-floored bars and the food, which you eat in the flagged conservatory, lives up to the surroundings. Local-game terrine with gooseberry chutney, roast monkfish with smoked ham risotto and chervil beurre blanc and caramelised lime tart should satisfy the hungriest walker; lunchtime sandwiches are good, too. And most of the bedrooms in the newly converted barn have that glorious view.

directions	M6 junc.16; A500 for Nantwich; A534 for Wrexham; right opp. Copper Mine pub; right for Burwardsley after 1 mile. At post office bear right & follow signs.
meals	12pm-2.30pm; 6.30pm-9.30pm. Main courses £3.95-£17.95.
rooms	10: 8 doubles, 2 twins, £70-£100. Singles £55.
closed	2.30pm-6.30pm.

Simon McLoughlin
The Pheasant Inn,
Higher Burwardsley,
Cheshire CH3 9PF
tel   01829 770434
web   www.thepheasant-burwardsley.com

♿ 🏃 🥄 🖃 🐕 🍺 🍷 👟

map: 8 entry: 49

The Cholmondeley Arms
Cholmondeley

The gabled Victorian schoolhouse, with its unusual, octagonal bell tower, stands virtually opposite Cholmondeley Castle and Gardens. It metamorphosed into a pub when the school closed in 1982 but is still part of the Viscount's estate and keeps that airy 'schoolroom' atmosphere with its high-roofed halls, large windows and huge radiators. Nowadays, it also has smart, pastel-painted walls, open fires, stripped pine tables, assorted old pews and family heirlooms. Educational relics in the form of old school desks, blackboards and easels fill a gallery above the bar and antique blackboards have been put to good use – of course; one is chalked up with the daily-changing choice of interesting bar food, the other lists the wines available by the glass. The clean and comfortable bedrooms are across the old playground in the former headmaster's house. Then it's back to school in the morning to report in for slap-up bacon and eggs.

directions	On A49, 6 miles north of Whitchurch.
meals	12pm-2.15pm; 6.30pm-10pm. Main courses £6.95-£15.
rooms	6 twins/doubles £65.

Guy & Carolyn Ross-Lowe
The Cholmondeley Arms,
Cholmondeley, Malpas,
Cheshire SY14 8BT
tel   01829 720300
web   www.cholmondeleyarms.co.uk

♿ 🏃 🖃 🐕 🍺 🍷 👟

map: 8 entry: 50

Cheshire

The White Lion
Barthomley

An inn since 1614 and a siege site in the Civil War, the wonderfully unspoilt White Lion, wonky with aged black and white timbers and a thick thatched roof, stands beside a cobbled cart track close to the fine sandstone church. Step inside and you find three delightfully, unspoilt rooms that exude aged charm, as well as head-cracking oak beams, moulded black panelling, tiny latticed windows and quarry-tiled floors. No music or electronic games, just the crackling of log fires and chatty conversation from contented locals. Lunchtime food is listed on a straightforward chalkboard menu. You sit at scrubbed wooden tables on ancient settles, and may wash down your sausages and mash, hearty ploughman's lunch or daily roast with a well-kept pint of Cheshire-brewed Burtonwood Top Hat — or opt for the regularly changing guest ale. Summer seating is at benches on the cobbles, with pretty views onto the village.

directions	M6 junc.; 3rd exit for Alsager; left for Barthomley
meals	12pm-2pm. Main courses £5.
closed	Thursday lunchtimes.

Terence Cartwright
The White Lion,
Barthomley,
Crewe,
Cheshire CW2 5PG
tel 01270 882242

map: 9 entry: 51

Cheshire

Harrington Arms
Gawsworth

You'd barely know it was a pub. The creeper-covered, red-brick building started life as a farmhouse in 1663 and still looks as if it might be part of a working farm (it is). The outside may have grown but the inside has barely changed; it wasn't long ago that they were serving beer here only from the cask. Off the passageway are a bar and a quarry-tiled snug, just big enough to take a settle chair, a table and an open fire. Then two more public rooms: the traditionally furnished Top Parlour, and the Tap Room, a red and black quarry-tiled room with simple, scrub-top tables — where they hold Friday's folk club sessions. The Wrights have a certified organic dairy herd and their high standards are reflected in the quality of the ale they serve; it's said that you won't get a finer pint of Robinsons than at the Harrington. Lunchtime snacks are of the pork pie and slab-sandwich variety — simple and good.

directions	On A536, 2.5 miles from Macclesfield.
meals	12pm-2pm. Sandwiches & soup £2.50-£3.
closed	3pm-6pm.

Ian Bailey Wright
Harrington Arms,
Church Lane,
Gawsworth, Macclesfield,
Cheshire SK11 9RR
tel 01260 223325

map: 14 entry: 52

Cheshire

The Ship Inn
Wincle

The red sandstone building – one of Cheshire's oldest – houses a small and well-loved local. Its two little taprooms are utterly simple and unspoilt, one with half barrels as ends for its counter, the other with stone-flagged floor and solid-fuel stove. Food is taken seriously in the traditional red-carpeted dining room, ingredients are local and booking is essential at weekends. There's steak and ale pie for meat-lovers, gnocchi with wild mushroom sauce for vegetarians. The Ship is also known for its beers – usually four on handpump plus a traditional cider or perry – and its fruit wines. Outside, the super little country garden by the car park has tables and chairs shaded by mature trees and swings for the kids. The young owners are full of enthusiasm and know what makes a good pub. From the edge of the Peaks the views are all they're cracked up to be and walks stretch in every direction.

directions	From Congleton A54 for Buxton for 7 miles; right at Clulow Cross for Wincle, 1.5 miles.
meals	12pm-2.30pm (3.30pm Sundays); 7pm-9pm; 6.30pm-9.30pm Fri & Sat; 5.30pm-8pm Sundays. Main courses £8.50-£14.95.
closed	Mondays except Bank Holidays.

Giles & Vickie Meadows
The Ship Inn,
Wincle,
Macclesfield,
Cheshire SK11 0QE

tel   01260 227217

map: 14 entry: 53

Cornwall

The Gurnard's Head Hotel
Treen

With the rugged Penwith Moors to one side and wind-swept cliffs to the other, this old Cornish pub shines like a beacon. On a night of driving Atlantic rain, walking into the Gurnard's stone-flagged bar with its blazing log fire is about as good as it gets. Book into one of the pine-furnished bedrooms, then head for the bar and a pint of Skinner's Cornish Knocker. The menu is influenced by the ocean. Warm up with seafood broth – a ravishing concoction of scallops, cockles, mussels, prawns, whitefish and crab with cider and herbs; then try John Dory, fried in butter and served with pickled marsh samphire. For hungry walkers there are steaks and ham and cheese platters. Puddings are served with lashings of local clotted cream. Twice a week, folk musicians draw the crowds. *New owners as we went to press.*

directions	On B3306 between St Ives & Land's End.
meals	12pm-2.15pm; 6.30pm-9.15pm (7pm Sundays). Main courses £7.50-£15.
rooms	6: 4 doubles, 1 twin, 1 family £55-£80.

The Gurnard's Head Hotel,
Treen, Zennor, St Ives,
Cornwall TR26 3DE

tel   01736 796928
web   www.gurnardshead.fsnet.co.uk

map: 1 entry: 54

The Star Inn
St Just

Entrenched in the wild landscape close to Land's End is the 'last proper pub in Cornwall'. This authentic 18th-century gem, St Just's oldest inn, proudly shirks the trappings of tourism and remains a drinkers' den. Bands of locals sink pints of Tinners Ale in the low-beamed, spick-and-span bar, old pub games thrive and the place is the hub of the local folk scene, with live music, sing-a-longs and joke-telling all part of the Monday evening entertainment. If you're here late on a Friday the local male voice choir may break into song. The dimly-lit bar is jam-packed with interest and walls are littered with seafaring and mining artefacts; coals glow in the grate on wild winter days. Food takes second place to St Austell ale and the 'craic', of course, but you'll find sustenance in the form of hearty soups, decent sandwiches and homemade pies. A Fifties' juke box, mulled wine in winter and that pub rarity: a great little family room.

The Halzephron
Gunwalloe

An opera singer running a remote smuggler's inn – irresistible! Looking out across the bay, the white-washed inn has been taking in guests (and smugglers: there's an underground passage) for 500 years. It reopened in 1958 as the Halzephron, old Cornish for 'cliffs of hell' and testament to the numerous ships dashed onto this stunning but treacherous stretch of coastline. Angela, exuberant and charming, has created some delightful eating areas around the bar, such as the 'sea cove' in wood-panelled marine-blue. Food is taken seriously. Freshly cooked and carefully presented: Mrs Kearsley's crab salad platter, seafood chowder with aioli, and roasted John Dory or chorizo with red wine sauce. Blow away the cobwebs on the cliff-top walk to Gunwalloe's 13th-century church beside the sand, or visit the wildlife haven of Looe Pool. Return to cosy bedrooms with deep-sprung beds, patchwork quilts, the odd heirloom, fresh fruit and real coffee.

directions	A3071 from Penzance. On right-hand side of square in centre.
meals	12pm-2pm. Soups, pasties & sandwiches c.£5.
rooms	2 doubles, 1 with shower room, 1 sharing shower, £20-£28.

directions	A3093 from Helston for The Lizard; right for Gunwalloe; 2 miles to pub.
meals	12pm-2pm; 7pm-9pm. Main courses £7-£17.
rooms	2 doubles £80. Singles £45.

Rosie Anguin
The Star Inn,
Fore Street,
St Just,
Cornwall TR19 7LL
tel 01736 788767

Angela Thomas
The Halzephron,
Gunwalloe,
Helston,
Cornwall TR12 7QB
tel 01326 240406

map: 1 entry: 55

map: 1 entry: 56

The Cadgwith Cove Inn
Cadgwith

Smack on the Cornish coastal path, in a thatched fishing hamlet on the rugged Lizard Peninsula sits this 300-year-old smugglers' inn. The two dimly-lit little bars with two open fires, furnished simply and decked with mementos of seafaring days, serve five ales on draught and pub grub from printed menus. For fresh and fishy daily specials, perhaps pan-fried sea bass with bacon and garlic or poached hake Florentine, look to the chalkboard. Mullet, sea bass, lobster and crab for delicious soup and sandwiches is landed on the beach below. Or try the lightly battered cod and chips, or a hearty bowl of plump mussels served with chunks of crusty bread – perfect after a cliff-path stroll to beautiful Church Cove and accompanied by a malty pint of Sharps Doom Bar. Say goodbye to a hard week on Friday and ensconce yourself in the bar for some traditional Cornish singing: the rafters resonate to the refrain of a male voice choir. In summer, lap up the views across Cadgwith's tiny working cove from the sunny front terrace.

| directions | Off A3083 between Helston & The Lizard. |
| meals | 12pm-3pm; 7pm-9pm. Main courses £5.95-£11.95. |

David & Lynda Trivett
The Cadgwith Cove Inn,
Cadgwith, Ruan Minor,
Helston, Cornwall TR12 7JX
tel   01326 290513
web   www.cadgwithcoveinn.com

map: 1 entry: 57

The Shipwright's Arms
Helford

Helford straggles beside a tidal creek on the wood-fringed waters of the river. Reachable only by foot (park in the car park and walk down), the pretty thatched pub has a gorgeous terraced garden of flowers and palms, with picnic benches on the water's edge. It was built in 1795 as a farmhouse – the shipwright connections came later – and as a summer pub is exceptionally popular… certainly on summer evenings, once the barbeque has got going. The interior is special, staunchly traditional, with simple country furnishings and open fires, full of nautical bits and pieces. Yachtmen tie up outside, then swap stories by the bar – there's always a buzz. The black panelled bar dispenses Sharps Doom Bar Bitter and buffet lunches. Walk off your ploughman's on the long distance coastal path that passes the front door – or the shorter circular walk via Frenchman's Creek – a smuggler's hideaway made famous by Daphne du Maurier and absolutely thrilling at high tide.

directions	On south side of Helford river & via Helston on The Lizard penninsula.
meals	12pm-2pm; 7pm-9pm. Main courses £8-£13.
closed	2.30pm-6pm; Sunday & Monday evenings in winter.

Charles Herbert
The Shipwright's Arms,
Helford,
Helston,
Cornwall TR12 6JX
tel   01326 231235

map: 1 entry: 58

Cornwall

Trengilly Wartha Inn
Nancenoy

Hard to navigate a car down the steep lanes to this rural hidey-hole near the Helford River — but worth it. Trengilly started life as a simple crofter's house and the pub has grown organically winning awards along the way. Honourable ales, real ciders, comfy wooden settles and good meals; *all* the locals come here. Wine is important, too; they have their own merchant business, based in the old piggery. Enjoy seasonal, modern British cooking (crab, scallops, Cornish fillet steak) in the pastel restaurant; families can use a no-smoking conservatory. There are pool and bar games, and a small sitting room away from the buzz with an open fire and books. Bedrooms are well done: those above the bar have more character than those in the annexe; nearly all have valley views. In summer, the six-acre garden fills with a happy throng.

directions	On A39 for Constantine for 7 miles. Inn signed left, then right.
meals	12pm-2.15pm (2pm Sundays); 6.30pm-9.30pm (7pm Sundays). No food Christmas Day. Main courses £5-£15; set dinner £21.50 & £27.
rooms	8: 5 doubles, 1 twin, 2 family £78-£96. Singles £49.

Nigel Logan & Michael Maguire
Trengilly Wartha Inn,
Nancenoy, Constantine,
Falmouth, Cornwall TR11 5RP
tel   01326 340332
web   www.trengilly.co.uk

map: 1 entry: 59

Cornwall

The Pandora Inn
Mylor Bridge

Yachtsmen moor their craft at the end of the pontoon that reaches into the creek. The building, too, is special: thatched and 13th-century. Originally The Passage House, it was renamed in memory of the *Pandora*, a naval ship sent to Tahiti to capture the mutineers of Captain Bligh's *Bounty*. The pub keeps the traditional layout on several levels, along with some dauntingly low wooden ceilings, panelled walls, polished flagged floors, snug alcoves, kitchen range, log fire and loads of maritime mementos. But it's not only the position, patio and pontoon that makes this one of Cornwall's best-loved inns; the bar food has something to please everyone, with fresh seafood dominating the 'specials' board. Arrive early in summer — by wheels or by boat — as the place gets packed and parking is tricky. On winter weekdays it's blissfully peaceful, and the post-prandial walking along wooded creekside paths easy.

directions	A39 from Truro; B3292 for Penryn & Mylor Bridge; descend steeply to Restronguet.
meals	12pm-2pm (2.30pm weekends); 6.30pm-9pm (9.30pm Fri & Sat). Main courses £6.95-£14.

John Milan
The Pandora Inn,
Restronguet Creek,
Mylor Bridge, Falmouth,
Cornwall TR11 5ST
tel   01326 372678

map: 1 entry: 60

Cornwall

The Roseland Inn
Philleigh

Beside a peaceful parish church, two miles from the King Harry Ferry and the river Fal, a cob-built Cornish treasure. The front courtyard is bright with blossom in spring, climbing roses in summer. Indoors: old settles with scatter cushions, worn slate floors, low black beams and winter log fires. Local photographs, gig-racing memorabilia and a corner dedicated to rugby trophies scatter the walls. The place is spotlessly kept and run with panache, and attracts locals and visitors in search of real ale and good food. Menu and blackboard dishes range from decent sandwiches and ploughman's platters to potted Cornish crab, local venison with red onion marmalade and sweet potato mash, and herb-crusted halibut with roasted sweet pepper jus. Staff are full of smiles — even when the pub doubles as the Roseland Rugby Club clubhouse and the lads down pints of Sharp's Doom Bar on winter Saturday nights.

directions	Off A3078 St Mawes road or via King Harry Ferry from Truro (Feock) to Philleigh.
meals	12pm-2pm; 6.30pm-9pm. Open all day in summer. Main courses £4.25-£14.
rooms	2 doubles £50. Singles £25.

Colin Phillips
The Roseland Inn,
Philleigh,
Truro, Cornwall TR2 5NB
tel 01872 580254
web www.roseland-inn.co.uk

map: 1 entry: 61

Cornwall

The Plume of Feathers
Mitchell

A sanctuary off a lonely stretch of carriageway. It was an inspired move of chef-patron Martyn Warner to transform the run-down, 16th-century coaching inn (where John Wesley once preached) into a stylish pub-restaurant with rooms. With food available all day, the inn has proved a hit with weary motorists and draws an appreciative crowd thanks to its imaginative cooking. Low, stripped beams, half-boarded walls hung with modern art, fresh flowers, candle-studded tables and subtle spotlighting make a relaxing backdrop to a roast rack of lamb with pumpkin ratatouille and wild mushroom confit — followed, with a bit of luck, by chocolate truffle tart. There's also a lively bar area with TV, piped music and Sharp's Doom Bar on tap. The once-dilapidated rear stables contain five stylishly simple bedrooms, replete with big brass beds, large-screen TVs and great bathrooms. Something different from the Little Chefs and the Travel Inns you passed by.

directions	Off junction of A30 & A3076.
meals	12pm-10pm. Main courses £7.25-£14.95.
rooms	5 doubles £55-£95. Singles £41.25-£71.25.

M F Warner
The Plume of Feathers,
Mitchell,
Truro,
Cornwall TR8 5AX
tel 01872 510387

map: 1 entry: 62

Cornwall

The Falcon Inn
St Mawgan

Traditional pubs are an endangered breed in Holiday Land; the Falcon is one of them, and a pub-lover's delight. In an attractive village, deep in the Vale of Lanherne and a stone's throw from its tiny stream, this 16th-century wisteria-draped inn is utterly unspoilt and a summer haven for those escaping the bucket-and-spade brigade on the beach. The muzak- and game-free main bar is neatly arranged and decorated with pine farmhouse tables and chairs. Chef-landlord Andy Banks sources fish and seafood from Newlyn (fresh cod in beer batter and Fowey mussels in cider and cream) and local meats, seasonal fruits and vegetables for his above average pub dishes listed on daily-changing blackboards. The dining room has a rug-strewn flagged floor, a pine dresser and French windows leading out into the cobbled courtyard. Beyond the rose-covered arch is a splendid terraced garden, ideal for summer quaffing.

directions	A30 for Newquay airport; right for St Mawgan. At bottom of hill by church.
meals	12pm-2pm; 6.30pm-9pm. Main courses £7.25-£14.
rooms	4 twins/doubles £50-£70.
closed	3-6pm (7pm Sundays).

Andy Banks
The Falcon Inn,
St Mawgan, Newquay,
Cornwall TR8 4EP
tel 01637 860225
web www.falconinn.net

map: 1 entry: 63

Cornwall

The Earl of St Vincent
Egloshayle

Open the door to an Aladdin's cave. The 15th-century inn is filled to the rafters with Edward Connolly's favourite things: rich furnishings, paintings, prints and an absolutely amazing collection of clocks, from grandfather to antique ball-bearing. All are in perfect working order. One bar is so tiny it resounds with ticking clocks; noon – and 'time' – is called by a cacophony of chimes, bongs and cuckoos. The Earl of St Vincent which hides in the oldest, most rambling part of Egloshayle started life as a boarding house for the masons who built the church, and was named after one of Nelson's admirals. Once a run-down local, it is now a beamy, atmospheric and civilised public house. Food is of the liver and bacon, ham and eggs and mixed grills variety; well-kept beers include Tinners and Tribute. While away a sunny afternoon in the garden – a prizewinning, floral wonderland.

directions	On Bodmin to Wadebridge road.
meals	12pm-2pm; 12.15pm-1.45pm Sun; 7pm-9pm. No food Sun evenings. Main courses £6-£14.
closed	3pm-6.30pm (7pm Sundays).

Edward, John & Anne Christine Connolly
The Earl of St Vincent,
Egloshayle, Wadebridge,
Cornwall PL27 6HT
tel 01208 814807

map: 1 entry: 64

St Kew Inn
St Kew

Lost down a maze of lanes in a secluded wooded valley, the St Kew is a grand old inn that stands next to the parish church. Though its stone walls go back 600 years – it was built for the masons working on the church – it has been welcoming visitors for a mere 200. Reputedly haunted by a Victorian village girl discovered buried beneath the main bar, it is an irresistibly friendly, chatty place with a huge range and a warming fire, a dark Delabole slate floor, winged high-backed settles and a refreshingly unspoilt atmosphere – no intrusive music or pub paraphernalia here. Meat hooks hang from a high ceiling, earthenware flagons and old-fashioned mincers embellish the mantelpiece, fresh flowers brighten the bar. Local St Austell ales are served in the traditional way, straight from the barrel. In summer, the big streamside garden is the place to be.

Port Gaverne Inn
Port Gaverne

Owners of a relaxed country house B&B on the south coast, Graham and Annabelle have turned their attentions to this north coast gastropub with rooms. The food, cooked fresh in a modern English style – sweet pepper soup, mussels, baked wing of skate – has come on in leaps and bounds since they took over. The 17th-century inn is set back from rocky, funnel-shaped Port Gaverne near the pretty fishing village of Port Isaac where people come for the sea and quiet relaxation. In the warren-like bar, snug cubby-holes warmed by a woodburner are ideal for recuperating with a pint after a hike along the coast – walks start from the door. A wonderful stained-glass picture of a rigger leads to the formal restaurant. Bedrooms in the oldest part of the building have beams, those in the modern wing have been updated by the Sylvesters, and some have access to a small balcony. Once an ordinary seaside hotel, now a stylish little inn.

directions	From Wadebridge for Bude on A39 for 4 miles; left after golf club. 1 mile to St Kew Churchtown.
meals	12pm-2pm; 7pm-9.30pm (9pm in winter). No food Christmas Day & Boxing Day evening. Main courses £6.75-£11.95.
closed	2.30pm-6pm (7pm Sundays). Open all day July-August.

directions	From Wadebridge B3314; B3267 to Port Isaac. There to Port Gaverne. Inn up lane from cove on left.
meals	12pm-2pm; 6.30pm-9pm. Main courses £5-£10.95; set menu £25.
rooms	15 twins/doubles £75-£95.

Des & Ginny Weston
St Kew Inn,
St Kew Churchtown,
Bodmin,
Cornwall PL30 3HB

tel   01208 841259

Graham Sylvester
Port Gaverne Inn,
Port Gaverne, Port Isaac,
Cornwall PL29 3SQ

tel   01208 880244
web   www.portgaverne.co.uk

map: 1 entry: 65

map: 1 entry: 66

Cornwall

The Mill House Inn
Trebarwith

You come down a steep winding lane to get to the old mill house in its pretty woodland setting. The atmosphere in the bar is family-friendly easy: a rustic slate floor, wooden tables and chapel chairs, a battered armchair by a wood-burning stove. The dining room over the old mill stream has light, elegance and a bistro feel: sea blues, white linen, subtle lighting that creates a tongue-in-cheek formality. Settle down to mussel and monkfish curry or a plate of West Country cheeses in the bar, plus a pint of rich Sharp's Doom Bar... or roast cod with bacon, crushed potatoes and gravy, followed perhaps by lemon zest and coconut tart. Delicious, and there are tables by the stream for summer dining. Chic, affordable bedrooms, too, and all you need a walk away: a glorious sandy beach, rolling surf and coastal trails that lead to Tintagel, official home of the Arthurian legends.

directions	From Tintagel, B3263 south, to Trebarwith Strand.
meals	12pm-2.30pm; 7pm-9.30pm; 1pm-7pm Sundays. Main courses £6-£8.95.
rooms	9 twins/doubles £70-£80. Singles £40.

Nigel Peters
Mill House Inn,
Trebarwith, Tintagel,
Cornwall PL34 0HD
tel 01840 770200
web www.themillhouseinn.co.uk

map: 1 entry: 67

Cornwall

The Springer Spaniel
Treburley

If only more roadside pubs were as bustling as The Springer. Long a favoured haunt of local foodies, the pub has a excellent new licensee in Richard Beaman, who has carefully restored it and is injecting new vigour. The neat, parquet-floored main bar has an unusual high-backed settle and two farmhouse chairs hugging a wood-burning stove, comfortable wall benches and rustic tables. There's a pleasing absence of fruit machines and piped music, but much happy chat. Up the steps to the beamed dining-room, where lunch and dinner menus are long and list a good mix of traditional and modern pub dishes, all fresh and homemade. Quaff a pint of Sharp's Doom Bar, take your fill of Cornish reared beef or local game, fish landed at Looe, and cheeses and cream from the Cornish famers' cooperative, Plough to Plate. Chalkboard specials feature, in season, wild boar terrine, honey-roasted wild duck, plaice with bacon and beurre blanc. In summer there's a secluded side garden to retire to, tucked away from the traffic.

directions	On A388 midway between Launceston & Callington.
meals	12pm-2pm; 6pm-9pm. Main courses £6.50-£13.95.

Craig Woolley & Richard Beaman
The Springer Spaniel,
Treburley,
Launceston,
Cornwall PL15 9NS
tel 01579 370424

map: 2 entry: 68

Cornwall

The Bush Inn
Morwenstow

After a romantic walk along the cliffs – where the eccentric 19th-century local vicar and poet, Robert Hawker, built a little shack to contemplate the sea and the greater questions – the simple, traditional Bush Inn, a genuinely ancient pub, makes the perfect resting place. Once a monastic rest-house, it dates back in part to 950 when it was a hermit's cell. A Celtic piscina carved from serpentine is set in one wall, while slate-flagged floors, a huge stone fireplace and lovely old wooden furnishings preserve the timeless character of this individual, immutable tavern. Weary walkers will find excellent St Austell HSD on draught, and hearty pub food – try the homemade soups and stews. There's seating on the front lawn, and a view out to sea. Visit the parish church to learn more about Robert Hawker, an extraordinary man who spent 40 years serving a multitude of smugglers, wreckers and dissenters.

directions	Off A39, 9 miles south of Bude.
meals	12pm-2pm. No food Sundays. Main courses £4.50.
closed	Mondays in winter.

Beryl Moore
The Bush Inn,
Crosstown,
Morwenstow, Bude,
Cornwall EX23 9SR
tel 01288 331242

map: 2 entry: 69

Cumbria

Shepherds Inn
Melmerby

The Eden Valley conceals a string of fellside villages. Melmerby is one of them, its sandstone cottages overlooking a green, its footpaths leading to the long climb up Hartside. The village has had a foodie reputation since the 1970s, thanks to the now legendary Village Bakery. Locals Garry and Marcia Parkin took over in 2002 and give classic pub dishes a modern twist (delicious Cumberland sausages), while wonderful cheeses and homemade bread come with the Ultimate Ploughman's Lunch. The pub is inviting at any time of year, with its sheltered sunny frontage and its winter comfort: an open fire in the top lounge and a wood-burning stove in the converted barn. There's a games area with pool, children are welcome, and the choice of cask ales, whiskies, wines and fruit wines is fantastic – good news after a day out on the wild Pennine moors.

directions	M6 junc. 40; A686 to Alston. 9 miles out of Penrith.
meals	11.30am-2.30pm (12pm Sundays); 6pm-9pm (7pm Sundays; 9.45pm Fridays & Saturdays.) Main courses £6-£10.
closed	3pm-6pm (7pm Sundays).

Gary & Marcia Parkin
Shepherds Inn,
Melmerby, Penrith,
Cumbria CA10 1HF
tel 017688 81217

map: 16 entry: 70

Cumbria

Old Crown
Hesket Newmarket

Some years ago Hesket Newmarket Brewery was saved by a cooperative, as was its pub. The Crown's tiny front room with bar, settles, glowing coals, well-thumbed books, pictures and a mass of memorabilia manages to squeeze in a dozen. There's another room with darts and pool, and a simply furnished dining room. Not only is this the only pub where you can sample all of Hesket Newmarket's distinctive beers but it is the focal point of the community – even supporting the fragile village post office, whose postmistress repays the pub in puddings and pies. The Old Crown is also known for its unpretentious grub: local bangers and mash, ham and eggs, fine curries, Sunday roasts. Its sheer authenticity draws people from miles around to explore the Caldbeck Fells; from the higher ground views reach over the Solway Firth to Scotland.

directions	M6 junc. 41 for Wigton on B5305. After 6.5 miles turn for Hesket Newmarket.
meals	12pm-2.30pm; 6.30pm-8.30pm. No food Sunday evenings; Monday & Tuesday evenings in winter. Main courses £5-£9.50.
closed	Monday & Tuesday lunchtimes in winter.

Lewis Hogg
Old Crown,
Hesket Newmarket,
Carlisle,
Cumbria CA7 8JG
tel   016974 78288

map: 16 entry: 71

Cumbria

Mill Inn
Mungrisdale

By a tumbling burn at the foothills of Blencathra... the setting could not be more idyllic. The village inn has a solid northern feel and is there to provide a down-to-earth yet comfortable welcome. The neat, simple bar has a warming fire and a wooden counter that dispenses Jennings ales to locals and walkers. A light and airy room at the back doubles for games and families and there's a riverside garden for summer. Since their arrival a few years ago, Jim and Margaret Hodge have built up a reputation for home-cooked country dishes – and they organise an annual pie festival. Evening specials may include a pie of wild venison and fresh cranberries marinated in port, or Moroccan lamb tagine – and there are homemade scones for tea. Upstairs rooms at the 16th-century inn are not huge but are freshly decorated and excellent value.

directions	From M6 junc. 40, A66 for Keswick for 10 miles; right for Mungrisdale; 1.5 miles to inn.
meals	12pm-2.30pm; 6pm-8.30pm; 5.30pm-9pm weekends in summer. Main courses £6.25-£15.50.
rooms	6: 3 doubles, 2 twin; 1 twin with separate bath £60. Singles £40.
closed	25-26 December.

Jim & Margaret Hodge
Mill Inn,
Mungrisdale, Penrith,
Cumbria CA11 0XR
tel   017687 79632
web   www.the-millinn.co.uk

map: 13 entry: 72

Cumbria

The Queen's Head Inn
Tirril

William Wordsworth and his brother sold the inn in the early 1800s to a Mr Bewsher after whom one of Tirril Brewery's ales is named. Chris Tomlinson brewed here before expanding operations at nearby Brougham Hall, but the whitewashed village inn is still the 'brewery tap' and hosts the Cumbrian Beer and Sausage Festival each August. Inside, oodles of charm with low beams, wooden settles and several open fires including a vast inglenook – whose logs smoulder, even, occasionally, in June – with its original hooks for smoking meat. At the back is a lively bar and games room. Sit down to some well-priced food in the bar or the cosy, carpeted, non-smoking restaurant, where braised shoulder of Lakeland lamb with redcurrant gravy will set you up for a day on England's highest peaks. Other chalkboard specials may include whole grilled sea bream and fresh pasta. Comfortable rooms, with bathrooms, ice this particular cake.

directions	On B5320, 3 miles south of Penrith.
meals	12pm-2pm; 6pm-9.30pm; 6.30pm-9pm Sundays. Main courses £7.95-£15.50.
rooms	7: 5 doubles, 2 twins £70. Singles £40.

Chris Tomlinson
The Queen's Head Inn,
Tirril, Penrith,
Cumbria CA10 2JF
tel 017688 63219
web www.queensheadinns.co.uk

map: 13 entry: 73

Cumbria

Brackenrigg Inn
Watermillock

The front terrace and bay windows have breathtaking views across the water to the fells and this 18th-century inn draws drinkers and diners in droves. Attention to detail is the thing here, and service is swift and friendly. The part-panelled bar with polished old boards, darts and open fire has a homely feel, as does the carpeted lounge-dining room where families are welcome. Expect Black Sheep and local Jennings beers on tap and an unusual wine list – ask about the wine appreciation weekends. The idea here is "food without fuss" and menus have a modern British slant; Cumberland sausage with apple mash in the bar, maybe, roast lamb rump with balsamic roasted tomatoes and madeira jus in the restaurant, glazed lemon tart for pudding. Sunday lunch is particularly good value. Newly done-up stable cottages have excellent bedrooms and family-sized suites, several suitable for wheelchair-users.

directions	M6 junc. 40 A66 for Keswick; A592 for Ullswater; Watermillock 5 miles.
meals	12pm-2.30pm; 6.30pm-9pm. Main courses £7.50-£12.95; set menu £18.95 & £21.95.
rooms	17 twins/doubles £54-£77.
closed	3pm-5pm November-March.

Garry Smith
Brackenrigg Inn,
Watermillock, Penrith,
Cumbria CA11 0LP
tel 017684 86206
web www.brackenrigginn.co.uk

map: 13 entry: 74

Cumbria

Shepherds Arms
Ennerdale Bridge

Beside a rushing stream in pretty Ennerdale Bridge, the immaculate Shepherds Arms strikes the balance between community pub and small hotel. It's also 'Overnight Stop 2' on Wainwright's Coast to Coast Walk, so they're used to muddy boots. Pass the ancestral portraits in the entrance – to reach the peaceful lounge with fine old furnishings, settles and armchairs; then go down the Victorian tiled passage to the cosy bar – a bookcase, daily papers, an open fire; then a conservatory at the back where doors open in summer to gardens bordering the stream. The Maddens' enthusiasm for real ale draws aficionados from miles and their eagerness to support local food suppliers and producers results in some fine home cooking: goat's cheese tartlet, half shoulder of fellside lamb with mint and garlic jus, rum and raisin pudding – beautifully served in a Georgian panelled dining room. Eight cosy bedrooms too.

directions	East from A5086, by Ennerdale Water.
meals	12.30pm-2pm; 6.30pm-9pm. Main courses £5.95-£14.95.
rooms	8: 5 doubles, 3 twins £58-£74. Singles £37.50-£44.50.
closed	Christmas Day.

	Steve & Val Madden
	Shepherds Arms,
	Ennerdale Bridge,
	Cumbria CA23 3AR
tel	019468 61249
web	www.shepherdsarmshotel.co.uk

map: 13 entry: 75

Cumbria

Bridge Hotel
Buttermere

The old coaching inn is a walkers' pub with the feel of a country hotel. The beamed, flagged bar sports built-in settles at shining wooden tables; another room has blue upholstered chairs and copper-topped tables at which you can eat. When the sun shines, it's onto the flagstoned terrace for sensational views accompanied by good booze; there are three cask ales and several excellent wines. Bar food is tasty and homemade: unusual sandwiches, baguettes and tortilla wraps, homemade burgers, butterbean casserole, Borrowdale trout. A belt-loosening five-course dinner is served in the hotel's formal, cream and yellow dining room, overlooking a tumbling stream. For residents there's a lounge with beautiful pale sofas and an open fire, while lushy decorated bedrooms are as comfortable as can be, some with balconies with views, all (thanks to poor reception!) free of radios and TVs.

directions	A66, turn at Braithwaite for Newlands Pass into Buttermere.
meals	10.30am-9.30pm. Bar food £2.25-£7.50.
rooms	21: 10 doubles, 7 twins, 2 singles, 2 four-posters. £110-£170. Singles £60.

	John & Adrian McGuire
	Bridge Hotel,
	Buttermere,
	Cumbria CA13 9UZ
tel	017687 70252
web	www.bridge-hotel.com

map: 13 entry: 76

Cumbria

Old Dungeon Ghyll
Great Langdale

In frontier land, a barn of a place – with flag floor, cattle-stall seating and a big fire to toast in front of. To hikers ruddy from the day's exertions, full of stories of courage in the face of adversity – mist, driving rain, mobile phone failure and the like – it serves decent grub and mugs of tea as well as God's own beer, Yates. The atmosphere is infectious – but avoid Bank Holidays at all costs. In wild weather you feel cocooned within the substantial stone walls; when it's fine there are tables outside with Tolkeinian views in every direction. Next door is the hotel, once a farm: not all bedrooms have their own bathrooms but they are pretty with pine furniture and patchwork quilts. The dining room has great breakfasts, suppers are farmhouse-style feasts.

directions	From Ambleside, A593 for Coniston, right on B5343. On right after 5 miles, signed, past Great Langdale campsite.
meals	12pm-2pm; 6pm-9pm. Main courses £7-£9.
rooms	14 family, doubles, twins, single rooms; some en suite. £39-£88. .
closed	4 days at Christmas.

Neil Walmsley
Old Dungeon Ghyll,
Great Langdale, Ambleside,
Cumbria LA22 9JY

tel 015394 37272
web www.odg.co.uk

map: 13 entry: 77

Cumbria

The Britannia Inn
Elterwater

Being everyone's secret, this pub is always busy, with happy customers spilling out onto the terrace, garden and maple-shaded village green. At the centre of lovely Elterwater, with Great Langdale Beck tumbling past into the tarn close by, it's a brilliant starting point for walkers. Drinking and eating happen together in the low-ceilinged rooms, corridors and the little velvety snug – ever welcoming with old settles, oak seats, open fires and homely touches. A fine range of ales is always on tap (they have their own champion beers festival in November) and menus carry satisfying lunchtime sandwiches or tasty main dishes. In the evening, food has more of a restaurant style. Book ahead if you want to stay: the Britannia's atmosphere is compulsive.

directions	A593 for 3 miles; right at Skelwith Bridge onto B5343, after a mile cross cattle grid. Next left is Elterwater; in middle of village.
meals	12pm-9.30pm. Main courses £6.95-£14.
rooms	9: 7 doubles, 2 twins £84-£92. Singles £74-£82.

Clare Woodhead & Christopher Jones
The Britannia,
Elterwater, Ambleside,
Cumbria LA22 9HP

tel 015394 37210
web www.britinn.co.uk

map: 13 entry: 78

The Drunken Duck Inn
Ambleside

At an isolated crossroads where narrow winding lanes meet stands this old inn, enfolded by high peaks and craggy tree-covered fells, small tarns and green fields enclosed by stone walls or high hedges. It is a stunning, quintessential Lakeland scene. The Duck has long been a popular watering hole among walkers and still is, in spite of its fresh contemporary face. Traditionally furnished small rooms with beams, picture-lined walls and open fires radiate from the solid bar – sheer joy for real ale enthusiasts, with all four home-brewed Barngates beers on handpump, and the Cracker Ale really living up to its name. There are also 20 wines available by the glass. Simple lunchtime menus may include bread with Cumbrian cheeses, or Holker Hall venison pie; on the more elaborate evening menu – fresh, seasonal – maybe ginger-marinated fillet of pork with garlic jus, or baked red snapper with fig and lemon confit. Bedrooms – in the old pub and a new building – are smartly kitted out and have impeccable bathrooms. All have views and one a balcony overlooking the garden – yours to explore, along with 60 glorious acres of woodland and tarn.

directions	From Ambleside B5286 for Hawkshead for 2.5 miles; right at inn signpost.
meals	12pm-2.30pm; 6pm-9pm. Main courses £11.95-£18.75.
rooms	16: 15 doubles, 1 twin £85-£190. Singles from £56.

Stephanie Barton
The Drunken Duck Inn,
Barngates, Ambleside,
Cumbria LA22 0NG
tel   015394 36347
web   www.drunkenduckinn.co.uk

map: 13 entry: 79

Cumbria

Queen's Head Hotel
Troutbeck

The Queen's Head crouches at the foot of the Kirkstone pass, with sweeping views over moor and valley. Inside it is a warren of fascinating rooms. The flagged bar is built around a magnificently carved Elizabethan four-poster. Old instruments hang above beams, stuffed birds and beasts gaze down from mantelpiece and alcove. In the dining room upstairs are a carved giant's chair and two big windows for the view, while blazing logs in the large open fireplace are a focal point on chilly days. Food is taken seriously, and there's masses of choice. Try the homemade bread and soup for a quick lunch, or go for salmon with lemon grass and ginger. There's even proper food for children. The bar appeals just as much to those in search only of a drink, with its fine cask beers (some local), and a wide choice of wines by the glass. Bedrooms are fancy with amazing views.

directions	M6 junc 36; A591 for Windermere; right on A592 to Patterdale. 2.5 miles on left.
meals	12pm-2pm; 6.30pm-9pm. Main courses £9.95-£14.25.
rooms	14: 6 doubles, 8 four-poster bed £37.50-£52.50. Singles £55-£70.
closed	Christmas Day.

Mark Stewardson & Joanne Sherratt
Queen's Head Hotel,
Townhead, Troutbeck,
Windermere, Cumbria LA23 1PW
tel   015394 32174
web   www.queensheadhotel.com

map: 13 entry: 80

Cumbria

Burnmoor Inn
Boot

Eskdale is one of England's most inaccessible valleys. Get here via the Cumbrian coastal road, or over the steep and challenging Hardknott Pass: either is a treat. Burnmoor was a farmhouse in 1578 and an inn two centuries later. Harry and Paddington Berger took it on in 1998 and have modernised comfortably. There's a roaring log fire in the cosy main bar, a play area outside, a games room in, and hearty home cooking: meals are served throughout the day; you state whether your appetite is "normal or starving". Plenty of local and organic food, game in season, and a slim but thoughtfully chosen wine list supported by four or more Cumbrian ales. In fine weather it's a joy to sit out. Many who come here stay the night: the nine bright bedrooms all have views, and a hearty breakfast sets you up for the path to England's highest point, Scafell Pike. Fido is welcome, too.

directions	From M6 junc. 36 for Broughton-in-Furness, then for Ulpha to Eskdale & Boot.
meals	11.30am-9pm (8.30pm Sundays). Main courses £6.50-£14.
rooms	9: 6 twins/doubles, 1 single, 1 family. £56-£60; singles £28-£38.

Harry & Paddington Berger
Burnmoor Inn,
Boot,
Cumbria CA19 1TG
tel   019467 23224
web   www.burnmoor.co.uk

map: 13 entry: 81

The Sun
Coniston

Coniston skirts the edge of Coniston Water – famous, of course, for Donald Campbell's world water-speed trials in *Bluebird*. Off its busy hub sits the Sun. At the front is the hotel with its Edwardian façade, at the back, the old inn. Inside, stone flags, beams, settles and a 19th-century range. It's an honest, no-nonsense little pub, the ideal place in which to quaff a fine selection of local cask ales. Wines too are well-chosen with at least six by the glass. Wooden agricultural implements add to the old-fashioned Cumbrian feel, as do the stools at the bar, the dartboard, and the blackboard of tasty dishes, nothing too fancy – steak and kidney cobbler, that sort of thing. For summer there's seating outside on a flagged area, and a tree-sheltered garden in front of the hotel's conservatory dining room, with views. The simply furnished bedrooms are decently priced and are gradually being upgraded.

directions	Up hill from bridge in village centre, off A593 Ambleside road.
meals	12pm-2.30pm; 6pm-9pm. Main courses £8.50-£16.
rooms	10: 4 doubles, 2 twins, 3 family, 1 single, £80-£90.

Alan Piper
The Sun,
Coniston,
Cumbria LA21 8HQ
tel   015394 41248
web   www.thesunconiston.com

map: 13 entry: 82

Manor Arms
Broughton-in-Furness

Unspoilt, grey-stoned Broughton-in-Furness – complete with village stocks – is a market town that feels like a village. In a corner of its Georgian square stands the 18th-century Manor Arms, a modest inn that has been in the Varty family for years. This is not a foody's pub, though hot snacks are on tap all day – pizzas, sausages, homemade soup and the like. Its main fascination lies in its traditional bar and its several ales; on handpump may be Coniston Bluebird, Plassy Bitter, Felinfoel Dark, with more in the cellar. In his unpretentious quest for perfection David Varty goes to some lengths to ensure his beers are in top-class condition. Cosy up on the bay window seat with children's books and games – little ones are welcome here. Logs burn in a rare 'basket' fireplace into whose oak mantel drinkers have scored their names down the centuries. Negotiate the stairs to three comfortable bedrooms; look forward to local sausages and free-range eggs at breakfast.

directions	On A593, 10 miles south west of Coniston.
meals	12pm-10pm. Snacks, sandwiches & soup only.
rooms	3 doubles £50.

David Varty
Manor Arms,
The Square,
Broughton-in-Furness,
Cumbria LA20 6HY
tel   012297 16286

map: 13 entry: 83

Cumbria

Blacksmiths Arms
Broughton Mills

An utterly unspoilt little local – there are few this good in the north of England. In the land of rugged hills and wooded valleys, you approach down a winding lane between high hedges; once you are round the final bend, the low-slung farmhouse-inn comes into view. Inside are four small, slate-floored rooms with beams and low ceilings, long settles, big old tables and several log fires. It couldn't be more 'homely' with its ornaments, dominoes and darts. The bar is strictly for drinking – indeed, there's not much room for anything else; there are three cask ales (two local, one guest) and traditional cider in summer. Across the passage, a room serving proper fresh food, snacks or full meals, and two further dining rooms that sparkle with glass and cutlery. The blackboard advertises dishes with a contemporary slant plus organic bread from the Broughton bakery. The food is seriously good, so it gets busy; in summer you can spill onto the flowery terrace.

directions	1 mile off A593, Broughton to Coniston road.
meals	12pm-2pm; 6pm-9pm. Main courses £6.95-£11.95.
closed	Christmas Day.

Michael & Sophie Lane
Blacksmiths Arms, Broughton Mills,
Broughton-in-Furness,
Cumbria LA20 6AX
tel   01229 716824
web   www.theblacksmithsarms.com

map: 13 entry: 84

Cumbria

The White Hart
Bouth

The main bar has a central counter dripping with brass, jugs and hops; walls and shelves are strewn with agrarian implements, clay pipes, old photos, washboards, taxidermy, tankards and mugs. It's a friendly, sleepy-village local, where regulars mingle happily with visitors over foaming pints of Black Sheep and Hawkshead Bitter. There are loads of malts, too, and a no-nonsense menu that includes rare-breed meat from nearby Abbots Reading farm. They source locally, and there are small portions for children. An age-polished, slopey flagged floor reflects the light from the window; grand fires at both ends are log-fuelled in cold weather. There's also a fresh smoke-free zone off the main bar where you can eat. Bedrooms with stunning views have been recently added; the walking's marvellous and both pub and village fit snugly into the ancient landscape of wooded valleys and tight little roads.

directions	Off A590 Barrow road after Lakeside & Haverthwaite Steam Railway.
meals	12pm-2pm; 6pm-8.45pm. Main courses £7.25-£11.95.
rooms	6: 3 twins, 3 doubles £40-£70.
closed	Mondays & Tuesdays.

Nigel Barton
The White Hart,
Bouth, Ulverston,
Cumbria LA12 8JB
tel   012298 61229
web   www.whitehartbouth.co.uk

map: 13 entry: 85

The Mason's Arms
Bowland Bridge

Slake your thirst with damson beer – or gin: the Lyth valley is known for its fruit. The countryside is gentle and the pub sits high on a steep wooded hillside; from the terrace you can see for glorious miles. Getting here may test your map reading skills but don't give up: this is no ordinary local. Over 100 bottled beers are on sale – continental beer engines gleam next to ebony handpumps – with a range of nearby Hawkshead Brewery beers plus others. There's charm too: open fires, old flag floors, black beams, Jacobean panelling and a family parlour. Dishes range from baked bass to vegetarian lasagne to good old steak and kidney pud. Eat in the bar rooms or in the upstairs dining areas, furnished with understated style. Window tables have stunning views.

The Punch Bowl
Crosthwaite

A reassuring old inn in a gentle setting, overlooking the valley. Through the flower-tubbed entrance into a high raftered bar with a minstrel's gallery; then to a dining room of intimate corners. Open fires, paintings and polished pieces make this a civilised and handsome country pub, while framed accolades tell of Steven Doherty's relationship with the Roux brothers: he was head chef at Le Gavroche. Superb sandwiches are available but it would be a shame to miss the saddle of rabbit with a wild mushroom sauce, or fillet of salmon on tagliatelle, or steamed white chocolate and vanilla sponge… The two-course lunch menu is terrific value, accompanied by 21 wines by the glass and a flurry of real ales. Comfortable rooms with four-posters beckon.

directions	M6 junc. 36; A591 to Kendal for 3.5 miles; A590 for Barrow-in-Furness; 2 miles onto A5074 for Bowness & then B. Bridge. Just beyond village.
meals	12pm-2.30pm; 6pm-9pm. All day in summer. Main courses £8-£14.
rooms	2 cottages: 1 for 6, 1 for 4. 3 suites: 2 suites, 1 suite for 4. £80-£150.
closed	3pm-6pm in winter.

directions	M6 junc. 36; A591; left onto A590; right onto A5074; hotel on right, over small bridge for Kendal. At end of road left; next to church.
meals	12pm-2pm; 6pm-9pm. Main courses £8.95-£14.95; set menus £10.95 & £13.95 (lunch), £15.95 & £17.95 (Sunday lunch).
rooms	3 doubles, half-board, £115. Singles, half-board, £60.
closed	Sunday evenings & Mondays.

John & Diane Taylor
The Mason's Arms,
Strawberry Bank, Bowland Bridge,
Cartmell Fell, Cumbria LA11 6NW
tel 015395 68486
web www.strawberrybank.com

Steven Doherty
The Punch Bowl,
Crosthwaite,
Kendal, Cumbria LA8 8HR
tel 015395 68237
web www.punchbowl.fsnet.co.uk

map: 13 entry: 86

map: 13 entry: 87

Cumbria

The Wheatsheaf
Beetham

A timeless air pervades the village of Beetham. The Wheatsheaf traces its origins back to the 16th century, hence the leaded windows, dark wood panelling, fine mouldings and wide open stairs. Comfortable furnishings and pictures lend an easy air. Beyond the intimate bar is a classic tap room with a big open fire and old prints while the first-floor dining room has a country-house feel. Lunchtime bar food ranges from generous sandwiches to dishes like Thai-spiced crab and salmon fishcakes or Cumberland sausages with creamy mash. Pan-seared duck marinated in honey, coriander and cumin appear in the evening and fine wines from Frank Stainton of Kendal join cask ales from Jennings and a local brewer to keep drinkers happy. Bedrooms are decorated with flair.

directions	Off A6, 1 mile south of Milnthorpe.
meals	12pm-2pm (2.15pm Sundays); 6pm-9pm; 6.30pm-8.30pm Sundays. Main courses £7.95-£16.95; set menu £9.95-£11.95 (Sunday lunch).
rooms	5: 4 doubles, 1 twin £40-£80. Singles £55.
closed	2.30pm-5.30pm (6pm Sundays).

Mark & Kath Chambers
The Wheatsheaf,
Beetham,
Milnthorpe, Cumbria LA7 7AL

tel 015395 62123
web www.wheatsheafbeetham.com

map: 13 entry: 88

Cumbria

The Moorcock
Garsdale Head

Wild and remote it may be, but the locals beat a path to this pub's door. The Moorcock crouches in an isolated moorland spot at the meeting of roads from Kirkby Stephen, Sedbergh and Hawes at the top end of Wensleydale. The outside looks straightforward enough but the inside is a surprise: the young owners, who took over three years ago, have decorated with massive originality and flair. The traditional bar area, with bar stools and solid fuel stove, is cheerfully fronted by a sofa, cushioned seating and a mix of tables, objects and plants. There's a quirky stylishness that is striking in such an utterly unworldly setting. The bar stocks up to four cask ales, mostly local, and there's an impressive array of malts. Food is the best of traditional pub grub. All is bright, welcoming and comfortable, including the attractive bedrooms upstairs, one perfect for families. They have worked wonders in their first three years.

directions	On A684, just after Garsdale station.
meals	10am-9pm. Main courses £3.25-£12.95.
rooms	2 twins/doubles £50.
closed	Christmas Day afternoon.

Mark Edward Owens
The Moorcock,
Garsdale Head,
Sedbergh, Cumbria LA10 5PU

tel 01969 667488
web www.moorcockinn.com

map: 13 entry: 89

Cumbria

Fat Lamb Country Inn
Ravenstonedale

No juke box, no pool – just a cheery, lived-in feel. Paul Bonsall's rambling, 17th-century farmhouse-inn has a carpeted main bar warmed by logs in an old black range, a lounge overlooking a patio and a lawned garden edged by ash trees and fields of sheep. At the bottom of the lower field is his wetland nature reserve, and what started as a hobby has "run away with itself". Over the years the Fat Lamb has built up a reputation for friendly service and good food: treat yourself to local Bessy Beck trout with a fresh fennel and ginger butter sauce, or roast leg of local lamb with redcurrant jelly and mint gravy. The table d'hôte dinners served in the low beamed and stone-walled restaurant are very popular – do book. Views sweep across fells and moor – if you're keen to spend a few days exploring by foot or by car, put up here. Spotless bedrooms are well-equipped, and those on the ground floor are perfect for wheelchairs.

directions	On A683 midway between Sedbergh & Kirkby Stephen.
meals	12pm-2pm; 6pm-9pm. All day in summer. Main courses £6.50-£12.50
rooms	12 twins/doubles £70-£85. Singles £45-£48.

Paul Bonsall
Fat Lamb Country Inn,
Crossbank, Ravenstonedale,
Kirkby Stephen, Cumbria CA17 4LL
tel   015396 23242
web   www.fatlamb.co.uk

map: 13 entry: 90

Derbyshire

The Plough
Hathersage

Expect a big welcome from Bob and Cynthia and their team at their 16th-century free house, once a corn mill, on the banks of the river. Acres of grounds and a riverside garden high in the National Park are the perfect backdrop to a perfect inn. Imaginative dishes – from good-value bar meals to more eclectic à la carte – are the order of the day and, with over 40 main dishes to choose from and a good range of hand-pulled ales and several decent wines, there's something for everyone. The atmosphere is unpretentious and homely in the cosy, convivial, split-level bar; settle down to log fires, exposed beams and brickwork, good solid furniture and, beyond, the intimate country restaurant area. Cross the cobbled courtyard at the back to find two excellent new bedrooms, in addition to three cottagey ones in the main building. Breakfasts are as good as you'd expect and the service first class.

directions	On B6001 1 mile from Hathersage for Bakewell.
meals	11.30am-2.30pm; 6.30pm-9.30pm (12pm-9pm Sundays). Main courses £7.95-£16.95.
rooms	5: 2 twins, 3 doubles from £69.50. Singles £55.

Bob Emery
The Plough,
Leadmill Bridge,
Hathersage,
Derbyshire S32 1BA
tel   01433 650319

map: 14 entry: 91

Derbyshire

Three Stags Heads
Wardlow Mires

Do not judge a pub by its cover. This unpretentious moorland inn with three stags' skulls fastened to the front by way of a sign may look a plain, squat, stark place on the outside (especially in driving rain) and scuffed around the edges inside, but it's a gem. It's a walkers' pub; dressed in anything other than waterproofs and gaiters, you may feel out of place. The small, plain front bar has a coal-burning kitchen range and there's another fire in the slightly larger dining room next door – just the thing for drying out muddy boots. Pat and Geoff Fuller have a splendidly relaxed attitude and run things their way, which means erratic opening hours (so check opening days and times) and a great sense of fun. Food is wholesome, hearty and local, with just a few dishes chalked up on the board: usually pasta, often rabbit or pigeon, or steak and kidney pie, no puddings. The beers, from Abbeydale Brewery, are excellent.

directions	At junction of A623 & B6465 south east of Tideswell.
meals	12.30pm-4pm; 7.30pm-9.30pm. Main courses £6.50-£10.50.
closed	Monday-Thursday; Friday lunchtimes.

Geoff & Pat Fuller
Three Stags Heads,
Wardlow,
Tideswell,
Derbyshire SK17 8RW
tel   01298 872268

map: 14 entry: 92

Derbyshire

Devonshire Arms
Beeley

Classic Peak District scenery surrounds stone-built Beeley and this splendid Georgian public house. It started life as three cottages, then become a coaching inn on the busy road from Bakewell to Matlock – and is popular today because of its proximity to glorious Chatsworth House. Wisely open all day, it's a civilised, upmarket stopover for Chatsworth visitors and well-heeled locals – and an obvious harbour for walkers exploring the estate footpaths. All is as neat as apple pie within, the three beamed rooms enticing with log fires, cushioned antique settles and tasteful prints. A separate stone-flagged tap room welcomes the booted walkers, refreshing them with expertly-kept Black Sheep and Theakston ales. Decent bar food ranges from soups and ploughman's lunches to braised lamb knuckle with rosemary sauce, followed reassuringly by Bakewell pudding. Friday is fresh fish night and on Sunday there's a sumptuous Victorian breakfast complete with bucks fizz and newspapers. Perfect!

directions	Off B6102, 5 miles north of Matlock.
meals	12pm-9.30pm. Main courses £7.10-£16.50.

John Grosvenor
Devonshire Arms,
Beeley,
Matlock,
Derbyshire DE4 2NR
tel   01629 733259

map: 14 entry: 93

Derbyshire

The Bull's Head
Ashford-in-the-Water

Lovely carved settles, cushions, clocks and country prints – this is pub heaven. There are newspapers and magazines to read, light jazz hums in the background, and, on chilly days, coals glow in the grate. The Bull's Head has been in Debbie Shaw's family for half a century and she and Carl have been at the helm for the past four. Carl cooks, proudly serving "bistro food, not a laminated menu"; everything, down to the bread and the cheese biscuits, is homemade. With a strong emphasis on local and seasonal produce, there's asparagus and coriander tartlet with Greek yogurt topping, steak with dripping-roasted potatoes, pan-fried liver with buttered cabbage, sticky toffee pudding with black treacle sauce. Service is swift and friendly and, this being a Robinson's pub, Best Bitter, Stockpot and seasonal Hartley's Cumbria Way are on handpump. Roses round the door, tables round the back, and a pretty village with a bridge from which to throw bread at the ducks. A civilised place.

directions	Off A6, 2 miles north of Bakewell.
meals	12pm-2pm; 6.30pm-9pm (7pm Sundays). No food Thursdays in winter. Main courses £7.50-£13.

Debbie Shaw
The Bull's Head,
Church Street,
Ashford-in-the-Water,
Bakewell, Derbyshire DE45 1QB
tel   01629 812931

map: 14 entry: 94

Derbyshire

Druid Inn
Birchover

A Dales pub that, inevitably, lures the knapsack crowds. At lunchtime, walkers in their stockinged feet – no muddy boots, please! – will be downing pints of specially-brewed Druids Ale or Marston's Pedigree. If possible, they'll be catching some sun on the sheltered terrace, too. There can be a hundred diners tucking into candlelit supper on a busy night – yet the kitchen remains unfazed. Menus make comforting reading and there's a massive choice for vegetarians, traditionalists and lovers of good old-fashioned puddings. Garlic mushrooms, roast whole pheasant with port and redcurrant sauce, vegetable curries and Sunday roasts, warm bakewell pudding, sherry and fruit trifle. In each of the plain, beamy bars you may toast your feet by the glowing coals in the grate – there's classical music in the background, malts by the shot, wines by the glass. The smarter Garden Room and a further, two-tier dining room are 20th-century additions to the old, creeper-clad pub, both with a light and airy restaurant feel.

directions	From A6; B5056; turn to Birchover.
meals	12pm-2pm; 7pm-9pm. Main courses £8.90-£15.80.
closed	Mondays.

Brian Bunce
Druid Inn,
Main Street, Birchover,
Derbyshire DE4 2BL
tel   01629 650302
web   www.druidinnbirchover.co.uk

map: 9 entry: 95

Derbyshire

Ye Olde Gate Inne
Brassington

One of the most charismatic pubs in Derbyshire, built from timber salvaged from the wrecks of the Armada. Furnishings are plain: ancient settles, rush-seated chairs, polished tables, gleaming copper pans, a clamorous antique clock, a collection of pewter. In winter a fire blazes in the blackened range that dominates the flagged main bar. In the smaller, dimly-lit bar, another glowing range, and candlelight. There's a short, regularly changing blackboard menu and traditional tucker: ploughman's, filled baguettes (delicious roast beef with onions and mushrooms), venison and red onion sausages, curries, Derbyshire specialities like fidgit pie (layers of ham, potatoes and cheese), lemon tart. Superbly kept Marston's Pedigree on handpump and a number of malts. Mullioned windows look onto a sheltered back garden, perfect for the popular evening barbecues that are held from Easter until October.

directions	Midway between Ashbourne & Wirksworth off B3035.
meals	12pm-1.45pm (2pm Fridays & Saturdays); 7pm-8.45pm (9pm Fridays & Saturdays). Main courses £4.95-£12.95.
closed	Mondays except Bank Holidays.

Paul Burlinson
Ye Olde Gate Inne,
Well Street,
Brassington, Wirksworth,
Derbyshire DE4 4HJ
tel   01629 540448

map: 9 entry: 96

Derbyshire

The Red Lion Inn
Hognaston

Three inns used to serve the packhorse trade in hillside Hognaston, but only the Red Lion is left. Pip Price's unassuming tavern is in tremendous walking and shooting country. You'll be drawn to its gloriously aged character – the beamy L-shaped bar, the rug-strewn quarry-tile floors, the old tables candlelit at night, the comfortable settles, soft classical music and three log fires. Browse the papers or a well-thumbed copy of Country Life as you sip country wine and Old Speckled Hen. The chalkboard lists, changed every day, suggest modern-style, imaginatively prepared pub dishes made with fresh local produce. Beyond soup and sandwiches, more substantial meals are whisked in on enormous white plates – perhaps Moroccan lamb tagine or fillet steak with a green peppercorn and brandy sauce. There's a back room with a big table for private parties, and three comfortable bedrooms upstairs. A warm, unspoilt and thoroughly civilised local.

directions	On B5035 between Ashbourne & Wirksworth.
meals	12pm-2pm; 6.30pm-9pm. No food Mondays or Sunday eve. Main courses £8.95-£14.95.
rooms	3 doubles, £80. Singles £50.
closed	3pm-6pm (7pm Sundays).

Pip Price
The Red Lion Inn,
Hognaston, Ashbourne,
Derbyshire DE6 1PR
tel   01335 370396
web   www.lionrouge.com

map: 9 entry: 97

Derbyshire

The Red Lion Inn
Hollington

When Robin Hunter took over this edge-of-village pub three years ago it was in a sorry state. His dedication has paid off: the Red Lion pulls such a crowd at the weekends that bookings must be made well in advance – and this in spite of the pub recently growing. Modernisation has been sensitive to character and intimacy, and bar food keeps the traditional mood going with steaming chilli con carne and sticky toffee pudding. It is on the main, changing menu that Robin gets to show off, using fresh and seasonal ingredients, particularly game and perfectly cooked fish (like grilled plaice fillet topped with lemon gremolata). While the menu revels in being wide-ranging and up-to-date, Robin's style is commendably direct and simple. Staff go to great lengths to make you feel at home. If you are here just for a drink, there's Marston's Pedigree on handpump and good wines by the glass. And the pretty garden is delightful in summer.

directions	Off A52 between Derby & Ashbourne.
meals	12pm-2pm; 7pm-9pm. No food Monday lunchtimes. Main courses £9.75-£16.95.
closed	Monday evenings.

Robin Hunter
The Red Lion Inn,
Main Street,
Hollington,
Derbyshire DE6 3AG
tel 01335 360241

map: 9 entry: 98

Derbyshire

Nag's Head Inn
Castle Donington

Donington is famous for its racetrack, so you might expect to see bikers wearing Viking helmets and peeing into pint pots wherever you go. Not a bit of it – the Nag's Head oozes gentility. It also sells good beer, has a very cosy bar, a dining room with a charming mural, and serves excellent food… it could hardly be more salubrious. On race days, of course, they shift a bit more beer than usual, but this local serves it well all year round. Its proximity to three motorways also means that it attracts more than just locals – some use the pub as a superior alternative to a service station. Hardly surprising, when dishes include breast of chicken in stilton sauce and lemon sole with caper and parsley butter.
Accompany all that with a good pint or a glass of wine and you've beaten all-day breakfast at Leicester Forest East into the proverbial cocked hat.

directions	From M1 junc. 23A or 24 take A453 past airport. At next traffic lights right to mini-roundabout. First left, go down hill, pub on right.
meals	12pm-2pm; 5.30pm-9.15pm. Main courses £14.95-£16.95.
closed	2.30pm-5.30pm (7pm Sundays).

Ian Davison
Nag's Head Inn,
Hill Top,
Castle Donington,
Derbyshire DE74 2PR
tel 01332 850652

map: 9 entry: 99

Devon

The Mason's Arms
Knowstone

The Mason's is a folksy old pub with a new and smiling Dutch landlord. Leaving windswept Exmoor behind, arrive through fern or twisting lane. Wood is stacked against the 13th-century walls, you are drawn to enter. The dim, low, flagged bar, with inglenook and elaborate burner (ever lit), fills with drinkers once the sun's gone down, here for Exmoor ale from the barrel. But who would imagine, down worn stone steps, the restaurant that shelters below? Served at a jumble of candlelit tables is food fit for kings – French-born son Hugo has cooked at starred restaurants in Provence and is causing a bit of a stir. Go for a starter of lobster fricassée, move on to Toulouse cassoulet with local sausages and French duck, finish with passion-fruit mousse. For lunch there's a perfect plate of French charcuterie.

directions	M5 junc. 27; A361 for Barnstaple; Knowstone signed on right after 20 miles. Into Knowstone, right at bottom of hill & pub on left.
meals	12pm-2pm; 6pm-9pm. Main courses £5.95-£14.95.
closed	3pm-6pm (4pm Sundays).

Edward Van Vliet
The Mason's Arms,
Knowstone,
Devon EX36 4RY
tel   01398 341231
web   www.masonsarmsinn.com

map: 2 entry: 100

Devon

Duke of York
Iddesleigh

Built to house the 14th-century stonemasons working on the church next door, the thatched Duke of York of today is a cracking local: heart-warming food, real ale and a big welcome from farmer-pub landlord Jamie Stuart and his wife. Pass a parked tractor on your way in to find farmers, shooters and the odd slaughterman parleying around the single bar over pints of Cotleigh Tawny tapped from the cask. Scrubbed oak tables have fresh flowers and candles, there are village photographs on the walls, banknotes on the beams, a huge fireplace stuffed with logs – it's an enchanting place. With fish fresh from Clovelly and Brixham and beef, lamb and pork from Jamie's farm, diners enjoy the heartiest home cooking: steak and kidney pudding, T-bone steak, whole baked sea bass with lemon butter, glorious puddings. Simple bedrooms are split between the pub and the cottage across the lane, and the all-day breakfasts are not for the faint-hearted.

directions	On B3217 between Exbourne & Dolton, 3 miles north-east of Hatherleigh.
meals	8am-10pm. Main courses £8-£12.
rooms	7 twins/doubles £60. Singles £30.

Jamie Stuart & Pippa Hutchinson
Duke of York,
Iddesleigh,
Winkleigh,
Devon EX19 8BG
tel   01837 810253

map: 2 entry: 101

Dartmoor Inn
Lydford

Tavistock has the only goose fair in the country and you may find goose on the menu here. Karen and Philip Burgess are self-confessed foodies and their imposing dining pub turns out some seriously good dishes. Step into the relaxed atmosphere to be greeted by big smiles and an invitation to find a table in any of the many dining rooms that takes your fancy. Everywhere there are up-dates on coming events: gourmet evenings and seasonal celebrations, a Parisian bistro supper or a hot Brazilian jazz night. Menus match the occasion and are seasonal while locals can, and do, take advantage of monthly set lunches. In June you might start with asparagus soup with nutmeg cream — faultless — then dive into a mixed grill of sea fish with lemon and herb butter and courgette flower fritters with a green mayonnaise... and finish with peach melba. In November, by candlelight, there are sardine toasts with garden lettuces, roasted pheasant with bacon and crab-apple jelly, pistachio meringues. Walkers and their dogs stride straight in from the moors — and squeeze into the bar for Dartmoor Best Bitter and organic bottled cider.

directions	On A386 between Okehampton & Tavistock.
meals	12pm-2.15pm; 6.30pm-9.15pm. Main courses £7.75-£16.75; set menu £11.75 & £14.95 (lunch).
closed	Sunday evenings & Mondays.

Philip & Karen Burgess
Dartmoor Inn,
Lydford,
Devon EX20 4AY

tel   01822 820221

map: 2 entry: 102

Devon

The Peter Tavy Inn
Peter Tavy

An atmospheric 15th-century inn on the flanks of desolate Dartmoor. Originally a tiny cottage built to house the masons working on the church, it graduated from being the parish poorhouse to an ale house, frequented for 200 years by grateful moorland walkers and local drinkers. Some years ago it was sensitively extended and is now one of Dartmoor's noted food pubs. There's masses of charm here, in black beams, gleaming, polished slate floors, long pine tables, high-backed settles and woodburners in huge hearths. Follow an invigorating walk with a pint of Princetown Jail ale and a lunchtime snack — perhaps steak and kidney pie or a Devon cheese ploughman's. Food in the evening steps up a gear, with beef fillet with mushroom sauce and red mullet with lemon and coriander on the imaginative chalkboard menu. Devon farm cider, country wines and fine malt whiskies are there for those adverse to West Country ale.

directions	2 miles off A386, 4 miles north of Tavistock.
meals	12pm-2pm; 6.30pm-9pm. Main courses £5.95-£13.95.
closed	3pm-6pm.

Graeme & Karen Sim
The Peter Tavy Inn,
Peter Tavy,
Tavistock,
Devon PL19 9NN
tel   01822 810348

map: 2 entry: 103

Devon

The Ship Inn
Noss Mayo

At the head of a tidal inlet, a 16th-century pub remodelled with a nautical twist. While visiting boats can tie up alongside (with permission, of course), high-tide parking is trickier. When the tide is in, you enter via the back door on the first-floor level; when out, it's a quick stroll over the 'beach' and in by the front entrance. Downstairs are plain floorboards, a light wood bar, solid-wood furniture and walls richly caparisoned with maritime prints. Open fires, books and newspapers add to the easy feel. Upstairs the Galley, Bridge and Met Office areas have views and a happy, dining buzz. The menu strikes a modern cord, and is fish-friendly, naturally, with sautéed Cornish scallops alongside Devon lamb and 'comforting' puddings. They have well-kept beers from Devon breweries (Summerskills and Princetown), many malts and eight wines by the glass: take your drink to the sunny patio at octagonal tables and make the most of the watery views. This is a civilised stop-off for walkers on the South Devon coast path.

directions	South of Yealpton, on Yealm Estuary.
meals	12pm-9.30pm. Main courses £7-£14.

Bruce & Lesley Brunning
The Ship Inn,
Noss Mayo,
Devon PL8 1EW
tel   01752 872387
web   www.nossmayo.com

map: 2 entry: 104

Devon

Tradesman's Arms
Stokenham

Nick Abbot swapped a thriving Chiltern's dining pub for the good life in South Hams. His new project is a 14th-century, part-thatched building, formerly a brewhouse with three cottages, it's in a sleepy village inland from Slapton Sands and takes its name from the tradesmen who used to call in for a jug of ale while trekking the coastal bridlepath. You may well find a tradesman or two here today, downing a pint in the main bar. Beamed, not smart but attractively rustic, it has an open fire and antique dining tables, and views that reach across the valley. The short blackboard menu chalks up some innovative pub food, created by loyal chefs who followed Nick to Devon. As well as the usual lunchtime sandwiches, the daily-changing and seasonal selection includes fresh Brixham fish, scallops from the bay and game – perhaps venison steak with red wine sauce. Brakspear Bitter – Nick's favourite tipple – is on handpump, fondly recalling his Chiltern Hills days.

directions	1 mile from Slapton Sands & Torcross, off A379.
meals	12pm-2.30pm; 6.30pm-9.30pm. Main courses £6.95-£14.95.
closed	3pm-6pm (6.30pm Saturdays; 7pm Sundays)

Nicholas Abbot
Tradesman's Arms,
Stokenham,
Kingsbridge,
Devon TQ7 2SZ
tel   01548 580313

map: 2 entry: 105

Devon

The Start Bay Inn
Torcross

Arguably the best pub fish and chips in Devon can be found at this 14th-century thatched inn, superbly slotted-in between the beach at Slapton Sands and the freshwater lagoon of Slapton Ley. Landlord and fisherman Paul Stubbs contributes to the vast amount of fresh fish that is delivered daily. The modest bar and dining areas are simply furnished and every available seat is taken soon after opening, especially in summer – arrive late at your peril. Fish and chip connoisseurs return time and time again to sample the delicious battered cod, haddock and plaice, available in three sizes and accompanied by properly plump chips. Also on the menu are daily fish specials, while fresh crab is cooked and dressed on the premises and used in their platters and sandwiches. The rest of the menu lists standard pub food that will not disappoint, and both meat-eaters and vegetarians are extremely well looked after. No wonder it's such a popular place.

directions	On A379 between Kingsbridge & Dartmouth.
meals	11.30am-2pm; 6pm-9.30pm (10pm in summer). Main courses £4.80-£12.90.

Paul Stubbs
The Start Bay Inn,
Torcross, Kingsbridge,
Devon TQ7 2TQ
tel   01548 580553
web   www.startbayinn.co.uk

map: 2 entry: 106

Devon

The Ferry Boat Inn
Dittisham

Little has changed at this waterside pub since it was built three centuries ago. The only inn right on the River Dart, it used to serve the passenger steamers plying between Dartmouth and Totnes – you can still arrive by boat. Inside, big windows show off the view over to the wooded banks of the Greenway Estate (once Agatha Christie's home, now owned by the National Trust: shake the old bell and catch the ferry to visit). Arrive early and bag the best seats in the rustically charming, unspoilt little bar with its bare boards, crackling log fire, nautical bric-a-brac and unmissable, all-important 'high tides' board. If you happen to have overlooked the village car park, negotiated the steep lane and parked on the 'beach', then do check the board before ordering your pint. Similarly, the tide dictates whether or not you can dine outside in summer… Expect a rousing welcome from landlord Ray Benson and decent home-cooked pub food. Gents can 'spray and pray' next door in the converted chapel.

directions	Off A3122, 2 miles west of Dartmouth.
meals	12pm-2pm; 7pm-9pm. No food Sunday evenings. Main courses £6.95-£12.

Ray Benson
The Ferry Boat Inn,
Manor Street,
Dittisham,
Devon TQ6 0EX
tel   01803 722368

map: 2 entry: 107

Devon

The Maltsters Arms
Tuckenhay

The setting is spectacular – down on the quay of wooded and beautiful Bow Creek – so grab a table outside this ravishingly rustic house. The 1550s pub was once owned by 'gastronaut' Keith Floyd and is still more lively London brasserie than rural Devon inn. Interconnecting rooms have deep red walls, scrubbed tables, boarded floors, log fires and big windows looking up the creek. The quayside bar, with barbecue, is open all day and a boon in hot summers. Daily menus use local ingredients, from West Country ploughman's or Brixham plaice with dill and lemon to pot-roasted local partridge with bacon, red wine and redcurrants, and there's a good children's menu. Behind the bar local ales and farm ciders vie for attention among wines, spirits and organic juices. Three super bedrooms await in the converted winery next door; from your bed watch the birds on the ebbing tide.

directions	Off A381, 2.5 miles south of Totnes.
meals	12pm-3pm (4pm Sundays); 6.30pm-9.30pm. Main courses £7.95-£16.95.
rooms	5: 4 double, 1 four-poster £65-£125.

Denise & Quentin Thwaites
The Maltsters Arms,
Bow Creek, Tuckenhay,
Totnes, Devon TQ9 7EQ
tel   01803 732350
web   www.tuckenhay.com

map: 2 entry: 108

White Hart Bar
Dartington

Keep going down the never-ending drive past farmland and deer until, finally, the Dartington Hall complex peeps into view. Here are the splendid college, conference centre, arts centre, dairy farm – and the 14th-century hall built for a half-brother of Richard II. Sneaked away in the corner of the courtyard, which is dotted with picnic tables in summer, is the White Hart. The informal bar and restaurant is characterfully 21st century, with chunky beams, York stone floor, smouldering log fires, round light-oak tables and windsor chairs. Organic and local produce are the mainstay of both the seasonal and the chalkboard menus, notably Brixham fish and farm beef and lamb. For lunch: doorstop sandwiches, warm salads and traditional sausages and mash. In the benched and trestled dining hall, well-above-average pub food comes in the form of fish chowder, confit of duck on fennel with flageolet bean blanquette, rack of lamb with redcurrant and rosemary sauce, bitter chocolate tart with clotted cream. Beers are from Princetown Brewery, there are eight unusual wines by the glass and as many organic juices and ciders as you could hope for. Walk off a very fine lunch with a stroll through the sweeping 28 acres that border the Dart.

directions	Off A385, 2 miles north west of Totnes.
meals	12pm-2pm; 6pm-9pm. Main courses £5.95-£12.95.

	Ben Harmer White Hart Bar, Dartington Hall, Dartington, Totnes, Devon TQ9 6EL
tel	01803 847111
web	www.dartingtonhall.com

map: 2 entry: 109

Devon

Rising Sun
Woodland

The farmhouse on the edge of Dartmoor was once a tearoom. Now the plushly-furnished open-plan bar, cosy with beams and log fire, delivers Princetown Jail ale, Luscombe cider and fine wines. Fresh market produce is what landlady Heather Humphreys likes to serve, her daily menus listing fish from Brixham, game from local estates and smoked meats and fish from Dartmouth's smokehouse. Hearty ploughman's come with a selection of four Devon cheeses, while shortcrust-pastry-topped pies are generously filled with venison with stout and juniper, or wild rabbit. Children have toys and dressing-up clothes in the family room; in the big garden are swings and an old tractor. There's a sunny terrace, too. Sleep tight in cottagey bedrooms, wake to a first-class breakfast.

directions	Off A38 before Ashburton junction heading west for Plymouth.
meals	12pm-2.15pm (3pm Sundays); 6pm-9.15pm (7pm Sundays). Main courses £7.95-£12.95.
rooms	2: 1 double, 1 twin £50. Singles £38.
closed	Mondays in winter; Monday lunchtimes (except Bank Holidays).

Heather Humphreys
Rising Sun,
Woodland,
Ashburton, Devon TQ13 7JT
tel   01364 652544
web   www.risingsunwoodland.co.uk

map: 2 entry: 110

Devon

Rugglestone Inn
Widecombe-in-the-Moor

Beside open moorland and walking distance from the village – and named after the Ruggle Stone, a huge mass of granite nearby – is a rustic, 200-year-old stone building whose two tiny rooms lead off a stone-floored passageway. Few of the hordes who descend on this honey-pot village in the middle of Dartmoor know of the Rugglestone. Yet it is an unspoilt gem. The delightful, old-fashioned parlour has exposed beams, an open log fire, simple furnishings and a deeply rural feel. Both rooms are satisfyingly free of modern intrusions, the locals prefering time-honoured games such as cribbage, euchre and dominoes. The tiny bar serves local farm cider; Butcombe Bitter and St Austell Dartmoor Best are tapped straight from the cask. From the kitchen come simple bar meals, from ploughman's lunches and homemade soups to hearty casseroles. Across the babbling brook at the front is a lawn with benches and moorland views.

directions	200yds from centre of Widecombe; signed.
meals	12pm-2pm; 7pm-9pm. Main courses £5.95-£8.95.
closed	3pm-6.30pm.

Rod & Diane Williams
Rugglestone Inn,
Widecombe-in-the-Moor,
Devon TQ13 7TF
tel   01364 621327

map: 2 entry: 111

Devon

The Anchor Inn
Cockwood

The vine-covered veranda of the 400-year-old fisherman's cottage is a super spot from which to watch the bobbing yachts and colourful crabbing boats of Cockwood's tiny landlocked harbour. Beyond lies the expanse of the Exe estuary and its teeming birdlife. Although added-to over the years, the rustic main bar is still dark, cosy and oozes atmosphere, with black panelled walls and head-cracking ceilings, a motley assortment of old tables and chairs and intimate little alcoves in three snug areas, one of which has a welcoming coal fire. Local fishermen and retired naval folk swapping yarns mix with tourists in the busy summer season. Local seafood, especially shellfish, is the big attraction on the mind-bogglingly long printed menu. Tuck into scallops, mussels and oysters from local beds along the Exe, all available with an endless choice of sauces. There's an excellent range of real ales, over 30 whiskies and an abundance of country wines. Nearby parking can be tricky.

directions	Off A379 Exeter to Torbay road.
meals	12pm-3pm (2.30pm Sundays); 6.30pm-10pm (9.30pm Sundays). Main courses £4.95-£14.95.

Terry Morgan & Alison Sanders
The Anchor Inn,
Cockwood,
Dawlish, Devon EX6 8RA
tel   01626 890203
web www.anchorinncockwood.com

map: 2 entry: 112

Devon

The Rock Inn
Haytor Vale

Originally a watering hole for quarrymen and miners, the 300-year-old inn stands in a tiny village high on Dartmoor's windswept southern slopes. Run by the same family for 20 years, this civilised haven has a characterful interior: polished antique tables and sturdy settles, a grandfather clock, decorative plates and fresh flowers, two log fires. Retreat to the cosy beamed bar for a pint of Dartmoor Best and peruse the supper menu that highlights local, often organic, produce. If all that fresh country air has made you ravenous, tuck into pan-fried pheasant with roasted shallots, smoked bacon, chestnuts and red wine (and then sticky toffee pudding). Lunchtime meals range from soup, sandwiches and ploughman's to local sausages in onion gravy. Traditional, individually decorated bedrooms feature period pieces of furniture; all are named after Grand National winners and two look over the moor.

directions	At Drumbridges roundabout A382 for Bovey Tracey; B3387 to Haytor. Left at phone box.
meals	12pm-2.15pm; 6.30pm-9pm. Main courses £9.95-£12.95; set menu £17.95 (2 courses).
rooms	9: 8 doubles, 1 twin £75.95-£105.95.

Christopher & Susan Graves
The Rock Inn,
Haytor Vale,
Bovey Tracey, Devon TQ13 9XP
tel   01364 661305
web www.rock-inn.co.uk

map: 2 entry: 113

The Nobody Inn
Doddiscombsleigh

Nothing has been said over the years about The Nobody that is not worth repeating. Ten years ago we remember an incomparable cheese and wine lunch and little has changed... the Butcombe bitter is still racked on an up-turned crate behind the bar. Nick Borst-Smith also has his own wine company (800 bins), the wines of the moment standing on an uneven counter; pick up a bottle and the others glide into place. Settles and tables are crammed into every corner, lanterns dangle from beams, there's an inglenook crackling with logs and a part of the bar dates from Tudor times. Choose a succulent tranche of pork and apple pie followed perhaps by chocolate truffle cake. Sweet and spicy Nobody soup is made from chicken stock, vegetables and local fruit; smoked eel comes from Dartmouth; local quail is stuffed with rice and apricots; the Devon cheeses are unsurpassed, and much the same can be said of the 240 whiskies. Their own Nobody's beer comes in old pint glasses. The village is buried down a maze of lanes but it's not hard to find and if a modest room is required, either in the pub or at their medieval manor, early booking is advised. It's old, rambling, eccentric, fun.

directions	Off A38 at Haldon Racecourse exit, then 3 miles.
meals	12pm-2pm; 7pm-10pm. No food 25-26, 31 Dec & 1 Jan. Main courses £6.90-£11.
rooms	7: 5 doubles, 2 twins £70. Singles £38.

Nick Borst-Smith
The Nobody Inn,
Doddiscombsleigh,
Exeter, Devon EX6 7PS

tel   01647 252394
web   www.nobodyinn.co.uk

map: 2 entry: 114

Devon

The Drewe Arms
Drewsteignton

Long, low and thatched, in a pretty village square above the wooded slopes of the Teign valley, the Drewe Arms is better known as Auntie Mabel's. Why? In honour of Mabel Mudge, once Britain's longest-serving landlady, who retired in 1996 aged 99. No longer quite in the time-warp it once was, it does remain an unpretentious and well-loved local. Beer straight from the cask is served from two hatchways, one opening to a front room with rustic benches and tables; a second room across the flagged passageway has sturdy old pine tables and a roaring log fire. Mabel's Kitchen, now the dining room, keeps the original dresser and old black cooking range. Home-cooked food using fresh local produce is listed on a daily-changing blackboard menu. Appropriately free of TV or telephone, charming upstairs bedrooms have old pine furnishings and original Victorian fireplaces. Stride off through National Trust woodland to Castle Drogo – the walks are wonderful.

directions	Off A382, 2 miles south of A30, 8 miles west of Exeter.
meals	12pm-2pm; 6.30pm-9pm. Main courses £6-£12.
rooms	3 doubles, 2 with separate bathrooms £60.

Janice & Colin Sparks
The Drewe Arms,
The Square,
Drewsteignton,
Exeter, Devon EX6 6NQ
tel   01647 281224

map: 2 entry: 115

Devon

The Bridge
Topsham

Cut across the bridge too fast and you miss one of Devon's last traditional ale houses. Unchanged for most of the century – and in Phyllis Cheffer-Heard's family for as long – the 16th-century Bridge Inn is a 'must' for every ale connoisseur. And for all who appreciate a genuine pub furnished in the old-style, all high-back settles and ancient floors. (The Queen chose to drop in on Tthe Bridge on her first official 'visit to a pub'.) Years ago it was a brewery and malthouse; Phyllis's great-grandfather was the last publican to brew his own here. This is beer-drinker heaven – fizzy lager lovers should note their favourite tipple is banned – with up to 10 real ales drawn from the barrel. There's cider and gooseberry wine, too. Cradle your pint to the background din of local chatter in the Inner Sanctum, under a grandfather clock by a blazing log fire. With bread baked at the local farm, home-roasted hams, homemade chutneys and cracking cheeses, the sandwiches and ploughman's are unmissable.

directions	In Topsham A376 for Exmouth; Elmgrove Road into Bridge Hill.
meals	12pm-2pm. Bar meals £2-£5.90.
closed	2pm-6pm (7pm Sundays).

Phyllis Cheffers-Heard
The Bridge,
Topsham,
Devon EX3 0QQ
tel   01392 873862
web   www.cheffers.co.uk

map: 2 entry: 116

Devon

Digger's Rest
Woodbury Salterton

Months of searching led the Rushtons to this 500-year-old, fat-walled former cider house built of stone and cob. It is the quintessential Devon inn. A good looking makeover swiftly followed, the timbered interior revived: fresh yellow décor, new carpets, an eclectic mix of old dining tables, subtle wall lighting, tasteful prints. Arrive early to bag the sofa by the log fire. They've thought of everything; as well as the local Otter ales, the impressive list of wines (10 by the glass) and the relaxing atmosphere, there are organic soft drinks, Italian Gaggia coffee, soothing piped jazz, baby-changing facilities, daily newspapers and a brilliant pub menu that employs the best local produce. Treat yourself to Brixham fish (cod on garlic mash with red wine and shallot sauce), Devon Ruby Red beef (chargrilled burger with fries), and local Kenniford Farm pork, roasted for Sunday lunches. There's even a newly landscaped patio garden, and a play area for kids.

directions	Off A3052, 3 miles east of Exeter & 3 miles from M5 junc. 30.
meals	12pm-2pm (2.30pm weekends); 7pm-9.30pm. Main courses £7.75-£12.50.
closed	2.30pm-6pm Monday-Friday.

Steve Rushton
Digger's Rest,
Woodbury Salterton,
Exeter, Devon EX5 1PQ
tel 01395 232375
web www.diggersrest.co.uk

map: 3 entry: 117

Devon

Ye Olde Masons Arms
Branscombe

Approach straggling Branscombe down narrow lanes (good for honing reversing skills!) to this creeper-clad inn. The 14th-century bar has a traditional feel with dark ship's timbers, stone walls, slate floor and central fireplace that cooks spit-roasts to perfection. Quaff pints of Otter Bitter or Jack Rat scrumpy by the fire; on warm days, make for the sun-trapped terrace. Nothing is too much trouble for the staff, whose prime aim is for you to unwind. Local produce, including fresh crab and lobster landed on Branscombe's beach, is the focus of the modern British menu. There's creamy seafood chowder and Lyme Bay mackerel, salt-baked brill and organically reared beef fillet with pepper sauce. Carpeted bedrooms are divided between the inn (originally an 8ftx4ft cider house) and the cottages opposite; the pebbly beach is a 12-minute stroll across National Trust land.

directions	Off A3052 between Sidmouth & Seaton.
meals	12pm-2pm; 7pm-9pm. Main courses £6.95-£14.95; set menu £30.
rooms	22 twins/doubles, 2 sharing bathroom £50-£150.
closed	3pm-6pm in winter.

Murray Inglis
& Tim Manktelow-Gray
Ye Olde Masons Arms, Branscombe,
Seaton, Devon EX12 3DJ
tel 01297 680300
web www.masonsarms.co.uk

map: 2 entry: 118

Devon

The Blue Ball
Sandy Gate

Sibling to the much-lauded Drewe Arms at Drewsteignton, it's no surprise The Blue Ball is so popular – though it is perhaps more informal eatery than traditional pub. Handy for the motorway, the colourwashed, thatched, roadside inn offers a cracking respite to any savvy traveller. Brasserie-style food is generous and well presented, while a separate restaurant menu struts its stuff in the evening. There's an earthy pubbiness to the dimly-lit front bar, with its flagstones, low beams, reassuring settles and log fire. Pink walls may add a cosmopolitan touch, but the old handsaws hung around the fire reinforce its essential rusticity. A further bar has a lighter feel with polished floorboards, while the contemporary dining-room extension brings things bang up to date, with its airy atmosphere, blond-wood furniture, cord carpeting and modern art. A great open-hearted village local, and, with a play area in the garden, family-friendly too.

directions	M5 junc. 30 for Sidmouth. Round r'bout, back towards motorway. Left 200yds down lane.
meals	12pm-2pm; 6.30pm-9.30pm. Main courses £3.95-£12.
closed	3pm-6pm.

Colin & Janice Sparks
The Blue Ball,
Sandy Gate, Exeter
Devon EX2 7JL
tel   01392 873401

map: 2 entry: 119

Devon

The Jack in the Green
Rockbeare

Bustle and buzz in the dark wood bar, and good local brews on tap – Otter Ale, Cotleigh Tawny, Branscombe Vale Bitter. But this is more restaurant than pub: "For those who live to eat," reads the sign. Chef Matthew Mason's bar menu goes in for modern variations of tried and trusted favourites: braised faggot with creamed potato, steamed venison pudding with port and juniper jus… even the ploughman's is impressive. More ambition on display in the restaurant, where pan-fried pigeon breast with bacon lardoons and a madeira sauce, and confit of Creedy Carver duck legs with butternut squash are fine choices. Leather chesterfields by the woodburning stove are a cosy touch; for summer there's a lovely orchard garden away from the road, so sit back and soak up the views. Paul Parnell has been at the helm for 12 years and he and his staff do a grand job.

directions	5 miles east of M5 (J29) on old A30 just past Exeter Airport.
meals	12pm-2pm (2.30pm Fri & Sat); 6pm-9pm (10pm Fri & Sat); 12pm-9.30pm Sundays. Main courses £5.75-£15; set menu £25.
closed	25 December-6 January.

Paul Parnell
The Jack in the Green,
Rockbeare,
Exeter, Devon EX5 2EE
tel   01404 822240
web   www.jackinthegreen.uk.com

map: 2 entry: 120

Devon

The King's Arms
Stockland

After a week here you'll feel like a fully-fledged local — an overflowing notice board fills you in on any gossip you didn't catch at the bar. You'll also be a stone or two heavier with seemingly endless menus from the Swiss chef: masses of fish, locally-reared game and even ostrich. Here are crackling fires, patterned carpets, gilt-framed mirrors on stone walls, cosy low ceilings and a stone-flagged Farmer's Bar where you can sup Exmoor Ale and meet the "fair-minded, fun-loving" locals, who'll probably have you playing skittles in no time. As for Paul, he's "a tyrant to work for", according to one of his (contented) staff. Bedrooms are not grand but perfectly traditional, with maybe a walnut bed or a cushioned window seat. It is a working pub and won't be quiet until about 11pm so don't try to sleep earlier, just join in. Lose yourself in the Blackdown Hills or simply laze around inside with Princess Ida, the cat.

directions	Off A30 to Chard, 6 miles north east of Honiton
meals	12pm-1.45pm; 6.30pm-9pm. Main courses £7.50-£15.50.
rooms	3: 2 doubles, 1 twin £60. Singles £40.

Heinz Kiefer & Paul Diviani
The King's Arms,
Stockland, Honiton,
Devon EX14 9BS

tel   01404 881361
web   www.kingsarms.net

map: 3 entry: 121

Devon

The Drewe Arms
Broadhembury

Nigel Burge runs a relaxed ship — perhaps the secret of his long success. The 15th-century thatched Drewe is the cornerstone of a thatched Devon village. By the fire are the day's papers and magazines; on the bar, local Otter ales tapped straight from the cask and wines beyond reproach. It's a captivating little place. Beams are oak-carved, walls plank-panelled, there are country tables, wood carvings, walking sticks, flowers and a log-fired inglenook that crackles in winter. Food is way above average for a country pub, with fish from Brixham and Newlyn. Go for Scandinavian-style gravadlax with dill and mustard, or skate wings served in the traditional manner with a caper sauce. Plenty of classy modern touches, too: stilton and smoked haddock rarebit comes in both small and large portions, there's brill with horseradish hollandaise, and hand-dived scallops that are seared to perfection. All this, and a garden that's as dreamy as a country garden can be.

directions	M5 junc. 28; A373 Honiton to Cullompton.
meals	12pm-2pm; 7pm-9.15pm. Main courses £10-£20.
closed	Sunday evenings; 3pm-6pm.

Kerstin & Nigel Burge
The Drewe Arms,
Broadhembury,
Honiton,
Devon EX14 3NF

tel   01404 841267

map: 2 entry: 122

Devon

Culm Valley Inn
Culmstock

Don't be put off by the unkempt exterior of Richard Hartley's pub by the river Culm. It may not be posh but inside there's a good aura: deep pink-washed walls, glowing coals, flickering candles, warmth and panache. Settle in with the locals to sample some micro-brewery beers; rub shoulders with the gentry who've come for unusually good food. Easy-going chef-patron Richard and his efficient band of beauties behind the bar make this place tick. Look to the chalkboard for south coast seafood (Ladram Bay crab, Exe estuary moules), cracking weekend fish specials like whole brill with quince aioli, Ruby Red Devon beef and wild boar from nearby farms, and a selection of tapas. From the English oak bar you can even order homemade sloe vodka, and French wines from small specialist growers. Deep in the Blackdown Hills, an idiosyncratic inn and a special place.

directions	On B3391, 2 miles off A38 west of Wellington.
meals	12pm-2pm; 7pm-9.30pm. No food Sunday evenings. Main courses £8-£18.
rooms	3: 1 double, 1 twin/double, 1 twin £50. Singles £30.
closed	3pm-7pm Monday-Friday.

Richard Hartley
Culm Valley Inn,
Culmstock,
Cullompton,
Devon EX15 3JJ
tel   01884 840354

map: 2 entry: 123

Dorset

The Shave Cross Inn
Shave Cross

Fancy a pint of Branoc and a spicy salad of jerk chicken? Once a busy stop-off point for pilgrims and monastic visitors (who had their tonsures trimmed while staying), the cob-and-flint pub now sits dreamily off the beaten track at the end of several tortuously narrow lanes. It was rescued from closure by the Warburtons, back from three years in the Caribbean. Life has stepped up a gear and the old hostelry thrives – thanks largely to the exotic cuisine. Where else in deepest Dorset can you tuck into roast creole duck breast with grilled plantain? There's simple pub grub at lunchtime and an evening table d'hôte for less adventurous palates, while surroundings remain strictly traditional: flagged floors, low beams, country furniture, a vast inglenook, and the oldest thatched skittle alley in the country. The garden, with goldfish pool and wishing well, is wonderful.

directions	B3162 for Broadwindsor; left in 2 miles for Broadoak. Follow unclassified road for 3 miles.
meals	11am-3pm; 5pm-9.30pm (6pm-8pm Sundays in summer). Main courses £3.50-£10.50; set menu from £14.94.
closed	Mondays except Bank Holidays.

Roy & Mel Warburton
The Shave Cross Inn,
Shave Cross, Marshwood Vale,
Bridport, Dorset DT6 6HW
tel   01308 868358
web   www.theshavecrossinn.com

map: 3 entry: 124

The Fox Inn
Corscombe

Clive, once an accountant, is now a licensee and his 17th-century inn is in the hands of a man who feels privileged to be running one of the most sought-after places to eat and sleep in the south-west. Everything about The Fox makes you feel good: the food, the people, the setting – Hardy's Wessex at its most peaceful and beautiful. The beer's not bad either, and there are farm cider and excellent wines. In the old days, drovers on the road to market would dip their sheep into the stream opposite and stop off for a pint of cider... the pub only received its full licence 40 years ago. In spite of modern changes the old feel has been kept; clever additions include a slate-topped bar, a flower-filled and benched conservatory, a long table made from a single oak felled by the storms of 1987. Be charmed by stuffed owls in glass cases, gingham tablecloths, paintings, flowers, flagstones, fires and six fish dishes a day. Bedrooms have a country feel, and you can almost smell the sea.

directions	From Yeovil, A37 for Dorchester for 1 mile; right for Corscombe, for 5.5 miles. On left, on outskirts. Use kitchen door to left of main entrance if arriving before 7pm.
meals	12pm-2pm; 7pm-9pm (9.30pm Friday-Sunday). Main courses £8.25-£18.25.
rooms	4: 3 doubles, 1 twin £80-£100. Singles £55-£75.
closed	Christmas Day.

Clive Webb
The Fox Inn,
Corscombe, Beaminster,
Dorset DT2 0NS
tel   01935 891330
web   www.fox-inn.co.uk

map: 3 entry: 125

Dorset

The Three Horseshoes
Powerstock

Known as The Shoes, it's a Victorian stone inn in a drowsy village down twisting lanes below Eggardon Hill (climb it to see the sea). Rebuilt in 1906, the pub's recent past has been a chequered one but fortunes were restored when the Preeces came onto the scene a year ago. The bustling bar and pine-panelled dining rooms are simply furnished and have good fires. People come from miles around for Andy's fresh, delicious food: he specialises in fish from local boats, organic Dorset lamb and in-season game. A meal might start with roasted pumpkin soup or seared scallops with lime and ginger, then roasted gurnard with garlic and rosemary butter and a steamed chocolate and stem-ginger pudding lasciviously coated in hot chocolate sauce. If you're not here to eat, you're probably downing a great pint of Palmers IPA – preferably on a balmy evening on the tiny terrace watching the sun slide over the valley.

directions	Off A3066 Bridport-Beaminster road.
meals	12pm-2.30pm (3pm Sundays); 7pm-9pm (8.30pm Sundays). Main courses £6.95-£10.50.
rooms	3 doubles £80. Singles from £40.
closed	3pm-6.30pm.

Andy & Marie Preece
The Three Horseshoes,
Powerstock, Bridport,
Dorset DT6 3TF
tel   01308 485328
web   www.threehorseshoesinn.com

map: 3 entry: 126

Dorset

The Acorn Inn
Evershot

Thomas Hardy called this 400-year-old inn The Sow and Acorn and let Tess rest a night here; had he visited today he might have let her stay longer. Todd and Louise are keen to improve upon the already high ideals of The Acorn but this is as much a place for locals to sup their ale as for foodies to sample some of the best meals in Dorset. The flagstoned locals' bar represents the heart of village life; old photographs of villagers cover the walls as stories are swapped over pints of Butcombe by an open fire. Walk through to the dining room and the atmosphere changes to rural country house with smartly-laid tables, terracotta tiles, soft lighting and elegant fireplaces; food is taken seriously, especially fresh local fish: red mullet in a celeriac salsa, scallops on tagliatelle. Bedrooms creak with age *and* style: painted shutters, uneven floors, draperies to soften the four-posters. Perfect Evershot lies at the door and rolling, anciently wooded countryside is there for the walking.

directions	Evershot 1 mile off A37, midway between Yeovil & Dorchester.
meals	12pm-2pm; 7pm-9.30pm. Main courses £3.75-£15.95.
rooms	9: 3 doubles, 3 twin, 3 four-posters £90-£130. Singles from £75.

Todd & Louise Moffat
The Acorn Inn,
28 Fore Street, Evershot,
Dorchester, Dorset DT2 0JW
tel   01935 83228
web   www.acorn-inn.co.uk

map: 3 entry: 127

Dorset

The Royal Oak
Cerne Abbas

Nothing is too much trouble for these affable hosts. A chatty welcome, a tasting of the five real ales before you decide, and every help in choosing from the printed and chalkboard menus. Crackling log fires throughout the three flagstoned rooms add to the charm – along with low oak beams, black panelled walls and rustic tables with candles and pots of herbs. In summer, you can use the enclosed back garden with decking, stone terracing and outdoor heaters. Food is traditional and inspired by the seasons, with fresh local ingredients in dishes like steak and Dorset blue vinney pie, rack of Kingston Maurward lamb with port and lemon sauce, and a platter of west country cheeses – try the Woolsert goat's cheese made in neighbouring Up Sydling. 'Light bites and walkers' favourites' lists sandwiches and local ham, egg and chips. Incidentally, the pub was built in 1540 from the ruins of a nearby Benedictine abbey.

directions	Off A352 between Dorchester & Sherborne. Next to church in centre of village.
meals	12pm-2pm (3pm in summer); 7pm-9.30pm (9pm Sundays). Main courses £5.75-£14.95.
closed	3pm-6.30pm (7pm Sundays).

David & Janice Birch
The Royal Oak,
23 Long Street,
Cerne Abbas,
Dorset DT2 7JG
tel 01300 341797

map: 3 entry: 128

Dorset

The Square & Compass
Worth Matravers

The name honours all those who cut stone from the nearby quarries. Built as a farm in the 17th century from slate and stone, this splendid old pub has been in the family for about 90 years and remains gloriously unchanged. A narrow (and rare) drinking corridor leads to two hatches from where young Charlie Newman draws Ringwood and Badger ales straight from the cask. With a pint of farmhouse cider and a homemade pastie – that's all they sell – you can chat in the flagged corridor or settle in the sunny parlour: with its painted wooden panels, old tables, wall seats, local prints and cartoons. The woodburner will warm you on a wild night. The rustic, stone-walled main room has live music; there's cribbage and shove-ha'penny; the family's fossil museum is next door. High on the edge of the village, gazing out across fields to the sea, the pub and its sunny front terrace – dotted, from time to time, with free-ranging chickens – is a popular stop for coastal path hikers. A timeless treasure.

directions	From A351, B3069 east of Corfe Castle. Through Kingston; right for Worth Matravers.
meals	Homemade pasties only.
closed	Sunday evenings in winter.

Charlie Newman
The Square & Compass,
Worth Matravers,
Swanage,
Dorset BH19 3LF
tel 01929 439229

map: 3 entry: 129

The Museum Inn
Farnham

Owing its name to the 'father of archaeology', General Augustus Lane Fox Pitt Rivers, this place fed and bedded people who came for his museum, now gone. There were three museums in all to house the collection and only the one in Oxford survives today; nor is there any sign of the yaks and zebu that the General once released into a nearby pleasure park. What you do find, however, is one of the most special inns in the south of England. Vicky, Mark and their mostly Ozzie staff have created a blissfully warm and happy place to stay: she does bubbly, he does laid-back. The refit of the big 17th-century bar has kept the period feel with flagstones, inglenook, fresh flowers and an engaging mismatch of wooden tables and chairs. It fills with smart country folk and their dogs but there are plenty of cosy alcoves to hide in; there's also a gorgeous, book-filled drawing room and a smart, white-raftered dining room. Chef Mark Treasure is as good as his name and serves the sea bass with crab, chives and spring onion potatoes with lime… far more fun to eat than to say. Puddings, too, are divine, sorbets a speciality. Impeccable bedrooms, breakfast worth getting up for and a village with roses round every door.

directions	From Blandford, A354 to Salisbury for 6.5 miles; left for Farnham.
meals	12pm-2pm; 7pm-9.30pm. Main courses £14.
rooms	8 doubles £75-£120. Singles £65.
closed	3pm-6pm Mon-Fri (7pm Sun).

Vicky Eliot
The Museum Inn,
Farnham, Blandford Forum,
Dorset DT11 8DE

tel	01725 516261
web	www.museuminn.co.uk

map: 3 entry: 130

Dorset

Coventry Arms
Corfe Mullen

A converted 15th-century watermill with its own island, and a fisherman for a landlord. John Hugo's freshly caught trout are sometimes reeled in by customers and may end up on your plate. Nowhere will you find more trout-inspired dishes than at The Coventry... baked with almonds, in pâté, in ploughman's, in salad. A display of antique fishing reels hangs above the beer barrels where pints are pulled straight from the cask; accompany your pint of local Ringwood Best with a glass-jarred nibble of spicy sesame peanuts or salami bites. The menu itself focuses on fresh ingredients cooked simply and well – the local butcher makes sausages and faggots to the pub's own recipe and game comes from the Drax estate. Low beams, logs in the grate, weekly musicians and tables by the stream: John and Alice's waterside pub is loved by all.

Durham

The Victoria
Durham City

Imagine an old Victorian public house with small rooms, high ceilings, marble fireplaces, etched and cut glass, a vast collection of porcelain ornaments and old prints. Such is the timeless and rather splendid Victoria in the centre of Durham city. Virtually unaltered since it was built in 1899, steeped in Victoriana, it has been it the Webster family for 27 years and has a strong loyal following – a newspaper article once called it "the jewel in the crown of watering holes". The three traditional rooms are spick and span, and above the bar servery is an unusual gallery with shining figurines and ornaments of Queen Victoria and the Prince Consort. Simple snacks are available but it is the Darwins Ghost Ale and other local and Scottish beers, the whiskies and the cosy camaraderie that makes this place so enticing. Upstairs bedrooms are simply furnished and good value.

directions	A31 between Dorchester & Wimborne; 2 miles from Wimborne.
meals	12pm-2.30pm; 6pm-9.30pm. All day on Sundays. Main courses £7-£14.
closed	3pm-5pm Monday-Friday.

directions	5-minute walk from Cathedral, Castle & Market Place.
rooms	5 twins/doubles £54-£64; Singles £40-£44.

	John Hugo Coventry Arms, Mill Street, Corfe Mullen, Wimborne, Dorset BH21 3RH
tel	01258 857284

	Michael Webster The Victoria, 86 Hallgarth Street, Durham, Durham DH1 3AS
tel	0191 386 5269
web	www.victoriainn.durhamcity.co.uk

map: 3 entry: 131

map: 17 entry: 132

Durham

The County
Aycliffe

Having won a Raymond Blanc scholarship in 1995, and worked with Gary Rhodes in London, Andrew Brown decided to take his skills north and restore the fortunes of a run-down pub. He chose The County overlooking Aycliffe's pretty green. Out with patterned carpeting and faded walls, in with bare boards, fresh paint and a minimalist feel. The award-winning food draws an eager crowd, while the open-plan bar is still the focal point of the community. Eat there, or in the stylish bistro. There are open sandwiches at lunchtime, and sausages with black pudding mash; in the bistro, crispy duck spring rolls with hoisin sauce, slow-cooked confit of pork with bean cassoulet, grilled tuna with fennel and a tomato ragout. The touch is light, bringing out textures and flavours superbly. Several real ales are on handpump, wines are mostly New World, service is swift, young and friendly.

directions	North of junc. 59 A1 (M), by A167.
meals	12pm-2pm (3pm Sundays); 6pm-9.15pm. Main courses £6.95-£16.95.
closed	Sunday evenings.

Andrew Brown
The County,
13 The Green, Aycliffe,
Darlington, Durham DL5 6LX
tel   01325 312273
web   www.the-county.co.uk

map: 14 entry: 133

Durham

The Rose & Crown
Romaldkirk

Few country inns match one's expectations as well as the Rose & Crown. Built in the 1750s when Captain Bligh, Romaldkirk's famous son, was still a young sprite, this dreamy inn is gently informal and utterly unpretentious. In the small locals' bar, warmed by an open fire while a few trophies peer down, sit at settles and browse the *Stockton Times* or the *Teesdale Mercury*. A shiny brass door latch reveals more: the elegant lounge where a grandfather clock sets a restful pace, and a bright, panelled dining room for more formal fare and breakfast. Food is excellent and fantastic value. Outside, a village green, with church and unblemished stone cottages, opens onto countryside as good as any in Britain. Alison and Christopher are easy-going perfectionists and the all-pervading sense of tradition is the perfect antidote to England's fickle clime.

directions	From Barnard Castle, B6277 north for 6 miles. Right in village towards green; on left.
meals	12pm-1.30pm; 6.30pm-9.30pm (7pm Sundays). Main courses £9.75-£13.95.
rooms	12: 7 doubles, 3 twins, 2 suites £110. Singles £75.

Christopher & Alison Davy
The Rose & Crown,
Romaldkirk,
Barnard Castle,
Durham DL12 9EB
tel   01833 650213

map: 14 entry: 134

Durham

Morritt Arms
Greta Bridge

Old-fashioned peace and quiet are the keynotes of the Dickens Bar of this well-loved coaching inn; the novelist stayed here while researching *Nicholas Nickleby*. The imposing building, right by the old stone bridge, invitingly floodlit after dark, has been welcoming travellers on the long road from Scotch Corner over Bowes Moor to Carlisle and Scotland since the 17th century. It's a warm and stylish stopover: the interior is effortlessly homely, polished block floors are graced with colourful rugs and deep chintz armchairs front open log fires in panelled lounges. The Dickens Bar has four local cask ales, views across the lawn to the river, and a wonderful mural painted in 1946 by John Gilroy, who selected well-known local figures and created a Dickensian theme around them. Food is available throughout the day in the bar. There are 23 modestly furnished rooms, some with four-posters, others traditional brass beds.

directions	Off A66, 10 miles west of Scotch Corner.
meals	12pm-9.30pm. Main courses £5-£12.95; set menu £21.
rooms	23 twins/doubles £59.50.

Barbara Johnson
Morritt Arms,
Greta Bridge, Barnard Castle,
Durham DL12 9SE

tel 01833 627232
web www.themorritt.co.uk

map: 14 entry: 135

Essex

Axe & Compasses
Arkesden

At the heart of an absurdly pretty village of thatched, timbered cottages with a stream running down its middle, the 400-year-old building resembles the perfect English pub. The rambling interior is a classic too: beamed ceilings, timbered walls, panelling, regiments of horse brasses gleaming in the light from little lamps, open fires, comfy sofas — and that's just the lounge bar. From the well-loved, lived-in feel to the attentive service, the place is nigh-perfect. It's all down to the Christou family, with father Themis at the head, whose pride in his pub over the past 11 years and respect for the traditions of English inn-keeping puts many English landlords to shame. Local Greene King ales are excellent; food is either traditional English — steak and kidney pie, lamb's liver and bacon, chicken supreme, wing of skate — or recognises the family's Greek Cypriot roots, with moussakas and Greek salads. It is all fresh, effortlessly cooked and generous.

directions	On B1038 between Newport & Clavering.
meals	12pm-2.15pm; 7pm-9.30pm. No food Sunday evenings in winter. Main courses £7.95-£13.95; set menu £16 (Sunday lunch).

Themis & Diane Christou
Axe & Compasses,
Arkesden, Saffron Walden,
Essex CB11 4EX

tel 01799 550272
web www.axeandcompass.co.uk

map: 10 entry: 136

The Cricketers
Clavering

It achieved fame as the family home and training ground of Jamie Oliver and, as such, draws a few passers-by... but this big 16th-century inn on the edge of Clavering handles its glory with good humour. Trevor and Sally Oliver's pub has low beams, original timbers and a contented, well-cared for air; light floods in, reflected in the highly polished tables and gleaming brass and glass. A serious commitment to local and seasonal food is obvious the moment you see the printed menu: plenty of comfort food and pub favourites like chicken and ham pie. For more contemporary ideas look to the daily changing blackboards, where fish takes pride of place along with meaty options including seasonal game and superb steaks. Another blackboard also lists good value wines of the month, many served by the glass – it's just as well you can stay the night. Choose between cottagey or contemporary bedrooms, all are in apple-pie order, as you'd expect from this pukka place.

The White Hart
Great Yeldham

This immaculate, Grade I-listed, black and white timbered pub is equally fine inside: dark panelling and exposed timbers, grand log-filled inglenooks, flagstones and polished oak. All deeply traditional – yet the food is punchy and modern. John Dicken's style is fresh and flexible: choose between the light menu or the full à la carte. Young staff serve you in the bar, the splendid dining room or at pretty tables under the trees on the lawned garden. Dishes range from Scottish steak sandwich and cod and chips to seared chicken terrine with garlic and shallot jus, medallions of beef on French beans, chocolate truffle with red fruit coulis. There are wines to match, with 12 by the glass, and real cider and organic fruit juices. It's not easy to please everyone, but judging from the mix of customers – young families, retired couples, business suits drinking well-kept Adnams as they whisper into their (banned) mobile phones – they've succeeded brilliantly.

directions	On B1038 between Newport & Buntingford.
meals	12pm-2pm; 7pm-10pm. Main courses £8-£16.
rooms	14 twins/doubles £100. Singles £70.

directions	On A1017 half-way between Haverhill & Braintree.
meals	12pm-2pm; 6.30pm-9.30pm. Main courses £11-£16.
closed	3.30pm-6pm.

	Trevor Oliver The Cricketers, Clavering, Saffron Walden, Essex CB11 4QT
tel	01799 550442
web	www.thecricketers.co.uk

map: 10 entry: 137

	John Dicken The White Hart, Poole Street, Great Yeldham, Halstead, Essex CO9 4HJ
tel	01787 237250
web	www.whitehartyeldham.co.uk

map: 11 entry: 138

The Sun Inn
Dedham

Piers Baker's transformation of this down-trodden, 15th-century village inn is remarkable. After five years running a successful gastropub chain in London, Piers wanted to get closer to the produce, and to the customers. With a sunny yellow theme throughout, the timbered Tudor ceilings and panelled walls, bare-boarded floors, panelling and log fires in grand grates take you back centuries. Piers' food, however, is entirely modern and, with a blackboard menu and no need to stick to the printed page, he changes his menus according to season and suppliers. He has taken his ideas from far and wide, as seen in dishes such as crab and spinach risotto with fennel and parsley, and beetroot soup with sautéed winter vegetables – all to be washed down with good wines (14 by the glass) and well-kept Greene King Abbot. Upstairs, four rustic-chic and panelled bedrooms display a trove of auction and junk shop finds. Busy in the tourist season, The Sun is a quiet, warm refuge on a cold winter's day – and refreshingly smoke-free with just one designated smoking room.

directions	From A12 towards Dedham & Stratford St Mary; pub 2 miles.
meals	12pm-2.30pm (3pm weekends); 7pm-9.30pm (10pm Fri & Sat). Main courses £8.50-£12.
rooms	4 doubles £60-£90.
closed	Sunday evenings in winter.

Piers Baker
The Sun Inn,
High Street, Dedham,
Colchester, Essex CO7 6DF
tel 01206 323351
web www.thesuninndedham.com

map: 11 entry: 139

Essessex

Carved Angel
Earls Colne

The pub is 15th-century, though modern beams now mix well with the originals. Contemporary lighting, colours and prints create a relaxed, informal eatery where good food is served with good cheer. Not that drinkers are discouraged: locals happily nurse pints of Adnams, Greene King and Carved Angel bitter (brewed for the pub) in the bar. Dishes range from traditional staples of, say, sausage and mash, to the more modern lime-pickled fillet of cod with tomato and basil butter, and there is a very good value, express-lunch menu of one, two, or three courses. You can sit either at a table in the light, bright modern conservatory (smoking), or in the snug, low-beamed rooms (non-smoking). Covered decking with outside heaters is an attractive, summer evening option. The civilised, clubby pool room is brilliant – standard setting stuff.

directions	On A1124 between Colchester & Halstead.
meals	12pm-2pm (2.30pm weekends); 7pm-9pm (10pm Fridays & Saturdays). Main courses £7.95-£15.95; set menus £9.95 (3-course lunch).
closed	3-6.30pm; 3.30-6.30pm weekends.

Michael & Melissa Deckers
Carved Angel,
Upper Holt Street, Earls Colne,
Essex CO6 2PG

tel	01787 222330
web	www.carvedangel.com

map: 11 entry: 140

Essex

The Swan
Little Totham

In a village of 300 souls who have no shop, post office or bus service, the highpoint has to be the village pub. Little Totham is lucky: Valerie and John Pascoe take their role as publicans seriously and their pretty 400-year-old cottage inn is as traditional as can be. There are quiz nights, special live music events of folk, blues and pop classics, a choice of old pub games, an award-winning array of real ales (Abbot Ale, Adnams, Crouch Vale, Fuller's London Pride) and old-fashioned pickled eggs on the bar. No glamour, no frills, just a real local with beams, open fires, soft lighting and bar room chat. Once you're here it is hard to tear yourself away. There's a splendid dining room, ideal for family gatherings, while lasagne, mixed grills, steaks and so on are listed on blackboards in the bar. The beer garden at the front is a lively spot in summer.

directions	A12; exit at Rivenhall for Great Braxted to B1022. Cross over to reach pub in 2 miles.
meals	12pm-2pm; 6pm-9pm; 12pm-6pm Sundays. No food Mondays & Tuesdays. Main courses £6-£12.95.

John & Valerie Pascoe
The Swan,
School Road, Little Totham,
Essex CM9 8LB

tel	01621 892689
web	www.theswanpublichouse.co.uk

map: 11 entry: 141

Essex

Square & Compasses
Chelmsford

Not many pubs can boast that the landlord shot the game offered on the winter menu. When he's not shooting, Howard Potts is fishing: his wild salmon is a very popular dish, smoked on the premises by chef Daniel. This is a genuine rural local where country pursuits are championed and local producers supported. The bar is a place for native gossip over a pint of Ridley's IPA or Nethergate Suffolk County, both tapped from the cask, but walkers and the sedentary are welcomed with equal affection. With their beams, standing timbers, a coal fire, wood-burning stove, local photos, prints, old farming tools, stuffed birds, the open-plan bars exude great warmth and character. Above all, you are here to eat: blackboards hanging over the bar list the choice, which can be as simple as a sandwich or as fancy as whole roasted mallard with cassis sauce And do leave room for co-owner Virginia Austin's puddings.

directions	Off A131 or A12, 5 miles west of Witham.
meals	12pm-2.15pm (3pm Sundays); 7pm-9.30pm (10pm Fri & Sat. No food Mondays or Sunday eve. Main courses £7.50-£14.75.

Howard Potts & Ginny Austin
Square & Compasses,
Fuller Street,
Chelmsford,
Essex CM3 2BB
tel   01245 361477

map: 11 entry: 142

Essex

The Viper
Mill Green

Isolated, but not lonely, this little pub is deep in magnificent woodland on an empty road. The snug, neat, open-plan front bar is warm and jolly – the place has been in the family since 1938 and they are determined to keep things simple. Locals will tell you, with a well-placed pride in their traditions, that these two plain simple rooms have stayed unchanged, bar the odd lick of paint, for 60-odd years. One blackboard lists a regularly changing selection of East Anglian real ales, such as Adnams Broadside, Mighty Oak Oscar Wilde or Ridleys IPA; another lists a decent choice of wine. The classic, good-value bar snacks are served at lunchtime only – sandwiches, soup, chilli, ploughman's – with the popular real-ale sausages at weekends. The setting is so quiet you can ignore the nearby A12; tables on the lawn overlook a cottage garden, resplendent in summer with flowers and shrubs. Super woodland and common-land walks start from the door.

directions	From A12 for Margaretting; left up Ivy Barn Lane; pub at top.
meals	12pm-2pm. Main courses £2.50-£5.50.
closed	3pm-6pm Monday-Saturday.

Roger Beard
The Viper,
The Common,
Mill Green,
Ingatestone, Essex CM4 0PT
tel   01277 352010

map: 11 entry: 143

The Bell Inn & Hill House
Horndon-on-the-Hill

Christine is an original fixture of this Great Inn of England: her parents ran The Bell for years. John is also a key figure, much admired in the trade, as is Joanne, their loyal manager, and friendly staff are predominantly, resolutely young. As a result, it is one of the few pubs in Essex of any real substance. The furniture is the requisite dark brown, there are oak-panelled walls and French wood carvings, plain flagstones or bare boards covered in rugs, an open fire, a grandfather clock, fine prints, ancient hot-cross buns hanging from beams – all bringing warmth and gregariousness to the various rooms. The bar bustles with working folk at lunchtime, downing a well-chosen wine or a pint from Greene King or Crouch Vale Brewers. In the smart restaurant,

which gets busy in the evenings, dishes can be as varied as smoked bacon macaroni cheese with poached egg or confit of pork belly with confit of cabbage and cockle sauce. The food rightly picks up awards – so should Christine's flower arrangements. Stylish bedrooms are available next door in Hill House but the suites upstairs at the inn are the best.

directions	From M25 (J30/31) A13 for Southend for 3 miles; B1007 to Horndon-on-the-Hill.
meals	12pm-1.45pm; 6.45pm-9.45pm. No food Bank Holiday Mondays, Christmas Day & Boxing Day. Main courses £8.50-£12.50.
rooms	16: 8 doubles, 3 twins, 5 suites £75-£105. Singles £50-£60.

John & Christine Vereker
The Bell Inn & Hill House,
High Road, Horndon-on-the-Hill,
Essex SS17 8LB

tel	01375 642463
web	www.bell-inn.co.uk

map: 5 entry: 144

Gloucestershire

The Bowl Inn
Lower Almondsbury

You'd never guess that the whitewashed row of 16th-century cottages-turned-pub would house a warren of frilly bedrooms – nor a proper restaurant. Yet the polish is obvious the moment you step into the swirly-carpeted bar, with a log fire at one end and a woodburner at the other. Half a dozen real ales, even more wines by the glass and a daily array of things to eat displayed on the chalkboards; nothing is too adventurous or over-complicated, but you can't go wrong with a Bowl club sandwich, chicken Caesar salad or braised half lamb shoulder with boulangere potatoes. Or good old-fashioned puddings. Sit outside among the flowering tubs in summer, take in the gentle views of the village green and church. The Alley family have bestowed on The Bowl a lifetime of investment and affection; their reward is a staunchly loyal clientele.

directions	M5 junc. 16; A38 for Thornbury. Left into Over Lane for Lower Almondsbury. Right into Sundays Hill; right into Church Road.
meals	12pm-2.30pm; 6pm-10pm. Main courses £6.75-£10.
rooms	13 twins/doubles £70-£97.50. Singles £44-£87.50.
closed	Christmas Day.

Elizabeth Alley
The Bowl Inn,
Church Road, Lower Almondsbury,
Bristol, Gloucestershire BS32 4DT
tel 01454 612757
web www.thebowlinn.co.uk

map: 3 entry: 145

Gloucestershire

King's Arms
Didmarton

This fine village inn has recently landed in the competent hands of Gamebird Inns' Nigel Pushman, under whose tutelage young Zoe Coombs is doing a great job. Slate floors, Cotswold stone lintels, terracotta walls, hops on beams and oak settles in the bar, and a separate, cheekily-bright dining room adorned with lithographs of the area. There's a big old fireplace for winter, darts and dominoes, too, and a garden for summer drinking. Light lunch dishes such as foie gras and free-range chicken on brioche toast turn up as starters at dinner. 'Something for everyone' on the daily boards might include fresh Cornish crab and locally made sausages with buttered mash and onion gravy. Bedrooms – and a couple of self-catering units in the barn – reflect the demands of the county set. You'll find Butcombe and Wickwar alongside oft-changing guest ales: "if they don't serve beer in heaven, then I'm not going", reads the sign behind the bar.

directions	On A433.
meals	12pm-2pm (2.30pm weekends); 7pm-9.30pm (9pm Sundays). Main courses £7.95-£19.95.
rooms	3 twins/doubles £70-80. Singles £45.
closed	3pm-6pm Monday-Thursday.

Zoe Coombs
King's Arms, The Street,
Didmarton, Badminton,
Gloucestershire GL9 1DT
tel 01454 238245
web www.kingsarmsdidmarton.co.uk

map: 9 entry: 146

Tipputs Inn
Horsley

A handsome Bath stone freehouse in a thriving little town once noted for the wool trade; now it's the place for riders and walkers. Its recent reincarnation is flashily modern with bare boards throughout, bar tables bunched around the open fire at one end and well-spaced, cast-iron dining tables more formally set at the other. Choose from large printed menus – light bites are served throughout the day (sandwiches till 6pm) and more stylish dishes for lunch and dinner. Early evening two-course menus are great value: soup or beef carpaccio, grilled tuna with sauce vierge or peppered rib-eye steak. Bite-sized additions include spiced Greek olives and variations on garlic bread – which go down very well indeed with one of the dozen decent house wines from Nick Beardsley's stable, or well-kept real ales from the likes of Hook Norton and Greene King.

The Tunnel House Inn & Barn
Coates

Follow the lane down from the church – "and don't give up," said the local builder upon our enquiry. He was right: the setting is idyllic (and one of John Betjeman's favourite places). Emerge via the portico tunnel of the Stroudwater canal to find a pretty Bath stone house in the clearing; it was built in the 1780s to house the canal workers. The new occupants have wasted no time in their considered conversion. There are ramps and wheelchair-accessible toilets, a simple, airy dining area and, in the bar, a cacophony of bric-a-brac (some on the walls, most on the ceiling!), an Ogygian juke box with decent tunes, and a mish-mash of sofas and tables around open fires. Pick up a printed menu – they change daily – and choose from Old Spot sausages, garlic-spiced sardines, hazelnut-crumbed brie, partridge pie, blackened fresh salmon. Cotswold Way from Wickwar and Archers' Village are appropriate ales to accompany the fresh, modern cuisine, and there's plenty of decent wine.

directions	On A46 2 miles south of Nailsworth.
meals	11am-10pm. Main courses £8.95-£16.25. set menu £7.

directions	Between Coates & Tarlton.
meals	12pm-2.15pm; 6.45pm-9.30pm. Main courses £7-£11.50.
closed	3pm-6pm Monday-Friday.

Jeremy Ingram
Tipputs Inn,
Bath Road,
Horsley, Nailsworth,
Gloucestershire GL6 0QE
tel 01453 832466

map: 9 entry: 147

Andrew Freeland
The Tunnel House Inn & Barn,
Tarlton Road, Coates, Cirencester,
Gloucestershire GL7 6PW
tel 01285 770280
web www.tunnelhouse.com

map: 9 entry: 148

Gloucestershire

Trouble House Inn
Tetbury

Busy road, another pub: but you would miss a Michelin star if you drove past this one. Say 'Wadworth' when you go to the bar and you won't go far wrong; then look at the chalkboards that spoil you for choice. The food is seasonal, exemplary modern British. For a snack go for crab thermidor with mixed leaves and fragrant homemade bread. Or choose Hereford rib-eye steak with the best-ever chips and a melt-in-the-mouth béarnaise… and finish with orange and rosemary syrup cake, or dark chocolate tart. Chef-patron Michael Bedford is another young cook who has swapped the glamour of the City for doing his own thing in a country pub, and the wine list is accessible and serious. Everything here is done with simplicity and integrity and that includes the interior of bare boards, open fires, warm pink walls and stripped pine. And the Trouble? The framed news clippings will explain that.

directions	On A433, 1.5 miles north east of Tetbury.
meals	12pm-2pm; 7pm-9.30pm (9pm Sundays). No food Sunday evenings October-May. Main courses £12.50-£16.
closed	Mondays.

Michael & Sarah Bedford
Trouble House Inn,
Tetbury,
Gloucestershire GL8 8SG
tel 01666 502206
web www.troublehouse.co.uk

map: 9 entry: 149

Gloucestershire

Seven Tuns Inn
Chedworth

As you nudge the brow of the hill and look down on the Seven Tuns, you know you've found a goodie. In 1610, and for a few centuries after, it was a simple snug; then they diverted the river and built the rest. Part-creepered on the outside, it rambles attractively inside, past open fires, aged furniture, antique prints and a skittle alley with darts. After a gentle walk to Chedworth's Roman Villa, buried in the wooded valley nearby, there's no finer place to return to for a pint of Young's Bitter. Mingle with cyclists, walkers and locals in the little lounge or rustic bar. If you're here to eat you can do so overlooking the garden through two gorgeous mullioned windows; a little further, across the road, is a raised terrace by a waterwheel and stream. Good food is listed on daily menus, from pub favourites (sandwiches, ploughman's, ham and eggs) to chef's specials. This is still the village hub, just as it should be.

directions	Off A429, north of Cirencester.
meals	12pm-2.30pm; 7pm-10pm. Main courses £7-£12.
closed	3pm-6pm Monday-Friday.

Alex Devonport-Jones
Seven Tuns Inn,
Queen Street, Chedworth,
Cirencester,
Gloucestershire GL54 4AE
tel 01285 720242

map: 9 entry: 150

Gloucestershire

The Bell at Sapperton
Sapperton

Note the tethering rail: the elegant community pub attracts horse riders, ramblers, drinkers and foodies. There's an engaging country mood, thanks to rug-strewn flagstones, stripped beams and woodburners, modern art on stone walls, country prints, fresh flowers and newspapers to browse. Sup on local Uley and Hook Norton ales, and eat a meal made with fresh local ingredients, including rare breed and organic meats. The monthly menus or daily specials are chalked up above the fireplace: ploughman's, fresh breads and olives, roasted garlic and tomato soup, chargrilled Dexter beef sirloin with brandy and peppercorn cream, roasted sea bass with fennel and lemon dressing, and so on. Puddings and cheese boards are first class, Sunday roast lunches hugely popular and you have 17 wines by the glass. There's also a walkers' menu. Summer eating can be outside on the glorious front terrace and spills over into the sun-trapping courtyard.

directions	Off A419, 6 miles west of Cirencester.
meals	12pm-2pm; 7pm-9.30pm (9pm Sundays). Main courses £10.50-£17.50.
closed	25 December; 31 December.

Paul Davidson & Pat Le Jeune
The Bell at Sapperton,
Sapperton, Cirencester,
Gloucestershire GL7 6LE
tel   01285 760298
web   www.foodatthebell.co.uk

map: 9 entry: 151

Gloucestershire

White Horse Inn
Frampton Mansell

Wonderful: a quirky-chic bar and restaurant, with good ales and first-class food. Emma and Shaun Davis have filled it with candlelit tables on seagrass floors, modern art on vibrant walls, Indian and Nepalese curios inspired by their travels. Expect an informal atmosphere and a big smile from Emma, who pulls pints of Uley bitter and oversees happy eaters in the restaurant. Fresh food is the mainstay of Shaun's imaginative and seasonal modern menus: rare-breed and traceable meats come from Chesterton Farm down the road, fish from Looe is delivered twice a week. Bread is baked daily, and hand-cut chips accompany lunchtime's home-glazed ham and free-range eggs. All this and hot cheese fritters with onion cream sauce, roast partridge with prune and red wine sauce, banana bread and butter pudding and six wines by the glass. It may not be very lovely and it may be next to a petrol station in the middle of nowhere – but what a pity to pass it by.

directions	On A419 6 miles west of Cirencester.
meals	12pm-2.30pm (3pm Sundays); 7pm-9.45pm. Main courses £8.95-£14.50.
closed	Sunday evenings.

Shaun & Emma Davis
White Horse Inn, Cirencester Road,
Frampton Mansell, Stroud,
Gloucestershire GL6 8HZ
tel   01285 760960
web   www.cotswoldwhitehorse.com

map: 9 entry: 152

The Butcher's Arms
Sheepscombe

Set in the folded hills and valleys of the glorious Cotswolds, the 17th-century Butcher's Arms is not easy to find. But persevere down these twisting, Gloucestershire lanes – it's worth it. A favourite with Laurie Lee, this has everything you would hope for in a village pub: friendly welcome, well-kept beer – Wye Valley and Hook Norton – and a good choice of traditional and modern pub food. The rustic bar is hung with old banknotes, postcards and brass, and leads into two tiny, no-smoking dining rooms. Try the handmade sausages on a leek and mustard mash with onion gravy, or ham, egg and chips, or a daily special of mixed game braised in cranberries and port. Picnic tables are scattered across the front courtyard and the precipitous garden has superb views over the village. Look out for the unusual pub sign with a carving of a butcher and pig over the Guild of Butchers' coat of arms – and don't set your watch by the clock over the bar.

The Five Mile House
Duntisbourne Abbots

In 300 years the interior has changed not a jot: bare wooden floors, open fires, two venerable curving settles, newspapers, cribbage. There is a fabulous flagstoned 'poop deck' of a snug for locals and a galley a few steps below; a more genteel wardroom – the owners' private parlour for a century or more – stands across the hall. Review here the pick of the day's produce, as it appears in baked codling fillets, neck of lamb with rosemary jelly, stilton, spinach and mushroom lasagne. The rest of the menu keeps things simple, with homemade soups and pâtés, local trout and plain grills accompanied by a sauce of your choice. All is cooked to order by Jo. Deserving more consideration than the proverbial swift half, the beer, which includes guests and Taylor's Landlord, is seriously good. You can hardly go wrong here, with serene views from the garden to the valley below. Above, the busy main road – now mercifully concealed by a bank and burgeoning hedgerows.

directions	On A417, turn at D. Abbots & 'Services' sign; successive rights; follow 'no through' road sign.
meals	12pm-2.30pm, 6pm-9.30pm; 7pm-9pm Sundays. Main courses £8.95-£11.75.

directions	Off A46 north of Painswick.
meals	12pm-2.30pm; 7pm-9.30pm. Main courses £5-£10.

Johnny & Hilary Johnston
The Butcher's Arms,
Sheepscombe, Painswick,
Gloucestershire GL6 7RH
tel   01452 812113
web   www.cotswoldinns.co.uk

map: 9 entry: 153

Jo & John Carrier
The Five Mile House,
Lane's End,
Old Gloucester Road, Cirencester,
Gloucestershire GL7 7JR
tel   01285 821432

map: 9 entry: 154

The Wheatsheaf
Northleach

When Northleach was a booming wool town, this was a coaching inn on the Fosse Way. Since then both pub and town have been through some tough times – but today the Cotswolds is, of course, thriving. Caspar Harvard-Walls took on The Wheatsheaf in 2002 and has breathed new life into the old place. The long, light, airy space has been divided into three: a flagstoned central bar, a floor-boarded dining area and a cosy lounge. Prints line light lofty walls and there's a fascinating collection of automata; beers are well-kept and several wines come by the glass. It's a popular pub, and its main business is food, with produce being both fresh and local. Apart from lunchtime soup and the sausage of the day – venison, perhaps, or Old Spot pork – the cuisine is modern British. Try roast breast of guinea fowl, cod in beer batter, fashionably traditional puddings. There's a lovely garden at the back and comfortable bedrooms upstairs.

directions	Off A429, between Stow & Burford.
meals	12pm-3pm; 7pm-10pm. Main courses £6-£14; set menu £12.50 & £15.
rooms	8 twins/doubles £55-£85. Singles from £45.

Caspar Harvard-Walls
The Wheatsheaf,
West End, Northleach,
Gloucestershire GL54 3EZ
tel   01451 860244
web   www.wheatsheafatnorthleach.com

map: 9 entry: 155

The New Inn
Coln St Aldwyns

Built by decree of Elizabeth I, this lovely coaching inn of roaring fires, low beams and swish bedrooms lays on old-fashioned hospitality at its best. The Kimmett family and their staff take the time to talk you through a local walk, the ales on tap, the malts, the wonderful menu. At beautifully dressed tables you feast on traditional dishes with a continental twist. There's a bar menu too: fish terrine, chicken with black pudding mash, caramelised lemon tart. The bedrooms have everything, and those in the dovecote come with views across meadows to the river Coln too. In summer, sip drinks outside under the generous shade of parasols. Brown-trout-fishing can be arranged; golf, biking and riding are nearby; and walks take you through some of England's loveliest villages and countryside.

directions	From Oxford, A40 past Burford, B4425 for Bibury. Left after Aldsworth to Coln St Aldwyns.
meals	12pm-2pm (2.30pm weekends); 7pm-9pm (9.30pm Saturdays). Main courses £8.50-£11.50; set menu £33.
rooms	14: 10 doubles, 3 twins/doubles, 1 single. £115-£148; singles £85-£99.

Roger & Angela Kimmett
The New Inn,
Coln St Aldwyns, Cirencester,
Gloucestershire GL7 5AN
tel   01285 750651
web   www.new-inn.co.uk

map: 9 entry: 156

The Village Pub
Barnsley

It's the 'jeans and jumper' twin of smart Barnsley House opposite and the name says it all. An old favourite of locals and regulars from far and wide, the Village Pub is a benchmark for village pubs everywhere. Classy bedrooms, English food based on the best local produce, good-quality beers and wines... there's something for everyone here. There's even a service hatch to the gas-heated patio at the back, so you can savour the sauvignon until the sun goes down. Cotswold stone and ancient flags sing the country theme. Past bar and open fires, quiet alcoves provide a snug setting that will entice you to stay. Well-balanced menus are sensibly short with dishes often changing at every season. On a typical December dinner menu you may find pumpkin and rosemary soup, roast duck with braised red cabbage, grilled sea bass with herb couscous and artichoke salad. Pudding-lovers could do worse than finish with orange and almond cake and clotted cream — all of it delicious. With Graham's award-winning cooking and such authenticity in a pub, who could ask for more?

directions	M4, junc. 15; A419 for Gloucester. Right onto B4425 for Bibury. Village 2 miles on.
meals	12pm-2.30pm (3pm weekends); 7pm-9.30pm (10pm Fri & Sat). Main courses £9-£13.
rooms	6 doubles, £65-£120.
closed	3.30pm-6pm; 4pm-6pm Saturdays (7pm Sundays).

Tim Haigh & Rupert Pendered
The Village Pub,
Barnsley, Cirencester,
Gloucestershire GL7 5EF

tel	01285 740421
web	www.thevillagepub.co.uk

map: 9 entry: 157

Gloucestershire

The Falcon Inn
Poulton

Look out for this old white stone pub as you swing round the bends through the village centre. New young owners of impeccable pedigree have given wing to this bird's potential – it is another superb dining pub for Gloucestershire. Two dining rooms face an open theatre kitchen, creating plenty of room for private dining without spoiling the feel of the traditional village bar and fireside tables at the front of the inn. Chef Robin Couling does not go in for towering lunches: simplicity is the key to his near-perfect crab risotto and spinach and potato cake with blue cheese rarebit. Dinner graduates to madeira-sauced duck breast and wild sea bass with pancetta and creamed cabbage. Whatever you eat, try the hand-cut real chips dusted with sea salt as an accompaniment (children cannot resist them), along with memorable guest beers such as West Berkshire's Good Old Boy, or one of several well-chosen wines by the glass.

directions	Beside A417, midway between Ampney Crucis & Fairford.
meals	12pm-2.30pm; 7pm-9pm. Main courses £5.50-£12.95; set 2-course Sunday lunch £14.95.
closed	Sunday evenings & Mondays.

Robin Couling
The Falcon Inn,
London Road, Poulton, Cirencester,
Gloucestershire GL7 5HN
tel 01285 850844
web www.thefalconpoulton.co.uk

map: 9 entry: 158

Gloucestershire

The Victoria
Eastleach Turville

The golden-stoned Victoria pulls in the locals, whatever their age, whatever the weather. Propping up the bar, welly-clad with dogs or indulging in great home-cooked grub by the inglenook, the locals and their laughter suggest a whale of a time is had by all. If frolic you must, this is the place to do it: summer brings river tug-o-war and the village's Frolic Day. (The highlight of which involves a large oak tree, children in sacks and a loaf of treacle-coated bread.) Refreshments are available for all from proprietors Stephen and Susan Richardson who, in spite of opening it up, have kept much of the character and cosiness of the low-ceilinged pub. Who could fail to enjoy warm smoked chicken, steak and mushroom pie, lamb shank on minty mash, accompanied by Arkells on handpump or a New World wine? Several wines are served by the glass, and there are picnic tables out front, from where you can look down onto the pretty stone cottages and the churches of the village.

directions	Off A361 between Burford & Lechlade.
meals	12pm-2pm; 7pm-9.30pm (9pm Sundays). Main courses £6.50-£14.50.

Stephen & Susan Richardson
The Victoria,
Eastleach Turville,
Fairford,
Gloucestershire GL7 3NQ
tel 01367 850277

map: 9 entry: 159

Gloucestershire

The Fox
Lower Oddington

Low ceilings, worn flagstones, a log fire in winter, good food and an exemplary host... people love it here. The comfortably stylish bar has scrubbed pine tables topped with fresh flowers and candles; newspapers, magazines and ales are on tap; rag-washed ochre walls date back years; the locals are lively. Eat here or in the elegant, rose-red dining room, or on the delightful garden terrace, heated on cool nights. Imaginative, sometimes elaborate dishes include smoked chicken and leek risotto, seared scallops in chive beurre blanc, lamb shank with rosemary and garlic, dark chocolate torte. Bedrooms that fall into the 'charming inn' category sometimes leave a lot to be desired, but these rooms, although above the unhushed bar, are a modest, old-fashioned treat, with antique beds, warm colours and prints of fox-hunting scenes. Before you leave, explore the honey-stone village and 11th-century church, known for its magnificent frescoes.

directions	From Stow A436 for 3 miles.
meals	12pm-2pm; 6.30pm-10pm; 7pm-9.30pm Sundays. Main courses £7.95-£13.75.
rooms	3 doubles, £68-£95.
closed	3pm-6pm; 4pm-7pm Sundays.

Ian McKenzie
The Fox, Lower Oddington,
Stow-on-the-Wold,
Gloucestershire GL56 0UR
tel   01451 870555
web   www.foxinn.net

map: 9 entry: 160

Gloucestershire

The Farriers Arms
Todenham

A tiny treasure: a couple of tables in front, a teensy dining room, a smallish bar with a room at the back, a few tables dotting the garden. But, being small, it's cosy — and wonderfully, reassuringly old-fashioned, with low, hop-hanging beams, polished flagstones, wonky walls and an inglenook with a wood-burning stove. Add great beers, real cider and perry, eight wines by the glass, an enjoyable menu and glorious views from the garden and you have a country pub worth a detour. Always busy, The Farriers is jam-packed on Sundays (lunch must be booked), as well as on Tuesday curry nights and Friday fish nights. Thomas Young, the landlord, describes the menu — without exaggeration — as "high quality pub food": fresh ingredients with tasty sauces. Try paupiettes of sole with salmon mousse, creamed spinach and tarragon sauce, or pheasant breast on black pudding with bubble-and-squeak cake and port sauce. The mellow-stone village is as pretty as the pub.

directions	Signed from Moreton-in-Marsh & from A3400.
meals	12pm-2pm; 7pm-9pm (9.30pm Fridays & Saturdays). Main courses £7.95-£16.95.
closed	3pm-6.30pm

Thomas Young & Charlotte Bishop
The Farriers Arms,
Todenham, Moreton-in-Marsh,
Gloucestershire GL56 9PF
tel   01608 650901
web   www.farriersarms.com

map: 9 entry: 161

Gloucestershire

The Churchill Arms
Paxford

The Churchill is fun. Walk into the bar, with stone floors and wooden tables, to a hub of happy chatter. Leo and Sonya are right to be proud of their creation – one guest described it as "Fulham in the country", and the locals sipping their well-kept Hook Norton like it that way. Many were reluctantly leaving when we arrived just after lunch. And the food is good, whether it's potato and horseradish soup or blade of beef with jus and soubise sauce – or the sticky toffee pudding which is perfect. Add good fabrics, pastel colours and country views from the heart of this picture-perfect village and you have something special. Bedrooms right above the bar are equally fun and stylish; two are small but you don't feel hemmed in. "Frills and drapes are not us," says Sonya; beams, old radiators and uneven floors are. The Churchill is a relaxed and engaging mix of the old and the new.

directions	A44 through Bourton-on-Hill; right to Paxford, via Blockley.
meals	12pm-2pm; 7pm-9pm. Main courses £8-£13.50.
rooms	4 doubles £70. Singles £40.

Leo & Sonya Brooke-Little
The Churchill Arms,
Paxford, Chipping Campden,
Gloucestershire GL55 6XH
tel   01386 594000
web www.thechurchillarms.com

map: 9 entry: 162

Gloucestershire

Red Lion
Chipping Campden

There are many classic Cotswold stone pubs in this village, all a huge draw for weekenders and walkers from the Home Counties and tourists from as far afield as New York and Tokyo. We chose this one for its history, from at least the 16th century, and its bedrooms in the old stables that have been so well done up by Jean and Roger Leigh. They take the same tack with food. Daily blackboard menus trumpet 'Flavours of the Three Counties' with nearby Worcester and Herefordshire playing their part. So look for local butcher's sausages, Evesham asparagus in spring, Hereford strawberries in summer and classic seared West Country scallops and Old Spot pork chops with grain mustard mash and sun-dried tomatoes. In the best tradition, real ales may be from Uley and Hook Norton, the wine list isn't half bad and, considering this is a tourist honey pot, the prices are pretty reasonable.

directions	On High Street at corner of Sheep Street.
meals	12pm-2pm; 7pm-9pm. Main courses £8.50-£14.50.
rooms	5 twins/doubles £70. Singles £50.

Roger Leigh
Red Lion,
Lower High Street,
Chipping Campden,
Gloucestershire GL55 6AS
tel   01386 840760

map: 9 entry: 163

The King's Arms
Stow-on-the-Wold

Peter was head chef at the chic Hotel Tresanton in Cornwall, until he and Louise moved to this 500-year-old, mellow-stone inn overlooking Stow's market square. With new life, style and panache breathed into it, and blessed with Peter's impeccable pedigree, the King's Arms was soon jam-packed with diners eager to get at his food. The fish travels from Cornwall every day, the local produce is as fresh as can be, with lamb and pork from surrounding farms, and the cooking is inventive and delicious — great white platefuls of spinach and ricotta risotto, grilled venison marinated in chilli, or lemon sole with fresh anchovies. The wine list is long, the ale is real (Greene King and Hook Norton), and the upstairs dining room — all damson walls and wonky polished floorboards — overlooks the charming town. Thanks to Louise, the old coaching inn is also a comfortable and friendly place to stay. Charles II stayed here during the Civil War; with what effect we don't know, but the rooms are unlikely to have been as stylish as they are today. The King's Arms is special, yet absolutely lacking in pretension; you'll feel thoroughly spoiled. Families are most welcome.

directions	Off A429, in centre of Stow-on-the-Wold.
meals	12pm-2.30pm; 6pm-9.30pm (10pm Saturdays); 7pm-9pm Sundays. Main courses £8-£13.
rooms	10 twin/doubles £60-£120.

Peter & Louise Robinson
King's Arms,
Market Square, Stow-on-the-Wold,
Gloucestershire GL54 1AF
tel   01451 830354
web   www.kingsarms-stowonthewold.co.uk

map: 9 entry: 164

Gloucestershire

The Plough Inn
Ford

Horses from the local stables gallop past, local shoots lunch here, race-goers stay overnight. The rustic walls of The Plough are lined with photographs of meetings at nearby Cheltenham: the place is dedicated to country pursuits. Cheltenham week is bedlam, and a marquee is erected in the garden, but – because of the food – every week is busy. The cooking has a loyal following, and the dining room is famous for its asparagus suppers. Aberdeen Angus fillet in a brandy and black peppercorn sauce tastes every bit as good as it looks. There are good local beers, real ciders and well-chosen wines. The building has been an inn since the 16th century, probably dates from the 13th and was once a courthouse, so bars are darkly cosy with low beams, flagstones and smouldering fires. In spite of its success, The Plough still pulls in the locals. Children will make a bee-line for the play fort in the garden.

directions	B4077 between Stow & Tewkesbury.
meals	12pm-2pm; 6pm-9pm; 12pm-9pm weekends. Main courses £6.95-£14.95.
rooms	3: 1 double, 1 family 1 single. £60; singles £35.

Craig & Becky Brown
The Plough Inn,
Ford, Temple Guiting, Cheltenham,
Gloucestershire GL54 5RU

tel	01386 584215
web	www.theploughinnatford.co.uk

map: 9 entry: 165

Gloucestershire

White Hart Inn
Winchcombe

Had you mentioned the Scandinavians in the sixth century, when Winchcombe was the Saxon capital of Mercia, there would have been a call to arms. But these Swedes have brought vibrant chic and warm hospitality to this 16th-century inn. The style is rural Swedish: scrubbed wooden floors, sisal matting, big windows and Gustavian blue-grey furniture. Nicole employs solely Swedish staff; all take it in turns to serve, clean, or cook authentic food: sil, marinated herring, is superb. They've even introduced Santa Lucia, a winter festival of song and candles and there's a pizzeria for those of a more southern persuasion. The best bedrooms have views of the high street; one has a four-poster.

directions	From Cheltenham, B4632 to Winchcombe. Inn on right.
meals	Bar snacks all day; à la carte from 6pm; Smorgasbord Wed eve, Fri & Sun lunch. Main courses £15-£16. Bar snacks from £5.
rooms	8: 2 doubles, 4 twins/doubles, 2 four-posters £65-£125; half-board (min. 2 nights) £75 p.p. Singles £55-£115.
closed	Christmas Day.

Nicole & David Burr
White Hart Inn,
High Street, Winchcombe,
Gloucestershire GL54 5LJ

tel	01242 602359
web	www.the-white-hart-inn.com

map: 9 entry: 166

Gloucestershire

The Boat Inn
Ashleworth

This extraordinary, tiny pub has been in the Jelf family since Charles II granted them a licence for liquor and ferry – about 400 years! It's a gem – a peaceful, unspoilt red-brick cottage on the banks of the Severn. Jacquie's a Jelf and she and husband Ron took over when Aunty Irene retired. You can sit in the no-smoking, gleaming front parlour – colourful with fresh garden flowers, a huge built-in settle and a big scrubbed deal table fronting an old kitchen range – or in the spotless bar. On sunny summer days you can laze by the languid river. Adjectives are inadequate: this place is cherished. "It's like letting people into your own home", says Jacquie. Real ale straight from the cask, Weston's farm cider, a bar of chocolate, a packet of crisps... but don't feed Sam, he's on a diet. There's no 'jus' here; Jacquie does lunchtime ploughman's and baps, some with homemade chutney. Perfect.

directions	On A417 1.5 miles from Hartpury, between Gloucester & Ledbury.
meals	Filled rolls, lunchtimes only. Main courses (rolls) £1.50-£2.
closed	Mondays; Wednesday lunchtimes; 2.30pm-7pm (3pm weekends).

Ron & Jacquie Nicholls
The Boat Inn, Ashleworth Quay,
Ashleworth, Gloucester,
Gloucestershire GL19 4HZ
tel 01452 700272
web www.boat-inn.co.uk

map: 9 entry: 167

Gloucestershire

The Glasshouse Inn
May Hill

If you are an aficionado of Bass and Butcombe, Weston's ciders and all good, nature-blessed produce, you have to come here. Ramshackle tables and open log fires are considered modern at this converted, 16th-century brick cottage where glass was once blown in wood-fired ovens and cider pressed in the shed. Guinness adverts, cartoons and horseracing prints decorate the place as do autographed England rugby shirts – and the chiming clock never serves as an invitation to leave. "We buy the best and mess around with it as little as possible," says exuberant landlady Jill – who adds that in her youth you never had a starter, unless it was somewhere posh, and if your kids were under 14 you wouldn't be eating out at all. Home-cooked ham and free-range eggs are from their livestock, beef from the Welsh borders is properly aged and the chips, in their vast portions, are all hand-cut. Eat outside on hidden seating canopied by a bridge of yew.

directions	Signed from A40 at Longhope, between Gloucester & Ross-on-Wye.
meals	11.30am-2pm; 6.30pm-9pm. No food Sundays. Main courses £6.50-£13.50.
closed	Sunday evenings in Jan & Feb.

Steve & Jill Pugh
The Glasshouse Inn,
May Hill,
Longhope,
Gloucestershire GL17 0NN
tel 01452 830529

map: 9 entry: 168

Wyndham Arms
Clearwell

"Life is short," says the menu, "eat dessert first." Pear and apple crumble with a glass of spiced apple wine or chocolate mousse with berry compote may have you obeying the edict. The inn dates back to 1347 and stands virtually in the shadow of Clearwell Castle: it feels very fitting that the place has been stripped back to reveal original wooden floors and brickwork. The setting also feels right for enjoying the local Freeminer's ale, organic Wye Valley cider and St Anne's country wines. There are regional cheeses such as Severn Sisters and Stinking Bishop and on the changing, seasonal menu is an inclusive two-course lunch or dinner that can include butternut squash and rosemary soup before poached salmon on saffron mash or pork medallions over apples with cider sauce. Its 20th-century bedroom additions may be a little less in keeping but they are arguably the best in the area.

The Ostrich
Newland

The antithesis of its well-heeled neighbours in Clearwell, the Ostrich is where the beer drinkers go. Across from All Saints Church, the famous 'Cathedral of the Forest', you'll rub shoulders with all manner of folk from huntsmen to trail bikers attracted by the huge log fire and massive portions of well-cooked pub food – from a Newland bread-and-cheese platter to rib-eye steak with lashings of fresh béarnaise. The nicotine-brown ceiling that looks in danger of imminent collapse is supported by a massive oak pillar in front of the bar where the locals chatter and where 1940s jazz CDs keep the place swinging. There's an intimate dining room where the weekly menu takes a step up in class and is excellent value for money. Energetic landlady Kathryn and her cook Sue keep the place buzzing. To the back is a grassy knoll of a garden – and the loos, 'just by there', beyond the coal sacks and guarded by the pub pooch.

directions	From Chepstow A48 for Gloucester; B4228 to Coleford. Clearwell signed after 12 miles.
meals	12pm-2pm (2.30pm Sundays); 7pm-9.30pm. Main courses £8.50-£14.50.
rooms	18 twins/doubles from £69. Singles from £32.50.

directions	Signed on lane linking A466 at Redbrook & at Clearwell between B4228 Coleford & Chepstow road.
meals	12pm-2.30pm; 6.30pm-9.30pm (6pm Saturdays). Main courses £7-£13.50.
closed	3pm-6.30pm.

Nigel & Pauline Stanley
Wyndham Arms,
Clearwell,
Gloucestershire GL16 8JT
tel   01594 833666
web   www.thewyndhamhotel.co.uk

Kathryn Horton
The Ostrich,
Newland, Coleford,
Gloucestershire GL16 8NP
tel   01594 833260
web   www.theostrichinn.com

map: 8 entry: 169

map: 8 entry: 170

Gloucestershire

The Red Hart
Awre

Sue says there's a ghost: "He sits in the restaurant with a beard and blue waistcoat: never speaks, just spooks people!" Ghost or no, there is little else that's spectral about Jerry Bedwell's 15th-century freehouse in the Severn flood plain. Here are open fires, hearty meals, real wines, real ales and a good welcome. Pine tables and chairs, old prints of the village of Awre, a bookcase of tomes on cookery and wine… It is pleasingly unprecious, with prices to match. Favourite nosh includes cod in beer batter, Old Spot sausages with bubble-and-squeak, crispy duck with lime, ginger and soy. They all wash down beautifully with a well-kept pint of Badger Tanglefoot or Weston's organic cider – or, indeed, wine. There's no standing on ceremony here: the place is rambler-, dog- and child-friendly. Follow the riverside walks from the maps outside, then foot it back to the tall, austere inn for some old-fashioned cheer.

directions	Off A48, 3 miles south of Newnham.
meals	12pm-2pm; 6.30pm-9pm (from 7pm Sundays). No food Sunday evenings in winter. Main courses £7.50-£15.95.
closed	Mondays in winter.

Jeremy Bedwell
The Red Hart,
Awre,
Gloucestershire GL14 1EW
tel   01594 510220

map: 9 entry: 171

Hampshire

The Yew Tree
Hollington Cross

The staff, smartly turned-out in long white aprons, may look daunting and 'upmarket' but are courteous and friendly. The contemporary and sympathetic makeover stitches the elegant and stylish dining room into the old fabric and character of the building; it is really more restaurant than pub. There are inglenooks, timbers and beams and light uncluttered walls, a vase of white lilies here, a leather sofa there, beige carpeting by the entrance. A spent magnum of Bollinger may stand alongside bowls of crisps and nuts on the bar. Around the bar area are solid tables and chairs on tiled floors softened by lamplight, the dining room's crisp white napery looks fine against a backdrop of exposed brick and timber, and the menu is suitably modern and British. Bedrooms are spotless; the peace is deep and sleep should be equally so, and you wake to hillside views.

directions	M4 junc. 13; A343 just after Highclere.
meals	12pm-3pm (4pm Sundays); 6pm-10pm; 7pm-9pm Sundays. Main courses £9-£10.
rooms	6: 4 doubles, 2 twins, £60.

Eric Norberg
The Yew Tree,
Hollington Cross,
Andover Road, Highclere,
Hampshire RG20 9SE
tel   01635 253360

map: 4 entry: 172

At the sign of the Four Seasons?
In celebration of seasonal, local and organic food

The renaissance of the British pub has been dramatic. A decade ago most of them peddled low-price Sunday roasts and mass-produced food; there were only a handful of outstanding ones in which to eat, drink and stay. Things have changed. With established players (Classic Country Pubs, Condor Pubs and Peach Pubs) taking on a greater variety of places, and more independents starting up (the Sun Inn at Dedham, Essex and the Mole Inn at Toot Baldon, Oxfordshire) new life is being pumped into depressed boozers, some on a shoestring budget and some with huge investment. If the new entrepreneurs take note that there are four seasons in the year, and talk to their suppliers rather than just place orders, there will be more and more delightful places to visit.

Out-of-season food used to be actively promoted by posh restaurants whose customers could afford it. Nowadays many dining pubs do so too.

From our research for this guide, it seems that many licensees still have no idea what is in season, be it fish, meat or vegetable. They hear that the trend is for local supplies and think 'let's go to Bernie down the road, he does veg', without thinking of asking where it really comes from.

A global marketplace dominated by powerful interests pursuing intensification and cheapness has driven our eating habits. We had a huge wake-up call with the foot and mouth epidemic in 2001. 'Local' suddenly became the buzz word. And the emphasis on local foods necessarily involves a response to the seasons.

Local supplies are generally fresher, not having been transported long distances; their provenance can be assured; and staying close to home encourages individuality: samphire in summer, for example. Scares about a cancer risk associated with eating farmed salmon bring a further point home: mass production comes at a cost. Given the choice between raspberries grown down the road or imported from Chile, there's a strong argument in favour of the former – as long as they have been grown with integrity. As the White Hart in Dartington, Devon puts it: "We appreciate all the arguments concerning local food, food miles, and organic produce. However, we use local producers primarily because the quality of their produce is outstanding."

We should not focus simply on giving business to the local greengrocer, fishmonger or butcher; we must ask where they are buying their produce. Talking to growers and producers tells you what is in, or coming into, season. Pubs like the Red Lion at Strathern, Leicestershire and the Tollgate at Holt, Wiltshire are confident enough to list their local suppliers.

When we asked all pubs and inns in this guide about organic supplies, many were ambivalent. Six years after the opening of the Duke of Cambridge, the first of two organic pubs owned by the Organic Pub Company, few have followed suit. Glyn Williams of the Randolph, in Reydon, Suffolk, is sceptical. He can trace his raw materials to local sources and refuses to commit to organic produce as so much is imported: "What could be fresher than something that has been killed or picked locally, recently, quickly? It has got to be better for you than imported organic produce".

One can only agree, yet we must beware of buying local food merely because it is local. At least organic food is regulated, while 'local' farming is not. So if a pub opts for local it should know its supplier well enough to trust him or her implicitly.

It helps to be close to an organic farm. As founder members of the Campaign for Real Food, the Corcorans of the Queen's Head, Bramfield, Suffolk support and promote 'real food' by working closely with local organic farmers. Janet Frank at the Moors Inn at Appleton-le-Moors, North Yorkshire works with a local organic farm at Fadmoor. It is worth the extra effort.

A last note: buy *The Little Food Book* (Alastair Sawday Publishing!). It's an easy but thought-provoking read and you will learn a huge amount about the food industry and its sometimes bizarre machinations.

Elizabeth Carter

Hampshire

The Red House
Whitchurch

A short stroll from the trout-filled Test, the sturdy, 16th-century country inn attracts those in search of fine food (it's packed on Saturdays) as well as the thirsty angler. Its pubby roots, however, are not forgotten: there's still a locals' bar. But it is the saloon bar that is the engine room of the place; large mirrors create an illusion of greater space, there's a small lightwood counter and a similarly modern floor, while low-beamed ceilings and a flagged inglenook (warmly glowing in winter) tell of the building's age. The cuisine has bags of style and could be loosely described as modern European. Well-presented dishes use excellent ingredients and are extremely tasty: scallops with crab meat and courgettes, chump of lamb in red wine jus, pistachio crème brulée. For summer, an excellent beer garden in which to sit back and relax with a hop-filled pint of Cheriton Pots, and a play area for well-behaved children. Nearby is the South's only working silk mill – worth a visit.

directions	Between M3 & M4; off A34 heading for Whitchurch B3400.
meals	12pm-2pm; 6.30pm-9.30pm (from 7pm Sundays). Main courses £3.95-£14.95.
closed	3pm-6pm (7pm Sundays).

Caroline & Shannon Wells
The Red House,
21 London Street,
Whitchurch,
Hampshire RG28 7LH
tel   01256 895558

map: 4 entry: 173

Hampshire

The Peat Spade
Stockbridge

It's a short drive through the glorious Test Valley from Mottisfont Abbey to Longstock, a straggling village of heavily thatched cottages with this striking gabled Victorian pub at its heart. Behind the little, lozenged-paned windows the feel is more private home than country pub, with a series of neatly furnished eating areas around an uncluttered bar. Chef-landlord Bernie Startup delivers a near-perfect version of country-pub food; he works to a short menu, avoids clichés, rings the changes, and buys local, seasonal and organic from first-class suppliers (notably Leckford Estate who supply his game). Handpumped beers include the locally brewed Ringwood Fortyniner and Hop Back GFB, and an organic ale from Brakspear. With the Test Way footpath almost passing the door and the famous trout stream only 100 yards away, it is popular with walkers and fishermen. There's a rear terrace for summer sipping and two pine-furnished bedrooms in a converted outbuilding.

directions	Off A3057, 1 mile north of Stockbridge.
meals	12pm-2pm; 7pm-9.30pm. Main courses £7.75-£13.50.
closed	Sunday evenings & Mondays.

Sarah Hinman & Bernard Startup
The Peat Spade,
Longstock,
Stockbridge,
Hampshire SO20 6DR
tel   01264 810612

map: 4 entry: 174

The Greyhound
Stockbridge

Thanks to the clear-running waters of the Test, civilised, one-street Stockbridge is England's fly-fishing capital. But you'll find more polo-necks than fishermen propping up the bar of the colour-washed Greyhound. With its blend of rusticity and sophistication the 15th-century coaching inn has been remodelled in style, and, though not entirely divorced from its pub roots – it's packed with drinkers at the bar – it is very much a dapper, food-and-wine-centred affair. And of some pedigree: chef-patron Darren Bunn worked at the Criterion Grill in the West End and used to buy wine for Marco Pierre White. Now his modern, brasserie-style dishes, based on impeccable produce, have netted him a Michelin star. Be won over by his pressed terrine of cornfed chicken, scallops, risotto, sea bream with linguini and meltingly rich fishcakes with a chive beurre blanc, jauntily topped with a poached egg. There's a separate lounge with a big red leather sofa and a chesterfield, and an open-plan dining area alongside the traditional bar. Fireplaces, log-burning stoves, low exposed beams, stripped floorboards and light wooden furniture encourage the cosy feel, while there's a pretty small garden overlooking the Test to which you may retreat with your glass of perfectly chilled chablis.

directions	On A30, 10 miles from Winchester.
meals	12-2.30pm; 7-9.30pm. No food Sunday evenings. Main courses £5-£25.
rooms	6 doubles (from August 2004) £90.

Darron Bunn
The Greyhound,
31 The High Street,
Stockbridge,
Hampshire SO20 6EY
tel   01264 810833

map: 4 entry: 175

The Plough Inn
Sparsholt

Children frolic in the flowery garden's wooden chalet and play-fort while grown-ups enjoy the views. The beer's good, too, with Wadworths ales on draught. Walkers come here for a lunchtime snack of beef-and-horseradish sandwiches with relish. Inside, the pub is smart and open-plan, with pine tables, hop-garlanded beams and an open log fire. The 200-year-old cottagey front rooms are particulary cosy places to have dinner and the enthusiastic tenants, Richard and Kathryn Crawford, with a loyal and hard-working team, run this busy pub with good humour. Blackboards proclaim the dishes of the day; favourites, like lamb's liver and bacon, are given a modern twist, and restaurant-style main courses show imagination and flair. Try cod with olives, crushed potato and herb oil, followed by fruits of the forest crumble. Wines are taken seriously and 12 are available by the glass.

The Star Inn
East Tytherley

Come for comfort and good food to this 16th-century inn overlooking Tytherley's cricket pitch. In summer the front terrace is festooned with flowers, replete with big brollies and chessboard; in winter, there's a pew by the fire in the modernised bar. Although food is the main attraction, Paul and Sarah have kept the village pub atmosphere, with Ringwood Best on tap and a nice little skittle alley. Tuesdays and Saturdays in summer see The Star filled with thirsty cricketers. Eat in the bar or in the restaurant; the menu is modern British. Choose from old favourites like steak, kidney and Guinness pie and freshly battered cod and chips, or something more elaborate, such as exquisitely presented seared scallops with smoked salmon kedgeree, or beef fillet with potato rösti, foie gras and madeira jus. There are also sandwiches and filled jacket potatoes, and comfortable bedrooms in a building by the cricket pitch.

directions	Off B3149 Winchester to Stockbridge road.
meals	12pm–2pm; 6pm–9pm. (9.30pm Fridays & Saturdays). Main courses £7.95–£16.95.
closed	3pm–6pm.

directions	Off B3084 north of Romsey.
meals	12pm–2pm; 7pm–9pm. Main courses £7–£17.
rooms	3 twin/doubles £70. Singles £50.
closed	Mondays except Bank Holidays; 26 December.

Richard & Kathryn Crawford
The Plough Inn,
Sparsholt,
Winchester,
Hampshire SO21 2NW
tel   01962 776353

Paul & Sarah Bingham
The Star Inn,
East Tytherley, Romsey,
Hampshire SO51 0LW
tel   01794 340225
web   www.starinn-uk.com

map: 4 entry: 176

map: 4 entry: 177

Hampshire

The Three Tuns
Romsey

There's a great deal more than three tuns of beer or wine on offer these days. Inside all is change: a recent remodelling delivering a contemporary makeover in keeping with the best of gastropubs. Flagstones, dark beams and timbers, a huge fireplace (with gas log fire) and a strong local following keep pubby roots in check, while a lightwood bar with glass-backed and under-lit shelving and modern spotlighting help create a clean, uncluttered space and a rustic-chic feel. Off to one side, there's informal, restaurant-style dining. Here redwood panelling lends a drawing-room note, while twinkling tea-lights help to soften the hard edges of a high-volume atmosphere. Modern brasserie-style food from a compact and appealing menu delivers light, well-presented and balanced dishes that well deserve the gastropub tag, alongside a more traditional bar menu at lunchtimes. It's the perfect place to drop in for bite after visiting Broadlands or the town's Norman abbey.

directions	Opposite Broadlands estate, on main Romsey by-pass.
meals	12pm-2.30pm; 7pm-9.30pm. No food Sunday evenings. Main courses £4.50-£8.

Jon Hughes
The Three Tuns,
58 Middlebridge Street,
Romsey,
Hampshire SO51 8HL
tel   01794 512639

map: 4 entry: 178

Hampshire

The Rose & Thistle
Rockbourne

A thatched Hampshire dream with a dovecote to match and a rose-tumbled garden. Like many rural pubs, it started life as two cottages so the interior, with its two huge fireplaces, comes as no surprise. It is a perfect mix of heavy oak beams and timbers, carved benches and flagstone or tiled floors. Add country-style fabrics, dried flowers, tables strewn with magazines and you have an enchanting place to return to after a visit to Rockbourne's Roman villa. Landlord Tim Norfolk has been here 11 years and has built up a good reputation for his steaks and sauces. Ever-changing blackboard specials make use of fresh local produce, like estate game in season and south-coast fish. At lunchtime you might find it hard choosing between smoked salmon and scrambled eggs, prawns by the pint and chicken, mustard and tarragon pie. The more elaborate evening menu favours fish, such as John Dory with lime and coriander butter. Rockbourne is a delight to discover.

directions	3 miles north-west of Fordingbridge, off B3078.
meals	12pm-2.30pm; 7pm-9.30pm. Main courses £5.95-£17.95.
closed	Sunday evenings November-March.

Tim Norfolk
The Rose & Thistle,
Rockbourne, Fordingbridge,
Hampshire SP6 3NL
tel   01725 518236
web   www.roseandthistle.co.uk

map: 4 entry: 179

The Royal Oak
Fritham

A small, ancient, thatched, off-the-beaten-track New Forest inn and an ale-lover's delight. There's no truck with fruit machines or muzak here: the atmosphere is one of quiet, old-fashioned bonhomie. Locals sup pints and exchange stories around the bar; ramblers and dogs are equally welcome. Huge fires glow through the winter and the smell of logs seduces one to linger. Neil and Pauline McCulloch believe in local, homemade produce and deliver honest, unpretentious pub lunches (seldom evening meals): ploughman's with pâté, hearty soups, quiches and pies, no chips. Though rustically simple, the three small rooms are well turned out, with light floorboards, solid cottagey tables and spindleback chairs, homely touches, darts, dominoes and cribbage. Beers are drawn straight from the cask – Cheriton Pots, Hop Back Summer Lightning, Ringwood Best. Outside, a large garden for summer barbecues and there's a beer festival in September.

White Star Tavern & Dining Rooms
Southampton

Placing the city on the gastropub map, the former seafarer's hotel – built in the heyday of the ocean-going liner – has been stylishly revived. Large etched windows carry the White Star logo, while a cluster of lounges round a lofty, dark wood bar are kitted-out with suede banquettes, leather armchairs and retro-mirrors. Open fires add warmth. The raised dining room has impressive wooden panelling, an open-to-view kitchen and the original chandeliers. Reclaimed wooden dining furniture, black leather banquettes and shipping photographs add to the metropolitan mood. Up-to-the-minute dishes hit all the right notes – potted crab with roast tomato salad, crispy pork and cassoulet, chocolate amaretto tart – while the bar flaunts cocktails, champagnes, wines by the glass and real ales. Pavement tables are just the thing for fine-weather drinking, accompanied by the papers.

directions	M27 junc. 1; B3078 to Fordingbridge; turn for Fritham after 2.5 miles. Follow signs.
meals	12pm-2.30pm (3pm weekends). Main courses £4.50-£5.
closed	3pm-6pm Monday-Friday.

directions	A33 to Southampton city centre & head for Ocean Village & Marina.
meals	12pm-2.30pm (3pm Fri & Sat); 6.30pm-9.30pm (10pm Fri & Sat); 12pm-9pm Sundays. Main courses £7.50-£15; set menus £9.95, £12.95 & £14.95.

Neil & Pauline McCulloch
The Royal Oak,
Fritham,
Lyndhurst,
Hampshire SO43 7HJ
tel 023 8081 2606

Mark Dodd
White Star Tavern & Dining Rooms,
28 Oxford Street, Southampton,
Hampshire SO14 3DJ
tel 023 8082 1990
web www.whitestartavern.co.uk

map: 4 entry: 180

map: 4 entry: 181

Hampshire

Harrow Inn
Steep

The 17th-century Harrow is a gem. Unspoilt, brick-and-tiled, it hides down a sleepy country lane that dwindles into a footpath by a little stream. Formerly a drovers' stop, it has been in the McCutcheon family since 1929 and they keep it today very much as it must always have been. Two small bar rooms have boarded walls, an old brick inglenook fireplace, scrubbed wooden tables and a hatch-like serving counter, behind which barrels of local ale rest on racks, with bundles of drying flowers hanging above. There's a small orchard garden, and some weather-worn rustic benches and tables to the front – only the distant hum of the hidden A3 disturbs the bucolic calm. Food is limited to a few wholesome snacks, generously-filled sandwiches, a split-pea and ham soup full of fresh vegetables served with great chunks of bread and a ploughman's platter of home-cooked ham. Loos are a quick dash across the lane.

directions	A272 at Steep west of Petersfield, left opp. garage; left at church; cross A3 to reach pub.
meals	12pm-2pm; 7pm-9pm. Main courses £3.60-£10.50.
closed	Sunday evenings in winter.

Ellen McCutcheon
Harrow Inn,
Steep,
Petersfield,
Hampshire GU32 2DA

tel   01730 262685

map: 4 entry: 182

Hampshire

The White Horse Inn
Priors Dean

Locally known as 'The Pub with No Name' – there being no sign in the cradle on the nearby road – this isolated pub is fiendish to find. But worth the effort for it is a perfectly wonderful 17th-century farmhouse pub of utterly simple charm. Untouched by modernity, the two splendid bars have open log fires, a motley collection of old tables, a wealth of memorabilia from old clocks to farming implements and a rich, warm patina on the walls, achievable only by age. The ticking of a grandfather clock and the gentle motion of the rocking chairs in front of the fire transport the visitor to an earlier age. First World War poet Edward Thomas used to drink here and the pub inspired his first published work, *Up in the Wind*. The White Horse stands 750 feet up on the top of the Downs, with peaceful views rolling out on every side. Expect up to eight real ales on handpump, interesting pub food and a raft of country wines.

directions	Between Petersfield & Alton. 6 miles from Petersfield, beyond Steep.
meals	12pm-2.30pm; 6.30pm-9.30pm; 7pm-9pm Mondays & Sundays. Main courses £8.95-£15.50.
closed	3pm-6pm (7pm Sundays).

Paul Stuart
The White Horse Inn,
Priors Dean, Petersfield,
Hampshire GU32 1DA

tel   01420 588387
web   www.stuartinns.com

map: 4 entry: 183

The Flower Pots Inn
Cheriton

Ramblers and beer buffs beat a path to Pat and Jo Bartlett's door, where award-winning pints of Pots Ale and Diggers Gold are brewed in the Cheriton Brewhouse to the side. Open fires burn in two traditional bars: one a wall-papered parlour, the other a quarry-tiled public bar with scrubbed pine and an illuminated, glass-topped well. Ales are tapped from casks behind the counter hung with hops, and drunk to the accompaniment of happy chat; music and electronic games would be out of place here. In keeping with the simplicity of the place, the menu is short and straightforward: baps with home-cooked ham, sandwiches toasted or plain, home-cooked hotpots, spicy chilli with garlic bread, hearty winter soups. Curry-lovers come on Wednesdays for authentic Punjabi dishes; Morris dancers drop by in summer. Stay the night in spotless bedrooms in a converted outbuilding.

Chestnut Horse
Easton

In the beautiful Itchen valley, this rather smart 16th-century pub was done up by experienced chef-landlord John Holland some time ago. A decked terrace leads to a warren of snug rooms around a central bar, warmed by log fires and cheered by a vast collection of jugs, teapots and country pictures. At night it is cosy and candlelit; you can eat either in the low beamed Red Room, with its wood-burning stove, cushioned settles and mix of dining tables, or in the panelled and plate-filled Green Room. On weekdays before 7.30pm try the two or three course menu (Caesar salad, confit of duck with green beans, treacle and lemon tart – all good value). Or tuck into fresh crab, homemade steak and kidney pudding or beer-battered fish and chips. Great local ale from Itchen Valley Brewery and decent wine and champagne by the glass.

directions	Off A272 E of Winchester on B3046.
meals	12pm-2pm; 7pm-9pm. No food Sunday & Bank Holiday evenings. Main courses £4.50-£8.
rooms	4: 1 double, 3 twins £60. Singles £40.
closed	2.30pm-6pm (7pm Sundays).

directions	1 mile off B3047 (Winchester to Alresford road), 4 miles east of Winchester.
meals	12pm-2.30pm; 6.30pm-9.30pm; 12pm-8pm Sundays (4pm winter). Main courses £5.95-£12; set lunch £13.95.
closed	Sunday evenings in winter.

Joanna & Patricia Bartlett
The Flower Pots Inn,
Cheriton,
Alresford,
Hampshire SO24 0QQ
tel   01962 771318

map: 4 entry: 184

John Holland
Chestnut Horse,
Easton,
Winchester,
Hampshire SO21 1EG
tel   01962 779257

map: 4 entry: 185

Hampshire

Bush Inn
Ovington

Down a meandering lane alongside the clear running waters of the river Itchen, the 17th-century inn is brimful of character – a jewel in the county crown. In winter it's dark and atmospheric, with a roaring log fire (Real-fire Pub of the Year 2001, no less), walls and ceilings are painted dark green and lit by gas lamps and candles on tables. In summer the cottagey garden comes into play, and there's the added bonus of a stroll along an idyllic stretch of the river. Cottage furniture and high-backed pews fill the series of small rooms around the bar, while walls are hung with fishing and country paraphernalia; among these, a stuffed 41lb salmon's head in its showcase! The atmosphere is calm, cosy and friendly, the clientele well-heeled. The kitchen deals in fresh local produce and presents its appealing modern menu with flair – venison steak, perhaps, with spiced red cabbage and a whisky and sherry vinegar sauce – but there are simpler dishes and lighter bites too.

directions	Off A31 between Winchester & Alresford.
meals	12pm-2.15pm; 7-9pm (9.30pm Fri & Sat). No food Sunday evenings. Main courses £9-£16.50.
closed	Christmas Day.

Nick & Cathy Young
Bush Inn,
Ovington,
Alresford,
Hampshire SO24 0RE
tel   01962 732764

map: 4 entry: 186

Hampshire

The Globe on the Lake
Alresford

The Globe delivers "the best views in the world" over Alresford's lake. It rests at the foot of the aptly named Broad Street, in this quaint little town known for its watercress and steam railway. Tables on the lawn present a gorgeous vista across the water and are a magnet for both customers and ducks. These residents are not chalked up on the menus, but the best of local produce is – in watercress soup, or Meon Valley pork and leek sausages with mash and onion gravy. Well-kept beers, several wines by the glass, flowers on the tables, pictures on the walls, candles… The main bar of this 16th-century, tile-hung inn oozes character, its vibrant red walls echoing some of the menu's more mediterranean-influenced dishes, while beams, wooden furniture and two warming fires add that cosy, traditional touch. There's a separate dining room at one end and a permanent marquee tagged onto the back, but the hub of the place is the bar – *the* place to be.

directions	Off A31 between Winchester & Alton, 7 miles from Winchester.
meals	12pm-3pm; 6.30pm-9pm. No food Sunday evenings in November. Main courses £8.25-£15.
closed	3pm-6pm.

Marc Duveen Conway
The Globe on the Lake,
The Soke, Alresford,
Hampshire SO24 9DB
tel   01962 732294
web   www.theglobeonthelake.co.uk

map: 4 entry: 187

Hampshire

Herefordshire

The Sun Inn
Bentworth

Stonehenge Pigswill, Badger Tanglefoot, Brakspears Bitter, Cheriton Pots... a parade of hand pumps (eight in all) pulls the beer buffs in. There's charm, too: the newly extended, flower-decked local was once a pair of 17th-century cottages. Surprisingly little has changed. On ancient bricks and bare boards find a rustic mix of new pine tables and oak benches and settles; beams are hung with horse-brasses, walls adorned with prints and plates; there are fresh and dried flowers, candlelight and smart magazines. Two cosy log-fired inglenooks warm the interlinking bars, and a third room has been added to make more space, but still holds on to the traditional character. Food is mostly perfect English: onion and cider soup, steak and kidney pie, lamb chops, Sunday roasts, wicked puddings. Hidden down a tiny lane on the edge of a village in deepest Hampshire the Sun Inn could scarcely be more rural. There's a garden at the back and footpaths radiate from the door.

The Riverside Inn
Aymestrey

Edward IV might, apparently, have had a celebratory noggin here after a decisive incident nearby in the Wars of the Roses. He was declared king soon afterwards. It is much altered: stylish bedrooms have been created in once-derelict outhouses, and inside there's an easy mix of antiques, fresh flowers, hops and pine. Menus change with the seasons and the seductive dishes include locally smoked salmon with cream cheese parcels, confit of duck legs with their own pak choi, and local venison with beetroot rösti and blackcurrant jus. Wander from the bar into linked rooms with log fires; order a pint of Wood's from nearby Wistanstow or a house wine from Italy, Chile, Australia. And look for the map of the kitchen gardens from which so much of the fruit and vegetables come: an interesting idea which we wish others would copy. The setting is bucolic, tucked back from a stone bridge over the river Lugg, alive with river trout for you to fish.

directions	Off A339, 2 miles from Alton.
meals	12pm-2pm; 7pm-9.30pm. Main courses £6-£12.95.
closed	3pm-6pm Monday-Saturday.

directions	On A4110, 18 miles north of Hereford.
meals	12pm-2.15pm; 7pm-9.15pm. Main courses £7.25-£14.95.
rooms	5 twins/doubles.
closed	Sunday evenings & Mondays.

Mary Holmes
The Sun Inn,
Sun Hill,
Bentworth, Alton,
Hampshire GU34 5JT

tel 01420 562338

map: 4 entry: 188

Richard & Liz Gresko
The Riverside Inn,
Aymestrey, Leominster,
Herefordshire HR6 9ST

tel 01568 708440
web www.theriversideinn.org

map: 8 entry: 189

The Stagg Inn
Titley

It took some courage – six years ago – for Steve Reynolds to take on a tiny village pub in the back of beyond and, defying all odds, become a Herefordshire hero. What strikes you is the attention to detail on the daily boards: the only thing you're not told is the name of the bird from which your pigeon breast (perfectly served with fig and port sauce) came. Cheeses from The Marches are listed by the dozen and most of the produce is organic. "How can you fault the place?" said another chef we met. (They fully deserve their Michelin star – the first for a British pub.) Simply no argument: there were seared scallops on parsnip purée with black pepper oil, traditional roast grouse with game chips and bread sauce, and puddings to die for: three crème brûlées of vanilla, coffee and cardamom; roast plums with vanilla panna cotta. If this guy is a star it is because he sets out his stall as he sees it and has never wavered from his belief that where good food exists people will seek it out. The flagstoned bar is perfect (and dog-friendly), there's beer from Hobsons, cider from Dunkerton's and classy wines. And you can stay the night.

directions	On B4355 between Kington & Presteigne.
meals	12pm-2pm; 6.30pm-10pm.
	Main courses (bar) £7.50-£8.50.
	No bar snacks Saturday evenings.
rooms	4 doubles £70-£100. Singles £40.
closed	Sunday evenings & Mondays.

Steve & Nicola Reynolds
The Stagg Inn,
Titley, Kington,
Herefordshire HR5 3RL
tel   01544 230221
web   www.thestagg.co.uk

map: 8 entry: 190

Salutation Inn
Weobley

Lording it at the top end of a village green that goes back to the Middle Ages, the old cider house creaks with age and beams. Drop by for a pint of Butty Bach from the Wye Valley Brewery, a local Stowford cider or a glass of Aussie wine... stay for ham and eggs, homemade soup and the steak and ale pie that has won awards. The lounge bar is divided by standing timbers and is nicely pubby, particularly in winter with logs burning in the grate. For dinner there's the Oak Room, its old booths separated by glass partitions; book a table and feast on Herefordshire sirloin steak and sweet Weobley lamb. We liked the Cornish mussels steamed in cider and a summer pudding packed with fresh wild berries (the area is famous for them). In summer, people crowd under the parasols on the back terrace. Smart bedrooms range from family room to romantic four-poster.

directions	Off A480 north west of Hereford.
meals	All day in summer; by arrangement in winter. Main courses £6-£10.
rooms	4: 1 double, 1 family, 1 twin, 1 four-poster £74-£80.
closed	3pm-7pm in winter.

Mike Tai
Salutation Inn,
Market Pitch,
Weobley,
Herefordshire HR4 8SJ

tel   01544 318443

map: 8 entry: 191

The Old Black Lion
Hay-on-Wye

Heaven for historians, antique-book-lovers and foodies in equal measure. Oliver Cromwell lodged here while laying siege to Hay Castle and the main building is packed with oak beams, ancient artefacts and conspiratorial nooks and crannies. The Wye Valley Brewery provides their own Black Lion bitter but ciders come from Somerset. Seasonal bar favourites keep the kitchen working flat out through every session with fairly priced Scrumpy pork and fresh whole plaice; local produce such as Brecon game and Wye salmon play their part. The 20-seat restaurant steps upmarket for those with more time and money to spare at night: Caesar salad with anchovies, fallow venison loin with parsnip purée; with a bottle of decent wine, expect to pay accordingly. Recently up-graded bedrooms provide the modern comforts demanded by the huntin', shootin' and fishin' types – not to mention the book-lovers.

directions	2-minute walk from centre of Hay.
meals	12pm-2.30pm; 6.30pm-9.30pm. Main courses £4.25-£17.50.
rooms	10: 5 doubles, 2 twins, 2 singles, 1 suite. £80-£110; singles £43-£50.

Vanessa King
The Old Black Lion,
26 Lion Street, Hay-on-Wye,
Herefordshire HR3 5AD

tel   01497 820841
web   www.oldblacklion.co.uk

map: 8 entry: 192

Herefordshire

The Pandy Inn
Dorstone

Dating way back to 1165, a half-timbered, Herefordshire gem. Inside are heavy beams, much smoke-stained stone, a vast oak lintel over the old log grate and an intimate dining room beyond the red velvet curtain. This is the county of Dorothy Goodbody and Butty Bach ales, Old Rosie and 'cloudy' scrumpy. On the menu: moules and pizzas, big Hereford beef steaks and home-spun specials, and wicked puddings from the South African-born landlady. For hungry walkers there are filled baguettes, hearty vegetable soup and homemade chicken-liver pâté with first-class bread. Booting across the well-worn flagstoned floor, stay sharp lest you tread – or sit – upon one of the resident cats. Children may chat to the parrot, or spill into the garden with its picnic tables and play area in summer. You are in the so-called Golden Valley, so set off for Abbey Dore, Arthur's Stone or bookish Hay-on-Wye, a short drive.

directions	Signed from B4348 Hereford to Hay-on-Wye, 5 miles from Hay..
meals	12pm-2.30pm; 7pm-9.30pm. Main courses £7.50-£14.95.
closed	Monday lunchtimes, except Bank Holidays, in summer; Mon in winter.

Paul & Marja Gardner
The Pandy Inn,
Dorstone, Hay-on-Wye,
Herefordshire HR3 6AN
tel   01981 550273
web   www.pandyinn.co.uk

map: 8 entry: 193

Herefordshire

The Bull's Head
Craswall

Craswall is not so much a village as a tangle of country lanes below the famous Black Hill of Bruce in the Black Mountains. A drovers' inn dating back 400 years, it is beautifully unspoilt and not hugely altered since the arrival of electricity. With bedrooms, stabling for your horse and rough camping available, the pub is in the hub of some fine walking and trekking country. The food follows suit and is as hearty as you would hope for, with lots of class and bags of flavour. Try the individual Craswall pies of beef, bacon and beer served with huge hand-cut chips, helped along with a pint of Butty Bach straight from the drum. Home-baked chunky bread 'Huffers' ensure that passing hikers will stride off fully fuelled. Hiker or not, be sure to plan for a sleepover after a big 12oz Hereford rib-eye steak and a bottle of Los Vilos Cabernet, lest the endless unmarked roads get to you on the journey home.

directions	On country lanes between B4350 at Hay-on-Wye & A465 at Pandy.
meals	12pm-9pm (3pm Sundays). Main courses £5.25-£10.95.
rooms	3: 2 doubles, 1 family £45-£50.
closed	Sunday evenings in winter.

Denise Langford
The Bull's Head,
Craswall,
Herefordshire HR2 0PN
tel   01981 510616
web   www.thebullsheadcraswall.com

map: 8 entry: 194

Herefordshire

Three Crowns
Ullingswick

Down winding lanes it's easy to get lost – but this is worth any amount of missed turns. You walk into a single flagstone bar to find the day's lunch or early evening specials chalked up to tempt you; since chef-landlord Brent Castle arrived on the scene we've never had a poor meal. The food is often organic and the ingredients are fresh and local whenever possible. There is real skill in some dishes, such as goat's cheese and potato terrine, or rump of lamb with chive mash and a shallot madeira sauce. And the food is often surprising. You'd be forgiven for thinking that this is more of a restaurant than a country pub, but there's always a table set aside for drinkers and you'll get a delicious pint of Wye Valley ale – or Hereford cider and the odd bargain wine. Hop-strewn beams and settles in the bar, open fires, candles on tables, cribbage – all that you'd expect of an old-fashioned English pub. Extras like home-baked bread and cafetière coffee are beyond reproach; kids are welcome too.

directions	1.5 miles from A417, 1 mile from A465, north-east of Hereford.
meals	12pm-2.30pm; 7pm-9.30pm. Main courses £13.75.
closed	Mondays.

Brent Castle
Three Crowns,
Bleak Acre, Ullingswick,
Herefordshire HR1 3JQ
tel 01432 820279
web www.threecrownsinn.com

map: 8 entry: 195

Herefordshire

Crown & Sceptre
Bromyard

Think 'village pub and country restaurant combined' and paper-wrapped linen napkins on tables and you have the essence of Nik, Kay and John's bubblingly successful new enterprise. The Grade II-listed, red-brick local has been given a thoroughly modern makeover. The Walls were finalists in the Flavours of Herefordshire awards within months of opening but it's good to see that in this foodie heaven the tiny bar's pool table remains – along with darts and cards. Behind a timbered screen on the far side are pine tables, high-backed, wicker-seated chairs and seasonal menus full of local ingredients. Be prepared to take your time; this is not a fast food kitchen. Imaginative dishes are cooked to perfection – worth the wait. You'll not need a tatty bun with your homemade Hereford beef and coriander burger: dressed fresh leaves are infinitely preferable, and the chips are fat and moreish. Take a delicious Wye Valley ale into the pretty courtyard in summer.

directions	At bottom of town, off A44.
meals	12pm-2.30pm; 6pm-10pm. Main courses £5.95-£13.95; set menu £9.75 (Sunday lunch).
rooms	1 double.

Nik & Kay Wall
Crown & Sceptre,
7 Sherford Street,
Bromyard,
Herefordshire HR7 4DL
tel 01885 482441

map: 9 entry: 196

Herefordshire

Herefordshire

The Butcher's Arms
Woolhope

Martin produces thoroughly reliable food from his fully modernised kitchen, and there are log fires and smiling Cheryl – to settle you in. Surrounded by walking country, opposite Marcle Ridge and close to the Forestry Commission's Haugh Woods, a half-timbered, low-beamed 'magpie' house that goes back to the 14th century. Recently taken over by returning locals it has undergone a restoration that it deserved long ago. From the central bar, hung with Weston's cider lithos and sepia prints, French windows open onto a garden that stretches down to the village brook – eat out here. In the evening, dine by candlelight in the tiny non-smoking restaurant from a menu that tempts with big salads in summer and, in winter, local game. Certainly worth a sleepover for those with weary feet; it's romantic and peaceful, and the gentle rustle of the leaves will lull you to sleep.

Lough Pool
Sellack

The words 'Lough' and 'Pool' are almost synonymous and, perversely, the pool and stream by which the pub once stood, deep in the bosky folds of Herefordshire, have long run dry. Here, celebrated chef Stephen Bull has hit upon a modus operandi that finds favour with the local country lifers. Stock-in-trade are good real ales from Wye Valley Brewery, strong draught ciders from Stowford Press and wines by the glass of surprising quality; try a glass of organic French fizz. Equal care goes into his sourcing of local produce wherever possible; they appear on the plate as heavenly reincarnations of English pub food: rich haggis fritters with beetroot relish, roast pork with spiced orange, ginger cake with treacle ice cream. Book ahead for your evening party and try not to be late: they've been known to shut on closing time with startling alacrity.

directions	Off B4224 between Hereford & Ross-on-Wye.
meals	12pm-2pm; 6.30pm-9pm. Main courses £6.95-£13.95.
closed	Monday lunchtimes Jan-Feb.

directions	Off A49, 3 miles north-west of Ross-on-Wye.
meals	12pm-2.15pm; 7pm-9.30pm. Main courses £10.50-£15.50.
closed	Sunday evenings; Mondays October-March.

Martin & Cheryl Baker
The Butcher's Arms,
Woolhope,
Herefordshire HR1 4RF
tel 01432 860281

Stephen Bull
Lough Pool,
Sellack,
Ross-on-Wye,
Herefordshire HR9 6LX
tel 01989 730236

map: 8 entry: 197

map: 8 entry: 198

Herefordshire

Penny Farthing Inn
Aston Crews

This is worth a long detour – a 17th-century inn and former blacksmith's shop standing high on an escarpment above the Wye valley, with the Malvern Hills as a backdrop. The ladies in charge are sisters and they breathe new life into the word 'welcome'; they are unfussy and hospitable. In front of coal-effect fires, a hairy Chow is available to add warmth to your toes. The food is cockle-warming, and there has been plenty of praise for the fresh fish (flag snapper and Cajun-spiced swordfish included), country-style bowls of lamb knuckles in rich-scented gravy, game in season and Hereford beef steaks from local farms. Here are real ales of high quality (Wadworth 6X and Greene King Abbot, perhaps), wines from Tanners and cups of fresh coffee re-filled at the table before you've had a chance to ask. Eat informally anywhere in the bar or at plainly-set tables in the cottagey restaurant, from the same menus that give you the widest choice at night. There are views from the garden and footpaths from the door.

directions	Off A40 in Lea.
meals	12pm-2.15pm; 6.30pm-9pm. Main courses £6.95-£11.95.

Dorothy Mellor
Penny Farthing Inn,
Aston Crews,
Herefordshire HR9 7LW
tel 01989 750366

map: 9 entry: 199

Hertfordshire

Bricklayer's Arms
Flaunden

When The Bricklayers came onto the market Alvin Michaels pounced, eager to restore the fortunes of his run-down local. Within two weeks the regulars had given him the thumbs up; now he and his staff are run off their feet. He's been in catering all his life and has no problem whatever turning out a fine roast Barbary duck with peach and pear compote. Or chicken breast stuffed with mozzarella, wrapped in Parma ham and served with a lime and coriander sauce – or good old steak and kidney pie, equally delicious. As well as installing skilled kitchen staff, Alvin has also remodelled the interiors and removed some less than sympathetic earlier renovations. The pretty, 18th-century building has low beams, a log fire and, now, white-painted, timbered walls. There's an excellent selection of beers, wines, ports and cognacs. As for the exotically named Hogpits Bottom, 'hog' is a dialect word for shale.

directions	M25 junc. 20; A41; 1st left to Chipperfield; 1st right to Flaunden.
meals	12pm-3pm (4pm Sundays); 6pm-9.30pm. Main courses £4.50-£14.95.

Alvin Michaels
Bricklayer's Arms,
Hogpits Bottom, Flaunden,
Hertfordshire HP3 0PH
tel 01442 833322
web www.bricklayersarms.com

map: 10 entry: 200

The Alford Arms
Frithsden

It isn't easy to find, so be armed with a detailed map or precise directions before you set out – David and Becky Salisbury's gastropub is worth any amount of missed turns. It's in a hamlet next to Frithsden Vineyard, enfolded by acres of National Trust common land – bring the walking boots. Inside, a rabbit warren of interlinked rooms, bright, airy, with soft colours and fresh flowers. Scrubbed pine tables and Georgian chairs sit on wooden or pattern-tiled floors, there are prints on the walls and fine drapes at sash windows. This is still a village local and the ales are good, with Marston's Pedigree, Brakspears Bitter, Flowers Original and Morrells Oxford Blue on handpump. Food, too, is taken seriously and ingredients are as organic, maize-fed and delicious as can

be. On a no-nonsense menu that divides dishes into small plates and main meals, there is potted ham with apple chutney, pan-roast lamb rump with puy lentils and roasted root veg, Nettleden honey-roast duck breast with rosemary dauphinoise potatoes, rhubarb and elderflower crumble. This is skilled cooking, and wine drinkers have the choice of 13 by the glass and a short but judiciously chosen list. Service is informed, friendly and alert. Arrive early on a warm day to take your pick of the teak tables on the sun-trapping front terrace, shaded by posh brollies.

directions	Phone for directions.
meals	12pm-2.30pm (3pm Sun); 7-10pm. Main courses £9.25-£12.75.

David & Becky Salisbury
The Alford Arms,
Frithsden, Berkhamsted,
Hertfordshire HP1 3DD
tel   01442 864480
web   www.alford.arms.co.uk

map: 10 entry: 201

The Valiant Trooper
Aldbury

Aldbury is an ancient site. A Roman road – now the Ridgeway Path – runs past, and the Saxon name means 'old fort'. Named in honour of the Duke of Wellington, said to have held a meeting here during the Napoleonic wars, the dear little brick and tiled cottage has been a pub since 1752. Now it caters for a mixed bunch: booted ramblers, diners escaping town, families (there's a little play house in the garden). You'll find dark beams on rough-plaster walls, bare brick, blazing log fires, tiled floors, rustic country furnishings and a hearty welcome from landlord Tim O'Gorman, who's been pleasing customers for over 20 years. Walkers can slake a thirst with a decent pint of ale from a chalked-up choice of five and refuel on ciabatta sandwiches or cottage pie. The light and airy stable restaurant groans with lunchers on Sundays. Come for roasts and sound English dishes: pork medallions layered with black pudding and red wine sauce, roast partridge, bread and butter pudding.

directions	North of Berkhamsted off B4506 towards Aldbury Common.
meals	12pm-2.15pm; 6.30pm-9.15pm. No food Sunday evenings. Main courses £7.50-£16.

Tim O'Gorman
The Valiant Trooper,
Trooper Road,
Aldbury, Tring,
Hertfordshire HP23 5RW
tel   01442 851203

map: 10 entry: 202

The Brocket Arms
Ayot St Lawrence

In peaceful Ayot St Lawrence stands the Brocket Arms, a 14th-century brick-built gem with leaded windows, a courtyard and a walled garden. The landlord has been here for more than 20 years and keeps his ramshackle inn stocked with good beers, proper cider and decent wines. The pub has a strong local trade and also brings in visitors from far and wide. Its interior is striking: oak beams, low ceilings, quarry floors and an inglenook large enough to hide a few small boys in. Choose from bar food or a more exotic menu in the lamp-lit restaurant, maybe Zrazzy Nelson (sirloin in spicy herbal liqueur known as kummel) or pheasant with pâté and a port and mushroom sauce. There are beamy bedrooms upstairs – just the place for George Bernard Shaw buffs; his house is down the road.

directions	5 miles north west of Welwyn off B656 or B651.
meals	12.30pm-2.30pm; 7.30pm-10pm. No food Sunday & Monday eve. Main courses £4.50-£12; set menu £21.
rooms	4 twins/doubles £80. Singles £70.

Toby Wingfield Digby
The Brocket Arms,
Ayot St Lawrence, Welwyn,
Hertfordshire AL6 9BT
tel   01438 820250
web   www.brocketarms.com

map: 10 entry: 203

Hertfordshire

The Cabinet
Reed

In a small village stands an enchanting, white clapperboard building – a pub for 400 years. A few years ago it was yet another nondescript hostelry, but in the capable hands of TV chef Paul Bloxham it has been transformed. The moment you enter, you see the place is well-loved. Regulars are drawn to the bar with its log fire and darts, Nethergate's Suffolk County and Old Growler, and modern-rustic style. The smarter-dressed make for the crisp linened and fresh flowered tables of the candlelit restaurant. And there's food to match, in dishes based on local produce: rare-breed Tamworth pork, vegetables from an organic nursery, potatoes grown just the other side of the A10. Alfresco dining is a major pull in summer, with a wood-burning rotisserie and a charming outdoor eating area. It's a treat to see a place so buried in history (built on a Saxon burial ground, haunted by two ghosts) thrive through its modern makeover.

directions	Off A10 between Royston & Buntingford.
meals	12pm-3pm; 7pm-10.30pm. Main courses £12-£20.
closed	Sunday evenings; Mondays.

Paul Bloxham
The Cabinet,
High Street, Reed, Royston,
Hertfordshire SG8 8AH
tel   01763 848366
web   www.thecabinetinn.co.uk

map: 10 entry: 204

Isle of Wight

The New Inn
Shalfleet

Built in 1746 on the site of a church house, this old fisherman's haunt is worth more than a passing nod – especially if you are on the 65-mile, coastal path trail. Or have arrived by boat and moored at Shalfleet Quay. The place now draws a cheerful mix of tourists, walkers and sailors to a spick-and-span bar with 900-year-old flagstones, beams and old fireplaces, and a series of pine-tabled dining rooms decked with nautical bits and bobs. Refreshment includes thirst-quenching pints of island-brewed Ventnor Golden and fabulously fresh seafood marked up on the daily-changing chalkboard. The huge platter (£50 for two) is a treat; other (considerably cheaper) fish choices might include sea bass cooked with lemon or simply grilled plaice. Mouthwatering fresh crab and lobster are landed at Newtown Quay; the crab sandwiches are memorable, as is the lobster salad. Carnivores are not forgotten, the menu reaching to prime steak, game in season and traditional pub grub.

directions	On A3054 between Yarmouth & Newport.
meals	12pm-2.30pm; 6pm-9.30pm. Main courses £6.95-£15.95.

Mr M Bullock
The New Inn,
Main Road, Shalfleet,
Yarmouth, Isle of Wight PO30 4NS
tel   01983 531314
web   www.thenew-inn.co.uk

map: 4 entry: 205

Isle of Wight

The Seaview Hotel
Seaview

Seaview is one of the island's institutions – smart, buzzing, by the sea and full of thirsty sailors. The terrace, with its railings, mast and flag, is like the prow of a boat – a great place to sit in summer. In the back bar, learn your knots; in the front, brush up your semaphore. Wander past portholes, ships' wheels, lanterns, even sails, for a plateful of roast monkfish with crab mash and chilli sauce in the restaurant – or seared scallops with squid ink pasta or crispy parma ham and lemon oil. In the bar, order island-brewed Goddard's Special and the famous hot crab ramekin; if you're here on a Sunday, don't miss the roast sirloin of beef. Bedrooms have all you need but it's the service that sets the place apart. Beds are turned down, staff couldn't be nicer and nothing is too much trouble.

directions	B3330 from Ryde; left into Puckpool Hill for Seaview.
meals	12pm-2pm; 7pm-9.30pm. Main courses £6.95-£11.95; set menu £26.
rooms	16 twins/doubles £70-£135. Singles from £55.

N W T Hayward
The Seaview Hotel,
High Street, Seaview,
Isle of Wight PO34 5EX

tel	01983 612711
web	www.seaviewhotel.co.uk

map: 4 entry: 206

Kent

The Swan on the Green
West Peckham

West Peckham may be the back of beyond – albeit a well-heeled beyond – but there's nothing backward about Gordon Milligan's 16th-century pub. People are drawn by its growing reputation for good food and beer that comes straight from the micro-brewery parked outside. The décor is fresh, contemporary and open-plan: blond wood, rush-seated chairs, big flowers, modern black and white photographs. Under the Swan Ales label, half a dozen brews are funnelled from the central bar, enticingly named Ginger Swan, Swan Mild, Trumpeters Best, Whoopers Pale Ale. The printed menus are a compendium of updated pub classics such as pork and leek sausages with mustard mash and gravy, steak and ale pie, and stilton burgers in ciabatta. In spite of clear gastropubby leanings, Gordon and his team have created a balanced mix of drinking bar – replete with locals – and dining areas. You may even borrow a rug and eat on the village green.

directions	From A26 north, 2nd left off B2016.
meals	12pm-2.15pm; 7pm-9.15pm. No food Sunday evenings. Main courses £6.50-£10.95.
closed	Sunday evenings in winter

Gordon Milligan
The Swan on the Green,
The Village Green, West Peckham,
Maidstone, Kent ME18 5JW

tel	01622 812271
web	www.swan-on-the-green.co.uk

map: 5 entry: 207

Spotted Dog
Smarts Hill

It's an enchanting old English country pub: ancient-looking and rambling on the outside, low beamed, panelled, nooked and crannied on the inside. Less traditional are Ben Naude and Kirsten Price, the talented young couple who run the place, and their daily-changing menus — to the point and full of surprises. The food is consistently brilliant here whether it's fillet of beef with wild mushrooms and a tangy red wine sauce, wild boar and apple sausages, Kentish pork chops or a simple, classic club sandwich — unpretentious and strong on flavour, country dishes blended with current trends. The ales are equally good. Sit back with an expertly kept pint of Larkins or Harveys Best at an ancient settle by an inglenook fire — there are four and one is huge; in summer, stroll into one of the tiered beer gardens at the front and back. The back would be famous for its view were it not for an inherited spat with neighbours who have planted trees that cut it out. (Hopes are pinned on a petition to restore the view.) The Spotted Dog is a textbook English pub, friendly and fun; its loyal regulars include *Private Eye*'s Ian Hislop. Plans include four bedrooms for summer 2004.

directions	Off B2188, 1.5 miles from Penshurst.
meals	12pm-2.30pm; 6pm-9.30pm; 12pm-8pm Sundays. Main courses £8.25-£15.95.
closed	3pm-6pm Monday-Thursday.

Ben Naude & Kirsten Price
Spotted Dog,
Smarts Hill,
Penshurst,
Kent TN11 8EE
tel   01892 870253

map: 5 entry: 208

Kent

The Hare
Langton Green

As you negotiate the green and the surrounding roads in the quest for somewhere to park, you'd be forgiven for thinking The Hare is hardly Kent's best-kept secret. Don't be put off. The feel inside is stylish and relaxed and the food among the best in the area (and is available all day). Large light rooms create some marvellous eating areas, with gleaming, well-spaced tables on polished floorboards, and yet more character from old prints, paintings, books and a collection of chamber pots dangling over broad doorways. The blackboard menu has pub classics such as home-cooked ham, free-range eggs and hand-cut chips as well as more ambitious dishes like line-caught sea bass with stir-fry veg and hoisin dressing. Cheerful staff dispense Greene King Abbot Ale and guest beers such as Ruddles County and Archers. Wine is taken seriously too; the well-balanced wine list has 16 by the glass.

Kent

Swan at the Vineyard
Lamberhurst

Real ale, real flowers, real food and real English wines: the Swan is a genuine country pub, a locals' pub too, friendly and welcoming. The building's 15th-century origins are pretty apparent in old, worn but highly polished floorboards, the low ceiling in the utterly charming little bar, the beams, timbering and fireplaces. Lovely dining rooms, one casual with a blackboard specials menu, the other a posher restaurant, sandwich the small bar. Vanessa and Sean Arnett have put in a lot of hard work to achieve this look and atmosphere – for years the Swan was a run-down boozer – and their efforts are paying off. Folk are drawn by the chance to sample Lamberhurst wines from the vineyard next door, drink local ales and get stuck into food known for its seasonal focus and generous portions. The glorious outside terrace overlooking the children's play area is a summer treat.

| directions | On A264 3 miles west of Tunbridge Wells. |
| meals | 12pm-9.30pm (9pm Sundays). Main courses £6.95-£14.95. |

Chris Little
The Hare,
Langton Green, Tunbridge Wells,
Kent TN3 0JA
tel 01892 862419
web www.brunningandprice.co.uk

map: 5 entry: 209

directions	From A21 in Lamberhurst B2100 for Wadhurst; right at crossroads.
meals	12pm-2pm; 6.30pm-9pm. Main courses £6-£18.
closed	Sundays & Monday evenings in winter.

Sean & Vanessa Arnett
Swan at the Vineyard,
The Down,
Lamberhurst,
Kent TN3 8EU
tel 01892 890170

map: 5 entry: 210

Kent

Three Chimneys
Biddenden

Ramble through tiny, unspoilt rooms – all rough panelling, stripped brick, faded paintwork, old flags, ancient timber and several smouldering fires. Yet there are only two chimneys. During the Napoleonic wars French officers imprisoned nearby were allowed to wander as far as the point where the three paths – 'trois chemins' – met (hence the name)... so, nothing to do with chimneys at all. The cooking is modern, in contrast to the rest, and tasty; try grilled sirloin with garlic butter followed by chocolate and praline torte with pistachio ice cream. You may eat in the bars, apart from the spartan public one, and in the charming restaurant, built 20 years ago to look like a barn from reclaimed wood. In summer, tables spill out onto a stylish and sheltered patio. They get the balance just right here between pub and restaurant – prop up the bar for as long as you like. There's farm cider and Adnams Best Bitter drawn straight from the cask.

directions	On A262 2 miles west of Biddenden.
meals	12pm-2pm; 6.30pm-9.45pm (9pm Sundays). Main courses £11.95-£18.95.

Craig Smith
Three Chimneys,
Hareplain Road, Biddenden,
Kent TN27 8LW
tel   01580 291472
web   www.travelguide.co.uk

map: 6 entry: 211

Kent

The Chequers
Smarden

The clapboard inn opposite the church dates from the 14th century; the village is perfect. Inside, low beams, standing timbers, soft lamplight and open fires create a warm and soporific glow. When Lisa and Charlie took over a few years ago they wisely kept the old feel but introduced bold colours to the two dining rooms and gorgeous old furniture. First and foremost, the Chequers is a village local full of unpretentious good cheer; in the main bar, a longcase clock sets a restful pace and they certainly know how to serve a decent pint, whether it's Adnams Bitter or the more local Harveys. The other big attractions are food and board: bedrooms have a classy, comfortable country look, and the often-changing menu includes straightforward dishes such as steak and kidney pie, or coq au vin in generous portions. Summer throws the spotlight on the back terrace, which overlooks a lovely garden and pond.

directions	From M20 junc. 8 A274 for Sutton Valence; left for Smarden.
meals	11am-2.30pm (12pm-3pm Sundays); 6pm-9.30pm (10pm Saturdays). Main courses £7-£15.95.
rooms	5: 3 doubles, 1 twin, 1 suite £70-£90.

Lisa & Charles Bullock
The Chequers,
The Street, Smarden,
Kent TN27 8QA
tel   01233 770217
web   www.thechequerssmarden.co.uk

map: 6 entry: 212

Dering Arms
Pluckley

Pluckley claims to be the most haunted village in England (16 ghosts at the last count) and the gothicky Dering Arms contributes its share. The former hunting lodge is hidden down country lanes almost two miles from the village. Owner-chef James Buss has given this civilised place a fantastic reputation for food and drink. Stone floors, blazing logs, old wooden tables and chairs and two bars garlanded with hops, farming implements, guns and prints – feast amid it all on fine produce and fish that will have you hooked: provençal soup perhaps, or fresh sardines grilled with rosemary butter. Or dine more formally in the pretty restaurant, candlelit at night. The blackboard also lists seasonal game, pie of the day, confit of duck. Dering Ale on handpump is brewed for the pub by Goachers of Maidstone; wines and whiskies galore. The bedrooms are big, and breakfasts delicious.

The Ringlestone Inn
Harrietsham

Two boss-eyed sisters once ran the Ringlestone; if they liked the look of you, they'd lock you in; if they didn't, they'd shoot at you. Michael and his daughter Michelle have let that tradition slip, preferring to run their 1635 ale house with a lighter, more convivial touch. Tankards dangle above the bar, a woodburner throws out heat from the inglenook and old *Punch* cartoons hang on the original brick and flint walls. They stock 30 fruit wines and liqueurs as well as excellent local ales to sup in settles or on quirky, tiny, yet comfy chairs. Across the lane in the farmhouse, lovely bedrooms have oak furniture and crisp linen. The food is good – panini or penne for lunch, maybe, game pie with redcurrant wine for dinner. There are waterfalls in the gardens, space for big parties, and the occasional vintage car rally. As for the breakfasts, they'll keep your strength up for a week.

directions	8 miles west of Ashford (M20 south junc. 8). Signed from Pluckley, by railway station.
meals	12pm-2pm; 7pm-9.30pm. Main courses £8.45-£15.95.
rooms	3 doubles £45. Singles £35.
closed	3.30pm-6pm.

directions	M20 junc. 8.; left after 0.25 miles at 2nd r'bout to Hollingbourne. Through, up hill, right at sign. Pub in 1.5 miles.
meals	12pm-2pm; 7pm-10pm. Main courses £5.50-£15.
rooms	3 twins/doubles £99-£120. Singles £89.

	James Buss Dering Arms, Station Road, Pluckley, Kent TN27 0RR
tel	01233 840371
web	www.deringarms.com

	Michelle Stanley The Ringlestone Inn, Ringlestone, Harrietsham, Kent ME17 1NX
tel	01622 859900
web	www.ringlestone.com

map: 6 entry: 213

map: 6 entry: 214

Kent

Froggies at the Timber Batts
Bodsham

Winding lanes lead to Bodsham, with glorious views of the North Downs. Wander into the splendidly rural Timber Batts – built in 1485 – for a pint of Woodforde's Wherry or Adnams Best; you are in for a surprise. Along with the bar menu of baguettes, sausages or ham, egg and chips is a slate of regional French dishes with the emphasis on seasonal: game from local shoots, Rye Bay fish. At traditional tables under hop-hung beams treat yourself to stuffed mussels, duck-leg confit and tarte tatin. Owner-chef Joel Gros juggles the best of English with French food and wine; the house wines come from a cousin's vineyard in the Loire. In winter, nurse a whisky by one of three fires, in summer enjoy the garden with its lush Kentish views.

directions	M20 junc.11; B2068 for Canterbury; left for Wye & Bodsham; 1st left fork, on for 1.5 miles; right for Wye; right for Bodsham; pub 300yds up on top of hill.
meals	12pm-2.30pm (12.30pm Sundays); 7-9.30pm. No food Sunday eve. Main courses £12-19; set menu £19 (Sunday lunch).
closed	Mondays except Bank Holidays when closed Tuesdays.

Joel Gros
Froggies at the Timber Batts,
School Lane,
Bodsham,
Wye, Kent TN25 5JQ
tel   01233 750237

map: 6 entry: 215

Kent

White Horse Inn
Bridge

The old staging-post inn on the Dover to Canterbury road has a new lease of life. It preserves its pubby atmosphere well, with a log-burning inglenook and several real ales. But under the guidance of young Ben Walton (dad Alan is the landlord), the White Horse has developed as an informal brasserie and a serious restaurant. The bar-brasserie is the seat of much action, blackboards list contemporary dishes where good materials, good farmhouse cheeses and really fresh vegetables are the components for excellent value food prepared with huge enthusiasm. A slate listing roasted pear, cobnut and goat's cheese salad, clams steamed in garlic, fennel and cider cream sauce, and lamb, tomato and rosemary stew, is tempting, especially when accompanied by a bottle from a well-researched wine list. A separate menu and a degree of peace and quiet can be had in the dining room where price and ambition are both high.

directions	On A2050, 3 miles south of Canterbury.
meals	12pm-2pm; 6.30pm-9pm. Main courses £6-£18.50; set menu £18.50-£22.50.
closed	Sunday evenings.

Alan Walton & Ben Walton
White Horse Inn,
53 High Street, Bridge, Canterbury,
Kent CT4 5LA
tel   01227 830249
web   www.whitehorsebridge.co.uk

map: 6 entry: 216

Griffin's Head
Chillenden

Jerry and Karen's hugely attractive Shepherd Neame pub – a Wealden hall house from the 14th century – will charm you. Dominated by a log fire in the tiny, flagstoned, central bar and back-to-back with its doppelganger hearth in the snug, attractive restaurant, this is a superb winter pub. Pale beams and standing timbers are everywhere, ceilings are low and the beams above the bar are a mass of glass beer mugs. Lovers of fizz know they've come to the right place the moment they step in and spot the blackboard listing champagne. Wine is taken seriously too, with a fair choice by the glass – three reds, three whites; you can always try a taster before you commit. Good country cooking is of the creamy garlic mushrooms, steak and kidney pie, roast partridge in cranberry sauce variety, and very delicious it is too. In spring the gorgeous garden is surrounded by wild roses. Particularly popular with the Kent cricketing fraternity.

directions	A2 from Canterbury; left along B2068 for Wingham. Follow signs for Nonnington & Chillenden.
meals	12pm-2pm; 7pm-9.30pm. Main courses £8-£16.
closed	Sunday evenings.

Jeremy Copestake
Griffin's Head,
Chillenden,
Canterbury,
Kent CT3 1PS
tel   01304 840325

map: 6 entry: 217

The Red Lion
Stodmarsh

A genuine country pub reached down rutted lanes that wind through bluebell woods. The tiny, 15th-century rooms have bare boards, log fires, garlands of hops, fresh flowers and candles on every table... and prints, framed menus from France, old wine bottles, milk churns, trugs and baskets, tennis rackets and straw hats. Then there's Robert Whigham, one of life's characters; the perfect landlord. A basket of freshly-laid eggs (chickens in the garden), locally-made chutney and a sign for the sale of locally-smoked ham – and two lazy cats – add to the rural feel. Greene King IPA and Old Speckled Hen are tapped direct from barrels behind the bar and everyone here is a regular – or looks like one. The blackboard menu changes every couple of weeks depending on what's available from local farms and shoots, food arrives on huge, individually painted plates and the quality is high.

directions	Off A257 Canterbury to Sandwich road.
meals	12pm-2.30pm; 7pm-9.30pm. Main courses £12.95-£17.95.
rooms	3 doubles £60.

Robert Whigham
The Red Lion,
High Street,
Stodmarsh,
Canterbury, Kent CT3 4BA
tel   01227 721339

map: 6 entry: 218

The Sportsman
Seasalter

On your way to Whitstable, slip off to Seasalter for a meal you won't forget. Brothers Phil and Steven Harris's pub is a gastronomic haven in the most unlikely setting, amid wastes of marshland with the North Sea somewhere behind. There's even a dominating wall, plus caravan sites and faded beach huts in between. In defiance of its bleak surroundings, the Sportsman is one of the most exciting dining spots in Kent. Happy eaters fill the three large, light-filled rooms, spreading across the stripped pine floors, pine wheelback chairs, chunky tables built from reclaimed wood and winter log fire. It's simple, fresh, unprecious: red stools at a cream-boarded bar, neat lighting, modern prints on white walls (they're for sale), and a glassed-in front porch, a fine place for soaking up the winter sun. The blackboard menu is short and sweet with everything seasonal and often local, and a big emphasis is placed on fish. It's fantastic food at reasonable prices, this "haute cuisine stripped bare". Thornback ray and balsamic vinaigrette, new-season lamb with pommes Anna, roast baby pineapple and coconut sorbet only hint at the skill, dedication and astonishing flavour combinations. On handpump are Shepherd Neame beers.

| directions | On coast road between Faversham & Whitstable. |
| meals | 12pm-2pm; 7-9pm. No food Mon. Main courses £11-£17. |

Phil Harris
The Sportsman,
Faversham Road,
Seasalter,
Kent CT5 4BP
tel   01227 273370

map: 6 entry: 219

The Dove
Dargate

In winter, woodsmoke hangs in the air, in summer, it's the heady scent of roses. This is an idyllic rural pub in the gloriously named Plum Pudding Lane. Enter through a series of small rooms with bare-boarded floors, scrubbed wooden tables and plain solid chairs to a hop-garlanded bar and winter fire. Nigel Morris cooks with skill and imagination using the freshest ingredients he can get his hands on. It's not your usual pub grub and raw materials are mostly regional: pheasant and partridge from local shoots, lemon sole, plaice and hake from Hythe. There could be roast shank of lamb, or a smashing confit of duck. Lunchtime snacks include soups, baguettes and a never-off-the-menu marinated chicken with mint. The sheltered, formal garden has tables under fruit trees, a swing for children, a dovecote with doves. Remember to book to eat, especially in the evening. There are Shepherd Neame ales on handpump and a short, good-value wine list.

directions	Off A299, 4 miles south west of Whitstable.
meals	12pm-2pm; 7pm-9pm. Main courses £5-£18.
closed	Mondays except Bank Holidays.

Nigel & Bridget Morris
The Dove,
Plum Pudding Lane,
Dargate, Canterbury,
Kent ME13 9HB
tel   01227 751360

map: 6 entry: 220

Shipwright's Arms
Faversham

It's been called the loneliest pub in the world. Surrounded by salt marshes, the below-sea-level-building and boatyard are protected by a dyke from inundation by the tidal creek above. Its isolation means the pub has to be self-sufficient: water is still drawn from a well and propane gas used for cooking. Plain and simple just about sums up the three tiny bar rooms separated by standing timbers and wooden partitions, all warmed by open fires or stoves and with booths formed by black-panelled settles. Furniture is ancient and there's no shortage of boating paraphernalia. Beers are from Kent brewers Goachers and Hopdaemon and are expertly kept, food sustains sailing folk and walkers on the Saxon Shore Way, and Derek and Ruth are lovely people. Join the summer crowd in the garden, sup a pint and sit on the sea wall.

directions	From A2 signs to Sittingbourne. Through Ospringe, right at r'bout on to western link road; right at end (T-junc.). Right again opp. school in 0.25 miles. Cross marsh to pub.
meals	12pm-2.30pm; 7pm-9pm. No food Sunday evenings. Main courses £5.95-£7.95.
closed	Mondays in winter.

Derek & Ruth Cole
Shipwright's Arms,
Hollowshore,
Faversham,
Kent ME13 7TU
tel   01795 590088

map: 6 entry: 221

Mulberry Tree
Wrightington

A big jewel in Lancashire's crown, the old wheelwright's workshop – then a brewery, later a forge – has now become a freehouse and restaurant with a Wrightington-born chef who trained under the Roux brothers and headed the kitchen at Le Gavroche. It's a vast, rambling place that's been reworked to create a fresh, modern look that matches the cooking. There's a smart lounge with a long bar, an intimate private dining room and an airy, open-plan eating area – subtly lit, softly hued, warmly carpeted, un-self-conscious. And chef-patron Mark Prescott's verve in the kitchen makes the Mulberry Tree one of the best gastropubs in the north-west. Order something as simple as rump steak with pepper sauce from the bar and be stunned by the presentation and finesse. Or book for a serious meal and enjoy some best-ever, flavour-packed, neo-peasant food. Start with Tuscan white bean soup with pesto, then plunge into roast rump of Cumbrian lamb with French beans and rosemary-flavoured sauce, or breast of wood pigeon with wild mushrooms, pancetta and rich merlot sauce. Puddings are to kill for: bread and butter pudding with apricot coulis, rhum baba with chantilly cream.

directions	M6 junc. 27; B5250 for Eccleston; on right in 2 miles.
meals	12pm-2pm; 6pm-9.30pm (10pm Fri & Sat); 12pm-9.30pm Sundays. Main courses £9.95-£15.25; set Sunday lunch £17.95.
closed	26 December-1 January.

Mark & Annie Prescott
Mulberry Tree,
9 Wrightington Bar,
Wrightington, Wigan,
Lancashire WN6 9SE
tel   01257 451400

map: 13 entry: 222

Lancashire

The Eagle & Child
Bispham Green

There's an old-fashioned pubbiness here *and* a sense of style — an informality touched with zing. The candlelit main bar welcomes you in with its rug-strewn flagged floors, well-used tables and chairs, hop-flower-decked beams and open fire, and the other two rooms are equally engaging — one hessian-carpeted with burgundy walls, the other cosy, with a cast-iron fireplace. Hand pumps line the bar (with beers from lesser-known brewers like Anglo-Dutch), the shelves parade an army of malts, and the wine cellar has some fine and unusual offerings, including English fruit wines. The staff seem to enjoy themselves as much as the customers and the food is good: olive and tomato bread pizza, spicy sausages and mash. The pub's reputation, however, lies with its cask ales, and a weekend beer festival in May packs the place out with beers and beer buffs.

directions	From M6 junc. 27, A5209 for Parbold; right along B5246; left for Bispham Green. Pub in 0.5 miles.
meals	12pm-2pm; 6pm-8.30pm (9pm Fridays & Saturdays); 12pm-8.30pm Sundays. Main courses £7.50-£12.
closed	3pm-5.30pm Monday-Saturday.

Martin Ainscough
The Eagle & Child,
Malt Kiln Lane,
Bispham Green, Ormskirk,
Lancashire L40 3SG
tel 01257 462297

map: 13 entry: 223

Lancashire

Oddfellows Arms
Mellor

Mellor is a small village on the outskirts of Manchester with fabulous views and this pub is a typical three-storey Pennine building, on the roadside opposite a car park. Unremarkable on the outside but inside a civilised tavern. Three cosy, low-beamed areas carpeted in warm colours, a stone-flagged central bar, well-spaced tables, old prints on the walls, a stove and open fires create a lovely informal mood. The smallish bar is attractively set out with four cask ale pumps and excellent wines are advertised on a blackboard, along with daily specials: chicken tikka tortilla, catalan fish stew, chocolate torte. The inn combines good food and drink with a great deal of comfort and an uncompromising respect for tradition. Because the building is set into the hillside space is at a premium; loos and restaurant are upstairs.

directions	M60 junc. 1 to Marple A626. After 6 miles to Marple Bridge & Mellor, for 2 miles.
meals	12pm-2.30pm (2pm Sundays); 6.30pm-9.30pm. Main courses £7.95-£14.95.
closed	Mondays; 25-26 December; 1 January.

Robert Cloughley
Oddfellows Arms,
73 Moor End Road,
Mellor, Stockport,
Lancashire SK6 5PT
tel 0161 449 7826

map: 14 entry: 224

Lancashire

The Church Inn
Uppermill

Next to the church on the way to the open moors – it's not easy to find. Julian Taylor brews their own Saddleworth beers and is involved in everything, including DIY. At the top end of the long curved bar, there's a grand fire with some window tables; at the other end, a big log burner in an old fireplace, with a heavily framed mirror above. Seating is a mix of padded benches, settles, chairs and a pew named Hobson's Choice. There's a fine atmosphere: lofty beams, leaded windows, lamps on sills, nightlights on tables, brass plates, Staffordshire jugs and fresh flowers. The soft background music is entirely bearable. Eat in the no-smoking dining room with valley views: the food is honest, unpretentious and good value, as are the beers. The inn is home to the world-famous Saddleworth Morris Men, with several lively events taking place here including the Rush Cart Festival on the August bank holiday weekend. A friendly place loved by all ages. Dogs are welcome, too.

directions	Saddleworth signed from Oldham. From Uppermill go up New St for 1 mile. Pub on left, next to church.
meals	12pm-2.30pm; 5.30pm-9pm. Main courses £3.50-£11.95.

Julian & Christine Taylor
The Church Inn,
Church Lane,
Uppermill, Sasddleworth,
Lancashire OL3 6LW
tel   01457 872415

map: 14 entry: 225

Lancashire

The Rams Head Inn
Denshaw

High on the moors between Oldham and Ripponden, with glorious views, the inn is only two miles from the motorway but you'd never know. It is unspoilt inside and out, with a genuinely old-farmhouse feel. The small rooms, with winter log fires, are carpeted, half-panelled and beamed; window panels display the white rose for Yorkshire, the red for Lancashire (you're on the borders here). Until recently beer was served from the cask; there's still an old sideboard behind the bar to remind you of former days. Blackboards announce a heart-warming selection of home-cooked food, and a serious effort is made to ensure that ingredients are fresh and in season. There's game and venison, and their own delicious sausages, homemade bread and ice cream. If you pop in for a drink you'll probably stay for a meal. A wonderfully isolated Lancashire outpost, with great staff too.

directions	M62 junc. 22 for Oldham & Saddleworth, 2 miles on right.
meals	12pm-2.30pm; 6pm-10pm; 12pm-8.30pm Sundays. Main courses c.£9.95.
closed	Mondays, except Bank Holidays.

Mr G R Haigh
Rams Head Inn,
Denshaw,
Saddleworth,
Lancashire OL3 5UN
tel   01457 874802

map: 14 entry: 226

Lancashire

What is real ale?

Keg or cask ale – what's the difference? One's a living organism, the other isn't. After the brewing process, cask-conditioned green beer ('real ale') is put into barrels to allow a secondary fermentation, producing a unique flavour and bubbles that are natural. Keg beer is beer that has been filtered and sterilised and, like lager, it's dead – until the gas is pumped back to give the distinguishing bubbles. Stored in sealed containers it tastes more like bottled beers – also put through the same process. Their advantage? They have a longer shelf life, and are easier to dispense.

In the 1960s and early 1970s the big breweries flooded the market with keg beers and lager. Then, in 1971, CAMRA (The Campaign for Real Ale) was founded. Their success in inspiring the real ale revival has been a dramatic example of a consumer group in action, forcing the brewing industry to rethink its stategy and produce real ales.

The new century has seen a flowering of craft breweries across the country, with beer being brewed on farms, on industrial estates and in sheds behind pubs. The Progressive Beer Duty was introduced in 2002 to give micro-brewers a further boost; there are over 400 independent breweries in Britain.

Assheton Arms
Downham

Assheton is the family name of the Lords of Clitheroe and Downham is their village. It has remained splendidly preserved and virtually untouched since the 16th century, its stone cottages strung out along a stream; it recently remodelled itself as Ormston in the BBC TV series *Born and Bred*. In the best traditions of country life, the pub stands opposite the church – it's the community's hub. The rambling, low-beamed bar bustles more often than not with both village regulars and hikers fresh from a wild moorland walk up nearby Pendle Hill. Diners drop by (or rather, pre-book) for the seafood, the huge grills, the hearty country casseroles and the rib-sticking puddings. As in the village, tradition reigns supreme: the atmosphere of an old inn has been preserved, right down to the huge stone fireplace and the horse brasses on the walls. Sit at solid oak tables on wing-back settles and bask in the absence of electronic games. In summer the front terrace entices you out to its serene pastoral views.

directions	Off A59, 3 miles NE of Clitheroe.
meals	12pm-2pm; 7pm-10pm; 12pm-10pm Sundays in summer. Main courses £7-£15.

David Busby
Assheton Arms,
Downham, Clitheroe,
Lancashire BB7 4BJ
tel   01200 441227
web   www.assheton-arms.co.uk

map: 13 entry: 227

The Inn at Whitewell
Whitewell

Richard was advised not to touch this inn with a bargepole. The old deerkeeper's lodge sits just above the River Hodder with views across parkland to rising fells in the distance. Merchants used to stop by and fill up with wine, food and song before heading north through notorious bandit country; the hospitality remains every bit as good and the most that will hold you up today is a stubborn sheep. Richard, officially the Bowman of Bowland, wears an MCC tie and peers over half-moon glasses with a soft, slightly mischievous smile on his face, the moving spirit behind all this informal pleasure. In the restaurant-with-views, tuck into cornfed Goosnargh chicken, peppered beef salad, homemade ice creams and great wines, including their own Vintner's. In the bar there's fish pie plus local bangers. Spend the day fishing on their own seven miles, then retire to bedrooms that are warm and cosy, with comely art and Bose music systems, overlooking the river. Views reach across parkland to rising fells in the distance. Mildly eccentric and great fun.

directions	M6 junc. 31a; B6243 east through Longridge; follow signs to Whitewell for 9 miles.
meals	12pm-2pm; 7.30pm-9.30pm. Main courses £6.50-£13.50.
rooms	17 twins/doubles £89-£133. Singles £66-£83.

Richard Bowman
The Inn at Whitewell,
Whitewell,
Forest of Bowland, Clitheroe,
Lancashire BB7 3AT
tel   01200 448222

map: 13 entry: 228

Lancashire

Ye Horns
Goosnargh

It's not an old pub though it likes to give that impression. Indeed, it was a house until 1952, when the owner's grandfather felt the village needed its own local and added the mock-Tudor facade. Inside, too, feels more house than pub, with separate rooms and the bar a partition between them. Rooms are snug and comforting, with old settles and polished furniture, log fires for winter days, prints, plants, ornaments and fresh flowers. Hearty food is a big draw, with Mark Woods, proprietor, starring in the kitchen. Fill your boots with roast local Goosnargh duck, steak and kidney pie and sticky toffee pudding. There are good wines, choice malts and (soon to come) cask ales; you can even buy wines to take home. The comfortable bedrooms in the barn annexe, have been done up in country-house style and there's a great big garden to spill into on warm days.

directions	From M6 junc. 32 for Garstang; right at 1st lights to Goosnargh. Follow signs for Horns Dam Fishery.
meals	12pm-2pm; 7pm-9pm. Main courses £8.25-£11.50; set menu £14.50.
rooms	6: 4 doubles, 2 twins £79.
closed	Monday lunchtimes.

Mark Woods
Ye Horns,
Horns Lane, Goosnargh, Preston,
Lancashire PR3 2FJ
tel   01772 865230
web   www.yehornsinn.co.uk

map: 13 entry: 229

Lancashire

Bay Horse Inn
Forton

The Wilkinsons have been in the saddle for a number of years during which their son Craig has become an accomplished chef. Lancashire produces some marvellous ingredients and Craig takes full advantage of them in his modern British cooking; specialities include slow-cooked Goosnargh duckling, suckling pig sausages, a delectable pear and almond tart. Yet the Bay Horse does not consider itself to be a true gastropub, there's too much of the traditional pubby atmosphere for that and great importance attached to a range of cask beers. Interconnecting areas are comfortably furnished with a mix of old chairs and cushioned seating in bay windows, the dining room sparkles and the bar is warm and inviting with its low beams, soft lighting and open fire in winter. Gentle background jazz adds to the relaxed mood and the service is friendly and professional. Beware: the inn is easy to miss on the corner of a country lane.

directions	From M6 junc. 33 A6 for Preston, 2nd left; pub on right.
meals	12pm-1.45pm; 7pm-9.15pm. No food Sunday evenings. Main courses £10.95-£17.95.
closed	Mondays.

Craig Wilkinson
Bay Horse Inn,
Bay Horse, Forton, Lancaster,
Lancashire LA2 0HR
tel   01524 791204
web   www.bayhorseinn.com

map: 13 entry: 230

Lancashire

Lunesdale Arms
Tunstall

A soft, wide, undulating valley, the Pennines its backdrop – this is the setting of The Lunesdale Arms. A traditional pub with a fresh, modern feel: Pimms in the summer, mulled wine in the winter, good ales and good cheer. Comfort is deep: big sofas and wood-burning stoves, cushioned settles in yellow and blue, newspapers to browse and oil paintings to consider – even to buy. A big central bar separates drinkers (three local cask ales, whiskies and wines) from diners. Sit down to locally-reared produce, home-baked bread and seasonal, often organic, vegetables at tables away from the bar. Emma Gillibrand delivers wholesome food full of flavour – country pâté, sugar-spiced salmon, damson fool – and encourages children to have small portions. (And there's always homemade pizza or pasta with tomato sauce if they prefer.) The Lunesdale is a great little local for all ages, with a popular games room.

directions	M6 junc. 34 A683 for Kirkby Lonsdale.
meals	12pm-2pm (2.30pm weekends); 6pm-9pm. Main courses £7.50-£12.
closed	Mondays except Bank Holidays.

Emma Gillibrand
Lunesdale Arms,
Tunstall, Kirkby Lonsdale,
Lancashire LA6 2QN
tel   01524 274203
web   www.thelunesdale.com

map: 13 entry: 231

Leicestershire

The Nevill Arms
Medbourne

A flurry of white doves greets you, making for the safety of the dovecote. You cross an arched footbridge over a duck-patrolled river to reach the Nevill's golden stone walls: it is idyllic in summer. And inviting in winter too, with two bars, one unusually backed by mirrors, and an inglenook fireplace. There's a separate dining room serving food that is relatively traditional – goujons of lemon sole, say, or pork in white wine and mushroom sauce – and there are five real ales on handpump and two dozen country wines. The Halls have been running the pub for years and simply love the place. There are darts and dominoes for the grown-ups, toys and table football (on request) for the kids, and every Easter Monday the village of Medbourne takes on neighbouring Hallaton in the hare-pie scramble and bottle-kicking contest: a football match in which a small barrel of beer is knocked about before being consumed. The good bedrooms are in two neighbouring cottages – stay for breakfast.

directions	On B664 between Market Harborough & Uppingham.
meals	12pm-2pm; 7pm-9.45pm. Main courses £5-7.95.
rooms	8 twins/doubles £55. Singles £45.

Nicholas & Elaine Hall
The Nevill Arms,
Medbourne, Market Harborough,
Leicestershire LE16 8EE
tel   01858 565288
web   www.thenevillarms.co.uk

map: 10 entry: 232

Leicestershire

The Baker's Arms
Thorpe Langton

A sleepy-village treasure with oodles of atmosphere beneath 16th-century thatch. A series of intimate little areas have been stylishly kitted out with long scrubbed pine tables, antique pews, settles on rug-strewn floors and paintings and prints on warm terracotta walls. The Bakers is more foodie than boozey though the pubbiness remains and the odd soul looking for just a pint of Tetleys will not be disappointed. But most come for Kate Hubbard's first-rate cooking (and it's important to book). Produce is impeccable, menus change daily. Chalked up on the boards are treats such as pan-fried scallops with a honey, mustard and lemon dressing, confit of duck leg and breast with parsnip and apple compote, baked sea bass with spinach, mushrooms and prawn jus, white chocolate and raspberry trifle. Wines, too, are good, and may come mulled in winter.

directions	Off A6 10 miles south of Leicester.
meals	12pm-2pm; 6.30pm-9.30pm. No food Sunday evenings. Main courses £9.95-£16.
closed	Weekday lunchtimes; Mondays.

Kate Hubbard
The Baker's Arms,
Thorpe Langton,
Market Harborough,
Leicestershire LE16 7TS
tel   01858 545201

map: 10 entry: 233

Leicestershire

The Bell
East Langton

Peter Faye and Joy Jesson took over the 16th-century village pub and its on-site brewery in 2003. In the now rather expensive Langton village, overlooking the cricket pitch, The Bell draws a loyal crowd. Subtle changes will soon see a fresher look to the long stone-walled bar with its dauntingly low beams, uneven floors and winter log fire; plans are also afoot for the bedrooms. Gone are the laminated menus in the dining room; in their place are agreeably short, daily menus devoted to the freshest produce. Caught-that-day cod is lightly battered and served with homemade chips and mushy peas, mussels are simmered in garlic, white wine and cream, shank of lamb is slow-cooked in red wine. The Caudle Bitter and Bowler Strong Ale nurtured in the brewery behind are a treat, and there's a pretty walled garden for summer supping. Reports on the changes are welcome.

directions	From A6, turn for East Langton on B6047.
meals	12pm-2pm; 7pm-9.30pm. Main courses £8.50-£13.50.
rooms	2 doubles £55.
closed	2.30pm-7pm Mondays & Sundays (6pm Thursdays & Fridays; 6.30pm Saturdays).

Peter Faye
The Bell,
Main Street, East Langton,
Market Harborough,
Leicestershire LE16 7TW
tel   01858 545278

map: 10 entry: 234

Leicestershire

The Cow & Plough
Oadby

The Cow and Plough sounds as if it should be a post-modern bar in Notting Hill. It is, in fact, a pub-restaurant housed in the former milking sheds of a working farm just outside Leicester. Barry and Elizabeth Lount founded it in 1989 and filled it with good beer and a hoard of brewery memorabilia: the two back bars are stuffed with period signs, mirrors and bottles. It later became an outlet for their range of Steamin' Billy ales, named after Elizabeth's Jack Russell who really did steam after energetic country pursuits. When the foot and mouth epidemic closed the farm's visitor centre, the Lounts established a restaurant there instead. Most of their dishes are made with local organic produce. The pub has built up a great reputation, winning awards and becoming a place for shooting lunches, and is also popular with the Leicester rugby team. And there's the new conservatory with its iron-topped and wooden tables, piano, plants and beams decked with dried hops.

directions On B667 north of town centre & A6.
meals   12pm-2pm; 7pm-9pm. No food Sunday & Monday evenings. Main courses £8.95-£14.95; set Sunday lunch £11.95/£14.95.

Barry Lount
The Cow & Plough,
Gartree Road, Oadby, Leicester,
Leicestershire LE2 2FB
tel   0116 272 0852
web   www.steamin-billy.co.uk

map: 9 entry: 235

Leicestershire

The Crown
Old Dalby

It looks like a private house: creeper-covered red brick at the front, and sweeping lawns, sheltered terrace and pétanque at the back. The 300-year-old pub has long been loved for its ales and food. Small, unspoilt rooms are a warren of ancient oak settles, antique tables, glowing coal fires, fresh flowers and a quaint hatchway bar from which village-brewed Belvoir and changing guest beers are tapped from the cask. And there's a bistro-style dining room, with seasonally changing menus promoting fresh local produce. At lunchtime there are soups and sandwiches, as well as spinach and ricotta tartlet, delicious fresh fish – whole sea bass, grilled brill – and dishes to delight the carnivore: ham hock and black pudding terrine, Moroccan chicken, sirloin steak with a stilton sauce. Jazz on the lawn is perfect on lazy summer days and the village is a charmer.

directions From Nottingham A606; at Nether Broughton right for Old Dalby; there 1st right, then left.
meals   12pm-2.30pm; 6.30pm-9.30pm. No food Sunday & Monday eve. Main courses £3.95-£9.95 (bar); £10.95-£16.95 (restaurant).
closed   Monday lunchtimes.

Mr & Mrs Hayle
The Crown,
Debdale Hill,
Old Dalby,
Leicestershire LE14 3LF
tel   01664 823134

map: 10 entry: 236

Leicestershire

Red House
Nether Broughton

The owners of the Fat Cat Café chain have brought a dash of cosmopolitan chic to the country; when the builder's swathes were removed in 2002 the villagers were stunned by the transformation. What was once the Red Lion, an old coaching inn, has become two snazzy bars, one with darts and a telly for football, the other more sophisticated: soft leather sofas, vases of flowers, a bar made out of books and a big open fire. At the back is an airy, chic, 75-seat restaurant where the chef from Nottingham's famous restaurant bluu presents a modern British menu and uses the finest local produce: confit of lamb with red onion tarte tartin and creamy mash, breast of chicken with wild mushrooms and madeira cream. There are cocktails, of course, locally-brewed Belvoir Beaver Bitter and 13 excellent wines available by the glass. And so to bed – after a fudge nut brownie and a perfect glass of sauternes. Eight bedrooms, kitted out with every conceivable modern luxury, are named after their headboards: choose between Green Suede, Red Leather, Smoked Mirror. Breakfasts are of croissants, sweet pancakes, fresh fruit or "a good old fry up".

directions	On A606 between Nottingham & M. Mowbray, 5 miles from Melton.
meals	12pm-2.30pm (6pm Sun); 6pm-9.30pm. No food Sun eve. Main courses (bar) £4-£11, (restaurant) £8-£11.
rooms	8: 6 doubles, 2 twins £100-£120.

Robin Kemp
Red House,
23 Main Street, Nether Broughton,
Leicestershire LE14 3HB

tel	01664 822429
web	www.the-redhouse.com

map: 10 entry: 237

Red Lion
Stathern

Count on stylishness and cheerful service. The rambling Red Lion feels like a home, with its books and papers, deep sofas and open fires; the flagstoned bar is more pubby. A trusted network of local growers and suppliers fills the kitchen with game from Belvoir estate, cheeses from the local dairy, fruits and vegetables from nearby farms. Menus are on blackboards dotted around, with a choice that leaps between fashion and tradition: fish and chips and mushy peas, sausages with sage mash and onion gravy, venison with parsnip mash, glazed beetroot and elderberry sauce. The set Sunday lunch is fantastic value at £14.50. The wine list has been created with imagination; beers include village-brewed Brewsters Bonnie and Grainstore Olive Oil from Oakham, and children have homemade lemonade. The outdoor play area will keep them happy, too.

directions	Off A607 north east of Melton Mowbray; through Stathern; past Plough; pub signed on left.
meals	12pm-2pm (3pm Sundays); 7pm-9.30pm (from 6pm Fridays). Main courses £7.75-£14.75; set menu £9.50 & £11.50 & £14.50..
closed	Sunday evenings.

Ben Jones
Red Lion,
Red Lion Street, Stathern,
Leicestershire LE14 4HS
tel   01949 860868
web   www.theredlion.co.uk

map: 10 entry: 238

Peacock Inn
Redmile

The Peacock has been given a complete makeover. There's still a pub bar, where you can eat pub food in pub surroundings, or drink good beer, or any of seven wines by the glass, but the rest of the place has been transformed into something much less traditional: a stylish country inn. Six fireplaces create a warm atmosphere throughout the polished, stone-flagged ground floor. The Garden Room is a light, airy restaurant in which you may take your fill of game, in season, and fish – or wild mushroom bouchés followed by medallions of venison in a port and peppercorn sauce. The individually designed bedrooms are in a traditional country style, some with four-posters, all with their own bathrooms; they're smart but not overdone. You're met at your door by a trompe l'oeil painting of a creature, such as a pig or an owl, peering from one corner. Worth seeking out following a visit to nearby Belvoir Castle.

directions	Off A52, 6 miles west of Grantham.
meals	12pm-2pm (3pm Sundays); 7pm-9pm (9.30pm Fri & Sat). Main courses £10-£15.
rooms	9 twins/doubles £80-£115. Singles from £55.

Stephen Hughes
Peacock Inn,
Church Corner, Main Street,
Redmile, Leicestershire NG13 0GA
tel   01949 842554
web   www.traditional-freehouses.com

map: 10 entry: 239

Lincolnshire

Lincolnshire

Wig & Mitre
Lincoln

When Major Hope left the army in the year of the Silver Jubilee, he and Valerie decided to open a pub in Lincoln. Here they still are, 27 years on, sandwiched between the cathedral and the courts. (They could have called it the Mitre and Wig: though lawyers dine here, the first ever pint was drawn by the Bishop of Lincoln.) Downstairs has a French café feel: old oak boards, exposed stone, sofas to the side; a civilised place for late breakfast and the papers. Upstairs, a cosy series of dining rooms and an open fire. In the Seventies it was hard to find decent food in any pub, let alone one in Lincoln. Valerie's kitchen became one of the finest in the area, serving a mix of dishes – baked cheese soufflé with rocket, tournedos of beef with red wine jus – strongly influenced by French and mediterranean cooking; the Wig and Mitre could perhaps claim to be the first gastropub. The regular visits of visiting High Court judges have, of course, nothing to do with late supper license.

directions	On Steep Hill leading down from Castle.
meals	8am-10.30pm. Main courses £10-£15; set lunch £11.95 & £13.95.

	Valerie Hope
	Wig & Mitre,
	Steep Hill, Lincoln,
	Lincolnshire LN2 1TL
tel	01522 538902
web	www.wigandmitre.com

map: 15 entry: 240

Hare & Hounds
Fulbeck

The old stone coaching inn was established in the early 1600s, grew in the 18th and 19th centuries, and was used as a maltings until 1910. David and Alison Nicholas took over six years ago and have created a successful small business: not only a comfortable and friendly bar with an excellent restaurant attached, but eight bedrooms in the former stables, some on the ground floor. Their reputation has grown and the restaurant menu flaunts some elaborate dishes; fillet steak with field mushrooms baked with pâté and roast shallots swirled with a madeira jus is one of David's favourites. The bar menu also invites you to eat more traditional pub food, and a fair selection of beers and wines. In spite of the fact that there are no well-known links between Fulbeck and France, a 'boules piste' has proved a major attraction in summer, and there's a big parasoled courtyard at the front. Fulbeck is a delight, with its steep streets and old stone houses.

directions	On A607 btwn Lincoln & Grantham.
meals	12pm-2pm; 7pm-9pm. Main courses £7-£14.
rooms	8: 4 doubles, 3 twin, 1 family £50-£70. Singles from £39.
closed	2pm-6pm (7pm Sundays).

	David & Alison Nicholas
	Hare & Hounds,
	The Green, Fulbeck,
	Lincolnshire NG32 3JJ
tel	01400 272090
web	www.hareandhoundsfulbeck.co.uk

map: 10 entry: 241

Lincolnshire

Chequers Inn
Woolsthorpe-by-Belvoir

A coaching inn for 200 years, The Chequers has built a reputation over the last five for being one of the best dining pubs in the area; so much so that Uma Thurman dropped by for a visit when filming at Belvoir Castle. There's luxury and deep comfort, with a flurry of open fireplaces, two dining rooms and two bars, armchairs, sofas, prints on rag-rolled walls. You have three beers on handpump, 24 wines by the glass, 50 whiskies, several fruit pressés and a humidor on the bar. The Monday evening set menu is very reasonable; there's seasonal game and steak and kidney pie on a daily-changing menu, home-cured gravadlax, small helpings on request. In summer The Chequers plays host to the village cricket team on what must be one of the slopiest pitches in England. Settle in and stay: the Vale of Belvoir is as beautiful as it sounds and comfortable beds in the stableblock await.

directions	Off A52, west of Grantham at Bottesford.
meals	12pm-2.30pm (3pm Sundays); 7pm-9.30pm. £8-£15; set Sunday lunch £10; set menu £10 & £12.50 (Mondays).
rooms	4 twins/doubles £50. Singles £40.
closed	Sunday evenings.

Justin Chad
Chequers Inn, Main Street,
Woolsthorpe-by-Belvoir,
Grantham, Lincolnshire NG32 1LU
tel   01476 870701
web   www.chequers-inn.net

map: 10 entry: 242

London

French House
London - Soho

This is something of an exception. As the French House does not serve pumped ale, it would not, by some lights, qualify as a pub – but no guide to British inns and public houses would be complete without it. This legendary Soho haunt, once patronised by members of the French Resistance, has been – and still is – befriended by famous Londoners (Freud, Melly), international figureheads and a welter of journalists, writers and bohemians who spend their days and nights in Soho. Dylan Thomas lost the only manuscript of *Under Milk Wood* here while on a bender. Despite the gentrification of Soho and the pub's renown, 'The French' has a delightfully scuffed-around-the-edges feel and attracts a friendly, bacchanalian crowd from many walks of life. There's bar food in the small, packed, smoky bar, and a cosy, funky restaurant upstairs with a late license – but this is first and foremost a drinking den (half pints of John Smith's, Beamish, Guinness) and a vastly atmospheric one at that.

directions	Nearest tube: Leicester Square.
meals	12pm-3pm; 6pm-11pm. No food Sundays. Snacks £2.50-£5.

Noel Botham
French House,
49 Dean Street,
Soho,
London W1D 5BG
tel   020 7437 2477

map: 5 entry: 243

London

Windsor Castle
London – Paddington

One of the joys of exploring London is that sometimes you chance upon an unexpected find – like the Windsor Castle, an extraordinary distillation of 20th-century pubbery in a quiet backwater off the Edgware Road, guarded by a model soldier. Run for 16 years by Michael Tierney, who was a publican in Marylebone for several more, it brims with plaques, coins, statues, signed photos of patrons (Peter O'Toole, George Best) and, above all, royal and Sir Winston Churchill memorabilia. (Republicans are welcome.) You'd be forgiven for thinking it was an antique shop. It is, however, an extremely friendly pub. Known as 'God's Waiting Room' – its clientele not being in the first flush of youth – it is also the monthly meeting place of that great British institution, the Handlebar Moustache Society, whose magnificent achievements are photographically illustrated by the entrance. Decent Thai food is served in the bar and in the wee, warm restaurant upstairs.

directions	Nearest tube: Edgware Road.
meals	12pm-3pm; 6pm-10pm. No food Saturday lunchtimes. Main courses £5.95-8.95.

Michael Tierney
Windsor Castle,
29 Crawford Place,
Marylebone,
London W1H 4LJ
tel   020 7723 4371

map: 5 entry: 244

London

The Seven Stars
London – Holborn

Nudging the backdoor of the Royal Courts of Justice, the Seven Stars is primarily a barristers' and litigants' den. Here since 1602, it was originally the haunt of Dutch sailors, and named after the seven provinces of the Netherlands. Having survived the Great Fire by a whisker it's been here longer than the courts themselves. Until recently it was looking tired, even exhausted; in the last three years it has been transformed by the exotically named Roxy Beaujolais, landlady and head chef. The glorious single bar has hung on to its boarded floors, low beams, old mirrors and narrow wood settles, and framed vintage legal film posters line the red walls. In 2003 the utterly old-fashioned, unspoilt and diminutive Seven Stars won the *Time Out* London Pub of the Year award, and has been dubbed "near-perfect". The menu is short and bistro-like: roast chicken and aioli, rib-eye steak sandwich, a plate of charcuterie. Harveys bitters are the house beers and there is a very decent selection of wines.

directions	Nearest tubes: Chancery Lane & Temple.
meals	12pm-3pm; 6pm-9pm. Main courses £6.50-£9.50.
closed	Sundays.

Roxy Beaujolais
The Seven Stars,
53 Carey Street,
Holborn,
London WC2A 2JB
tel   020 7242 8521

map: 5 entry: 245

The White Swan
London - Holborn

It had spent the previous 20 years as the Mucky Duck – and had become, of late, very mucky indeed. In 2003, brothers Tom and Ed Martin restored the original name and created a cool, new swan. The bar with a vast mirror on one wall evokes a classic, city pub feel. At plain tables on fashionably unpolished boards, City traders quaff real ales (there are four) and fine wines (20 by the glass). Upstairs is a mezzanine level, a stylish banquette-seated restaurant with a mirrored ceiling and some unusually good modern European cooking. Dishes are an enticing, flavoursome mix of robust (rump of lamb with crushed olive-oil potato and salad niçoise; gnocchi with pear, sherry and blue cheese) and subtle (fricassée of monkfish with fennel, chervil and truffle oil). The accompanying homemade foccaccia is wonderful. Cheese and wine lists are encyclopaedic, vegetables and side dishes expensively 'extra'. Uniquely, they have lockers for regular customers in which to store a bottle of unfinished wine. The bar menu veers from £5 sourdough sandwiches to dishes that change with seasons... with a bit of luck you'll find seared rabbit with roast tomatoes, chorizo, basil and crème fraîche on yours.

directions	Nearest tube: Chancery Lane.
meals	12pm-3pm; 6pm-10pm.
	Main courses £5-£9;
	set menus £18 & £22.
closed	Weekends; 3pm-6pm.

Tom & Ed Martin
The White Swan,
108 Fetter Lane, Holborn,
London EC4A 1ES
tel   020 7242 9696
web   www.thewhiteswanlondon.com

map: 5 entry: 246

Old Bank of England
London - Holborn

The solid Italianite exterior prepares you for the splendour within. It was built in 1888 as the Law Courts' branch of the Bank of England and it remained a bank right up until 1994. Then Fuller's Brewery, with help from the Heritage Committee, transformed it into a lavish pie-and-ale house. In the First World War the Crown Jewels were kept in steel-lined vaults downstairs – these now house the kitchens – while the two bars are linked by the most magnificent staircase. High ceilings are elaborately moulded, there are marble pillars, grand murals, glittering chandeliers. No. 194's other claim to fame is that it is on the site of a certain Mrs Lovett's pie shop. Mrs Lovett was the partner-in-crime of the demon barber, Sweeney Todd, who reputedly dug a tunnel from his shop 200 yards down Fleet Street along which he dragged his victims for use in Mrs Lovett's pies. Today's pies are less challenging – basic pub grub, in fact – while the beers are Fuller's best, and there's a long wine list.

directions	Nearest tube: Fleet Street.
meals	12pm–9pm.
	Main courses £7–£10.

Mark Maltby
Old Bank of England,
194 Fleet Street, Holborn,
London EC4A 2LT
tel   020 7430 2255
web   www.fullers.co.uk

map: 5 entry: 247

The Black Friar
London - Blackfriars

Across the Thames from the Tate Modern, the only Art Nouveau pub in London – perhaps the world. It was built in 1905 and the fact that it exists today is almost entirely due to Sir John Betjeman and his noble Sixties' campaign to save it from demolition. The building's amazing wedge shape is an echo of those narrow medieval streets, long since replaced by broad thoroughfares. It stands, soaked in history, on the site not only of a Dominican Friary but also of the courthouse in which Henry VIII achieved the annulment of his marriage to Catherine of Aragon. Art Nouveau mosaics romp over walls inside and out; in the arched room off the saloon, green and red marble alabaster is embellished with cavorting friars. It can get packed at lunchtimes and evenings so go off-peak if you can. No piped music, no plush – just bare boards, unpretentious pub grub courtesy of Mitchells and Butler and good solid ales from Adnams and Tetley. But it's the architecture that's the real star here – there is no other like it.

directions	Nearest tube/rail: Blackfriars.
meals	11am–9pm.
	Main courses £5–£7.50.

David Tate
The Black Friar,
174 Queen Victoria Street,
Blackfriars,
London EC4V 4EG
tel   020 7236 5474

map: 5 entry: 248

London

Jerusalem Tavern
London - Clerkenwell

There's so much atmosphere here you could bottle it up and take it home – along with one of the beers. Old Clerkenwell – once a haunt of the Knights Templar – has reinvented itself; the quaint 1720 tavern, a former coffee house, epitomizes all that is best about the place. Its name is new, acquired seven years ago when the exemplary St Peter's Brewery of Suffolk took it over and stocked it with their ales and fruit beers. Step in to a reincarnation of a nooked and crannied interior, all bare boards and plain tables, candlelit at night with a winter fire; arrive early to bag the table on the 'gallery'. Lunchtime food is simple and English – bangers and mash, a roast, a fine platter of cheese – with ingredients coming daily from Smithfield market down the road. There's a good selection of wines by the glass but this is a drinker's pub: staff are friendly and know their beer, and the full, irresistible range of St Peter's ales is all there, from the cask or the specially designed bottle.

directions	Nearest tube: Faringdon Road.
meals	12pm-2.30pm.
	Main courses £6-£8.

John Murphy
Jerusalem Tavern,
55 Britton Street, Clerkenwell,
London EC1M 5NA
tel   020 7494 4281
web   www.stpetersbrewery.co.uk

map: 5 entry: 249

London

The Eagle
London - Faringdon

Still mighty, after all these years. The Eagle is the standard bearer of the new wave that saw off scampi-in-a-basket and similar horrors. No tablecloths, no reservations – just delicious food ordered from the bar. With its real ales and decent choice of wines, the appeal is as much for drinkers as for diners and at peak times it heaves. The atmosphere is louche and bohemian, no doubt because the offices of the *Guardian* and the *Face* are next door. In spite of the laid-back appeal of scuffed floors, worn leather chairs, mix-and-match crockery, background Latin music and art gallery upstairs, the Eagle's reputation rests firmly on its food. The long bar counter is dominated by a stainless steel area at which ravishingly beautiful squid, pancetta and Mediterranean vegetables are prepared. Pasta, risotto, peasant soups, spicy steak sandwiches... it's worth the trek to get here. And how many gastropubs have a best-selling cookery book to their name?

directions	Nearest tube: Faringdon Road.
meals	12.30pm-3pm (3.30pm weekends);
	6.30pm-10.30pm.
	Main courses £8-£12.
closed	Sunday evenings.

Michael Belben
The Eagle,
159 Faringdon Road,
Faringdon,
London EC1R 3AL
tel   020 7837 1353

map: 5 entry: 250

The Peasant
London - Islington

A huge, nicely old-fashioned 19th-century pub with a fireplace in the corner, a massive, dark wooden bar and acres of ceilings. Over five years the Wright brothers built up a reputation for good wine, beer, cocktails and food. Now they have improved what was already a slick and sophisticated set-up, and brought in new blood to spice up the menus. Expect the freshest ingredients and quite a few surprises: grilled kangaroo with globe artichoke stuffed with shiitake mushrooms and peanuts; roast cod on fennel; edamame (soybean) and saffron broth with pickled cucumber. Mezze are served downstairs throughout the day – marinated olives and peppers, good cold meats and decent bread. The restaurant, too, has had a shake-up: a light, polished, first-floor room with a painted corner bar and a conservatory with a balcony attached. It's brilliantly positioned for antique shops, markets and visiting the design centre or Sadlers Wells.

directions	Nearest tube: Angel.
meals	12pm-3pm (4pm Sundays); 6pm-11pm. Main courses £6-£13. Mezze £3-£4.50.
closed	Saturday lunchtimes.

Gregory & Patrick Wright
The Peasant,
240 St John Street, Islington,
London EC1V 4PH

| tel | 020 7336 7726 |
| web | www.thepeasant.co.uk |

map: 5 entry: 251

The Westbourne
London - Notting Hill

Come to see and be seen, if that is your thing. Danny Boyle and Olly Daniaud took the place on a few years ago and gave it a thorough going over. Westbourne Park Villas promptly became the trendiest place in England and it's worth arriving early… 11am perhaps. London's beau monde amasses throughout the day at this shabby-chic gastropub, keen to spend gaily for decent beers and scrummy food. In the main bars is a collection of old tables and chairs, with some lush sofas at the back; walls spill over, bistro-style, with posters, photos and original art. The terrace at the front with its gas heaters is an all-year drinking spot – and just about handles the overflow. Chef Neil Parfitt's style is robust modern British and the ingredients he uses are the freshest: oysters, salmon, grilled fish, pan-fried duck breast with juniper jus, chargrilled venison steak with braised red cabbage. But most are here for the scene as much as the food.

directions	Nearest tube: Westbourne Park.
meals	12.30pm-3pm (3.30pm weekends); 7pm-10pm (9.30pm Friday-Sunday). Main courses £8-£12.50.
closed	Monday lunchtimes.

Wood Davis
The Westbourne,
101 Westbourne Park Villas,
Westbourne Green, London W2 5ED

| tel | 020 7221 1332 |
| web | www.thewestbourne.com |

map: 5 entry: 252

London

Ladbroke Arms
London - Holland Park

The warm glow emanating from the sage-painted sash windows is enough to tempt anyone into the Ladbroke Arms. Cream-painted and ginger hessian walls, benches plump with autumnal-hued cushions, long shiny tables, paintings, books... and beers to please real enthusiasts: Fuller's London Pride, Greene King IPA and Abbot Ale, Adnams Bitter. The intimate Ladbroke takes its food seriously, too, the chef buying cheese twice weekly from a touring supplier and placing orders with a fishing fleet every day. The bar is adorned with a sparkling collection of olive oils, vinegars and bottled fruit; in the raised restaurant area foodies tuck into intensely flavoured dishes such as aubergine, tomato and taleggio tart, sea bass with squid and risotto nero and braised lamb faggots with rosemary jus. Sunday roasts are a favourite among well-heeled locals; the hot chocolate fondant pudding is legendary. Sup under the parasols in summer as Notting Hillbillies smooch by.

directions	Nearest tubes: Notting Hill Gate & Holland Park.
meals	12pm-2.30pm (3pm weekends). Main courses £9.50-£14.50.

J Shubrati
Ladbroke Arms,
54 Ladbroke Road, Holland Park,
London W11 3NW
tel   020 7727 6648
web www.capitalpubcompany.co.uk

map: 5 entry: 253

London

Portobello Gold
London - Notting Hill

A fun little place off Ladbroke Grove – a bar, a restaurant, an internet café and a place to stay. Sit out on the pavement in wicker chairs and watch the fashionistas stroll by. Or hole up at the bar with a pint of malty Spitfire and half a dozen oysters, as Bill Clinton did on his last visit to Britain as president (and left without paying). Tiled floors, an open fire and monthly exhibitions of modern art fill the walls. At the back, the conservatory restaurant with its retractable glass roof feels comfortably 'jungle'. Dine – to the sweet song of canaries – on roast sea bass with rosemary and garlic (seafood's a speciality), venison casserole or spaghetti with mushroom ragout. Linda writes about wine, so you'll drink well. Bedrooms are basic, with small shower rooms and good beds; the backpacker room is amazingly cheap. Ideal if the hippy in you is still active, or you're after a quirky place to stay where you eat and drink.

directions	Nearest tube: Notting Hill Gate; follow signs for Portobello Market.
meals	10am-10pm (12pm Sundays). Main courses £5-£12.95; set menu £20.50.
rooms	7 doubles £22-£160.

Michael Bell & Linda Johnson-Bell
Portobello Gold,
95-97 Portobello Road,
Notting Hill, London W11 2QB
tel   020 7640 4910
web www.portobellogold.com

map: 5 entry: 254

London

The Scarsdale
London - Kensington

We can only be grateful to the French builder who believed Napoleon would invade and built The Scarsdale as living quarters for the French army. The immaculate Edwardes Square could only have been built by the French. This is a delightful little pub with a summer terrace of hanging baskets and bags of Victorian character. The old stained glass, dark panelling and burgundy walls provide a distinguished foil for old paintings in heavily gilded frames and various empty magnums of champagne, while the happy hum of quaffers flows from cosy corners as easily as the ales. Fabulous smells emanate from the kitchen hatch heralding the arrival of slow-roasted lamb shoulder with haricot blanc and minted gravy, expertly followed by hot chocolate pudding. Eat in the busy bar or in the swagged dining room. You could happily go on a first date here, or bring the parents.

directions	Nearest tube: High Street Kensington.
meals	12pm-10pm (9pm Sundays). Main courses £8-£14.
closed	Christmas Day.

Roy & Sarah Dodgeson
The Scarsdale,
23a Edwardes Square,
Kensington,
London W8 6HE

tel   020 7937 1811

map: 5 entry: 255

London

Churchill Arms
London - Kensington

It's hard to say which comes first in the popularity stakes, the publican or the pub: Gerry O'Brien is an influential figure and this is a terrific pub. The Churchill is not only a shrine to the great prime minster but to Gerry's collections of memorabilia and his irrepressible Irish humour. To the left of the counter in the bar – smoky, cosy with open fire – is Chamber Lane (115 chamber pots suspended from the ceiling that Gerry is "potty about") while the walls of the leafy, glass-roofed Thai restaurant – once, unbelievably, a garage – display his prized butterflies. Never mind the tourists; come for great Guinness and beers, oriental feasts that don't break the bank, bags of atmosphere and a big dollop of tradition. On the annual celebration of Sir Winston's birthday unsuspecting drinkers are amazed to see everyone dressed in 40s style; sausage and mash can be bought for a shilling and the evening's takings go to the Cabinet War Office Museum. You have been warned!

directions	Nearest tube: High Street Kensington.
meals	12pm-9.30pm. Main courses £5.85.

Gerry O'Brien
Churchill Arms,
119 Kensington Church Street,
Kensington,
London W8 7LN

tel   020 7727 4242

map: 5 entry: 256

The Grenadier
London - Belgravia

Down a cobbled alley on the Grosvenor estate, the tiny Grenadier is unmissable, with its fanfare of patriotic paintwork, tumbling flowers and red sentry box. It is a magnet for tourists and their cameras. Small, uneven steps lead to a cosy interior with a military theme – a reflection of this little watering hole's glorious past. Originally the Duke of Wellington's officers' mess, it later became a popular place for King George IV to enjoy a pint. The dimly lit Mess Bar, with smouldering coal fire, is stuffed with memorabilia: gleaming breast plates, swords, bearskins and bugles. Behind, in the small restaurant, squeeze in and settle down to beef Wellington or fish and chips at battle-themed bench seats and tables dressed in starched white linen. In September, the ghost of an officer – accidentally flogged to death after cheating at cards – returns to haunt the place, while the infamous Bloody Marys are best sampled on Sundays, from a specially erected bar. A small place with a big heart, and once frequented by Madonna.

directions	Nearest tube: Hyde Park Corner.
meals	12pm-1.30pm (3pm Sundays); 6pm-9pm. Main courses £5-£8.50.

Mr Cellan Williams
The Grenadier,
18 Wilton Row, Belgravia,
London SW1X 7NR
tel   020 7235 3074
web   www.thespiritgroup.com

map: 5 entry: 257

The Nags Head
London - Knightsbridge

Once known as the smallest pub in London, the Nags Head expanded in Victorian times, but modestly; it could still lay claim to its title today. This wooden-floored and panelled boozer may be small but it has huge personality. The tiny bar is low enough to serve passing gnomes, hence the sunken floor behind, allowing bar staff to meet seated drinkers eye to eye. Walls and ceilings are packed with interesting memorabilia, including a squadron of nicotine-stained matchstick bi-planes and a 'What the Butler Saw' machine – operational in exchange for a donation to the pub's charity pot. No fruit machines, no mobile phones, but music hall songs from the 20s and 30s, open fires and loads of nostalgia; it's a great little place to quaff Adnams ales or a glass of Aspall's Suffolk cider. Downstairs, on checked cloths, a great spread of home-cooked meats, pies, cheeses and salads can be scoffed at lunchtime, along with other hot 'Kitchen Favourites', such as real ale sausages.

directions	Nearest tube: Hyde Park Corner.
meals	11am-9.30pm. Main courses £6.50-£10.50.

Kevin Moran
Nags Head,
53 Kinnerton Street,
Knightsbridge,
London SW1X 8ED
tel   020 7235 1135

map: 5 entry: 258

Builders Arms
London - Chelsea

You wouldn't expect such an exquisite little pub in the back streets of the King's Road. Enter and be seduced: the country-living-room feel is so comforting you might want to move in. Pints of London Pride are downed among large puffy armchairs, low table lamps, walls in soft greens and creams, and in a ruby-red snug behind the bar. 'Never trust a builder without a tattoo' reads the sign on the wall, but the people here, and their pooches, are as immaculate as the interior. This popular watering hole draws a lively mix of locals, business folk and shoppers. The Builders is a stylish pub, even if labelling the loos 'Builders' and 'Ballerinas' is a bit twee. The food is modern British – smoked haddock, saffron and spring onion risotto, grilled rib-eye steak with garlic and parsley butter, attractively presented. Avoid Friday lunchtimes: they're packed.

Coopers Arms
London - Chelsea

A refreshing pit-stop not far from the glitzy King's Road – you'd be forgiven for thinking you'd stepped into the 1930s, and a station waiting room at that. Find wooden floors, dark furniture, high ceilings, cream and burgundy paintwork, old railway posters on the walls. Yet there's a contemporary feel to it all and the space is big, airy and light. Head to the bar for Young's Bitter and Special, Smiles' IPA or some wholesome pub food. The homemade lamb burgers, with ingredients fresh from proprietor Charles Gotto's organic farm, are a big hit, along with roast pimento and tomato soup and traditional temptations like apple and berry crumble and custard. Upstairs, a newly done-up function room with long trestle table; downstairs, a stuffed brown bear, a mounted moose head and organic eggs for sale. This is an uncomplicated, down-to-earth pub with some fun and original touches – you could happily stay for a pint or two on a Sunday with the papers.

directions	Nearest tubes: Sloane Street & South Kensington. Behind King's Road, between Sydney Street & Chelsea Green.
meals	12pm-3pm; 7pm-9.45pm. Main courses £8.95-£13.95.

directions	Nearest tube: Sloane Square.
meals	12.30pm-3pm; 6.30pm-9.30pm. No food Sunday evenings. Main courses £7.50-£12.

Rupert Clevely
Builders Arms,
13 Britten Street, Chelsea,
London SW3 3TY
tel 020 7349 9040
web www.geronimo-inns.co.uk

Charles Gotto
Coopers Arms,
87 Flood Street, Chelsea,
London SW3 5TB
tel 020 7376 3120
web www.thecoopers.co.uk

map: 5 entry: 259

map: 5 entry: 260

London

Chelsea Ram
London – Chelsea

A quiet residential street at the bottom of the Lots Road seems an unlikely place to find a corner pub bursting with bonhomie. It used to be a junk shop; now the fine arched shop windows with etched glass are complemented by soft and subtle mustards and terracottas, tongue-and-groove cladding, a dark green wooden bar and colourful local art. A carpeted area to the back, with its small alcoves, soft lighting and shelves of thumbed books, is a intimate spot in which to be treated to enticing dishes: settle down to smoked haddock and spinach perhaps ("posh fish pie"), then chocolate pudding with Baileys sauce. The scrubbed wooden tables are a great place for lively card games (please bring your own) over coffee. Close to the large storage depot of Bonhams the auctioneers, this popular pub has done well for itself and is worth the few minutes' walk from the end of the King's Road.

directions	Nearest tube: Sloane Square.
meals	12pm-10pm (9.30pm Sundays). Main courses £3.95-£11.95.

Jeremy Lee
Chelsea Ram,
32 Burnaby Street,
Chelsea,
London SW10 0PL
tel   020 7351 4008

map: 5 entry: 261

London

Fox & Hounds
London – Battersea

As you pass beneath yet another dripping railway bridge you start to wonder if you're heading the right way. You probably are; and the moment the bright little corner pub comes into view you'll know the trek from Clapham has been worth it. With its excellent beers, including Harveys, and its photos of pints on deep cream walls, you'd think the place was a shrine to the golden brew. It's still a popular hangout for locals but, as with its sister pub, The Atlas (see entry 265), the food is now the star, and mediterranean-style dishes that flow from the trendy open kitchen attract diners in droves. Food-conscious train-spotters will think they've gone to heaven as they tuck into Italian chicken casserole at a scrubbed pine table (or Turkish meatballs...) and watch the Connex South Central trains whizzing by. There's a laid-back atmosphere here, and a good little garden for summer.

directions	Nearest rail: Clapham Junction. Left towards lights; up Lavender Hill. At Police Station left onto Latchmere Rd.
meals	12.30pm-2.30pm (3pm Friday-Sunday); 7pm-10.30pm (10pm Sundays). Main courses £6.50-£11.50.
closed	Monday lunchtimes.

George & Richard Manners
Fox & Hounds,
66 Latchmere Road, Battersea,
London SW11 2JU
tel   020 7924 5483
web   www.thefoxandhoundspub.co.uk

map: 5 entry: 262

Earl Spencer
London – Southfields

The main drag of Merton Road is not where you expect to find a pub run with passion. But the grand old Earl Spencer's spit 'n' sawdust days are over, its fine Edwardian interior stylishly restored. Now, to a clean backdrop of deep cream and dark blue, gilded ceiling mouldings and a winter fire, you will discover some of the best pub food in south London. Chef Mark Robinson and his team bake bread twice a day, have a smokery on the premises and a collection of cookery books to tempt you at the bar. Above the central fireplace the blackboard is chalked up with an ever-changing seasonal menu and inventive dishes popping up every day; perhaps fish soup with aioli and chive; pheasant, pigeon and Parma ham terrine with gooseberry chutney; roast monkfish with saffron mash, spinach, piquillo peppers and gremolata; shoulder of lamb to be shared among four; poached pear, honey and brandy parfait. Proprietor Jonathan Cox has not forgotten the Earl Spencer's roots, so there's a fine selection of wine (10 by the glass) and ales (Hook Norton, Shepherd Neame Spitfire) and Hoegaarden on tap. A place to unwind... fresh flowers and papers, laid-back staff, happy drinkers, contented dogs.

directions	Nearest tube: Southfields.
meals	12.30pm-2.30pm (3pm Sundays); 7pm-10pm (9.30pm Sundays). Main courses £7.50-£12.

	Jonathan Cox Earl Spencer, 260-262 Merton Road, Southfields, London SW18 5JL
tel	020 8870 9244

map: 5 entry: 263

London

The Harwood Arms
London - Fulham

Of all of the gastropubs in Rupert Clevely's impressive chain, the Harwood Arms stands out. Unusual, too, to find a pub so close to Chelsea football ground that dares depart from the strictly traditional. There's an unashamedly contemporary feel here, and Rupert flaunts his love of Africa: wonderful earthy colours — reds, oranges, aubergines, browns and creams — wooden floors and a slightly more formal dining area with seagrass woven in deep colours creates the perfect backdrop for exotic *objets d'art*. Texture is king — huge feather-filled velvet cushions, some bright orange tribal hats, a striking canvas of thick bright oils, a row of black and white African portraits in wide wooden frames. The Harwood encourages an easy informality where, over a pint of Youngs or Spitfire, you dine on good modern dishes, cut your own bread (homemade, of course) and help yourself to oils & vinegar from a long central table.

directions Nearest tube: Fulham Broadway. Pub on corner of Walham Grove & Farm Lane.

meals 12pm-2.45pm (4pm Sundays); 7pm-9.45pm (9.30pm Sundays). Main courses £5.95-£10.50.

Ben Hurley
The Harwood Arms,
29 Walham Grove, Fulham,
London SW6 1QR
tel 020 7386 1847
web www.geronimo-inns.co.uk

map: 5 entry: 264

London

The Atlas
London - Fulham

Up high, golden letters on wooden panelling proclaim London Stout, Burton Bitter and mild ales. The Atlas is a great little place in which to delve into more modern brews: Fuller's London Pride, Caledonian Deuchars IPA, Adnams Broadside. A glazed wooden partition — a prop for the 'Wine of the Moment' blackboard — divides the bar in two. Other Thirties' features remain: floorboards, attractive black and white tiling around the foot of the bar and three brick fireplaces, two of which add a glow in winter. The third, its mantelpiece piled high with lemons and limes, has been converted into a serving hatch for mediterranean-inspired dishes — grilled sardines, Italian sausages, Spanish sliced meats; the wine list trumpets 24 wines by the glass. Doors lead to a walled suntrap garden (open from May till October) where puffa-jacketed Fulham-ites flock under the rain and wind cover. In spite of its modest frontage on a residential street, the pub is next to a big Pay & Display, so not hard to find.

directions Nearest tube: West Brompton.

meals 12.30pm-3pm; 7pm-10.30pm (10pm Sundays). Main courses £6.50-£12.

George Manners
The Atlas,
16 Seagrave Road,
Fulham,
London SW6 1RX
tel 020 7385 9129

map: 5 entry: 265

London

White Horse
London - Fulham

The pub on the green is reputed to have the best-kept beers in Europe. Mark Dorber's remarkable knowledge of real ale is the fruit of years working with the best tasters and encouragement from good trade journalists. His place is a shrine, his glorious two-day beer festival in November brings buffs from far and wide to consume 300 British ales, and the ever-changing list of guest ales above the log fire is within reading distance of some deeply comfortable sofas. Bar food is of the best sort, from ploughman's with unusual cheeses to fried bass with garlic mash, and the menu usefully suggests the best accompanying liquor. Inside, terracotta walls, slatted wooden blinds, lovingly polished pumps and beer memorabilia; outside, a big terrace overlooking the green and a Sunday barbecue. The pub may be a hotbed of Fulhamites, but whoever dubbed it 'The Sloaney Pony' was misguided; given such a passion for beer, 'The Frisky Fermenting Filly' might seem more appropriate.

| directions | Nearest tube: Parsons Green. |
| meals | 12pm-3.30pm; 6pm-10.30pm; 12pm-10.30pm weekends. Main courses £7.75-£13.95. |

Mark Dorber
White Horse,
1 Parsons Green, Fulham,
London SW6 4UL
tel   020 7736 2115
web   www.whitehorsesw6.com

map: 5 entry: 266

London

Swag & Tails
London - Knightsbridge

Hidden down a pretty mews in one of the most fashionable parts of town, the little whitewashed pub with blue shutters and well-clipped topiary is an easy walk – even in Jimmy Choos – from the main Harvey Nichols-Harrods drag. Escape the crowds and rest weary feet in the warm, yellow-and-blue interior where wooden floors and swagged curtains make a fresh and glamorous alternative to the heavy trimmings of the traditional Knightsbridge pub. The attractive tiled conservatory at the back – less noisy and smoky than the main bar – is a charming spot in which to tuck into seared king scallops with lemon dill sauce or chargrilled lamb chops, couscous and herbed yogurt. The food is stylish, modern and really very good. Staff are full of smiles and, if it takes an explorer to find this little place, the wonderful black and white photograph of Nare's Arctic expedition of 1875 – a present from landlady Annemaria to her husband – is a fitting first reward for your perseverance.

directions	2 minutes' walk from Harrods.
meals	12pm-3pm; 6pm-10pm. Main courses £7.50-£13.25.
closed	Weekends; Bank Holidays.

Annemaria Boomer-Davies
Swag & Tails,
10-11 Fairholt Street,
Knightsbridge, London SW7 1EG
tel   020 7584 6926
web   www.swagandtails.com

map: 5 entry: 267

Ship Inn

London - Wandsworth

Drinking a pint of Young's Special next to a concrete works doesn't sound all that enticing, but the Ship Inn is special enough that one visit will have you hooked. With a pint of ale in hand (or a glass of New World wine) the riverside terrace by Wandsworth Bridge is a dreamy spot. Chilly evenings still draw the crowds to this old pub, cosy with rustic old tables and new conservatory and wood-burning stove. The days when the ceilings were decked with plastic lobsters, and grub no more than a pie on a glass shelf, are long gone. Charles Gotto supplies ingredients for a swish, fresh menu from his own organic farm - Shorthorn beef, rare breed pork and lamb, eggs - and the popular summer barbecues rustle up grilled swordfish and lobsters alongside organic sausages and Angus rib-eye steaks. At peak times expect 'who can be the loudest' Fulhamites to pack out the front bar - but don't let that put you off. The Ship opens its arms to all, and families congregate under the marquee in summer.

| directions | From Wandsworth station left under railway bridge; inn down by river. |
| meals | 12pm-10.30pm (10pm Sundays). Main courses £8.50-£15. |

Charles Gotto
Ship Inn,
Jews Row, Wandsworth,
London SW18 1TB
tel   020 8870 9667
web   www.theship.co.uk

map: 5 entry: 268

Alma Tavern

London - Wandsworth

Each of Charles Gotto's enterprises has an individual quirk and the Alma is no exception. Charles was first attracted to this green-glazed corner pub opposite Wandsworth station by the whimsical notion of transforming it into a 'Hotel de la Gare'. Gone are the early promotional days of a Citroën H truck trumpeting *La Marseillaise* and handing out complimentary baguettes at East Putney tube. Fifteen years on, the Alma is as continental as ever and a stylish place in which to savour a pint – or a good wine – while relaxing into the original surroundings of rich-painted mirrors, gold mosaics, wooden panelling and etched glass. In the attractive, bare-boarded dining room, overseen by a baby-blue frieze of satisfied nymphs, diners exult in imaginatively modern dishes – guinea fowl with herb lentils, mussels with lemongrass and coriander, chorizo frittata, steak burger and fries. Many ingredients come from Charles's organic farm.

| directions | Straight across road from Wandsworth station. |
| meals | 12pm-10.30pm (10pm Sundays). Main courses £8.75-£14.75. |

Charles Gotto
Alma Tavern,
499 Old York Road,
Wandsworth, London SW18 1TF
tel   020 8870 2537
web   www.thealma.co.uk

map: 5 entry: 269

The Crown & Goose
London - Camden

From the outside it looks like a twee tearoom; inside it feels like a house occupied by friendly squatters. You might wonder where the border lies between bohemian and unkempt and some would argue that this popular little pub lies on the wrong side. However, the laid-back inhabitants of Camden (where Dickens had Bob Cratchit live) don't mind a bit… people are as happy here browsing the papers as gossiping with friends. There's one big room with an elaborate wooden bar and a vaguely Victorian mishmash of tables, sofas and chairs, an open fire and music in the background. Walls are largely bare but carry the odd piece of art; look out for an unusual bronze. Service is exuberant and warm, the beer plentiful and well-priced, the food simple modern British. Typical dishes are wild-boar sausages with roasted vegetables and beetroot and apple relish, and Cuban burgers with jalapeno salad. Some say the chips are the best in town.

The Lansdowne
London - Primrose Hill

Abuzz with music and conversation, the Lansdowne is worth crossing several postcodes for. Amanda Pritchett was one of the founders of the trail-blazing Eagle; eight years ago she set up the Lansdowne and followed a similar gastropub route. It's laid-back, open-plan and atmospherically lit, with big wooden tables and dark green tiles — and manages, at least downstairs, to keep its pubby feel, in spite of the emphasis on dining. Upstairs is an elegant and charming 60-seat restaurant where customers are treated to adventurous food — Jerusalem artichoke and red onion risotto, sea bass en papillotte, belly of pork with mash and shallots. Though the serious dining goes on up here, you can also eat down — the decibels are high, the atmosphere shambolic and everyone loves the pizzas (kids included). There are two draught ales and one real cider, but really this is a wine and lager place. Outside in summer is a little oasis to which you can retreat and leave the city far behind.

directions	Nearest tube: Camden Town.
meals	12pm-3pm; 6pm-10pm; 12pm-10pm Fridays & Saturdays (9pm Sundays). Main courses £8-£10.

directions	Nearest tube: Chalk Farm.
meals	12pm-3pm; 7pm-10pm. Main courses £8-£15.
closed	Monday lunchtimes.

Joe Lowry
The Crown & Goose,
100 Arlington Road,
Camden,
London NW1 7HP
tel   020 7485 8008

Amanda Pritchett
The Lansdowne,
90 Gloucester Avenue,
Primrose Hill,
London NW1 8HX
tel   020 7483 0409

map: 5 entry: 270

map: 5 entry: 271

The Engineer
London - Primrose Hill

Victorian superstar Isambard Kingdom
Brunel, whose silhouette decks the sign,
once had an office here. Artists are the
new stars and today the place is run by a
painter and an actress. Behind the half-
stuccoed 1850 edifice lies a cheerful,
friendly gastropub with a smart
bohemian feel and an outstanding
reputation for food. It is particularly
strong on fish cooked with a touch of the
mediterranean or Pacific Rim –
chargrilled squid with green papaya, say
– but there are roast rack of lamb, fat
homemade chips and creamy and
chocolately desserts to swoon over too.
Wines look to the New World and beer
is excellent. You can eat up or down: the
front bar is relaxed, bright and buzzing,
the restaurant up has white plates on
white cloths, mirrors in gilt frames and
art for sale. In summer, the large lush
garden catches the sun and seats up to
80. There's a good mixed crowd here
though the majority are hip and young.
The service is often praised, and the
parking is easy.

directions	Nearest tube: Camden Town.
meals	12pm-3pm; 12.30pm-3.30pm weekends; 7pm-10.30pm. Main courses £9.75-£16.

Karen Northcote
The Engineer,
65 Gloucester Avenue,
Primrose Hill, London NW1 8JH
tel 020 7722 0950
web www.the-engineer.com

map: 5 entry: 272

The Belsize
London - Belsize Park

Belsize Park was once a slightly down-at-
heel relation sandwiched between
affluent neighbours, but, like almost
every other building in the area, the
exterior of The Belsize has had a
fashionable lick of pastel paint. It used to
be an ordinary boozer; today it is a chic
and baroque dining pub with a cocktail
list and its own bread oven. Yet owners
Randall and Aubyn, who also own The
Ifield, have cleverly managed to hold on
to the old pubby feel. Enter an open bar
area with a raffish mix-and-match décor
that caters for a North London crowd:
chandeliers hang from ceilings, gilt-
framed mirrors cover the walls. There's
rap and reggae and an almost louche
feel, themed nights, exotic cocktails and
oceans of bottled beer. Menus change
regularly and are modern British in style,
with prices to reflect the area. Typical
dishes might include linguini and clams
with chilli, lemon and parsley and crispy
aromatic duck with herb and beanshoot
salad. There's also a room at the back
that can be hired for private parties.

directions	Nearest tube: Belsize Park.
meals	12pm-10.30pm. Main courses £4-£13.50.

Sam Freeman
The Belsize,
29 Belsize Lane,
Belsize Park,
London NW3 5AS
tel 020 7794 4910

map: 5 entry: 273

London

Ye Olde White Bear
London - Hampstead

Hampstead has jealously guarded its reputation as a village near London rather than as part of the sprawling suburbs; when you visit Ye Olde White Bear you feel it has succeeded in staving off the city's advances. There is still a villagey air to Hampstead, though there would no doubt be an outcry if anyone drove a herd of cows through the streets (there certainly was when McDonalds set up shop.) The Bear resembles a country pub on the outside and is marvellously quiet, buried down a backstreet, protected from the buses and bustle of the Heath Road. Inside, a higgledy-piggledy, reassuringly cosy local – with dark walls, a real fire, comfortable chairs. Friendly staff serve you a well-kept pint of bitter or a glass of one of their many wines, and, should you have built up an appetite by walking across that magnificent heath, there's a whole menu of nourishing pub grub – snacks, salads, sirloin steak – at reasonable (London) pub prices.

| directions | Nearest tube: Hampstead. |
| meals | 12pm-9pm.
Main courses £7-£10. |

Chris Ely
Ye Olde White Bear,
Well Road,
Hampstead,
London NW3 1LJ
tel   020 7435 3758

map: 5 entry: 274

London

The Junction Tavern
London - Kentish Town

From the stainless-steel, open-to-view kitchen flows food that is modern European and wide-ranging – from good old Sunday roast beef to poached langoustine with new potatoes and lemon butter and perfect fruit crumble. The daily menu is market-based and well-priced, particularly at weekday lunchtimes when main courses are endearingly affordable. Word has spread: at weekends you must book, as the place heaves. Young staff are friendly and – given that this is a 'chilled' place – cheerfully attitude-free. The interior is high-ceilinged, corniced, wood-panelled, with big leather sofas and an open fire. While half the pub is restaurant, the rest is old fashioned bar, serving beers and good wines. Enjoy a fresh glass of manzanilla in the garden in summer (or even in winter, thanks to the heaters), or in the conservatory in spring. Jacky Kitching and partner Chris Leach have a background in restaurants; they also own The Northgate in Islington. This is their second gastropub.

directions	Nearest tubes: Kentish Town & Tufnell Park.
meals	12pm-3pm (4pm weekends); 6.30pm-10.30pm (9.30pm Sundays). Main courses £6.50-£13.50.
closed	Xmas Eve & Day; New Year's Day.

Jacky Kitching
The Junction Tavern,
101 Fortess Road,
Kentish Town,
London NW5 1AG
tel   020 7485 9400

map: 5 entry: 275

London

Dartmouth Arms
London - Dartmouth Park

The pub has style *and* a sense of humour. Sitting unobtrusively in a Highgate side street, the Dartmouth Arms looks smart but unexceptional. Inside is another story. There's huge personality and the predominant theme is copper. It comes highly burnished, whether as water pipes, bar top or mirror frame. In the back room there's bold kitsch in a copper statue, fish in a TV-set tank and champagne bottles hanging from a chandelier. Furnishings are chic: a pine bar, black padded chairs, half-panelled walls painted vibrant red. Landlord Nick is passionate about food and beer. There are three perfectly kept cask ales, 10 wines by the glass and a modern British menu displayed on the inevitable copper boards. There's food for everyone: roast vegetable and goat's cheese tart, leek and Caerphilly sausages with tomato sauce and mash, pan-fried organic salmon. The background music is noisy at times and the pub attracts a lively crowd.

directions	Nearest tube: Tufnell Park.
meals	11am-10pm (10am Sundays). Main courses from £7.

Nick May
Dartmouth Arms,
35 York Rise,
Dartmouth Park,
London NW5 1SP
tel   020 7485 3267

map: 5 entry: 276

London

Paradise by Way of Kensal Green
London - Kensal Rise

The exotic name was poached from G K Chesterton. Locals were taken aback when the bohemian bar first opened. Now the area is full of the young and fashionable who little realise that The Paradise — all fairy lights and candles, background jazz and blues — stands on the site of the oldest pub in Brent. A statue of a fallen angel on the wall stares down in surprise on the battered reproduction Regency sofas, wrought-iron garden tables and chairs, and vast palm fronds growing in even vaster planters. The bar itself is small and not the most comfortable but there's still a pubby feel. The place isn't too self-obsessed (in spite of the odd C-list celebrity) and nor are the people who come here. Pop in for a pint of real ale and to look at the papers, or stay for a meal (must book). The menu is modern European with an oriental twist and the food extremely good: Thai green curry, penne with grilled aubergine, artichoke hearts, tomatoes and black olives, beef fillet with peppercorn sauce.

directions	Nearest tube: Kensal Green.
meals	12.30pm-4pm; 7pm-11pm (12.30pm-9pm Sundays). Main courses £8-£9; set menu £10.

Linda McConnell & Paul Halpin
Paradise by Way of Kensal Green,
19 Kilburn Lane,
Kensal Rise,
London NW10 4AE
tel   020 8969 0098

map: 5 entry: 277

The Drapers Arms
London – Islington

The Islington Labour Party was founded in the meeting room upstairs. Islington, the Labour Party and The Drapers have come a long way in the 100-odd years since but they have travelled together and today's Labour group would be just as happy here as their forebears. In the old days, there was probably only beer, sandwiches and Clause 4 on the menu; today's deliberations are more likely to be accompanied by gnocchi with gorgonzola, spinach and pinenuts or perfect foie gras, washed down with an Amarone della Valpolicella at £65 a bottle. There are, of course, less pricey vintages on offer... and delicious roasts on Sundays. In a quiet side street off Upper Street, the once ramshackle Drapers has rejoiced in its renaissance ever since Paul McElhinney took over two years ago. It has won a hatful of awards for its food and is friendly, airy and scrupulously clean. A terrific place in which to settle down on a comfy leather sofa with a jug of Bloody Mary. Outside there's a lovely little garden for summer.

directions	Nearest tube: Highbury & Islington.
meals	12pm-3pm; 7pm-10.30pm. No food Sunday evenings. Main courses £9-£16.

Paul McElhinney
The Drapers Arms,
44 Barnsbury Street,
Islington,
London N1 1ER
tel 020 7619 0348

map: 5 entry: 278

The King's Head Theatre Pub
London – Islington

Dan Crawford set up London's first pub theatre decades ago in the then unfashionable Islington. All these years later, both he and it are still going strong. Indeed, the King's Head has an international reputation and has Tom Stoppard, Kenneth Branagh and Antony Sher among its ardent and vociferous supporters. Book in advance, have dinner, see the show – the newly-tarted up 115-seat theatre is upstairs and is huge fun. But don't think the pub plays second fiddle to the drama: it's a vibrant local with a late licence and jumps with live music every night. There's food for those who watch the show; there are real ales (Adnams, Young's) and a couple of wines by the glass. The King's Head is all about performance and the energy that goes with it, so there's a terrific buzz in the heaving, wooden-floored front bar, and a heady mix of students, Islington trendies, thesps and late-night revellers.

directions	Nearest tubes: Angel; Highbury & Islington.
meals	Pre-theatre set menu £14.

Dan Crawford
The King's Head Theatre Pub,
115 Upper Street, Islington,
London N1 1QN
tel 020 7226 0364
web www.kingsheadtheatre.org

map: 5 entry: 279

London

The House
London - Islington

There's been a transformation here. The old Belinda Castle has become The House, and every day brings another accolade. The chef is a Marco Pierre White protegée — people travel far for the cooking. Mirrors gleam on pale lemon walls, one slice of the wedge-shaped building is given over to white-clothed tables, candles and twinkly lights, the other is a chic and charming bar, with a real fire. Food is simple, gutsy, modern: try courgette and aubergine fritters, roast bream with trompette mushrooms, braised lentils and basil coulis, or good old shepherd's pie. Save space for pudding... treacle pudding, crème brulée, chocolate parfait. It's Islington-cool and far from hushed, but you could relax with anyone here — or pop in just for a pint of their handpumped ale. A treasure.

directions	Nearest tubes: Highbury & Islington; Essex Road.
meals	12pm-2.30pm (3.30pm weekends); 5.30pm-10.30pm (6.30pm Saturdays; 9.30pm Sundays). Main courses £9.50-£22.50; set menu £12.95 & £14.95.
closed	Monday lunchtimes.

Barnaby Meredith
The House,
63-69 Canonbury Road, Islington,
London N1 2DG

tel	020 7704 7410
web	www.inthehouse.biz

map: 5 entry: 280

London

Duke of Cambridge
London - Islington

Geetie Singh and Esther Boulton are on a mission to raise people's awareness of food and where it comes from. At the Duke, the first of two all-organic London pubs run by Singhboulton, 'organic' and 'sustainable' are the watchwords: everything — wines, beers, spirits — is certified organic and they buy as locally as they can to cut down on food miles. Most of the beers are brewed in nearby Shoreditch, meat comes from a single farm, fish is purchased from sustainable sources. If you think it all sounds a touch saintly, note that this is not a meeting place for the worthier-than-thou but a proper pub with a reputation for terrific food, drink, service and atmosphere. Heavens, you can even smoke in the bar! It's a large, airy space with a comfortable, easy, shoestring minimalism; take your fill of the eclectic, mediterranean-influenced food in here or in the big non-smoking restaurant at the back. A great place of taste and intelligence.

directions	Nearest tubes: Angel; Farringdon.
meals	12.30pm-3pm (3.30pm weekends); 6.30pm-10.30pm (10pm Sundays). Main courses £9.50-£16.

Miss Geetie Singh
Duke of Cambridge,
30 St Peter's Street, Islington,
London N1 8JT

tel	020 7359 3066
web	www.singhboulton.co.uk

map: 5 entry: 281

The Garrison Public House
London - London Bridge

Do dinner and a movie – there's a rough-and-ready cinema downstairs with films on Sunday nights, and a great little restaurant up. Gastropub veterans Clive Watson and Adam White have taken on an old Victorian pub, kept the engraved glass windows and remodelled the rest into a light and airy, bare-boarded space. The furniture is silver-sprayed, lamps and objets fill every cranny. Fresh food, from apricots to Orkney mussels, arrives daily from the market down the road, and is reconstructed into dishes that are elaborate but not overly so. With a glass of rioja or a bottle of St Peter's, you'll polish off your roast cod with ribbon leeks and a shrimp and chive sauce in no time at all – or duck breast with shallots, thyme and fondant potato. Snacks include beans on toast. The kitchen is open, staff attractively laid-back, decibels are high, tables are crammed. The place is filled with fashionistas visiting the Fashion Museum and bounces with bonhomie. Forget hushed conversation.

Anchor & Hope
London - Southwark

It's been going for less than a year but has already been heaped with praise. Come for some of the plainest yet gutsiest food in London; chefs Jonathan Jones and Harry Lester will be names to watch in the years to come. Harry describes the cooking as 'English bistro', and give or take the odd foreign exception (a chorizo broth, a melting crème caramel), it is just that. The menu is striking in its simplicity: cockles, Bath chap and pickled onion, devilled kidneys and potato cake, plaice with leeks and herbs, Lancashire hot pot, rib of beef with chips, partridge with red cabbage and quince (a shared dish). The beer comes from the exemplary Charles Wells brewery, the wine list has 18 by the glass. Staff are youthful and eager, décor, in keeping with the 1930s architecture, is sober and understated. The restaurant area glows by candlelight. At the far corner of the rambling bar is the tiny theatre kitchen where you can watch the stars at work. It is seriously busy and you can't book – avoid peak times!

directions	Nearest tube: London Bridge.
meals	12.30pm-3.30pm (4pm Sundays); 6.30pm-10pm (9.30pm Sundays). Main courses £8-£12.

directions	Nearest tubes: Southwark; Waterloo.
meals	12pm-2.30pm; 6pm-10.30pm. Bar meals served all day. No food Mondays. Main courses from £10.
closed	Sundays.

	Clive Watson & Adam White The Garrison Public House, 99 Bermondsey Street, London Bridge, London SE1 0PA
tel	020 7089 9355
web	www.thegarrison.co.uk

	Robert Shaw Anchor & Hope, 36 The Cut, Southwark, London SE1 8LP
tel	020 7928 9898

map: 5 entry: 282

map: 5 entry: 283

London

Greenwich Union
London - Greenwich

Master brewer Alastair Hook has turned this Greenwich boozer into a shrine to his beers. The rich golds and browns of the interior reflect the hues of the glorious ales he painstakingly creates at the nearby Meantime Brewery; his Red, Golden, Amber and Chocolate ales slip down so easily that Sainsbury's has now made them part of their range. (If you're not sure which one to go for, helpful staff behind the bar are more than happy to give you a taster.) This quirky little pub also serves some fine food, the Spanish chef willing to concoct delicious tapas at short notice. On Sundays, the so-called Potty Roasters take over the kitchen, feeding eager diners with succulent roasts, fresh vegetables and "crazy gravy". All, including children and dogs, are welcome here, and the spontaneous creativity of local residents, fuelled by Alastair's beers, is a rich source of entertainment for a lively crowd on the famous, regular Open Mike Nights.

directions	Exit Greenwich station, left & 2nd right (Royal Hill), pub on right.
meals	12.30pm-10pm (5pm weekends). Main courses £5.50-£7.50.

Alastair Hook
Greenwich Union,
56 Royal Hill, Greenwich,
London SE10 8RT
tel   020 8692 6258
web www.meantimebrewing.co.uk

map: 5 entry: 284

London

Royal Inn on the Park
London - Hackney

There are many fine pubs clustered around Victoria Park but none of them as enjoyable as this one. A massive Victorian local guarding the edge of the park, it has all the faded grandeur its name suggests; high ceilings, dark corners, open fires – a truly pubby feel. There's also a bar that can be hired for private functions. In summer it's fantastic, with a big covered seating area outside and a garden that backs the park: relax with the children and watch the world go by. The place buzzes in the evening with a mix of fashionable – though not achingly so – new East Enders and traditional characters. Chalked up on the menu is some tasty pub grub: salmon and sweet potato fishcakes, bacon and dolce latte risotto, rib steak. Puddings are a speciality. To drink... a well-kept real ale or one of 12 decent wines available by the glass. The jukebox that favours jazz and funk is usually drowned out by the volubility of the crowd as the evening fizzes towards closing time.

directions	Nearest tube: Mile End.
meals	12pm-3pm; 6pm-9.30pm; 12pm-9.30pm Saturdays; 12pm-5pm Sundays. No food Sunday evenings. Main courses £7.50-£12.

John Cheeseman
Royal Inn on the Park,
111 Lauriston Road,
Hackney,
London E9 7HJ
tel   020 8985 3321

map: 5 entry: 285

Manchester

The White Hart
Lydgate

Decay was settling in at this 18th-century ale house when Charles Brierley took it over 10 years ago. It has since been transformed into a charming restaurant-pub. Relax in the bar with a glass of John Willie Lees, toast your toes by the wood-burning stove and admire its colourful lack of clutter, or have your drink in a room lined with Tibetan photographs. If you are hungry you could try out the homemade sausages (five, with five different kinds of mash) – or move upstairs to the restaurant, where more extravagant treats are in store. Delicacy combines with robustness in unusually fine cooking: smoked pigeon breast, feuilleté of wild mushrooms, pan-fried cod with tomato compôte. Stay the night: your host's knack of combining period pieces with modern style in the rooms might persuade you to. This is a beautiful village where, on a fine day, you can stretch your eyes to the Cheshire Plain.

directions	East from Oldham on A669 for 2.5 miles. Just before hill right onto A6050; 50yds on left.
meals	12pm-2.30pm; 6pm-9.30pm; 1pm-7.30pm Sundays. Main courses £11.75-£16.25.
rooms	12: 10 doubles, 2 twins £105. Singles £75.

Charles Brierley
The White Hart,
51 Stockport Road, Lydgate,
Oldham, Manchester OL4 4JJ
tel 01457 872566
web www.thewhitehart.co.uk

map: 14 entry: 286

Merseyside

Baltic Fleet
Liverpool

Alone on a dockland corner, this landlocked Fleet's Victorian fabric remains unchanged with no concessions to poshness – and people like it that way. The small marble-topped bar counter is crammed with handpumps (most ferrying beers brewed in the engine room below) and furnishings are engagingly timeworn: settles, plain chairs, marble-topped tables. Two rooms beyond offer more comfort. The first has a servery for baguettes, toasties and Scouse soup, its walls lined with pictures of Liverpool's past and Simon Holt's forebears – traders and shipowners when the Baltic was built. The second is a snug in the 'bows' with that Liver Building view; hole up here in front of the fire and imagine sailors swapping tales. Upstairs is a bistro serving gravadlax with dill mustard, trout en papillotte, pan-fried leg of lamb. An honest outpost with cheerful, hard-working staff; the more engaging the longer you stay.

directions	Liverpool city centre, opposite Albert Dock.
meals	12pm-2.30pm (4pm Sundays); 6pm-9.30pm. No food Sunday & Monday evenings. Main course bar £2.50-£3.95; bistro £7.95-£12.95.

Simon Holt
Baltic Fleet,
33a Wapping, Liverpool,
Merseyside L1 8DQ
tel 0151 709 3116
web www.wappingbeers.com

map: 13 entry: 287

The Philharmonic
Liverpool

The Phil was built by Liverpool brewers Robert Cain & Co in the style of a gentlemen's club: a place for bodily refreshment after the aesthetic excitements of the Philharmonic Hall opposite. There's ornate Victorian extravagance at every turn, impossibly high ceilings, elaborate embellishment, etched glass; the gents is decked in marble and mosaic, its porcelain fittings of historical importance. Sweep through the columned entrance into the imposing, mosaic-tiled central bar, gawp at the scale. Beyond, a succession of small rooms and snugs separated by mahogany partitions, then a Grand Lounge with a stately frieze and table service for lunch: you can settle down to baked potatoes or proper fish and chips, all reasonably priced. In spite of the remarkable surroundings – or possibly because of them – the Philharmonic is very popular with students. It is a great pub serving excellent beers, wines and whiskies and a huge dose of cheer.

The Red Cat
Crank

Chef Ian Martin is breathing life back into the very ordinary-looking Red Cat and drawing people in droves. It's still the village pub with real beer in the bar, but the food – fresh, modern, inventive – is a surprise. Local farms supply vegetables and local shoots provide game. There's a standard bar menu and a terrific-value two-course lunch. Try grilled haloumi and roasted vegetables, Lune salmon with Cajun spices and salad, free-range Bowland pork loin with asparagus and girolle mushroom sauce, hand-made noodles with roasted vegetables and basil sauce. Everything, including the bread, is made here. The wine list is amazing for a pub, with over 100 clarets from outstanding growths and vintages, at modest mark-ups; Ian will gladly steer you through his cellar which he's assembled with skill and passion.

directions	City centre; between the Cathedrals at corner of Hardman Street.
meals	12pm-6pm (3pm in summer); 12pm-3pm weekends (5.30pm weekends in summer). Main course bar £4.95-£7.95.

directions	Exit M6 junc. 23; A580/A570 & follow signs to Crank.
meals	12pm-2pm; 6pm-9.30pm; 12pm-8pm Sundays. No food Mondays & Tuesdays. Main courses £6.50-£15.95; set menu £9.95 (2 courses).

Marie-Louise Wong
The Philharmonic,
36 Hope Street,
Liverpool,
Merseyside L1 9BX
tel   0151 707 2837

map: 13 entry: 288

Ian Martin
The Red Cat,
8 Red Cat Lane,
Crank, St Helens,
Merseyside WA11 8RU
tel   01744 882422

map: 13 entry: 289

An evening in the life of The Griffin Inn

The smooth glide of the swan across the calm surface of water is, as we all know, entirely due to the frenzied paddling of two busy feet out of sight. I have often wondered whether successful pubs are similar – calm surface, chaotic inner workings. The Pullan family, who own the Griffin Inn (entry no. 441), had invited me to spend time behind the scenes, so I would see.

The Pullan parents, Nigel and Bridget, bought the Griffin Inn because it was a way of keeping four sons employed. Son James was in charge, directing events from a central bar that gleamed like the bar of an ocean liner. He poured me a glass of red wine then disappeared, leaving me with barman Charlie and the locals who had arrived for their evening drinks.

Our small, softly-lit wooden enclosure was an inviting place to stand and chat, to ponder the menu or daily papers. It was the hub of the pub, even of the village. While pulling local Harveys real ales, Charlie explained some of his daily tasks such as 'bottling up and down'

(restocking bottles and removing empties), and checking beer taste and pipelines. Although every skilled barman must know a 'White Russian' from a 'Black', every Sussex barman must also recognise a 'Mother-in-law' (half Harveys Old, half Harveys Bitter).

When a slight cloudiness crept into the ale it was time to take to the pub's cellar. Here Marcus, affectionately known by those at ground level as the 'Cellar Monkey', tends the beers at a constant temperature of around 52-58 degrees. With up to 90 gallons of Harveys served a week, pipes must be kept clean; the clarity of the beer must be checked (too cold and it will go cloudy) and any dead yeast settling around the tap must be drawn off. Before long a call of 'It's on' again brought clear mahogany ale to the taps upstairs and relief to the thirsty.

Back above ground James caught up with me and I joined him on his speedy and skilled round of inspection. An energetic operation was running, the feet were paddling hard. Then he led me to the kitchen.

Boxes lined a spotless central surface, their colourful contents ready to be blanched, fried, sliced or grated for the main courses. Large jars of richly coloured homemade jams and chutneys caught the bright overhead

lights. Anne was preparing for 'starters and puddings', chef Simon 'the mains' and Christine 'the washing up'. Since the morning meat and fish delivery much had already been done including the pounding of 12lb of bread dough.

Another brother, Daniel, appeared at the door having 'sat six'. Andrew, as Front of House, skimmed over to offer aperitifs to them. Before long food orders decorated the kitchen walls. Anne (who came to the Griffin to help with a wedding 25 years ago and never left) tossed sizzling seared scallops on a huge gas hob, while on a stainless steel shelf below, plump, homemade ravioli waited for a boiling plunge. Simon was preparing main courses such as pheasant and steaks on the char grill. On the call of 'service' the Pullan brothers collected plates and delivered them to the restaurant with panache. As diners surveyed their beautifully presented orders, James, armed with dazzling white cloth and gleaming bottle of Burgundy, circled the table like a matador.

It was nearly midnight before the brothers slowed their pace, when every diner had left. Daniel's local title as King of Cappuccino remained unchallenged and chef Simon had phoned orders in to that night's fishing fleet.

I sank into a luxurious four-poster in a soft, colourful bedroom with fine linen, a deep free-standing bath, fluffy robes, handmade soaps and shampoos – and slept beautifully.

The Griffin is clearly as loved by those who work there as by those who visit. As I left, Grace and Shirley were ironing freshly laundered sheets, barman Toby was delivering logs to the bar door and Harveys' draymen were rolling barrels down the street to the cellar – more unseen hard slog to keep a happy and successful inn running without a hitch.

Rebecca Harris

Norfolk

Wildebeest Arms
Stoke Holy Cross

In the 1990s Henry Watt decided to introduce good food to his country inn – a rarity in the days of starchy pub grub. A decade on, The Wildebeest is one of the most popular dining pubs in Norfolk, and booking for both lunch and dinner is essential. The 19th-century building may be no great shakes from the outside, but there's a special atmosphere within. Sympathetically modernised to create one long room simply split by a central bar, this is dominated by a cheerful log fire. Rich yellow walls offset dark oak beams, there are fresh flowers on polished tables and an African theme to match the pub's name. (A former partner was known variously as 'wild man' and 'beast'… it's a long story.) Ales include Adnams, there's a good choice of wines by the glass and an interesting list, and the menu is up-to-the-minute with everything freshly made. Who could resist pot-roast duck breast with cocotte potatoes, roasted butternut squash, crispy Alsace lardon and sautéed cabbage with redcurrant jus? Chef Daniel Smith may enjoy a bit of leonine bravura, but he is just as at home with good old English favourites like sausage and mash and sticky toffee pudding.

directions	Off A140, 3 miles south of Norwich.
meals	12pm-2pm; 7pm-10pm. Main courses £9.95-£18.50; set menu £14.95 (lunch).
closed	25-26 December.

Henry Watt
Wildebeest Arms,
82-86 Norwich Road,
Stoke Holy Cross, Norwich,
Norfolk NR14 8QJ

tel   01508 492497

map: 11 entry: 290

Norfolk

Norfolk

Walpole Arms
Itteringham

Enjoying fine food and wine should be an adventure, a voyage of discovery – so says Richard Bryan, ex-producer of BBC's *Masterchef*, and co-owner of this famous Norfolk pub. Exploration, one assumes, carries less guilt than indulgence. Sweating over a hot stove is Andy Parle, once head chef to Alastair Little. His daily menus reflect the seasons and a delight in fresh local produce: Cromer crab, Morston mussels, venison from the Gunton estate. Farm-fresh fruits and vegetables are used in chicken, ham and pepper terrine with home-pickled veg; braised lamb shank with garlic mash, gem lettuce, peas and mint; baked pumpkin custard with stem-ginger ice cream. You can eat in the bar, with rough brick walls, beamed ceilings, standing timbers and big open fire, or in the stylish dining room. There are fine East Anglian ales from Adnams and Woodforde's, and a first-class list of wines, 12 by the glass.

Buckinghamshire Arms
Blickling

This handsome, 17th-century coaching inn was originally the estate builder's house for Blickling Hall, by whose Jacobean gates it deferentially stands. Later it became the quarters for the servants and guests. Like the Hall, it is owned by the National Trust but functions as a self-contained inn, serving the locals in the winter and the sightseers in the summer, when the big lawn and sheltered courtyard have an outside servery. Tuck into baked potatoes and baguettes, with a pint of local cider or Woodforde's Wherry. In the evening: steak and kidney pie, grilled trout, Norfolk treacle tart. The charming and well-furnished bars have open fires, old pine and a small snug at the front, Spy cartoons on the walls, cribbage – utterly in keeping. Upstairs bedrooms have their own bathrooms and dramatic evening views across to the flood-lit Hall. Walk in the park and admire the lake, gothic folly and the pyramidal mausoleum; the Hall is open from April to October.

directions	From Aylsham towards Blickling, then 1st right to Itteringham.
meals	12pm-2pm (2.30pm Sundays); 7pm-9.30pm. Main courses £6.50-£16.
closed	3pm-6pm (7pm Sundays).

directions	From Aylsham B1354; pub opp.Hall.
meals	12pm-2pm; 7pm-9pm. Main courses £9.75-£13.95.
rooms	3 doubles £75-£85. Singles £50.
closed	3pm-6.30pm.

	Richard Bryan
	Walpole Arms,
	The Common, Itteringham,
	Aylsham, Norfolk NR11 7AR
tel	01263 587258
web	www.thewalpolearms.co.uk

	Robert Dawson-Smith
	Buckinghamshire Arms,
	Blickling,
	Aylsham,
	Norfolk NR11 6NF
tel	01263 732133

map: 11 entry: 291

map: 11 entry: 292

Norfolk

Saracen's Head
Wolterton

Close to Norfolk's bleakly lovely coast: food, real ale, good wines, a delightful sheltered courtyard and walled garden, this is why people come here. But the food is the deepest seduction. Robert and his team cook up some of Norfolk's "most delicious wild and tame treats". Morston mussels with cider and cream, pigeon, Cromer crab, venison, regal ribs of beef on Sundays, old favourites like treacle tart… vegetarians are not forgotten either. The bar is as chatty as a bar could be, a refreshing antidote to bars with piped music and fruit machines – Robert will have none of them. There's a parlour with a big brick fireplace, deep red walls, colourful plastic tablecloths, candles in wine bottles, a black leather banquette along two walls. Modest bedrooms have a Bloomsbury feel. The whole mood is of quirky, committed individuality – slightly arty, slightly unpredictable and in the middle of Norfolk's nowhere.

directions	From A140 follow signs for Erpingham. Pass church, follow road to Carthorpe & Wolterton.
meals	12.30pm-2pm; 7.30pm-9pm. Main courses £9.75-£13.95.
rooms	7: 6 doubles, 1 twin £70-£80. Singles £45.

	Robert Dawson-Smith Saracens Head, Wolterton, Erpingham, Norfolk NR11 7LZ
tel	01263 768909
web	www.saracenshead-norfolk.co.uk

map: 11 entry: 293

Norfolk

Red Lion
Stiffkey

Stiffkey overlooks a stretch of rare north Norfolk hill-country, a view once shared by three pubs. They, the Red Lion included, became victims of the Watney revolution in the 1960s. Then, in 1990, after three decades as a private house, the fine 16th-century brick and flint cottage was resurrected as a free house and has been thriving ever since. It attracts a loyal local clientele for its fresh fish from King's Lynn and its first-rate ales from East Anglian brewers. It is rustic not smart: three rooms have bare floorboards or aged quarry tiles, open log fires and a simple mix of stripped wooden settles, old pews and scrubbed tables. Chatty locals supping pints of Wherry rub shoulders with booted walkers and birdwatchers recovering from the rigours of the Peddars Way path and Stiffkey's famous marshes. After a day on the beach, the large and airy conservatory is great for families, as is the terraced garden overlooking the meadows and valley.

directions	From Wells 4 miles along coast road towards Cromer.
meals	12pm-2pm; 6.30pm-9pm. Main courses £8.50-£9.95.
closed	3pm-6pm.

	Andrew Waddison Red Lion, 44 Wells Road, Stiffkey, Wells-next-the-Sea, Norfolk NR23 1AJ
tel	01328 830552

map: 11 entry: 294

Norfolk

Three Horseshoes
Warham

An atmospheric jewel in a rural backwater, this former row of 18th-century cottages hides a mile from the coastal path. The three utterly plain, unspoilt rooms have barely changed since the 1930s – gas lights, rough deal tables, Victorian fireplaces and a pianola that performs... occasionally. Vintage entertainment includes an intriguing American Mills one-armed bandit converted for modern coins and a rare Norfolk 'twister' set into the ceiling – for playing village roulette, apparently. The food is in keeping. No chips, no 'international cuisine', just traditional English dishes based emphatically on Norfolk produce including fish and locally-shot game. Exemplary home-cooking is enhanced by top East Anglian ales straight from the cask. Alternatively, sample the local Whin Hill cider or the homemade lemonade.

directions	Warham off A149 between Wells-next-the-Sea & Stiffkey; 2 miles east of Wells.
meals	12pm-1.45pm; 6pm-8.30pm. Main courses £6.50-£9.
rooms	4: 1 double; 2 doubles, 1 single sharing bathroom. £48-£52; singles £24.

Iain Salmon
Three Horseshoes,
Bridge Street, Warham,
Wells-next-the-Sea,
Norfolk NR23 1NL
tel   01328 710547

map: 11 entry: 295

Norfolk

Crown Hotel
Wells-next-the-Sea

The interior of this handsome 16th-century coaching inn has been neatly rationalised yet is still atmospheric with its open fires, bare boards and easy chairs. And it's run by an enterprising landlord who knows how to cook. Order pub food at the bar and eat it in the lounges, the lovely modern conservatory or the Sun Deck: a hearty serving of Brancaster mussels, perhaps, with locally brewed Adnams Bitter. Bold colours, modern art and attractively-laid tables suggest there's life in the restaurant too, where local ingredients are translated into global ideas: Wells crab spring rolls with dipping sauce, roasted partridge with pancetta, red wine risotto and balsamic onions. The crisp elegance has also found its way to the bedrooms with their white linen and wicker chairs; front rooms facing the small green are the pick. A happy, relaxed place.

directions	On B1105, 10 miles north of Fakenham.
meals	12pm-2.30pm; 6.30pm-9.30pm. Main courses £8.50-£14; set menu £29.95.
rooms	11 twins/doubles £85-£95. Singles £60.

Chris & Jo Coubrough
Crown Hotel,
The Buttlands, Wells-next-the-Sea,
Norfolk NR23 1EX
tel   01328 710209
web   www.thecrownhotelwells.co.uk

map: 11 entry: 296

Norfolk

The Victoria
Holkham

Tom and Polly (Viscount and Viscountess Coke) took the place on a few years ago. The result is a stunning country pub-hotel at the entrance to Holkham Hall. The building is matchless 18th century, the interiors grand but unintimidating. A contemporary colonial theme runs through – it's hugely stylish, with much dark wood and vibrant furnishings from Rajasthan. Gentle staff are as happy for you to pop in for a ploughman's and a glass of Woodforde's Wherry in the sprawling bar-lounge as for a slap-up meal in the restaurant. Food is very good, with menus focusing on local produce, especially estate game in winter: carpaccio of venison with fig purée, beef with celeriac and baby beetroot, seafood from the Norfolk coast. Even the fish and chips are fabulous. Barbecues in the courtyard are a summer treat, and bedrooms are as seductive and as original as you'd expect.

directions	On A149, 3 miles west of Wells-next-the-Sea.
meals	12pm-3pm; 7pm-9.30pm. Main courses £7-£16.
rooms	11: 10 doubles, £110-£170; 1 suite £200-£490. Singles £55-£125; self-catering lodge for 4 £330-£950.

Tom & Polly Coke
The Victoria,
Park Road, Holkham,
Norfolk NR23 1RG
tel 01328 711008
web www.victoriaatholkham.co.uk

map: 11 entry: 297

Norfolk

The Hoste Arms
Burnham Market

As the brochure says, pub and owner are made for each other (that's Paul they are talking about): "both have struggled to avoid being popular country attractions". Brilliantly too – The Hoste has won almost every prize going. It's a luxurious place that has a genius of its own – successful mixtures of bold colour, sofas to sink into, panelled walls, an art gallery, log fires. And food to be eaten in rapture, anywhere and anytime. The "modern British with Pacific Rim influences" menu changes every five weeks – seared tuna with ginger and lemongrass, roasted ham hock, Burnham Creek oysters. Every bedroom is different: a tartan four-poster here, a swagged half-tester there, a leather telly console in the brand-new, state-of-the-art Zulu wing. There are bowls and blankets for your dogs, breakfast lasts as long as you like, and the ales on tap pull in a fascinating array of regulars, from fishers to film stars.

directions	Off B1155, 5 miles west of Wells-next-the-Sea. Inn by green & church in village centre.
meals	12pm-2pm; 7pm-9pm. Main courses £8.95-£16.50.
rooms	36 twins/doubles £108-£236. Singles £74.

Paul & Jeanne Whittome
The Hoste Arms,
The Green, Burnham Market,
Norfolk PE31 8HD
tel 01328 738777
web www.hostearms.co.uk

map: 11 entry: 298

The White Horse
Brancaster Staithe

Enter the dapper, white pub, pass the front bar — lively with locals downing East Anglian beers — and head for the conservatory dining room with its sweeping, astonishing views. The White Horse is surprisingly chic for these parts, with its Kensington-on-sea muted tones (sand, stone, aqua and terracotta), driftwood finds, contemporary paintings, sepia photographs and fresh flowers. Local oysters, crabs, mussels and smoked fish are matched by exemplary steaks, lamb and pork; make the most of prawns with lemon and dill mayonnaise, baked bream with a cassoulet of puy lentils, roast pear with brandy snaps. Browse the papers from a cushioned wicker chair, nurse a malt whisky or a wine by the glass. Bedrooms in a wavy extension facing the tidal marshes and North Norfolk Coastal Path have generous proportions and a patio each; the roof is grassed over so that the fine-weather sun deck, dining room and some of the main house bedrooms (ask for the split-level room at the top, with telescope) have a clean view that stretches all the way to Scolt Head Island. Comfort, huge sunsets, fine food, big breakfasts, and a lovely welcome for children and dogs.

directions	On A149 between Hunstanton & Wells-next-the-Sea.
meals	12pm-2pm; 7pm-9.15pm. Main courses £9.75-£15.95.
rooms	15: 10 doubles, 5 twins £104-£116. Singles £72-£78.

Cliff Nye
The White Horse,
Main Road, Brancaster Staithe,
Norfolk PE31 8BY

tel	01485 210262
web	www.whitehorsebrancaster.co.uk

map: 11 entry: 299

Lord Nelson
Burnham Thorpe

Once The Plough, the pub changed its name two years after the Battle of Trafalgar to commemorate Burnham Thorpe's most famous son (Nelson threw a dinner for the village here to celebrate his return to sea). It has barely changed in 100 years: ancient benches and settles, worn brick, tile floors, a servery instead of a bar, distinguish this marvellous place. If a tot of Nelson's Blood (a devilish concoction of cranberry juice and rum) doesn't tempt, order a pint of Woodforde's Wherry or Greene King IPA tapped from the cask. Nelson memorabilia reach into every corner of the small, characterful rooms — and into the Victory Barn restaurant where the annual Trafalgar Night Dinner is held on October 21st before an open fire. All in all, a unique local asset, with a family-friendly garden, imaginative food (terrine with redcurrant jelly, pork in cider and wholegrain mustard sauce) and a past that is well respected by David and Penny Thorley, the new licensees.

directions	Off A149, B1155 & B1355; 2 miles south of Burnham Market.
meals	12pm-2pm; 7pm-9pm. No food Sunday evenings. Main courses £7.95-£16.95.
closed	Mondays in winter.

David & Penny Thorley
Lord Nelson, Walsingham Road,
Burnham Thorpe, Burnham Market,
Norfolk PE31 8HL
tel   01328 738241
web   www.nelsonslocal.co.uk

map: 11 entry: 300

The Lifeboat Inn
Thornham

Ideal for some away-from-it-all, country-traditional, unpretentious good cheer. It's been an ale house since the 16th century and they still serve real cider and a decent pint: Adnams, Greene King, Woodforde's. The food is equally decent — try the bar, cosy with beams, glowing paraffin lamps and roaring fire, for its staples: steaming cauldrons of Norfolk mussels and chips and real ale-battered fish — or the more formal, richly coloured restaurant for dishes with a more sophisticated ring: halibut with a rice timbale and mild curry sauce, beef fillet with a brandy and mushroom cream sauce. The bedrooms are pine-furnished, not huge but entirely functional and well-equipped; most have mind-clearing views over Thornham harbour to the sea. Come when the wind blows and the hall fire flickers around damp dogs, while the odd stuffed animal looks on. Bask in the sheltered courtyard when it's sunny and let the children run. A place to be comfortable, relaxed and well-fed.

directions	From Hunstanton A149; 1st left on entering Thornham.
meals	12pm-2.30pm; 6.30pm-9.30pm. Main courses £8.50-£15.95.
rooms	12 twins/doubles.

Charles Coker
The Lifeboat Inn,
Ship Lane, Thornham,
Norfolk PE36 6LT
tel   01485 512236
web   www.lifeboatinn.co.uk

map: 11 entry: 301

Norfolk

Rose & Crown
Snettisham

Roses round the door in summer and twisting passages within, it is quintessentially English. Homemade burgers with red onion relish, and fish and chips with minted mushy peas will please the traditionalists among you, but the menu soon zooms into the dizzy realms of swordfish and spring onion, hot and sour soup, corn-fed chicken and sag aloo curried baked beans. There are also 30 wines on the wide-ranging list, half available by the glass. The Rose & Crown is still proud to be a pub, with good beers – Adnams, Greene King IPA, Bass – on handpump. The walled garden was once the village bowling green and young visitors will love the wooden play fort and the animals (guinea pigs and chipmunks!). Inside, a warren of rooms filled with old beams and log fires, and a further flurry of bedrooms for those who wish to stay – country-house chic with "not a drop of pine in sight".

directions	Off A149 north of King's Lynn.
meals	12pm-2pm (2.30pm weekends); 6pm-9pm (9.30pm Fri & Sat). Main courses £9-£14.
rooms	11 twins/doubles £70-£80. Singles £45.

Anthony & Jeannette Goodrich
Rose & Crown,
Old Church Road, Snettisham,
King's Lynn, Norfolk PE31 7LX
tel 01485 541382
web www.roseandcrownsnettisham.co.uk

map: 11 entry: 302

Northamptonshire

White Horse
Kings Sutton

In 1872 a UFO resembling a haystack flew over King's Sutton. It produced the same effect as a tornado, then vanished. It may be farfetched to suggest that the rustic White Horse is that UFO come to rest on the (very pretty) church green. But, like a UFO, it is super-modern inside. The White Horse had a complete overhaul in 2000 and is now a smart dining pub with a chic-rustic feel – chunky pine tables and chairs on light wooden floors, low beams, the odd rug and interesting picture, open fires, a country pub feel. Two flagstoned, no-smoking rooms are for eating in, and people come from miles to savour the likes of rump of lamb with creamy flageolet beans, thyme and roasted garlic, or pan-fried scallops with honey-roasted pears. Puddings, like coffee crème brulée, are a speciality, and there is a generous array of wines by the glass. Brakspears recently took the pub over but little has changed – apart from the beers.

directions	Off A4260 south of Banbury, just north of Adderbury.
meals	12pm-2pm; 12.30pm-3pm Sundays; 6pm-9pm. No food Sunday eve. Main courses £7.50-£14.

Matthew Stimpson
White Horse,
The Square,
Kings Sutton, Banbury,
Northamptonshire OX17 3RF
tel 01295 810843

map: 9 entry: 303

George & Dragon
Chacombe

It's an old pub – the building dates from 1640 and has been added to over the centuries – but a relative newcomer given that Chacombe appears in the Domesday Book. There's a great atmosphere at the George and Dragon, whose mellow front is festooned with flowers in summer. Like almost all successful country pubs, it's reputation has been built on its food. Ray Bennett has established a team of four who turn out modern, mouthwatering dishes – supreme of salmon with citrus couscous, or pasta with tomato, olives and tuna – as well as the good old favourites like steak and kidney pie. Almost all the ingredients are local, and there are two real ales and four wines by the glass. Expect flagstones, low beams, simple furnishings and a massive open fire. There are also three bedrooms, old and full of character yet well equipped and with their own bathrooms. Chacombe is a delightful conservation village.

Royal Oak
Eydon

Eydon is as remote as it is possible for a village in the south-east of England to be. It may not be isolated – it is only seven miles from the motorway – but it is secluded. The menu – fresh, short, regularly changing – is the big attraction. The pretty, 17th-century honey-stone pub has old flagstones, exposed stone walls, an inglenook and that Sunday-papers-and-a pint feel. You'll find chalked up not only the best of traditional pub food – Welsh lamb with rosemary and garlic and mustard mash – but also the best of exotic: grilled Australian goatfish with lemon grass and coriander, say, accompanied by a spicy lime and chilli salsa. The long bar is propped up by ale-quaffing regulars; the rest is made over to a darts room and three small dining areas. There are picnic seats out in front and tables in the courtyard, and a warm and family-friendly atmosphere.

directions	M40 junc. 11; A361 for Daventry; Chacombe signed in 1 mile.
meals	12pm-2pm; 6.30pm-9.30pm; 12pm-8pm Sundays. Main courses £8.50-£12.50.
rooms	3: 1 double, 1 twin, 1 family £64-£94. Singles £44.95.

directions	Off A361 midway between Banbury & Daventry.
meals	12pm-2pm; 7pm-9pm. Main courses £10.95-£12.95.

Ray Bennett
George & Dragon,
Silver Street,
Chacombe, Banbury,
Northamptonshire OX17 2JR
tel 01295 711500

J Lefevre
Royal Oak,
6 Lime Avenue,
Eydon,
Northamptonshire NN11 3PG
tel 01327 263167

map: 9 entry: 304

map: 9 entry: 305

The Star Inn
Sulgrave

George Washington's family lived in the village until 1700 so Americans have visited in their droves since the 1920s, and it was around then that The Star was set up by the Hook Norton brewery. Now it's run by Jamie and Charlotte King, who could not resist the inn's old-world charm. Low ceilings, small windows and polished flagstones make for a delightful atmosphere in both bar and restaurant; cushioned window seats, red carpeting and a big inglenook add comfort. Jamie cooked at the Harvey Nichols restaurant in London: you'll eat as well here. The blackboard chalks up some delectable-sounding food: Gressingham duck breast with minted leeks and sauté potatoes, perhaps, or sea bass with a mussel, prawn and parsley sauce. In summer dine under a vine-covered trellis at the back.

The King's Head
Wadenhoe

Richard Spolton had "cooked everywhere" before settling at the King's Head. At first glance the two make an unlikely couple: the cosmopolitan globetrotter and the 17th-century pub. But, this unconventional partnership really works. These days most village pubs need to draw folk from further afield to thrive. They come here to tuck into Richard's medallions of beef on a pâté-stuffed crouton with peppercorn sauce, or plaice and asparagus on field mushrooms with cream. The River Nene runs past the bottom of the big grassy garden – great for kids – so you can visit the pub by boat (some do). Arriving by car – down the deeply-wooded road over humpback bridges – feels special, too. No fruit machines or noisy concessions to the modern age here; just books, skittles, open fires and the irresistible waft of Richard's cooking. Well-kept beers include Adnams and Badger IPA.

directions	M40 junc. 11; A422; Brackley; B4525; follow signs to Sulgrave Manor.
meals	12pm-2pm (3pm Sundays); 6.30pm-9pm. No food Monday evenings. Main courses £9-£15.
rooms	3: 2 doubles, 1 twin £60-£70. Singles £35-£40.
closed	Sunday evenings; Monday lunchtimes Jan & Feb; Boxing Day.

directions	Off A605, 4 miles south west of Oundle.
meals	12pm-2pm; 7pm-9pm. No food Sunday-Tuesday evenings. Main courses £9.50-£13.50.
closed	Tuesdays in winter.

Jamie & Charlotte King
The Star Inn,
Manor Road, Sulgrave, Banbury,
Northamptonshire OX17 2SA
tel   01295 760389
web   www.starinnsulgrave.com

Richard Spolton & Louise Rowell
The King's Head,
Church Street, Wadenhoe, Oundle,
Northamptonshire PE8 5ST
tel   01832 720024
web   www.kingzed.co.uk

map: 9 entry: 306

map: 10 entry: 307

The Falcon
Fotheringhay

'Civilised' is the word for the Falcon, a smashing place serving wonderful food. (No surprise, really, as it's a member of the Huntsbridge Group – see the Pheasant at Keyston and the Three Horseshoes at Madingley.) Discreetly, stylishly modernised, it keeps its pub feel – darts in the tap bar, an open fire in the larger bar and well-kept Adnams on handpump – in spite of all the spoiling extras: soft colours, high-back tapestry-covered chairs, evening candlelight, fresh flowers. Richard III was born in Fotheringhay Castle and Mary Queen of Scots was executed here. The castle is now a mound, but the medieval church is worth a visit and the bar deftly picks up on the history in the prints on the walls. For a change of mood, head for the elegant, double conservatory; it has the same monthly-changing menu as the bar but the feel is more contemporary – light, open, with Lloyd Loom chairs and impressive church views. Ray Smikle's cooking is never over-elaborate, whether it's potato and chive tart, peppered and roasted loin of venison, panna cotta with preserved cherries or vanilla rice pud. Wines are good (of course) with an excellent selection by the glass.

directions	Off A605, 4 miles north east of Oundle.
meals	12pm-2pm; 6.30pm-9.30pm. Main courses £8.50-£12.50.
closed	3pm-6pm.

Ray Smikle & John Hoskins
The Falcon,
Fotheringhay, Oundle,
Northamptonshire PE8 5HZ
tel   01832 226254
web   www.huntsbridge.com

map: 10 entry: 308

Olde Ship Hotel
Seahouses

The Glen dynasty has been at the helm of this nautical gem for close on a century. The inn sparkles with maritime memorabilia to remind you of Seahouses' fine heritage and the days when Grace Darling rowed through huge seas to rescue stricken souls. Settle into the atmospheric main bar by the glowing fire with a decent pint (there are eight ales to choose from) and gaze out across the harbour to Farne Islands and the Longstone Light. In the bigger 'cabin' bar you can get stuck into some enjoyable, home-cooked food – fresh crab soup and sandwiches, steak and Guinness pie, liver and onion casserole, hearty fish stew. Rooms of all configurations, some quite small, are beautifully furnished, while bigger rooms in the building next door have superb views over the harbour. The place creaks with history.

Ship Inn
Low Newton-by-the-Sea

A deeply authentic coastal inn with tongue and groove boarding and flooring, old settles, scrubbed tables and a solid-fuel stove. Step in and you step back 100 years: landlady Christine Forsyth fell in love with the simplicity of the place and gives you provender to match. Good local beers (Wylam Gold Tankard and Landlord's Choice) and fair trade coffee and chocolate go well with a menu built around the best local produce – simple, fresh, satisfying. Local hand-picked-crab rolls (stotties), lobster from yards away, Craster kippers from two miles down the coast, ploughman's with local unpasteurised cheddar or New Barns free-range ham. In the evenings there's often a choice (venison, grilled red mullet) but book first. Park on a compulsory plot back from the beach and take the short walk to the sand, green and pub – worth every step.

directions	B1340 off A1 8 miles north of Alnwick; inn above harbour.	directions	From Alnwick B1340 for Seahouses for 8 miles to crossroads; straight over, follow signs.
meals	12pm-2pm; 7pm-8.30pm Main courses £6.50-£10.30.	meals	12pm-2.30pm; phone for evening opening & food times in winter. Main courses £6.50-£22.
rooms	18 twins/doubles £90-£96. Singles £45-£48.		

	Alan & Jean Glen Olde Ship Hotel, 9 Main Street, Seahouses, Northumberland NE68 7RD		Christine Forsyth Ship Inn, The Square, Low Newton-by-the-Sea, Alnwick, Northumberland NE66 3EL
tel	01665 720200	tel	01665 576262
web	www.seahouses.co.uk	web	www.theshipinnnewtonbythesea.co.uk

map: 17 entry: 309

map: 17 entry: 310

The Tankerville Arms
Eglingham

Exploring the rolling acres between Northumberland's dramatic coastline and the wild Cheviot Hills? Charming Eglingham has the best pub for miles. The long, stone-built tavern is a boon for ramblers and cyclists, and cheerfully mixes traditional and new. In the lounge and bar are carpeted and stone-flagged floors, blackened beams, coal fires, plush seating and old-fashioned dominoes; in the kitchen, a modern approach. John Blackmore, owner and cook, chalks up blackboard menus featuring fresh, local, seasonal ingredients — ham and duck confit terrine with toasted brioche; black pudding tart with goat's cheese, roasted vegetables and garlic sauce. Food goes traditional in good sandwiches and Sunday lunchtime roasts, served in one of the cosy bars or in the converted barn restaurant. Children are welcome and drinkers kept happy with a range of thoroughly respectable ales, including the local Hadrian and Border brews, and a well-balanced list of wines.

The Pheasant
Stannersburn

A really super little inn, the kind you hope to chance upon: not grand, not scruffy, just right. The Kershaws run it with passion and an instinctive understanding of its traditions. The stone walls hold old photos of the community, and bars are immaculate: brass beer taps glow, anything wooden — ceiling, beams, tables — shines, and the clock above the fire keeps perfect time. The attention to detail is staggering. Robin and Irene cook with relish, again nothing fancy, but more than enough to keep a smile on your face — game pies, salmon and local lamb, wicked puddings, Northumbrian cheeses. Real ales change weekly, there are over 20 malts and five wines by the glass. Bedrooms next door in the old hay barn are as you'd expect: simple, cosy, good value. Wonderful Northumbrian hospitality in the Northumberland National Park — they really are the nicest people.

directions	On B6346 towards Charlton & Wooler, 7 miles from Alnwick.
meals	12pm-2pm; 6pm-9pm. Main courses £7.50-£14.
closed	Christmas Day.

directions	From Bellingham to Kielder Water 7 miles. On left, before K. Water.
meals	12pm-2.30pm (2pm Sun); 7pm-8.30pm. Main courses £6.50-£11.95.
rooms	8: 4 doubles, 3 twins, 1 family £65-£85. Singles £40-£45.
closed	3pm-6pm (7pm Sundays).

	John Blackmore The Tankerville Arms, 15 The Village, Eglingham, Alnwick, Northumberland NE66 2TX
tel	01665 578444

	Walter & Robin Kershaw The Pheasant, Stannersburn, Kielder Water, Northumberland NE48 1DD
tel	01434 240382
web	www.thepheasantinn.com

map: 17 entry: 311

map: 17 entry: 312

Northumberland

Northumberland

Queen's Head Inn
Great Whittington

The sober stone frontage hides a deeply civilised and comfortable interior. The small bar is hugely appealing with its polished counter and gleaming beer engines disbursing Nick Stafford's ales, one specially brewed for the pub. Toast your toes from a carved oak settle in front of the fire and admire the intriguing mural above of the hunt passing through the village. Across the entrance passage is a stylishly comfortable lounge, and another magnificent log-filled grate for those bitter Northumbrian days. Beyond are the more formal dining areas. The place appears to run on wheels and everything is beautifully maintained. Chef Ian Scott uses fresh, local produce, including beef and lamb from nearby farms. As well as delicious sandwiches, daily menus may list seared lamb fillet with pear and redcurrant tart and a port and thyme jus, and pan-fried sea bass with king prawns, buttered noodles and a herb beurre blanc.

The Angel Inn
Corbridge

Even older than Hadrian's Wall, quaint Corbridge is a pretty place with the 17th-century Angel, full of history and character, at its hub. You walk straight into the splendid panelled lounge, cosy with its leather armchairs, heavy drapes, big open fire and newspapers to browse through. Off to the left, a plush dining room – deep carpeting, polished tables, sparkling glassware – and to the right, the bar. This is a big room, simply decorated in brasserie style with a bright, contemporary feel. Cask beers are available and the menu, chalked on a blackboard over the fire, reveals some imaginative dishes as well as more traditional roasts – and the Angel's fabulous Yorkshire pudding. There's a beer garden at the back, more places to sit at the front and five good, newly decorated bedrooms upstairs. A comfortable stopover on the long journey from north to south.

directions	In Corbridge, 2 miles off A69.
meals	12pm-2.30pm; 6pm-9pm. No food Sunday evenings. Main courses £10.50-£15.50; set menu £11.50 & £14.50.
rooms	5 twins/doubles £74-£85. Singles £49.

directions	Off B6318, 4 miles north of Corbridge.
meals	12pm-2pm; 6.30pm-9pm. Main courses £9.95-£18.95.
closed	Sunday evenings & Mondays.

Ian Scott
Queen's Head Inn,
Great Whittington,
Corbridge,
Northumberland NE19 2HP
tel 01434 672267

map: 17 entry: 313

Alan O'Kane
The Angel Inn,
Main Street,
Corbridge,
Northumberland NE45 5LA
tel 01434 632119

map: 17 entry: 314

Northumberland

The Feathers Inn
Hedley-on-the-Hill

Marina Atkinson has seen a few changes to the British pub scene in her 24 years — yet has not lost sight of The Feathers' old-fashioned pubby feel. It is a rare treat west of Newcastle to find such an authentic little place. In the two bars are old beams, exposed stonework, Turkey rugs, open fires and a cottagey feel. Furnishings are simple but comfortable: red benches and settles, ornaments and soft lights. So restful — you'd feel as much at home browsing the papers as enjoying a fireside chat. Beer is excellent, with four cask beers from local or micro breweries; wines are taken as seriously. The food — Greek beef casserole, tortillas and croustades, ginger pudding — is home-cooked and vegetarian- and vegan-friendly. Menus change twice a week, and dishes are deliberately unelaborate: Marina puts the focus on freshness and flavour. Hedley-on-the-Hill is as charming as its name.

directions	From Consett, B6309 north to New Ridley; follow signs to Hedley-on-the-Hill.
meals	12pm-2.30pm; 7pm-9pm. No food Monday evenings. Main courses £6.95-£8.95.
closed	Weekday lunchtimes except Bank Holidays.

Marina Atkinson
The Feathers Inn,
Hedley-on-the-Hill,
Stocksfield,
Northumberland NE43 7SW

tel   01661 843607

map: 17 entry: 315

Northumberland

The Manor House Inn
Carterway Heads

No wonder it's a popular place. Cheerful young staff, tasty food, a good bar with four cask ales and a cask cider, eight wines by the glass, a raft of malts. The large, light lounge bar, with wood-burning stove and blackboard menu, is a great spot for meals, though there's a dining room if you prefer. Chicken liver pâté comes with onion marmalade, pigeon breast with mushroom and juniper sauce. In the smallish public bar, modestly furnished with oak settles and old pine tables, is a big open fire; owners Chris and Moira Brown add a further warm touch. Take your pint of Theakstons Best into the garden in summer — your eye sweeps over the Derwent valley to the Durham moors. Upstairs, four en suite bedrooms are prettily decorated in a cottagey style. To expand the already thriving business, the Browns are planning a farm shop that will sell the best Northumberland produce.

directions	Beside A68 at junction with B6278; 3 miles west of Consett.
meals	12pm-9.30pm (9pm Sundays). Main courses £7-£17.
rooms	4 twins/doubles £60-£70. Singles £38-£48.

Moira & Chris Brown
The Manor House Inn,
Carterway Heads,
Shotley Bridge,
Northumberland DH8 9LX

tel   01207 255268

map: 17 entry: 316

Nottinghamshire

Caunton Beck
Caunton

Having hatched the hugely successful Wig and Mitre in Lincoln, Valerie Pascoe looked for a rural equivalent and found one in pretty little Caunton. The pub was lovingly reconstructed from the skeleton of the 16th-century Hole Arms and then renamed. Eight years on it is a hugely popular pub-restaurant, opening at 8am for breakfast – start your day with freshly squeezed orange juice, espresso coffee, poached eggs on toast – and staying open all day. Later, there are sandwiches, zucchini frittatas and fillet of beef. The puddings (make space for vanilla panna cotta with rhubarb ice cream) are fabulous. It's all very relaxed and civilised, the sort of place where newspapers and magazines take precedence over piped music and electronic wizardry. Come for country chairs at scrubbed pine tables, rag-rolled walls and a fire in winter, or parasols on the terrace in summer. Well-managed ales are on handpump.

Nottinghamshire

Waggon & Horses
Newark

The Whites have built up a fantastic reputation for their food. You can tell how keen they are just by looking at the menu with its mouthwatering exhortations to try each dish. The specials board announces whole roast partridge with a mushroom, port and thyme sauce, and Cornish bream with smoked salmon and scallops; even the lunchtime rolls are worth travelling for. Members of the Campaign for Real Food, they get almost everything locally, although the fish comes daily from Cornwall. The pub is small, beamed and softly lit with low ceilings and bold walls. In the open-plan bar divided into distinct sections, rush-seated chairs sit at sturdy tables, with the odd settle and masses of cricket memorabilia. An exotic metal grill separates the bar from the smoke-free dining area. Rebecca and William keep themselves busy offering a takeaway service and catering for parties as well as running the pub. It's a Thwaites' tied house, friendly and expertly run.

directions	6 miles NW of Newark past sugar factory on A616.
meals	8am-11pm. Main courses £8.50-£17.50; set menu £13.95.

directions	Off B6386 in Southwell for Oxton.
meals	12pm-2.30pm (4pm Sun); 6pm-9.30pm. No food Sun evening. Main courses £8-£12.50.
closed	3pm-5.30pm Monday-Friday.

Mrs Wendy Miller
Caunton Beck,
Main Street,
Caunton, Newark,
Nottinghamshire NG23 6AB
tel   01636 636793

William & Rebecca White
Waggon & Horses,
Mansfield Road,
Halam, Newark,
Nottinghamshire NG22 8AE
tel   01636 813109

map: 10 entry: 317

map: 10 entry: 318

Nottinghamshire

Ye Olde Trip to Jerusalem
Nottingham

Another pub that claims to be the oldest in England! The building dates from the 1600s and the name is older still. Certainly there has been brewing on the site since the 1170s (to supply the needs of the castle above) and the crusaders probably met here en route to Jerusalem. An amazing place carved into solid rock on which the castle sits; drinking here is like drinking in a cave, only warmer. There are rickety staircases, ancient chimneys that were cut up through the rock to assist medieval brewing, a cursed galleon, hairy with dust because the last three people who cleaned it died, and Ring the Bull, a pub game which involves swinging a ring on a string over a bull's horn. The Rock Lounge, with its sandstone ceiling and chimney, is aptly named, while the cellars stretch more than 100 feet beneath the castle. The Trip (meaning 'resting place') serves Hardys & Hansons to a mixed crowd – locals, tourists, students – and the food is standard pub stuff.

directions	From inner ring road follow A6005 'The North' to Castle Boulevard; right into Castle Road.
meals	12pm-6pm. Main courses £5-£8.

Karen Ratcliffe
Ye Olde Trip to Jerusalem,
1 Brewhouse Yard, Castle Road,
Nottingham NG1 6AD
tel   0115 947 3171
web   www.triptojerusalem.com

map: 9 entry: 319

Nottinghamshire

The Victoria
Beeston

There's a large picture of Queen Victoria ruling the main bar of this unpretentious and bustling city-suburb pub. It's an ex-Victorian railway hotel with bags of character, and it pulls in a crowd with its 12 ales, 18 wines by the glass and lethal selection of malt whiskies. The food's good, too, with a menu strong on vegetarian options. The civilised main bar, with fire, newspapers on racks and etched windows, sets the tone for the other rooms, all plainly painted in magnolia paint with woodblock flooring and scrubbed, dark-wood or brass-topped tables. Blackboards give the food and booze headlines. You get shepherd's pie, sautéed chicken with honey, ginger and chilli and veggie dishes to delight even non-vegetarians (pasta with fresh rocket pesto, stuffed vine leaves with mozzarella). At the back, there's a heated marquee area for cooler summer nights; dine as the trains go by. Service is efficient, friendly and laid-back. Try to catch the summer festival of ale, food and music.

directions	On A6005; follow signs to station.
meals	12pm-8.45pm (7.45pm Sundays). Main courses £6.50-£10.95.

The Victoria,
Dovecote Lane,
Beeston,
Nottinghamshire NG9 1JG
tel   0115 925 4049

map: 9 entry: 320

Nottinghamshire

Martin's Arms
Colston Bassett

The Elizabethan farmhouse became an ale house around 1700, and an inn a couple of hundred years later. Today it is a deeply civilised place. The bar exudes so much country-house charm – scatter cushions on sofas and settles, crackling logs in Jacobean fireplaces – that the bar seems almost an intrusion. You eat here or in the elegant restaurant; fresh, seasonal menus change daily in both. Bar snacks include special sandwiches, warm salads and splendid ploughman's lunches with Colston Bassett stilton. In the restaurant be treated to inventive and beautifully presented dishes, with Park Farm Estate game (woodcock, duck and pigeon, shot by the chef) the highlight of winter menus, and raspberry and marscapone shortbread with stem ginger, perhaps, for pudding. Behind the bar is an impressive range of real ales, cognacs and malts, and wines from Lay & Wheeler. The garden backs onto the Colston Bassett Estate and you can play croquet on the lawn in summer.

directions	Off A46, east of Nottingham.
meals	12pm-2pm; 6pm-10pm. Main courses £9.75-£18.95.
closed	3pm-6pm; Sunday evenings; Christmas Day evening.

Lynne Bryan Strafford
& Salvatore Inguanta
Martins Arms,
School Lane, Colston Bassett,
Nottinghamshire NG12 3FD
tel   01949 81361

map: 10 entry: 321

Oxfordshire

The White Lion
Crays Pond

Chef-patron Stuart and his wife Caroline bought the lease to this 300-year old pub two years ago and have been busy ever since. A well-heeled Henley and Goring crowd is drawn by Stuart's imaginative and daily-changing menu that mixes old favourites – fish and chips, calves' liver and bacon – with new ideas such as salt and pepper squid with spring onion and chilli, confit of duck leg with bubble-and-squeak and grain mustard sauce. Everthing is made freshly and in-house, from the pasta to the ice cream. Simple tables are topped with fat white candles in a dining room where deep red walls are lined with unusual prints and the floor is jauntily strewn with rugs. There's also a light and airy conservatory extension. Relax over the papers in the small bar with a pint of Greene King and a bowl of marinated olives, dip daintly into a pint of prawns or chew on a thick steak sandwich.

directions	3 miles N of Pangbourne on B471.
meals	12pm-2pm (2.30pm Sundays); 6pm-9.30pm. Main courses £8.95-£17.95.
closed	Mondays.

Stuart & Caroline Pierrepont
White Lion,
Crays Pond, Goring Heath,
Oxfordshire RG8 7SH
tel   01491 680471
web   www.innastew.com

map: 4 entry: 322

Oxfordshire

Perch & Pike
South Stoke

It's easy to fall for the Perch and Pike. Brick-and-flint-built in the 17th century and serenely restyled, the pub's fortunes have changed thanks to an inspired landlord and chef. In contrast to the traditional, low-beamed bar – with handpumped ales and winter logs – is a white-walled, sunlight-filled dining room in the barn. Glasses sparkle on ash-blond tables, striking art adorns the walls. Upstairs, in the same lovely conversion, are the funky bedrooms, one with a jacuzzi. Service is good-humoured, children are welcome and dogs are allowed (by arrangement). The food is an attractive blend of the modern and traditional with a monthly-changing dinner menu. Treat yourself to homemade pasta with seafood, fresh herbs and pesto; game casserole; chargrilled fresh swordfish with Thai-scented prawn broth; apple pie. Impressive light lunches and a first-class sandwich menu reel in Thames-side walkers and those in the know.

directions	On Goring to Wallingford road, 1.75 miles from Goring.
meals	12pm-2.30pm; 7pm-9.30pm. No food Sunday evenings. Main courses £7.95-£13.95.
rooms	4: 3 doubles, 1 twin £55-£75.

Edwin Pope
Perch & Pike,
South Stoke, Goring,
Oxfordshire RG8 0JS
tel   01491 872415
web   www.perchandpike.com

map: 4 entry: 323

Oxfordshire

Crooked Billet
Stoke Row

Dick Turpin apparently courted the landlord's daughter and Kate Winslet had her wedding breakfast here. Pints are drawn direct from the cask and the rusticity of the pub charms all who manage to find it: beams, flags and inglenooks, old pine, walls lined with bottles and baskets of spent corks. In the larger room, red walls display old photographs and mirrors; shelves are stacked with books... by candlelight it's irresistible. The menu is Italian/French provincial, and long: bouillabaisse, beef fillet with seared foie gras and red wine jus, sea bass with roasted vegatables and salsa verde. It's founded on well-sourced raw materials bolstered by a satisfying wine list; there are no fewer than six English puddings, and sweet wines by the glass. Occasional jazz, and a big garden bordering the beech woods where children can roam.

directions	5 miles west of Henley, off B481 Reading to Nettlebed road.
meals	12pm-2.30pm; 7pm-10pm (12pm-10pm weekends). Main courses £12-£18; set menu £12.95-£16.95.

Paul Clerehugh
Crooked Billet, Newlands Lane,
Stoke Row, Henley-on-Thames,
Oxfordshire RG9 5PU
tel   01491 681048
web   www.thecrookedbillet.co.uk

map: 4 entry: 324

Three Tuns
Henley-on-Thames

Gone are the days when the Three Tun's last orders prompted the first fights of the night. Few locals would have dared step inside, but now it's an elegant meeting place, wedged between shops on Henley's fine market square. The feel is more wine bar than pub: soft cream hues and old beams, a small interior with a huge personality. Arresting antiques are everywhere and can even be bought from the antiques 'menu', along with lunch or dinner and homemade goodies to take home. Funky chairs by one fireplace add a contemporary splash; fossils in another add a touch of whimsy. This eclectic mix extends to the food prepared by Keiron. It's seasonal, fresh, of the very best quality and served on crisply clothed tables. Salivate over four-cheese soufflé with truffled green bean salad, home-cured bresaola with aged balsamic, fillet steak sandwich with sauté potatoes. Evenings at the 'foodhouse' may bring spaghetti with wild cep, lemon and chilli, roast venison with fig gravy, and baked vanilla cheesecake with lime mascarpone. There's also a selection of mainly French wines, well-kept Brakspears and an elegant awning in the courtyard at the back.

directions	In centre square.
meals	12pm-3pm; 7pm-10pm.
	Main courses £8-£17.
closed	3pm-5.30pm in winter.

Keiron Daniels
Three Tuns,
5 Market Place, Henley-on-Thames,
Oxfordshire RG9 2AA
tel   01491 573260
web   www.thefoodhouse.com

map: 5 entry: 325

Oxfordshire

The Fox & Hounds
Christmas Common

In a hamlet in the hills – a few grand houses and this 15th-century brick and flint cottage: the civilised Fox and Hounds. Three years ago it was a rustic rural ale house, but Brakspears, with tenant Judith Bishop, have transformed it into a thriving food pub. Despite the changes, the 'Top Fox' (on its escarpment) has lost none of its charm and character. Enter a beamy, tiled bar full of cosy corners, logs glowing in a vast inglenook all year round, cribbage and cards, and pints of Brakspear tapped direct from the cask. In the bar are lunchtime doorstop sandwiches, while the foodie action takes place in the newly-built restaurant, with its wooden floors, open-to-view kitchen and chunky furniture. From farm-reared meats and locally grown fruit and vegetables come wholesome dishes like lamb shank in red wine, garlic and herbs, and baked halibut with coriander and rocket pesto. Make time for walks through the beech woods, look up for soaring red kites.

directions	From M40 junc. 5 follow old A40 to Christmas Common.
meals	12pm-2.30pm (3pm Sundays); 7pm-9.30pm (9pm Sundays). Main courses £6.50-£14.50.

Judith Bishop
The Fox & Hounds,
Christmas Common,
Watlington,
Oxfordshire OX49 5HL
tel   01491 612599

map: 10 entry: 326

Oxfordshire

Sir Charles Napier
Chinnor

The merry tumble of furnishings and sculptures will have you converted – along with all the others who beat a path to its door. Julie's place is rather more restaurant than pub, with stylish wines, good-humoured service and heli-pad in the garden. Yet the country pubby trappings remain: rough-hewn wooden bar, log fires, boarded floors, beams to duck. Add to that a battered mix of tables and chairs, sofas and lamps, well-kept Wadworths and a superb bar menu. It's a legendary place... Oxfordshire's worst-kept secret! The cashmered and jeaned arrive via road and air for handwritten menus that signal simple, unpretentious, modern European food. In the bar there's parsnip and chestnut soup, jugged rabbit with mash, seared tuna nicoise; in the restaurant, splash out on baked Cornish lobster with sauce vierge, or wild mallard with Jerusalem artichokes, chestnuts and madeira. Dine in summer on a wisteria-shaded terrace while red kites circle overhead.

directions	M40 junc. 6 to Chinnor; right at x-roads; up hill to Spriggs Alley.
meals	12pm-2.30pm (3.30pm Sunday); 6.30pm-10pm. Main courses £9.50-£12.50.
closed	Sunday evenings; Mondays.

Julie Griffiths
Sir Charles Napier,
Spriggs Alley, Chinnor,
Oxfordshire OX39 4BX
tel   01494 483011
web   www.sircharlesnapier.co.uk

map: 10 entry: 327

Oxfordshire

The Goose
Britwell Salome

At first glance, the modest 16th-century pub on the main through road of the village might not warrant a visit. Yet those in the know will tell of light, modern, remodelled interiors and fabulous food. Calming, pastel colours, light floorboards and matting, comfy armchairs and a fireside sofa create a civilised backdrop for this high-rolling, gastropub adventure. Owner-chef Michael North's innovative daily menus reflect the seasons; in November, say, parfait of foie gras with fig compote, or roast duck from Well Place Manor estate with green peppercorn and honey jus. The produce is fresh and local allowing flavours to shine, and service is from a young and professional team. The lightwood bar and white-linen-dressed tables further add to the chilled-out yet friendly feel. The back room (no smoking) continues the theme, and an enclosed garden with proper wooden furniture is tidily hidden at the back.

directions	On B4009 south of Watlington, 5 miles from M40 junc. 6.
meals	12pm-2.30pm; 7pm-9pm. Main courses £14-£17; set menus £12-£15.
closed	Sunday evenings.

Michael North
The Goose,
Britwell Salome,
Oxfordshire OX49 5LG
tel   01491 612304

map: 10 entry: 328

Oxfordshire

The Boar's Head
Ardington

If it's not the sweet smell of lilies, it's the irresistible aroma of fresh bread. With daily baking to tempt them, villagers arrive for a pint of the best then put in their orders – sun-dried tomato, granary, with or without olives. Here are good ales, fine wines, darts, dominoes and a welcome for kids. In a bar cosy with low beams, scrubbed wooden tables, checked curtains and log fires, sit down to a first-class seasonal menu created by a chef-patron who knows what's what. Bruce Buchan is inventive with fish from Newlyn and market-fresh produce from Newbury and Wantage; even the local black pudding has won prizes. His wife Kay keeps this lovely little pub running with friendly efficiency downstairs while supervising the bedrooms up; they are immaculate, with soft colours, waffle bedspreads and flat-screen TVs. A 400-year-old special place in a timeless estate village. Come to unwind.

directions	On A417, 2 miles east of Wantage.
meals	12pm-2pm; 7pm-9.30pm (10pm Fridays & Saturdays). Main courses £13.50-£18.50.
rooms	3 doubles £75-£120. Singles £65-£95.
closed	3pm-6pm.

Bruce & Kay Buchan
The Boar's Head,
Church Street, Ardington,
Wantage, Oxfordshire OX12 8QA
tel   01235 833254
web   www.boarsheadardington.co.uk

map: 9 entry: 329

Oxfordshire

North Star
Steventon

Despite a previous owner's hammering of the ancient walls with a JCB in a fit of New Year pique, the pub's 15th-century interior has remained miraculously intact. Enter down a narrow tiled corridor to four small rooms whose creaky latched doors have numbers – a throwback to the days when inns were taxed by the room. Real ale is served straight from the barrel through a hatch, there's no central heating, two open fires, and a huge L-shaped settle filling the low-ceilinged main bar. This used to be a popular venue for the old boys of the village; it's still a great place to catch up over a pint of Greene King. There's bar food at lunchtimes, tables outside, and a front gateway through an ancient yew. Recent photographs of the pub's restoration show workmen reconstructing the ancient walls (wattle and daub with horsehair plaster) overseen by the resident ghost.

directions	Exit A34 at Didcot/Milton junction for Steventon; right at lights; through village. Left at causeway; follow road.
meals	12pm-2.30pm. No food Sundays. Main courses £2.50-£6.95.
closed	3pm-7pm Sunday-Thursdays.

Kerry Tyrrell & Michael Toplis
North Star,
Stocks Lane,
The Causeway, Steventon,
Oxfordshire OX13 6SP
tel   01235 831677

map: 9 entry: 330

Oxfordshire

The Bull & Butcher
Turville

Landlady Lydia Botha ensures this little pub quenches the thirsts of all who come to visit one of the most bucolic film locations in Britain – it sits beneath the Chitty Chitty Bang Bang windmill, the village is the setting for *The Vicar of Dibley* and suspects from *Midsomer Murders* have propped up the bar. There's bags of atmosphere, and style, in cream walls, latched doors, a glass-topped 50-foot well, fresh flowers. Busy with Londoners at weekends, it's a jolly place in which to down a pint of Brakspears finest or take a tipple of homemade sloe gin. Food is good modern British: poached champagne salmon fillet, Vicar of Dibley pie, bangers and mash – and biltong, a dried meat speciality added to the menu by Lydia's South African husband. No piped music, no games, no pubby paraphernalia, just fine 17th-century beams, lovely log fires and friendly people. There's a garden for fine days and great walks through the Chiltern beechwoods.

directions	M40 junc. 5; through Ibstone; for Turville at T-junction.
meals	12pm-2.30pm (3pm Sun); 7pm-9.45pm. Main courses £7.50-£14.95.
rooms	6: 2 doubles, 4 twins £80. Singles £55.
closed	Christmas Day evening.

Hugo & Lydia Botha
The Bull & Butcher,
Turville, Henley-on-Thames,
Oxfordshire RG9 6QU
tel   01491 638283
web   www.thebullandbutcher.com

map: 10 entry: 331

White Hart
Wytham

Who says the traditional and the contemporary don't mix? In the White Hart, an interesting ancient stone building which was once a deeply rural drinkers' den but is now practically in Oxford, mad shaggy bolsters mingle whimsically with twig-framed mirrors. The different areas of the pub have distinctive characters, too: the Shaker-style 'green' room has wooden tables and a central bread block laid with fresh loaves; the cosy parlour has exotic coloured walls, and velvet and silk cushions. The upstairs bar is quite different, with open brickwork, wooden floorboards, a log fire and walls bearing, capriciously, peppers and a buxom tomato. The conservatory is where the shaggy bolsters lurk while, outside, the terrace has a rustic feel with Greek terracotta woodburners and a 15th-century dovecote. Expect real ales on handpump in the softly-lit bar, and modern cooking from the kitchen. Blackboards announce inventive pub food and monthly specials which are described as "divine" – seared scallops with basil dressing, pork fillet wrapped in Italian bacon with mustard cream sauce, chocolate fondant with chocolate sauce. Wytham means 'village on a bend'. *Inspector Morse* aficionados may recognise the pretty building and its Thames-side setting.

directions	A34 to Oxford, off at Botley interchange.
meals	12pm-3pm; 6.30pm-10pm. Main courses £11.95-£18.50.
closed	3pm-6pm Monday-Friday.

David Peevers
White Hart,
Wytham,
Oxfordshire OX2 8QA
tel   01865 244372

map: 9 entry: 332

The Mole Inn
Toot Baldon

The drunken mole logo reflects the celebratory mood that's been in the air since chef-patron Gary took over. Needless to say, The Mole has proved a hit with Oxford foodies who have flocked to experience the pub's renaissance... it is packed at weekends. Money and love have been lavished on the old boozer, as you can see from the impeccable stone exterior, the young landscaped garden and the ravishing bar. You'll be embraced by stripped beams and chunky white walls, black leather sofas, logs in the grate and a dresser that groans with breads and olive jars. The rustic-chic style continues into three dining areas: fat candles on blond wooden tables, subtle lighting, thick terracotta floors. The sun angling in on a plateful of red mullet with lemon parsley mash is one of life's pleasures. Chalkboard fish specials and daily dishes point to a menu that trawls the globe for inspiration, from Asian salmon fishcakes with aïoli and herbs to perfect Oxford bangers and mash. Whether you go for light salad and pasta bowl lunches or rack of lamb with aubergine, tomato, olives and mint oil, the food is big on looks and flavour. Scrumptious puddings, British cheeses, great wines, local Hook Norton ale and happy staff complete the picture, and ten new bedrooms are eagerly awaited.

directions	The 'Baldons' off A4074, 5 miles S of Oxford at Nuneham Courtenay.
meals	12pm-2.30pm; 7pm-9.30pm; 12pm-9pm Sundays. Main courses £7.95-£17.50.

	Gary Witchalls The Mole Inn, Toot Baldon, Oxfordshire OX44 9NG
tel	01865 340001
web	www.moleinn.com

map: 9 entry: 333

Oxfordshire

The Bear
Oxford

When a publican mentions 'ties' you might think he's talking about his relationship with the brewery. But at The Bear a former landlord was so fascinated by gentlemen's neckwear that he offered free pints for any tie he could remove from its owner. Many years' worth of framed, frayed ties now line this idiosyncratic little boozer's walls and ceilings. The beer must have been good. Today, there are several real ales on tap, Old Speckled Hen included, and a few guest beers. There's a good mix of town and gown here, with open-collared students arriving in their droves, and locals devotedly keeping to their end, a minute 10ftx6ft snug by the bar hatch. The Office, as it is commonly known, has housed over 30 drinkers on popular quiz nights, when locals compete – successfully, as often as not – with the university colleges. Oxford's oldest pub (1242) has a low-beamed, shambolic interior, no fruit machines, music or TV. It's absolutely perfect for short people in search of authenticity and good ale.

directions	Down lane by NatWest bank.
meals	12pm-4pm.
	Main courses £5-£11.

Ian Stevenson
The Bear,
6 Alfred Street,
Oxford,
Oxfordshire OX1 4EH
tel   01865 728164

map: 9 entry: 334

Oxfordshire

Boot Inn
Barnard Gate

It's not often you can down a pint of Hook Norton in a cosy Cotswold pub while pondering David Beckham's shoe size, Jasmin Le Bon's ankle and the flexibility of Roger Bannister's soles. The Boot's walls are covered with a rare collection of celebrity footwear, and the list is long: Stirling Moss, Henry Cooper, Prue Leith, Rick Stein. Expect standing timbers, bare board floors, good country tables candlelight at night and a huge log fire... a deliciously traditional atmosphere in which to settle back and enjoy some fresh, flavourful cooking: free-range chicken filled with cranberry compote, Moroccan vegetable casserole, rib-eye steak with garlic butter. After a slice of dark chocolate cheesecake there is an overwhelming temptation to don a pair of Ranulph Fiennes's record-breaking Polar bootliners and turn into an armchair explorer by the fire.

directions	Off A40; 4 miles from Oxford.
meals	12pm-2pm (2.30pm Saturdays; 3pm Sundays); 7pm-9.30pm (10pm Fridays & Saturdays). Main courses £7.95-£15.95.
closed	3pm-6pm.

Craig Foster
Boot Inn,
Barnard Gate, Witney,
Oxfordshire OX29 6XE
tel   01865 881231
web   www.theboot-inn.com

map: 9 entry: 335

Oxfordshire

The Royal Oak Inn
Ramsden

From opening time on, the jolly banter of the Royal Oak's regulars can be heard from the doorstep outside. Blazing winter fires, piles of magazines and well-thumbed books by the inglenook make this a fine place to down a pint of real ale; tuck into a cosy corner filled with plump scatter cushions. In the pubby bar – open-stone walls, cream and soft-green windows – some brilliant food can be had, as well as in the restaurant extension beyond, where glass doors open onto a pretty terrace with wrought-iron chairs in summer, and outdoor heaters keep you snug. With dishes such as wild boar and venison casserole, rack of English lamb cooked pink, chocolate and brandy ice cream and lovely Sunday roasts you cannot go wrong. This rural pub is refreshingly child- and dog-friendly, and the welcome from the pub's owners will be as genuine as that of the owners' young hound, Hero. Stay for breakfast: good rooms are in cottages to the side, and the village is a stunner.

directions	On B4022, 3 miles from Witney.
meals	12pm-2pm; 7pm-10pm.
	Main courses £12-£15.
rooms	4 twins/doubles £50. Singles £35.
closed	3pm-6.30pm.

Jon Oldham
The Royal Oak Inn,
Ramsden,
Charlbury,
Oxfordshire OX7 3AU
tel   01993 868213

map: 9 entry: 336

Oxfordshire

Fleece on the Green
Witney

Lee Cash and Victoria Moon dug deep into their pockets last year to buy the lease on the Fleece – a Georgian building overlooking the church green in genteel Witney. Wooden floors, plum-coloured walls, squashy sofas around low tables, a relaxed atmosphere and a continental opening time of 8.30am for decent coffee and bacon sandwiches. Moving the bar to the front has worked wonders, drawing in casual drinkers for pints of Greene King and bucket-sized glasses of wine. Thumbs-up from locals for the all-day sandwiches, salads and deli-board menu, the latter suggesting nibbles or starters of cheese, charcuterie, fish and anti-pasti – olive tapenade and marinated chillies. There are, too, stone-baked pizzas and modern brasserie-style dishes like salmon fishcake with tomato and chive butter sauce. Chic, aubergine bedrooms are due to be re-done soon.

directions	M40 junc. 15 or M6 junction 4.
	On green, near church.
meals	8.30am-11.30am; 12pm-2.30pm;
	6.30pm-10pm (9.30pm Sundays).
	Snacks served 2.30pm-6.30pm.
	Main courses £7.50-£13.
rooms	10: 9 doubles, 1 single £75.

Tina Baily
Fleece on the Green,
11 Church Green, Witney,
Oxfordshire OX28 4AZ
tel   01993 892270
web   www.peachpubs.com

map: 9 entry: 337

Masons Arms
South Leigh

A quintessentially English inn – with attitude – in somnolent South Leigh. Who would guess there's a gentlemen's club here? This is 'Gerry Stonhill's Individual Masons Arms'; dogs, children and mobile phones are unwelcome and vegetarians visit 'by appointment only'. Dickensian is the word that springs to mind! Fifteenth-century flagstone floors, crackling log fires, dark hessian walls clad with paintings, old oak tables, spent wine bottles and scattered cigar boxes on shelves. There are three rambling rooms to explore and be charmed by and a cosily clubby whisky-and-cognac-stocked bar. Burton Ale comes from the barrel and the wines are French. This is a smoking establishment, naturally, with Cuban cigars proffered at the end of the meal. Food is proper English: potted shrimps, wild smoked salmon, casseroles, roast duck, Angus steaks and the juiciest fish from the market, brought to the table to be admired before it's cooked.
Cash, cheques & American Express only.

Shaven Crown Hotel
Shipton-under-Wychwood

Stone-mullioned windows, ancient faded tapestries, grand fireplaces and suits of armour... hardly your average local. This marvellous Tudor stone building, built to a medieval design, is still loved by villagers today – in spite of, or perhaps because of its grand history as a monastic hospice-cum-hostelry turned royal inn. When Henry VIII disbanded the monasteries, Elizabeth I gave the 'Crown Inn' back to the village; residents still come first. Boules championships pull in the crowds in summer, while the Christmas sloe gin competition with courtyard pig roast brings pink cheeks to the faithful. To the passing traveller, the Shaven Crown is a marvellous place in which to savour both medieval architecture and a mixed game terrine – delicious with homemade apple and pear chutney. And at the end of a day of real ale and revelry there's always the old chapel four-poster bed to sink into upstairs.

directions	On A361, 4 miles NE of Burford.
meals	12pm-2pm; 5.30pm-9.30pm. Main courses £9-£11.20; set menu £25.
rooms	8: 5 doubles, 2 double/twin, 1 four-poster £85-£130. Singles £65.

directions	3 miles south east of Witney off A40 towards Oxford
meals	12.30pm-2.30pm; 7.30pm-10.30pm. Main courses £10-£25.
closed	Monday & Sunday evenings.

Gerry Stonhill
Masons Arms,
South Leigh,
Witney,
Oxfordshire OX29 6XN
tel 01993 702485

map: 9 entry: 338

Philip Mehrtens
Shaven Crown Hotel, High Street,
Shipton-under-Wychwood,
Oxfordshire OX7 6BA
tel 01993 830330
web www.shavencrown.co.uk

map: 9 entry: 339

Oxfordshire

The Lamb Inn
Burford

Old inn, new owners. Bruno and Rachel say they don't want to make big changes and in many ways there's no need. In 1420 it was a dormy house; centuries-worth of footsteps have worn a gentle groove into the pale stone. The smell of woodsmoke is irresistible... make a tour and you'll stumble across four fires. And two sitting rooms, mullioned windows, rambling corridors, polished brass and silver, thick rugs, a chintzy settle with a back high enough to keep the draught off a giant's neck – and a delicious, walled, cottagey garden. Bedrooms are just as good, with plump armchairs, oak beams, brass beds and antiques. Changes have been made in the kitchen under chef Ashley James's eagle eye with menus making the best use of seasonal food: smoked salmon with lime salsa, rib-eye steak with béarnaise sauce, real ice cream. The wine list is long and full of surprises; enjoy a glass in summer under a stylish parasol.

directions	Up High St; 2nd right into Sheep St.
meals	12pm–2.30pm (4pm Sundays); 7pm–9.30pm. Main courses £14.95–£21.
rooms	15: 11 doubles, 3 twins, 1 four-poster £130–£200. Singles £80–£120.

Rachel & Bruno Cappuccini
The Lamb Inn,
Sheep Street, Burford,
Oxfordshire OX18 4LR
tel   01993 823155
web   www.lambinn-burford.co.uk

map: 9 entry: 340

Oxfordshire

The Trout at Tadpole Bridge
Buckland Marsh

One misty-moist lunchtime, down by the river, one could almost expect to bump into Ratty and Toad toasting their toes in front of the wood-burning stove. The Trout is a drinking fisherman's paradise. Walls are adorned with bendy rods, children are welcomed, and your dogs may join the pub's. Landlord and chef, Chris Green knows breeds, cuts and quality of meat better than most; with lamb from the Blenheim estate, game from his family's farm and veg grown at the back, you can expect a treat. His father is in charge of the wine and Chris concentrates on wholesome dishes with a dash of fun. In summer the riverside garden comes alive as drinkers in search of real ale arrive by boat. Upstairs, pretty bedrooms are a temptation for weary fisherfolk – or pitch your tent at the pub's waterside camping site and catch a glimpse of *Wind in the Willows* magic.

directions	Off A420 between Oxford & Swindon
meals	12pm–2pm; 7pm–9pm. No food Sunday evenings. Main courses £7.95–£15.95.
rooms	6: 2 doubles, 4 twins £80. Singles £55.
closed	Sun eves; 25-26 & 31 December; 1 January; 1st week of February.

Christopher Green
The Trout at Tadpole Bridge,
Buckland Marsh, Faringdon,
Oxfordshire SN7 8RF
tel   01367 870382
web   www.trout-inn.co.uk

map: 9 entry: 341

Oxfordshire

The Swan
Swinbrook

No pool tables, no juke boxes, no fruit machines, no central heating, no soggy dogs – though "dry and on a lead" will do. This old water mill dating back to the 15th century in a lovely village on the Devonshire Estate – owned by the Duchess – and often with CAMRA representatives propping up the bar, is an ale lover's paradise. In the two small rooms of the open-stonework, listed building, customers down well-nurtured pints of Old Speckled Hen and vintage organic cider beneath hop-laden beams. The restaurant area with ceiling reaching to the sky must once have been the working hub of the mill; now chefs toil to serve a fresh menu using local ingredients. Despite the lack of radiators, the slow-roasted English lamb, the treacle and orange tart and the open fires will warm the cockles of anyone's heart, even on the coldest Cotswold day. Flagstones and settles, cheerful chatter, darts on Thursday and cribbage on Monday – it's almost perfect.

directions	From Oxford A40, through Witney. Village signed right, off A40.
meals	12pm-2.30pm; 6.30pm-9.30pm. Main courses £6.95-£13.95.
closed	3pm-6pm.

Andy Morris
The Swan,
Swinbrook,
Burford,
Oxfordshire OX18 4DY
tel   01993 822165

map: 9 entry: 342

Oxfordshire

Kings Head Inn
Bledington

About as Doctor Doolittle-esque as it gets: achingly pretty Cotswold stone cottages around a village green with quacking ducks, a pond and a perfect pub with a cobbled courtyard. The rambling 15th-century King's Head stands smack on the Gloucestershire border with its easterly wall resident in Oxfordshire. Archie and Nic are a young, affable couple and charming with locals and guests. The low-ceilinged bar is cosy and lively and long, and the flagstoned dining room with its pale wood tables most elegant. Food is cooked by a Swedish chef who is just as good with the locally sourced meat (shank of lamb with thyme and root vegetable casserole) as with fish (truly tasty mackerel and haddock fishcakes). Homemade puddings, serious cheeses, local Hook Norton ale, simple bedrooms with great colours and fabrics, and lovely unpompous touches like jugs of cow parsley in the loo.

directions	Burford-Stow A424; right to Idbury; Bledington, signed.
meals	12pm-2pm; 7pm-9.30pm . Main courses £4.50-£16.95.
rooms	12: 9 doubles, 2 twins, 1 four-poster £65-£90. Singles £50.
closed	3pm-6pm (6.30pm Sundays).

Archie & Nicola Orr-Ewing
King's Head Inn,
The Green, Bledington,
Oxfordshire OX7 6XQ
tel   01608 658365
web   www.kingsheadinn.net

map: 9 entry: 343

The Falkland Arms
Great Tew

Tradition runs deep here: a low-slung timbered ceiling drips with jugs, mugs and tankards; the hop is treated with reverence and ales are changed weekly; there are malt whiskies and country wines. Five hundred years on and the fire still roars in the stone-flagged bar, stocked with endless tins of snuff. In summer, Morris Men stumble on the lane outside while life spills out onto the terrace at the front and into the big garden behind. This lively pub is utterly down-to-earth and in very good hands. The dining room is tiny and intimate with beams and stone walls; every traditional dish is home cooked. Bedrooms are snug, cosy and fun: brass beds and four-posters, an uneven floor. The house remains blissfully free of modern trappings; in the bar active mobile phones meet with swift and decisive action.

The Stag's Head
Swalcliffe

Shakespeare is said to have supped here, though it was hardly his local. It is also rumoured that there's a tunnel leading from pub to church so that Catholics could go out for a pint, then sneak into the church for mass. Julia and Ian Kingsford took over four years ago and have built up a reputation for their food, both plain and posh: ham and eggs, Sunday roast, rump of lamb with garlic and rosemary butter. There's a children's menu too and puddings are mouthwatering. Julia uses home-produced herbs and eggs and buys all her meat locally. The pub takes its booze equally seriously, with three ales and nine wines by the glass. Inside, wooden settles and a woodburner in a low-beamed bar, two more rooms, oodles of character, newspapers, candles and books. Outside, a large terraced garden with palm trees, a pergola and tables, and a play area for little ones.

directions	Off A361 between Banbury & Chipping Norton.
meals	12pm-2pm; 7pm-8pm. No food Sunday evenings. Booking essential for evenings. Main courses £6.50-£12.95.
rooms	5 doubles £75-£100. Singles £50.
closed	2.30pm-6pm (7pm Sundays). Open all day at weekends in summer.

directions	Off B4035 in Swalcliffe, 6 miles west of Banbury.
meals	12pm-2.15pm (2.30pm Sundays); 7pm-9.30pm. No food Sunday evenings. Main courses £8-£17.
rooms	1 twin £60. Singles £35.
closed	Mondays.

Paul Barlow-Heal
The Falkland Arms,
Great Tew, Chipping Norton,
Oxfordshire OX7 4BD
tel   01608 683653
web   www.falklandarms.org.uk

map: 9 entry: 344

Ian & Julia Kingsford
The Stag's Head,
Swalcliffe,
Banbury,
Oxfordshire OX15 5EJ
tel   01295 780232

map: 9 entry: 345

Turf Tavern
Oxford

Towers, domes, steeples and quadrangles trumpet Oxford's historic and academic glory, and the Bridge of Sighs may draw eyes heavenwards. But watch out, for you could easily miss nearby St Helen's Passage and its spartan directions to The Turf. This narrow alleyway (once known as Hell's Passage) leads to a classic, 18th-century tavern in the shadow of the city wall and famous colleges – a real drinking den that was a site of vice for centuries with cockfighting and bear-baiting among the outlawed activities. Today, with 11 ales on handpump and some 200 guest ales served during the year, it's a rambling, low-beamed and lively haven of 'education and intoxication' where staff are proud to claim that lager-drinking 'freshers' are transformed into connoisseurs of real ale by the end of their degrees. After three pints of Cains Sundowner, Hook Norton Old Hooky or Badger Tanglefoot you may be bouncing off the walls, but light bar meals (sausage and mash, Caesar salad, steak and ale pie) should steady you. There are three flagstoned courtyards for summer; in winter, students and locals huddle beneath heaters around burning braziers over mulled wine and toasted chestnuts or marshmallows.

directions	Under Bridge of Sighs; St Helen's Passage between Holywell Street & New College Lane.
meals	12pm-7.30pm. Limited menu (till 3pm) on Sundays. Main courses £5.95-£7.

Darren Kent
Turf Tavern, Tavern Bath Place
via St Helen's Passage, Oxford,
Oxfordshire OX1 3SU

tel	01865 243235
web	www.theturftavern.co.uk

map: 9 entry: 346

Oxfordshire

Ye Olde Reindeer Inn
Banbury

Oliver Cromwell held court in the heavily wood-panelled Globe Room during the Civil War. The panelling was dismantled in 1909, almost sold to America, then returned in 1964... it is a magnificent feature in Banbury's oldest pub. Recently taken over by Tony and Dot Puddifoot, the backstreet local has a reputation for well-priced, home-cooked food, simply but perfectly done. Specialities include sirloin steak with mushroom sauce and delicious pies made of local meat and game. The bar is cosy with rugs on polished oak boards, solid furniture and a magnificent, carved, 17th-century fireplace, log-fuelled in winter. Hook Norton ales are served as well as country wines, including apricot and damson, that rival the beer in popularity. Parsons Street is tiny and runs off the Market Square yet the Reindeer is — as you'll see — unmissably signed.

directions	In town centre, just off Market Square.
meals	11am-2.30pm. No food Sunday lunchtimes. Main courses £4-£6.75.
closed	Sunday evenings.

Tony Puddifoot
Ye Olde Reindeer Inn,
47 Parsons Street,
Banbury,
Oxfordshire OX16 5NA
tel   01295 264031

map: 9 entry: 347

Rutland

The Grainstore Brewery
Oakham

Tony Davis, former master brewer at Ruddles, was driving past one day and realised that the Victorian building's three storeys would be perfect for a gravity-operated tower brewery. He and his partner Simon Davies went with the idea, converted the building and now brew a range of award-winning ales that supply pubs throughout the country. Attached to the brewery is The Tap. It serves pub food (including Dutch breakfast from the Dutch chef), wine by the glass and a fine range of ciders, but this place is generally and unashamedly about beer. Nine cracking ales are brewed and friendly staff are happy to pour you samplers. Don't expect any frills: you are in a working brewery and the open-plan bar is all bare board floors, vast ceiling joists (and noises above) and a long brick bar counter lined with bar stools. You can spot the brewery through glass doors and, with notice, Tony can give you a fascinating tour.

directions	Next to railway station.
meals	12pm-2.30pm. No food Sundays. Main courses £3-£6.50.

Tony Davis
The Grainstore Brewery,
Station Approach,
Oakham, Rutland LE15 6RE
tel   01572 770065
web   www.grainstorebrewery.com

map: 10 entry: 348

Olive Branch
Clipsham

There are so many blackboards here that you could be forgiven for thinking that Sean Hope, Ben Jones and Marcus Welford were ex-school teachers unable to let go. But it is, simply, the most immediate way to list the rare and speciality wines, the cigars and the daily-changing lunches. The Olive Branch is no ordinary pub, for it is one of a tiny handful to be awarded a Michelin star without abandoning its cheerfully relaxed pub personality. The food is not dressy, and the casual mood – derived from a ragbag of bar furniture, closely arranged tables and log-burning fires – is fully intended. Though the menu seems to borrow from every nation (chargrilled lemon sole, fennel potatoes, salsa verde, chocolate brownie with crème fraîche),

British cooking is still a strong point. Fish and chips, roast rib of beef, cottage pie, potted shrimps, Scotch egg with whisky mayonnaise, egg custard tart – all are revealed in a new and contemporary light. Real ales are taken seriously, with weekly changing guest ales such as Shepherd Neame Spitfire or Greene King Abbot Ale, and the wines are exceptional. There's a sheltered and attractive patio for you to use in the summer.

directions	2 miles off A1 at Stretton (B668 junction).
meals	12pm–2pm (3pm Sun); 7–9.30pm. Main courses £7.75–£15.95; set menu (lunch) £12.50 & £15.
closed	Sunday evenings; Dec 25–26.

Ben Jones
Olive Branch,
Main Street, Clipsham,
Rutland LE15 7PW

tel   01780 410355
web   www.theolivebranchpub.com

map: 10 entry: 349

Rutland

Finch's Arms
Upper Hambleton

Alone on its peninsula surrounded by Rutland Water, the Finch's has the greatest of rural views. Colin Crawford, who took over seven years ago, could have sat back and twiddled his thumbs and people would still have poured in. But he has not been idle, and has created a terrific team in the kitchen led by a Marseillaise chef. Décor is elegant wicker and wood, food is stylish, whether tagliatelle with artichokes in a pesto cream or steamed fillet of beef in a marrow and thyme dumpling. Or simply sausages with mash and onion. The menu changes frequently. There's also a friendly and efficient bar with a fine selection of ales and a great wine list, and a garden and a hillside terrace. It is a compliment to the way Colin runs this place that chef Yves believes English pubs have much to teach the French. Equally impressive are the bedrooms upstairs, each identified by a painting on the door, four with lakeside views.

directions	Off A606, east of Oakham.
meals	12pm-2.30pm; 6.30pm-9.30pm; 12pm-8pm Sundays. Main courses £6.95-£9.95; set weekday lunch £9.95/£11.95.
rooms	6: 4 doubles, 2 twins £65-£70. Singles £55.

Colin & Celia Crawford
Finch's Arms,
Oakham Road, Upper Hambleton,
Oakham, Rutland LE15 8TL

tel	01572 756575
web	www.finchsarms.co.uk

map: 10 entry: 350

Rutland

The Kings Arms
Wing

In medieval times, penitents would crawl round the turf maze on their knees. It's still there, in this quaint little village. The pub is merely 17th-century – and has been lavishly renovated by owner Jason Allen and his partner Richard. In two years they've transformed the place: smart bedrooms in the former stables and bakehouse, and a restaurant to which the locals flock. Jason describes the cooking as 'international'. Settle down at chunky new beechwood tables to Waldorf salad with Cajun chicken, honey-glazed lamb shank with chick pea salsa and marsala sauce and, finally, warm chocolate fondant. The bar with open fires is beautifully nooked and crannied, a fine spot for a pint of ale and a plateful of cider-and-apple sausages (stylishly topped with a 'nest' of fresh herbs). Ingredients are locally sourced and beers come from the excellent Grainstore Brewery in nearby Oakham (see entry 348).

directions	Off A47, 4 miles south east of Oakham.
meals	12pm-2pm; 6.30pm-9pm. Main courses £7.50-£12.95.
rooms	8 twins/doubles £50-£85.

Jason Allen
King's Arms,
Wing, Oakham,
Rutland LE15 8TL

tel	01572 737634
web	www.thekingsarms-wing.co.uk

map: 10 entry: 351

Rutland

Fox & Hounds
Exton

Exton is an unspoilt village of thatched houses and honey-coloured stone. On the sycamored village green sits the Fox and Hounds, looking more like an exquisite manor than the coaching house it used to be. Valter and Sandra Floris arrived two years ago, she a local girl, he, the chef, from Italy. No gastropubbery here, but they do have a reputation for food in both English and Italian styles: superbly authentic pizzas as well as more formal dishes. Or Valter combines the two, as in his roast leg of Rutland venison with polenta and a chianti jus. The lounge bar is country-smart with armchairs and sofa gathered round a roaring log fire; there's a white-walled dining room and a long public bar with darts. The large walled garden is brilliant for alfresco dining, and great for kids. Bedrooms have lovely views of garden or green; fall asleep to the hooting owl, wake to the hum of the distant tractor.

directions	Off A606 between Stamford & Oakham.
meals	12pm-2pm (2.30pm Sundays); 6.30pm-9pm. No food Sunday eve. Main courses £7-£14.
rooms	4: 2 double, 1 twin, 1 single sharing bathrooms. £42; singles £28.

Valter & Sandra Floris
Fox & Hounds,
19 The Green, Exton,
Oakham, Rutland LE15 8AP

tel	01572 812403
web	www.foxandhoundsrutland.com

map: 10 entry: 352

Rutland

Exeter Arms
Barrowden

Tip up on Thursday and you may be able to join a tour of the micro-brewery in the next-door barn. Peter and Elizabeth took over the solid, stone-built pub that stands by the duck pond and the green 10 years ago and have been brewing their own beers since 1998. The BBC (Blencowe Brewing Company) beers are all named 'Boys' – thus they serve Beach Boys (3.8%), Young Boys (4.1%) and Boys With Attitude (6%), among others. Inside there's bustle and bags of atmosphere, a long and cheery bar with an open fire and a thriving restaurant, and new dishes chalked up daily. There's lamb shank with honey, rosemary and garlic, or salmon-ish Arctic char in a mushroom and Pernod sauce, followed by lemon sponge or fruit crumble. Old-fashioned pub games inside, boules out, and themed supper evenings with blues and jazz. Bedrooms are simple.

directions	Off A47, between Leicester & Peterborough.
meals	12pm-2pm; 7pm-9pm. No food Sun & Mon evenings. Main courses £7.50-£14.
rooms	3: 1 double, 2 twins £60. Singles £30.
closed	Monday lunchtimes.

Pete & Elizabeth Blencowe
Exeter Arms,
Main Street, Barrowden,
Rutland LE15 8EQ

tel	01572 747247
web	www.exeterarms.com

map: 8 entry: 353

Rutland

The Old White Hart
Lyddington

In summer, the walled garden and 12(!) floodlit pétanque pitches fill with villagers and visitors. In winter, the spick-and-span bars, decked with old black beams, tiled floors, country prints and roaring log fires, bustle with locals downing Timmy Taylor's. Seasonal menus are appropriately British and traditional. Fruits, vegetables and herbs come from the pub's gardens and the local meat and game are top quality. Try Stuart's homemade Gloucester Old Spot sausages, or slow-roasted shoulder of lamb with garlic and rosemary – or go further afield for deep-fried Grimsby haddock with chunky chips. For pudding, why resist the rich chocolate and raspberry torte? Bedrooms have brass beds and valley views.

directions	1 mile south of Uppingham off A6003.
meals	12pm-2pm (2.30pm Sundays); 6.30pm-9pm. No food Sunday evenings. Main courses £8.95-£15.95; set menu £9.95 & £12.95.
rooms	5 twins/doubles £80-£85. Singles £55.

Stuart East
The Old White Hart,
Main Street, Lyddington,
Uppingham, Rutland LE15 9LR
tel   01572 821703

map: 10 entry: 354

Shropshire

The Waterdine
Llanfair Waterdine

"We've come for a ploughman's and been asked to wait while they bake some fresh rolls." Ken Adams's inn is charming and does brilliant food worth waiting for. Take a look at the tiny kitchen garden packed with herbs: a hint of what is to come. Fresh tomato soup with coriander pesto, roast mallard (wild not farmed) with parsnip mousse, Old Spot pork with chorizo, iced autumn berry parfait – take your fill in the conservatory or dining room. Bar food, too, shows skill and finesse: mushroom ramekins glazed with hollandaise, kipper terrine with dill and melt-in-the-mouth mayonnaise, Shropshire lamb. The garden, bordered by the river, is tailor-made for summer pleasure, to be enjoyed with a tasty drop of Woods' seasonal ales, a fine cider or perry. Modest bedrooms have amazing views, and the takeaway homemade pickles and preserves will have you dashing back for more.

directions	Off B4355, 4 miles west of Knighton.
meals	12pm-1.45pm; 7pm-9pm. Main courses £7.50-£15; set menus £16-£26.
rooms	3 doubles £90-£120. Singles £55-£70.
closed	Sunday evenings & Mondays (excluding Bank Holidays).

Ken Adams
The Waterdine,
Llanfair Waterdine, Knighton,
Shropshire LD7 1TU
tel   01547 528214
web   www.the-waterdine.co.uk

map: 8 entry: 355

Shropshire

Unicorn Inn
Ludlow

With its trio of Michelin-starred restaurants, Ludlow deserves at least one pub for foodies; the Unicorn is a contender for that title. It hides at the bottom end of town on the east bank of the River Corve as you approach the Shrewsbury road – and has a distinguished gastro neighbour in the Merchant House, run by Shaun Hill. The Unicorn, however, does not have to be booked as far in advance. And along with well-priced bar snacks there's some pretty decent tucker here. Fill your boots with proper food and plenty of it (rabbit in mustard sauce, sea bass with moules mariniere) served in front of a log fire in the panelled bar or at red-clothed tables in the dining rooms – or in the garden in summer. Ceremony here is about as out-of-place as Formula One tyres on a family Ford: no wonder it remains so popular. It's our pick of the pubs in town, and the beer is expertly kept.

directions	From A49, B4361 to Ludlow. After lights & bridge, bear right; bear left up hill. At top, down; after lights at bottom next right; 50yds on left.
meals	12pm-2.15pm; 6pm-9.15pm. Main courses £6-£13.50.
closed	3pm-6pm; 3.30pm-6.30pm Sundays.

Mike & Rita Knox
Unicorn Inn,
Lower Corve Street, Ludlow,
Shropshire SY8 1DU

tel   01584 873555
web   www.theunicorninn.com

map: 8 entry: 356

Shropshire

Roebuck Inn
Brimfield

When Peter and Julie arrived they took the village by storm. The old inn has been rejuvenated... here are well-kept ales, fine wines, new bedrooms and an inventive menu. The lounge bar's linen-fold panelling may be (a touch) dated, but not the kitchen's daily offerings. In a newly decorated, shiny-floored dining room, lemon-spiced gravadlax and quail-egg, fig and balsamic salad come as starters. For mains: a legendary fish pie – or roast chicken breast with caramelised button onions, smoked bacon and red wine. The cheese board, culled from the Marches and Welsh Borders, is possibly the best for miles around; it comes with freshly-baked bread, homemade biscuits and a glass of port. We'd travel the extra mile for the food and the welcome and for the attention to detail which includes proper coffee and homemade biscuits in the bedrooms.

directions	Off A49 4 miles south of Ludlow.
meals	12pm-2.30pm; 6.30pm-9.30pm; 7pm-8.30pm Sundays (bookings only). Main courses £8.95-£16.95.
rooms	3: 2 doubles, 1 twin £60-£70. Singles £45.

Peter & Julie Jenkins
Roebuck Inn,
Brimfield, Ludlow,
Shropshire SY8 4NE

tel   01584 711230
web   www.roebuckinn.com

map: 8 entry: 357

The Peacock
Boraston

Look out for Mrs Brown, a former landlady who drowned in the nearby river and is said to haunt the place. She pales into insignificance, however, in the presence of this wonderful inn. Step over the entrance stones, worn hollow by centuries of travellers, into a 14th-century, low-beamed bar. There's also an oak-panelled restaurant-lounge with a log fire, a loft bistro, a terrace for summer and bedrooms of which any ghost would be proud. The food gives a passing nod to France and the mediterranean; seasonal specials include tuna with sauce vierge, and local venison with redcurrant and port sauce. Regulars include a healthy blend of locals – whose preferred quaffing leans towards Hereford cider, Hobsons and Hook Norton ales – and those 'in the know' who come for the set-price, early evening dinners; Sunday lunches, too. A dozen or more wines come by the glass, and there's a whole fabulous raft of cognacs and malts.

directions	On A456, 2 miles east of Tenbury Wells.
meals	12pm-2.15pm; 6.30pm-9.15pm. Main courses £8.95-£15.95; set menu £13.
rooms	6 twins/doubles £60-£85.

James Vidler
The Peacock, Worcester Road,
Boraston, Tenbury Wells,
Shropshire WR15 8LL

tel	01584 810506
web	www.thepeacockinn-hotel.co.uk

map: 8 entry: 358

The Crown
Hopton Wafers

The tranquillity of the little valley makes this a lovely place to stay and bedrooms, though modest, have all the comforts expected by this generation's explorers. But bring with you an appetite after your hike on the moors – the food is mouthwatering. Daily specials might include broccoli and goat's cheese pancakes with a parmesan crust, pork and stilton sausages with apricot gravy, and Barbary duck breast with an orange and armagnac glaze. Real ale such as Hobsons and a wide selection of wines by the glass make admirable accompaniments. The chef's winter specials are very fairly priced (venison casserole with juniper berries and root vegetables at well under £10), and fresh fish choices above the norm for a pub so deeply set in middle England. Inside are beams, inglenook, paintings and flowers; outside: a country garden.

directions	On A4117 between Cleobury Mortimer & Ludlow, 2 miles west of Cleobury.
meals	12pm-2.30pm (3.30pm Sundays); 7pm-9.30pm. Main courses £6.75-£13.50.
rooms	7: 6 double, 1 twin £80. Singles £49.50.

Howard Hill-Lines
The Crown,
Hopton Wafers, Cleobury Mortimer,
Shropshire DY14 0NB

tel	01299 270372
web	www.crownathopton.co.uk

map: 8 entry: 359

Shropshire

The Cookhouse
Ludlow

We recommend the Cookhouse particularly for dinner which can be a treat – the sort of place where you can tuck into pot-roast partridge with thyme, garlic and red wine sauce. There are more than 50 individual dishes on the menu, and a big choice of house wines by the glass, so enjoy your deliberations. That said, you may drop into this handsome red-brick building at any time of day for a pint of Hobson's Best – accompanied by a salad niçoise, perhaps, or Cajun chicken strips with avocado in an orange and honey dressing, in small or large servings. Even the rare breed rump steak with chasseur sauce, or Cornish sole with parsley butter and dressed salad won't break the bank. The Cookhouse is not particularly 'pubby', apart from a very decent pint of Hobson's on handpump, so the drinkers are mostly locals. You might pass this place by the busy A49 without a nod unless we told you otherwise.

directions	2 miles north of Ludlow on A49.
meals	11am-3pm; 6pm-10pm (11am-10pm weekends). Main courses £7.95-£15.95.
rooms	15 twins/doubles £40-£65. Singles £25-£40.

Paul Brooks
The Cookhouse,
Bromfield, Ludlow,
Shropshire SY8 2JR
tel 01584 856565
web www.thecookhouse.org.uk

map: 8 entry: 360

Shropshire

Hundred House Hotel
Norton

Henry is an innkeeper of the old school, with a great sense of humour – he once kept chickens, but they didn't keep him. Having begun its life in the 14th century, the place rambles charmingly inside as well as out. Enter a world of blazing log fires, soft brick walls, oak panelling and quarry-tiled floors. Dried flowers hang from beams, herbs sit in vases, blackboard menus trumpet prime Shropshire sirloin, chicken blanquette with lemon and sage, grilled tuna in Moroccan spices. In the restaurant, Sylvia's wild and wonderful collage art hangs on wild and wonderful walls, and there's live music in the barn. Quirky bedrooms come in different shapes and sizes, with carafes of shampoo in the bathrooms and pillows sprinkled with lavender water – homemade, judging by the extraordinarily lush herb and flower gardens outside. Wander out with a pint of Heritage Mild and share a quiet moment with a few stone lions.

directions	Midway between Bridgnorth & Telford on A422.
meals	12pm-2.30pm; 6pm-9.30pm; 7pm-9pm Sundays. Main courses £7.95-£18.95.
rooms	10 twins/doubles £85-£150. Singles £75.

Phillips Family
Hundred House Hotel,
Bridgnorth Road, Norton, Telford,
Shropshire TF11 9EE
tel 01952 730353
web www.hundredhouse.co.uk

map: 9 entry: 361

Shropshire

Wenlock Edge Inn
Wenlock Edge

A E Housman's 'blue remembered hills' set the scene, high on a limestone ridge. Dave and Debbie's inn has a terrace with that view – and a beer garden – and a conservatory. This is walking and riding country, so set off down one of the many bridleways and come back hungry: you can look forward to some great food at the Wenlock. The menu is largely based on locally available produce, and the chef-landlord, being a Shropshire Lad, knows what's what. In the bar is Hobson's real ale and guests such as Archers Golden – each a fine accompaniment to the day's tomato and basil soup, oak-roasted Bradon salmon or tender shank of Shropshire lamb, plus fresh vegetables in generous portions. Settle into a cosy corner by the log stove... And if this militates against a long drive home, the newly spruced-up bedrooms are sublimely quiet and full of homely touches.

directions	On B4371 between Much Wenlock & Church Stretton.
meals	12pm-3pm; 7pm-9pm. Main courses £7.25-£12.95.
rooms	3 twins/doubles £70. Singles £50.
closed	Monday & Tuesday evenings; 3pm-7pm Wednesday-Sunday.

David & Debbie Morgan
Wenlock Edge Inn, Hilltop,
Wenlock Edge, Much Wenlock,
Shropshire TF13 6DJ
tel   01746 785678
web www.wenlockedgeinn.co.uk

map: 8 entry: 362

Shropshire

The Riverside Inn
Cound

The change of hands may be recent but there's already a buzz in this huntin', shootin' and fishin' inn standing on a wide bend of the Severn and looking out over open country towards the Wrekin and beyond. The Riverside Inn is worth seeking out for its open fires in winter and its dining conservatory with the amazing all year round view. Seasonal monthly menus might include starters of butternut squash soup or tuna and bean salad; main dishes could be cod with tarragon and pernod, or mediterranean chicken with feta cheese and sun-blushed tomato. Make the most of the Salopian beers and Broadland country fruit wines, and enjoy the lovely garden in summer, smartly furnished with patio and barbecue pit. You can fish from the bank. New bedrooms are big and comfortable.

directions	On A458, Shrewsbury road.
meals	12pm-2.30pm; 6.30pm-9.30pm. Main courses £7-£10.50.
rooms	7: 6 doubles, 1 twin £60-£75.
closed	3pm-6pm.

Peter Stanford Davies
The Riverside Inn,
Cound,
Cressage
Shropshire SY5 6AF
tel   01952 510900

map: 8 entry: 363

Shropshire

The Burlton Inn
Burlton

Gerry Bean's philosophy here is tried and successful: keep it simple. Well-stocked with real ales and wines of the month, the central bar has assorted pine tables in front of an open log fire. Recent additions include half a dozen smart bedrooms at the back – but not so classy that you can't take the the kids and the dog – and, 'in response to popular demand', this year's kitchen and dining room improvements. Yet the Burlton remains both intimate and personal. The staff are super, and there's nothing wrong with the food either, from home-cooked gammon or rare roast beef sarnies to roast rack of lamb with apricot and mustard glaze – or plaice fillets with smoked salmon, chablis and prawn cream. All are chalked up daily. Neither the building itself nor the road it stands on are the prettiest, but the minute you enter you know the warmth of the place is genuine – just like its owner.

directions	On A528 Wrexham road, 8 miles north of Shrewsbury.
meals	12pm-2pm; 6.30pm-9.45pm; 7pm-9.30pm Sundays. Main courses £5.50-£14.95.
rooms	6 twins/doubles, £80-£90. Singles £50.

Gerald Bean
The Burlton Inn,
Burlton,
Shrewsbury,
Shropshire SY4 5TB
tel   01939 270284

map: 8 entry: 364

Somerset

Royal Oak Inn
Withypool

It's a magical drive through twisting lanes shrouded in early morning mist to this haven of comfort – and the 300-year-old Royal Oak is sheer indulgence. Look on any map: Withypool is the point at which tiny roads across the moor meet, a small forgotten place, so remote that it has grown immune to outside cares. Food, all home-cooked, ranges from a pint of prawns to venison and redcurrant sausages; there are two real ales, six wines by the glass and the bar bustles comfortably. Oak trestles, beams and crackling log fires – just what you need after a walk to Tarr Steps. But heed Jake the barman's advice: an Exmoor mile is longer than an ordinary one; take time to absorb the barren embrace of stone and bog and heather that blazes a resplendent purple in summer. Divided between the main inn and two superb cottages across the courtyard, the bedrooms are fresh and stylish: *toile de Jouy* on the walls, maybe an antique half-tester, sheepskin rugs to cosset tired feet. There's no better place to flee.

directions	A369, left at Exebridge on B3222 to Dulverton. Withypool signed.
meals	12pm-2pm; 6.30pm-9.30pm. Main courses £8.25-£16.95.
rooms	8: 6 doubles, 2 twins £90-£110.

Gail Sloggett
Royal Oak Inn,
Withypool,
Somerset TA24 7QP
tel   01643 831506
web   www.royaloakwithypool.co.uk

map: 2 entry: 365

The Crown Hotel
Exford

Entering Hugo's mildly eccentric world in the middle of Exmoor is guaranteed to be entertaining – don't be surprised to find a horse propping up the bar! Following the success of the Rising Sun in Lynmouth, these generous hosts have an in-built knack of knowing how to spoil. Hugo, impeccably dressed beneath a shock of white hair, sharpens his wits playing bridge with seasoned oldies who "clout me over the head if I make a foolish bid". You're in wild, horsey country where the outlook of laid-back locals reminds you of easy-going rural Ireland. The building itself is Exmoor's oldest coaching inn, set in front of a village green, with a beautiful sloping water garden to the rear. Dine on teriyaki of salmon or shepherd's pie in the lively bar, warmed by a log fire, or sea bass with a lobster vierge in the more hushed dining room; then retire to serenely elegant bedrooms upstairs. Destined to get better and better.

Royal Oak
Luxborough

Five miles south of Minehead, as the pheasant flies, is Luxborough, tucked under the lip of the Exmoor's Brendon hills. This is hunting country and from September to February beaters and loaders traditionally lunch at The Oak. The food is fresh and first class, ranging from bar snacks to imaginative daily fish dishes, game from nearby estates and vegetable from local growers. A low-beamed, log-fired bar (with locals' table) leads to a warren of dining rooms beautifully kitted out with polished dining tables and hunting prints on deep green walls. There's a miscellany of aged furniture and wooden and millstone flooring in the two rustic bars. In spate, the river Washford can detour through the bar. One bedroom comes with benign mop-hatted, foot-licking ghost. Ask James about it!

directions	M5 junc. 25; A38 to Taunton; A358 for Minehead; B3224 to Exford, via Wheddon Cross; by village green.
meals	12pm-2pm; 7pm-9.30pm. Main courses £7.95-£12.75.
rooms	16: 10 doubles, 4 twins, 2 singles £95-£130. Singles £55.

directions	A358 for Minehead; left on A39. At Washford left for Mill & Abbey. Right at White Horse Inn; right after Valiant Soldier. Follow road to Luxborough.
meals	12pm-2pm; 7pm-9pm. Main courses £6.95-£14.95.
rooms	12: 9 doubles, 2 twins, 1 single £65-£85. Singles £55.
closed	2.30pm-6pm (7pm Sundays).

Hugo Jeune
The Crown Hotel,
Exford,
Somerset TA24 7PP
tel   01643 831554
web   www.crownhotelexmoor.co.uk

James & Siân Waller, Sue Hinds
Royal Oak,
Luxborough, Dunster,
Somerset TA23 0SH
tel   01984 640319
web   www.theroyaloakinnluxborough.co.uk

map: 2 entry: 366

map: 2 entry: 367

Three Horseshoes
Langley Marsh

A proper, traditional local and proud of it. Come for good beer and good food, kept and cooked by John and Marella. He's an MG man (owns four) and the pub is full of memorabilia, steering wheels, display cases, Dinky toys, and a unique collection of black and white photos of the racing greens. Beers are Fuller's London Pride, Otter Bitter and Palmers IPA tapped from the cask. As for meals – "home-cooked food from heaven", said a judge on TV's *Taste of the West*: Marella was a finalist. Pies and pizza, soup and sandwiches, specials on the board, all freshly made, no chips, nothing frozen, and veg from their own garden. Just so you see how seriously they take it, they list their suppliers on the back of the menu. In the bustling front room, polished tables, dark wallpaper dotted with banknotes, table skittles, dominoes, darts and a piano; in the dining room, old settles; in the garden, sloping lawns and a very good play area.

Blue Ball Inn
Triscombe

In 2003 the Blue Ball rolled down the hill from the original thatched building into its new home in the ancient stables below. Using old craftsmen's skills and plenty of vision, they then metamorphosed into a rather smart pub. Climb the fabulous beech stairs to a swishly-carpeted central bar that leads to two inviting dining areas, each with open fires, country furnishings and fabrics and high-raftered ceilings. Menus are imaginative, produce local. Treat yourself to warm goat's cheese salad, seared tuna with saffron and ginger potato chutney, or pan-fried Quantock rabbit with lemon grass. At the bar, lunchtime crusty rolls and excellent cheese ploughman's make this a popular walkers' pit-stop. There are four ales, drinkable wines by the glass and local farm ciders – in summer best sipped out in the decked garden with views across the Vale of Taunton.

directions	Off B3227 from Wiveliscombe.
meals	12pm-1.45pm; 7pm-9.30pm. Main courses £5.20-£11.50.
rooms	2 holiday cottages £60.
closed	Mondays in winter.

directions	From Taunton A358 for Minehead; just past Bishops Lydeard right to Triscombe.
meals	12pm-2pm; 7pm-9.30pm. Main courses £7.95-£16.95.
rooms	2 twins/doubles £70.
closed	3pm-7pm; Christmas Day.

John & Marella Hopkins
Three Horseshoes,
Langley Marsh,
Wiveliscombe,
Somerset TA4 2UL
tel 01984 623763

map: 2 entry: 368

Peter Alcroft & Sharon Murdoch
Blue Ball Inn,
Triscombe,
Bishops Lydeard, Taunton,
Somerset TA4 3HE
tel 01984 618242

map: 3 entry: 369

Somerset

Carew Arms
Crowcombe

You can't keep a good publican down. Supposedly retired, Reg Ambrose is back – if not behind the bar, then assisting son Simon in reviving this pub in the shadow of the Quantock Hills. It was, and still is, a mammoth task. But the outside loos have gone and the old skittle alley has been transformed into a bar-dining room where French windows lead to a sunny back terrace and young garden. The front room, with its hatch bar, flagstones, plain settles, pine tables with benches and vast inglenook remains the same – delightfully unspoilt. Down pints of Exmoor Ale, engage in lively conversation, be inspired by the menu and dishes such as homemade faggots with madeira gravy, olive-crusted sea bass with basil purée, locally farmed beef steaks and orange trifle. Bedrooms upstairs are smart. Picnic tables outside have gently rural wooded views.

Somerset

Rising Sun
West Bagborough

In 2002 the Sun rose from the ashes of a fire, and now shines brightly. Constructed around the original 16th-century cob walls and magnificent door, its reincarnation is bold and contemporary with 80 tons of solid oak timbers, a slate-floored bar, chunky-modern furnishings, spotlighting and swagged drapery. Modern art is for sale, a baby grand stands in one corner, and high in the rafters is a dining room with views unfurling across the Vale of Taunton. It's an impressive setting for impressive food. There's roasted red pepper risotto, fresh tuna with salad niçoise, steamed game pudding, fillet steak with mushroom sauce and mustard mash. Once here you'll want to stay: choose between a French-inspired room with painted furniture or a cosy four-poster. All this is the brainchild of one Russian-born landlady, formerly a translator with the UN. But that's another story.

directions	Off A358 between Taunton & Minehead.
meals	12pm-2.30pm; 7pm-10pm. No food Sunday evenings. Main courses £7.50-£11.50.
rooms	4: 3 doubles, 1 single, 2 sharing bathroom £69. Singles £39.

Simon Ambrose
Carew Arms,
Crowcombe, Taunton,
Somerset TA4 4AD
tel 01984 618631

map: 2 entry: 370

directions	Off A358 Taunton to Minehead road, 6 miles north west of Taunton.
meals	12pm-2pm; 7pm-9.30pm. Main courses £7.95-£16.95.
rooms	2: 1 double, 1 four-poster £80.
closed	Mondays except Bank Holidays.

Eleana Ellis
Rising Sun,
West Bagborough, Taunton,
Somerset TA4 3ES
tel 01823 432575
web www.theriser.co.uk

map: 3 entry: 371

Somerset

The Greyhound Inn
Staple Fitzpaine

Walls are decked with collages of pictures and fishing memorabilia. Let the eye wander while sitting at old, wooden tables worn nicely from frequent use and decorated with vases of wild flowers. A roaring hearth in winter, a flagstoned bar busy with friendly locals, and a good meal – fish delivered daily from Brixham, meat from within four miles. Then "retreat in good order", as one boxing print wisely suggests, to comfortable, hotel-style bedrooms. The Back Room restaurant serves a new fusion of fresh food. Ivor and Lucy bought the inn after leaving busy careers in pharmaceutics. "We still work long hours but we see each other now," says Ivor, obviously happy in his new role.

directions	M5, junc. 25, A358 for Ilminster for 4 miles; right for Staple Fitzpaine. Left at T-junc. Village 1.5 miles further. Inn on right at x-roads.
meals	12pm-2pm; 7pm-9.30pm (9pm Sundays). Main courses £8-£18.
rooms	4: 2 doubles, 1 twin/double, 1 twin £75-£90. Singles £49.95.
closed	3pm-6pm Monday-Saturday except on race days at Taunton.

Ivor & Lucy Evans
The Greyhound Inn,
Staple Fitzpaine, Taunton,
Somerset TA3 5SP
tel   01823 480227
web   www.the-greyhoundinn.fsbusiness.co.uk

map: 3 entry: 372

Somerset

Helyar Arms
East Coker

Aussie Ian McKerracher's gastropub and inn is worth a long detour for the lovely atmosphere, the food that goes from strength to strength, and for the handsome feudal village it lives in. Daily up-dated boards of seasonal dishes demonstrate the style of the new set-up: duck confit with fresh spinach, mash and red wine jus, roast venison with grain mustard and juniper berries, and a sticky toffee pudding that's served with a glass of Yalumba Muscat. Real ales, Somerset cider and global wines are well priced. For cheese lovers there might be Montgomery cheddar, Somerset brie and Dorset blue vinny. Low beams and a woodburner in the lounge, a raftered restaurant in the apple loft, a garden and skittles. Bedrooms are more than comfortable and serenely quiet. Come downstairs in the morning for fresh-baked pastries and, quite possibly, Puccini.

directions	From A37, on A30 follow signs to East Coker.
meals	12pm-2.30pm; 6.30pm-9.30pm; 12pm-9pm Sundays (till 4.30pm January-Easter). Main courses £8.95-£14.95.
rooms	6: 2 doubles, 3 twins, 1 single. £70-£80.; singles £59.

Ian McKerracher
Helyar Arms,
Moor Lane, East Coker, Yeovil,
Somerset BA22 9JR
tel   01935 862332
web   www.helyar-arms.com

map: 3 entry: 373

Somerset

Halfway House
Pitney Hill

Somerset's mecca for beer and cider aficionados. No music or electronic games to distract you from the serious sampling of up to eight ales tapped straight from the drum, heady farmhouse ciders and bottled beers from around the globe. Passionate real-pub-lovers will not be able to leave. The two simple and homely rooms, lined with old benches and pews at scrubbed tables on stone-slabbed floors have a friendly buzz. And three crackling log fires and daily papers to nod off over... A quick lunchtime pint can easily turn into two hours of beer-fuelled bliss. Blot up the alcohol with thick homemade soups, wonderful cheese ploughman's lunches served with huge slabs of crusty bread or prize-winning sausages and mash. In the evenings, the Halfway's revered homemade curries are gorgeous with pints of Butcombe, Branscombe and Hop Back ales.

directions	Beside B3153, midway between Langport & Somerton.
meals	12pm-2pm; 7pm-9.30pm. No food Sundays. Main courses £4.50-£6.50.
closed	3pm-5.30pm (7pm Sundays).

Julian Litchfield
Halfway House,
Pitney Hill, Langport,
Somerset TA10 9AB
tel 01458 252513

map: 3 entry: 374

Somerset

Red Lion Inn
Babcary

A lattice of hot white bread with unsalted butter arrives unannounced and with a cheery smile – and the girls will keep a benign eye out for you right through from starters to coffee. Best to book at weekends. This is another new Somerset revival that espouses the best of pub tradition with excellent food. There is a single central bar with a locals' Snug behind that dispenses real ale, local cider and house wines from France and Oz. To one side, hair-cord carpets, sofas and the cast-iron stove lend a welcome to the bright bar/lounge, while to the far right a dozen well-spaced country dining tables plainly set out on original flagstone flooring are part of an immaculate reconstruction. Daily menus offer as little or as much as you'd like, from small or large Caesar salads to salmon fillet with shellfish cream, and lamb rosettes with glazed garlic and rosemary.

directions	Off A37 & A303 7 miles north of Yeovil.
meals	12pm-2.30pm; 7pm-9pm (9.30pm Fridays & Saturdays). Main courses £6.95-£16.
closed	Sunday evenings.

Clare & Charles Garrard
Red Lion Inn,
Babcary
Somerton, Somerset TA11 7ED
tel 01458 223230

map: 3 entry: 375

Somerset

The Montague Inn
Shepton Montague

With scarcely another dwelling in sight, the 17th-century public house still looks like the grocer's it once was. It also happens to neighbour one of the south west's largest organic farms – so your breakfast eggs couldn't be fresher. Small remains beautiful, with real ales straight from the cask, log fires in the bar, candles on stripped pine tables, a recently extended dining area leading to gardens with country views and three bedrooms that are infinitely preferable to those on the trunk routes nearby. The food is simple yet imaginative: ciabattas, maybe, with bacon, brie and caramelised peppers and plenty of homemade pies such as lamb and apricot. And there's true quality in dishes such as duck breast with cherries and brandy sauce and salmon with lettuce, peas and bacon that feature on the daily à la carte. Good for a hearty meal, then, and a friendly country stopover away from it all.

directions	Off A359 2 miles east of Castle Cary, towards Bruton.
meals	12pm-2pm; 7pm-9pm. Main courses £5-£13.
rooms	3: 2 double, 1 twin £55-£70.
closed	Sunday evenings & Mondays.

Julian & Linda Bear
The Montague Inn,
Shepton Montague, Castle Cary,
Somerset BA9 8JW
tel   01749 813213

map: 3 entry: 376

Somerset

The Manor House Inn
Ditcheat

Just where it should be, at the heart of a quaint village, opposite the Post Office and one of England's last red telephone boxes. The villages around here are the stuff of postcards: smatterings of Somerset stone cottages among the gently rolling hills. The pub started as the focus of village life in the 17th century and, after playing all the possible variations on the theme of inn, has now been given a new song-sheet in gastro guise. The flagstone flooring is more ordered than most, the bar less scuffed and more polished and the atmosphere more formal than you'd expect of a typical village boozer. So's the food: grilled calves' liver and smoked bacon on parsnip bubble-and-squeak with a balsamic vinegar sauce. But there's a superb pint of Thatchers or Butcombe on tap and a belting fire in the main room. Children are welcome, there's a skittles alley, and outdoor tables.

directions	Between A37-A371, in village of Ditcheat, next to the church.
meals	12pm-2pm; 7pm-9.30pm. Main courses £7-£13.
rooms	3: 2 doubles, 1 twin £70. Singles £45.
closed	3pm-6.30pm (7pm Sundays).

James & Tania Finch
Manor House Inn,
Ditcheat, Somerset BA4 6RB
tel   01749 860276
web   www.destninationsuk.com

map: 3 entry: 377

Somerset

The Three Horseshoes
Batcombe

Down a web of country lanes, the Benson's honey-stoned coaching inn sits by the church. Step into a long, low bar, its beams painted cream, its pine scrubbed, its pink-sponged walls hung with Mediterranean landscapes. There are cushioned window seats and an inglenook with a wood-burning stove. David and Liz have created a relaxing place that appeals as much to locals in for a pint of Butcombe as to diners and families; there's a summer terrace and a great play area for children. The modern British menu is full of promise: start with smoked fishcake with horseradish and caper sauce, move on to marinated venison with grain mustard and red wine jus, finish with apple and blueberry crumble. If you're here for the ale, don't miss the chance of a quenching pint of Mine Beer from Blindmans Brewery in nearby Leighton.

directions	Off A359 between Frome & Bruton, 7 miles south west of Frome.
meals	12pm-2pm (2.30pm Sundays); 7pm-9.30pm (10pm Fridays & Saturdays; 9pm Sundays). Main courses £6.95-£16.95.
closed	Christmas Day.

David & Liz Benson
The Three Horseshoes,
Batcombe, Shepton Mallet,
Somerset BA4 6HE
tel   01749 850359

map: 3 entry: 378

Somerset

Waggon & Horses
Doulting Beacon

At first glance, a typical creeper-clad old coaching inn on the busy Wells-Frome road, with fine stone steps, leaded, mullioned windows and the odd furry trophy on the wall. Yet this is far more than a pub. The urbane, Columbian-born, Harvard-educated Francisco has poured his passions for classical music, wine and local fish and game into this hugely-popular meeting place. He's created an impressive international concert programme and gives gallery space to local artists in between creating tantalising dishes such as pot-roasted guinea fowl (right up HRH Prince Charles's street; he made a special visit to this windy spot on the Mendips). A wood-burning stove and the odd swirl on the carpet make sure this is still a pub, though the beers (Greene King IPA, Wadworth 6X) play second fiddle to a carefully-picked wine list. A solidly good pub with an imaginative twist.

directions	Follow signs at junction of A37 & A361, north east of Shepton Mallet.
meals	12pm-2pm, 6.30pm-9.30pm. No food Christmas Day. Main courses £8-£15.
closed	2.30pm-6pm; 3pm-7pm Sundays.

Francisco Cardona
Waggon & Horses, Frome Road,
Doulting Beacon, Shepton Mallett,
Somerset BA4 4LA
tel   01749 880302
web   www.music-at-the-waggon-and-horses.co.uk

map: 3 entry: 379

The Talbot Inn
Mells

The huge oak gate opens to a flowered, cobbled courtyard, with a big, rough-boarded, ever-so-friendly bar to one side, and restaurant and bedrooms to the other. Butcombe bitter flows straight from the cask, there are flagons of scrumpy and wines galore (three by the glass). Soak up any excess by a platter-full of tagliatelli with smoked salmon and asparagus in tarragon cream sauce; you can have it as a starter or as a main course. Dinner under the hop-strewn rafters highlights fresh Brixham fish such as brill fillets in nut-brown butter with capers, prawns and lemon; or go for a winter rabbit and vegetable stew with herb dumplings. You have here all the oak beams, archways and golden stones you could wish for from a 15th-century coaching inn in a Somerset village. And don't miss the Burne Jones windows in the beautiful, medieval church.

Tucker's Grave Inn
Faulkland

If only the essence of Tucker's could be bottled and preserved; 'to be used as emergency tonic for the despairing' the label would read. In an unassuming, almost-unsigned 17th-century stone building, Tucker's is defiantly informal. An unprecedentedly narrow, extremely wiggly corridor leads in from the garden door; you'd be forgiven for thinking you'd wandered into someone's living room as you stoop to enter the warmth. There's no bar and no fridge, just four beer casks and containers of local cider sitting in their jackets in the bay (no draught) and a stack of crisp boxes against the wall. You could pour your own beer... but that may not be allowed. A small open fire lends cosiness to the no-frills room next to the tiny wooden serving room. The interiors are as basic as they come but the atmosphere is roaring at weekends. In the words of one regular: "you can't come here without chatting to someone". And now there's a new skittles room in the big back garden.

directions	From Frome A362 for Radstock; left signed Mells in 0.5 miles.
meals	12pm-2.30pm; 6.45pm-11pm. Main courses £6.50-£14.50.
rooms	8: 7 twins/doubles, 1 with separate bath £75-£125. Singles £55.

directions	A362 Radstock-Frome; left onto A362; through Faulkland, pub near next junction.
meals	Sandwiches only c. £1.50.
closed	3pm-6pm (7pm Sundays).

Roger Elliott
The Talbot Inn,
Selwood Street, Mells, Frome,
Somerset BA11 3PN
tel   01373 812254
web   www.talbotinn.com

Glenda & Ivan Swift
Tucker's Grave Inn,
Faulkland, Radstock,
Somerset BA3 5XF
tel   01373 834230

map: 3 entry: 380

map: 3 entry: 381

Somerset

The Hunters' Lodge
Priddy

Pulling up at the windswept Priddy crossroads high on the Mendip Hills, you'd be mad to ignore this starkly rendered old building. A little pearl lies within. It's been in the same family since 1840 and Mr Dore is its proudest fixture, administering ale to cavers, pot-holers, hikers and the odd local for over 30 years. Lively chatter drowns the ticking clock and the crackling fire. The pristine main bar is delightfully devoid of a modern make-up – just simple wooden benches and tables, a shove-ha'penny board, old photographs on the walls, Exmoor Ale and Butcombe fresh from the barrel. There's a lounge bar and a rear room for families, equally plain. Food is straightforward, homemade, tasty, great value. Folk in muddy boots come for just-made bowls of chilli, cauliflower cheese, faggots and peas and chunks of bread and cheese. A totally unpretentious treat.

directions	1.5 miles up Priddy-Wells road; look out for the TV mast.
meals	11.30-2.30; 6.30-11pm. Snacks £1.80-£2.70.

Mr Dore
The Hunters' Lodge,
Priddy, Wells, Somerset BA5 3AR
tel 01749 672275

map: 3 entry: 382

Somerset

The Crown
Churchill

Once a coaching stop between Bristol and Exeter, then the village grocer's, now an unspoilt pub. Modern makeovers have passed this gem by, and beer reigns supreme, with up to 10 ales tapped from the barrel. For 18 years landlord Tim Rogers has resisted piped music and electronic games; who needs them in these little beamed and flagstoned bars? A wooden window seat here, a settle there... the rustic surroundings and the jolly atmosphere draw both locals and walkers treading the Mendips hills. Bag a seat by the log fire, cradle a pint of Bath SPA or RCH PG Steam Bitter, be lulled by the hum of regulars at the bar. If you're here at lunchtime you'll find a short, traditional, blackboard menu: winter-warming bowls of soup, thick-cut rare roast beef sandwiches, baked potatoes, winter casseroles, treacle pud. Evenings are reserved for the serious art of ale drinking, and it's packed at weekends, especially in summer.

directions	From Bristol A38 to Churchill, right for Weston S.M. Immed left in front of Nelson Pub, along lane.
meals	12pm-2.30pm. Main courses £2.90-£5.95.

Tim Rogers
The Crown,
The Batch, Churchill,
Somerset BS25 5PP
tel 01934 852995

map: 3 entry: 383

Bear & Swan
Chew Magna

The area just to the south-west of Bristol is a gastronomic desert, with this pub one of the few oases – a relief to frustrated foodies. It is a four-square Victorian pub in the middle of Chew Magna, a pretty, busy village six miles from Bristol in the Chew Valley (good walking country). The Pushman family rescued it from dereliction in 1999 and, with massive skill, have created a roomy and airy bar with a damned good restaurant. The floorboards were reclaimed and the stone de-plastered; bay windows hang low and a big log fire blazes in the bar. Ladderback chairs, candlelight and flowers, bottles racked on the wall... it's hard to resist a swift half before eating. Beers (Butcombe and John Smith), wines and an irresistible menu draw keen eaters from far and near. Choose from chicken liver parfait with apricot chutney, grilled goat's cheese on smoked salmon, mussel chowder – these are generous, and just the starters! Puddings are delicious: baked Alaska, chocolate Royale, fruit crumbles with their own jugs of custard. The menu changes daily, food is locally sourced and cooked to order, and there's lots of fresh fish. Last, and first, Caroline Pushman is a delightful, informal and ever-patient hostess, and her staff are unusually helpful.

directions	On B3130 between A37 & A38.
meals	12pm-2pm; 7pm-10pm.
	Main courses £4-£17.
rooms	2 doubles £80. Singles £50.
closed	Sunday evenings.

Nigel & Caroline Pushman
Bear & Swan,
South Parade, Chew Magna,
Somerset BS40 8SL
tel   01275 331100
web   www.chewmagna.co.uk

map: 3 entry: 384

Somerset

Queen's Arms
Bleadon

A curious spot, for the ineffable Weston-super-Mare is just round the corner. But just behind the village begin the Mendip Hills, whose bleak winter walks challenge the most hardy, and whose wild and beautiful woodland and fields sing in summer. The Queen's Arms, like many, is not especially seductive from the outside, but cheerfully sweeps you in to four terracotta rooms, much chat and laughter and some jolly good food (which sometimes goes French or Greek). There are hunting prints on the walls, wood in the burners, candles in bottles and proper pub dishes, from homemade pâté and ham and eggs to rump steak, duck breast, lemon sole, stilton and chicken supreme. Ales come from the barrel (Palmers IPA, Butcombe Bitter, Otter), cider is Thatchers, staff are swift and the family runs the place with good humour - not least on Sunday quiz nights.

directions	A370 from WSM; left towards Bleadon; 50yds from church.
meals	12pm-2pm (2.30pm Friday-Sunday); 7pm-9.30pm (6.30pm Fri & Sat). No food Sunday evenings. Main courses £5.90-£12.
closed	2.30pm-5.30pm Monday-Friday.

C & A Smith & M Sanders
Queen's Arms, Celtic Way, Bleadon,
Weston-super-Mare,
Somerset BS24 0NF

tel 01934 812080
web www.queensarms.co.uk

map: 3 entry: 385

Somerset

The Black Horse
Clapton-in-Gordano

A cracking pub. The Snug Bar once doubled as the village lock-up and, if it weren't for the electric lights and motors in the car park, you'd be hard pushed to remember you were in the 21st century. All flagstone and dark moody wood, the main room bears the scuffs of centuries of drinking. Settles and old tables sit around the walls, and cottage windows with dark, wobbly shutters let a little of the outside in. The fire – a real focus – roars in its vast hearth beneath a fine set of antique guns, just the sort of place to pull off muddy boots. Sepia prints of parish cricket teams and steam tractors clutter the walls and cask ales pour from the stone ledge behind the wide hatch bar. The food is unfancy bar fodder, with the odd traditional special. Ale is what's important and that's what takes pride of place; beneath a chalkboard six jacketed casks squat above drip pans (there are five wines too). There's plenty of garden; well worth leaving the motorway for.

directions	M5 junc. 19 for Portbury & Clapton. Left into Clevedon Lane.
meals	12pm-2pm. No food Sundays. Main courses £3.50-£5.
closed	2.30pm-5pm (Monday-Thursday).

Nicholas Evans
The Black Horse,
Clevedon Lane,
Clapton-in-Gordano,
Bristol, Somerset BS20 7RH

tel 01275 842105

map: 3 entry: 386

Staffordshire

The Holly Bush Inn
Salt

Geoffrey Holland came to the Holly Bush some years ago and has turned it into a thriving local. Indeed, all the emphasis is local – especially where food is concerned. Cheeses, vegetables, meat and game (hear the shoot from the pub garden) are local and almost exclusively organic; herbs are fresh from the garden. Even a few of the recipes, such as the oatcakes (pancakes not biscuits!), are strictly Staffs. Only the fish, and some of the beers (the Boddingtons comes from Manchester) are from further afield. But people come for miles to tuck into salmon with hollandaise sauce and the very popular steak and ale pie. The 'second oldest licensed pub in the country' is a characterful little place, quirky even – its menu is designed in the form of a Victorian newspaper – with separate cosy areas, open fires and the odd carved beam and settee. There are picnic tables on the big back lawn, and the village, listed in the Domesday Book, will charm you.

directions	Off A51 south of Stone & A518 north east of Stafford.
meals	12pm-2pm; 6pm-9.30pm; 12pm-9.30pm Saturdays (9pm Sun). Main courses £6.25-£11.95.
closed	3pm-6pm.

Geoffrey Holland
The Holly Bush Inn,
Salt, Stafford,
Staffordshire ST18 0BX
tel 01889 508234
web www.hollybushinn.co.uk

map: 9 entry: 387

Staffordshire

The Crooked House
Coppice Mill

Local big-wigs found coal here in about 1800 and started mining; shortly thereafter the pretty, 18th-century red-brick farmhouse fell into a hole. It has been buttressed ever since, but it is the most crooked building you are ever likely to see and makes you feel topsy-turvy the moment you walk through the door. Inside are two wonky little bars; it is quite an experience to be seated here. The grandfather clock, although upright, looks as if it is about to fall over, the red-tiled floors swim as you cross them, the bottled beers roll uphill. The whole place is faintly surreal: you could imagine yourself to be entering the world of *Alice in Wonderland*. The pub serves real ales such as Banks Bitter, farm cider and standard pub grub in a large (uncrooked) dining room, and sits in its own big garden near Himley Court.

directions	Off B4176 between Gornalwood & Himley.
meals	12pm-2.15pm (3.30pm Sundays); 6pm-9pm (9.30pm Fridays & Saturdays); 5.30pm-8pm Sundays. Main courses £6-£8.

Louise Pattern
The Crooked House,
Coppice Mill,
Himley,
Staffordshire DY3 4DA
tel 01384 238583

map: 9 entry: 388

Suffolk

Old Cannon Brewery
Bury St Edmunds

Brewing is a slow process, says Richard Eyton-Jones, and he should know; for the past four years he has been the chief brewer (and co-owner) of this admirable revitalisation of a Victorian brewhouse-cum-pub. Bare boards clatter, wooden tables are plain, a huge mirror vies with two gleaming stainless steel brewing kettles for decoration. The atmosphere is young, refreshingly friendly, and smoky and further enlivened by pints of own-brew Cannon Best and Gunner's Daughter. A surprising mix of contemporary dishes such as local sausages with onion gravy, grilled wing of skate with lemon grass and caper butter, and roast duck with sloe gin is to be expected. Five smart, modern bedrooms await in the old brewery, a couple of steps across the yard, with the breakfast room here too. You are a five-minute walk from the town and its treasures.

directions	From A14, Bury exit, for centre, left at r'bout to Northgate Street; right at Cadney Lane & into Cannon St.
meals	12pm-2pm; 6.30pm-9.30pm. No food Sunday evenings. Main courses £10-£15.
rooms	5: 4 doubles, 1 twin £62.
closed	Mondays.

Richard Eyton-Jones
Old Cannon Brewery,
86 Cannon Street,
Bury St Edmunds, Suffolk IP33 1JR
tel 01284 768769
web www.oldcannonbrewery.co.uk

map: 11 entry: 389

Suffolk

Beehive
Horringer

Look out for the beehive at the front or you'll miss the converted 19th-century cottages. Which would be a shame, for this is a local of the very best kind. It's well modernised inside yet the higgledy-piggledy feel remains, along with low beams and worn flagstone floors that ooze character. Several rooms, both smart and cosy, interlink, sharing soft lighting, old prints, wooden tables, evening candlelight, a woodburning stove. Greene King ales are on handpump but people come for more than the beer. Blackboards announce the daily menu, perhaps a lunchtime snack of Suffolk ham with salad and homemade chutney, or a winter-warming braised oxtail in a rich ale gravy, polished off with a date and walnut tart. Seven good wines are served by the glass and there are some well-priced bottles, too. The place can fill up quickly so do book, especially at weekends. The pub's popularity is proof of Gary and Diane Kingshott's hospitality, honed to perfection with 20 years' practice.

directions	3 miles south west of Bury St Edmunds on A143.
meals	12pm-2pm; 7pm-9pm. Main courses £6.95-£15.
closed	Sunday evenings.

Gary & Diane Kingshott
Beehive,
The Street, Horringer,
Bury St Edmunds,
Suffolk IP29 5SN
tel 01284 735260

map: 11 entry: 390

Suffolk

Star Inn
Lidgate

The garden is glorious on a summer's day. Inside it's snug, especially by the blazing fires; there are actually two snugs, each the centrepiece of an ancient-beamed bar. Indeed, the pretty Star, built in 1588, is one of the oldest buildings in the village – two cottages knocked into one – and is as English as can be. Yet the landlady hails from Spain. Maria Teresa Axon is Catalan and the rich aromas that reach you on entering may just as well come from a daube of beef or venison in port as from Spanish-style roast lamb, fabada asturiana (Asturian pork and bean stew) or parillada of fish. Bring a good appetite as portions will be generous, and book a table. Proximity to Newmarket brings racing types. There are darts and dominoes to get stuck into, Greene King beers on handpump – ask about the unusual handles – and Spain is deliciously represented in brandies and wines.

directions	On B1063, 7 miles south east of Newmarket.
meals	12pm-2pm (2.30pm Sundays); 7pm-10pm. No food Sunday evenings. Main courses £13.50-£15.50; set menu £10.50 (2-course lunch).
closed	3pm-5pm (6pm Sundays).

Maria Teresa Axon
Star Inn,
The Street, Lidgate,
Bury St Edmunds,
Suffolk CB8 9PP
tel   01638 500275

map: 11 entry: 391

Suffolk

Pumpk Inn
Little Grumple Snosher

The landlord has been here for 250 years, it seems, lending a patina of agelessness to the massive inglenook and flagstones. He is sometimes to be found deep in the inglenook, smoking a pipe and tenderly nursing a pint of OldeGrumpleSnosher. Rumour has it that it is the same pint he began with all those years ago. (Good stuff that Grumple – never loses its head, unlike the previous landlord who lost his in 1751 during the annual cheese-rolling competition when a Tipplebottom Blue hurtled out of control.) When you can lure him out he will draw a decent pint of the new local brew, Sleezeand Gerkin – but that's all, for he'll draw no other. Meg, his circular wife, does a fine line in banter. (We suggest you laugh with her and agree with her; she has been known to dash customers to the ground with a sweep of her gargantuan forearm.) This is the last of the spit-and-sawdust pubs in Britain, so tread carefully lest you leave with a spittoon clenched to your foot.

directions	Pub on left just past hedgehog.
meals	Only pumpkin meals served: pie (obviously), pudding, pancakes and NOT soup - they say it's too messy.
rooms	One – and not worth sleeping in.
closed	Often and abruptly.

Mr & Mrs O Lordy
Pumpk Inn,
Little Grumple Snosher,
Tipplebottom
Suffolk DO3 345
web   www.pumpk-inn-pub-online-./ :-)

map: 0 entry: 392

The George
Cavendish

Take an ancient inn on a perfect Suffolk green, decorate in neutral colours, add a dash of modern art, five delightful bedrooms and a talented chef and you have somewhere 'worth a detour'. The timbered, 600-year-old frame was rescued from near-collapse by Jonathan and Charlotte, who have brought cosmopolitan chic to a village pub. The ground floor has a smart country-restaurant feel, with every table laid for eating, but there are plenty of quiet corners in which to enjoy a pint of Woodforde's Wherry or Nethergate's Augustinian. The bar area leads onto a terrace with heated canopies and more dining tables: people come for the food. Jonathan (once head chef at Conran's Bluebird in Chelsea) and his team can be seen in the open kitchen whipping up modern dishes from colourful mediterranean – tortellini of lobster and truffle, Moroccan spiced lamb rump with stuffed piminto – to age-old favourites like game pudding with port wine gravy or roast pork with parsnip mash and sage jus. Service is charming, the wine list soars above most pub efforts, and the bedrooms have bright wool carpets and pretty views.

directions	On A1092 between Haverhill & Long Melford.
meals	12pm-3pm; 6pm-10pm; 6.30pm-9.30pm Sundays. Main courses £4.75-£19.85; set menus £13, £16.50 & £20.
rooms	5 doubles £70-£110. Singles £48.
closed	Mondays January-April.

Jonathan & Charlotte Nicholson
The George,
The Green, Cavendish,
Suffolk CO10 8BA

tel	01787 280248
web	www.georgecavendish.co.uk

The Swan
Monks Eleigh

The interior is not unlike that of a bistro with its polished wooden floors, but Nigel and Carol Ramsbottom's 16th-century thatched Swan is still pubby at heart. There's a large bar, Adnams on handpump and a good line in wines by the glass. The modernised interior is invitingly open with recessed ceiling lights, soft sage tones, and a winter log fire. Yet most folk come to eat. Nigel, in the kitchen, has created a menu to please both the traditionalist and adventurer, so dishes include simply grilled fillets of plaice with creamy leeks and new potatoes, grilled sea bass with orange and beetroot salad, whole roast teal with braised red cabbage, fabulous rice pudding. Fish can be relied upon to be beautifully fresh – raw materials are as local as possible – and puddings should not be resisted. Service, by Carol, is a lesson in how these things should be done: efficient, knowledgeable, cheerful and charming.

The Anchor
Nayland

The Bunting family, like many farmers, has been forced to diversify in recent years and cleverly bought the pub next to their land. They take huge pride in the local produce that appears on the menus: pheasant, duck and rabbit from farm shoots, eggs from their 120 bantams, their own lamb. Not only that, the smokehouse at the back produces game, fish and terrific treacle bacon for the menu (and to take home). When it came to updating the building they sensibly kept things simple. The pretty, butter-coloured pub successfully blends soft modern colours in traditional small rooms with open fires, and has a good big restaurant upstairs. Another draw is the setting, right beside the river Stour where summer barbecues bring out the best of the 120-seater garden. At weekends, at the Bunting's Heritage Centre behind the pub, rare Suffolk Punch draft horses plough the fields in the old way.

directions	On B1115 between Lavenham & Hadleigh.
meals	12pm-2pm; 7pm-9pm. Main courses £9.50-£16.50.
closed	Mondays & Tuesdays.

Nigel & Carol Ramsbottom
The Swan,
The Street,
Monks Eleigh, Lavernham,
Suffolk IP7 7AU
tel   01449 741391

map: 11 entry: 394

directions	From Colchester A134 for Sudbury. In 6 miles follow signs for Nayland.
meals	12pm-2.30pm (3pm weekends); 6.30pm-9.30pm. Main courses £6.95-£12.95.

Daniel Bunting
The Anchor,
26 Court Street, Nayland,
Suffolk CO6 4JL
tel   01206 262313
web   www.anchornayland.co.uk

map: 11 entry: 395

The Angel
Stoke-by-Nayland

Soft lamplight glows in the window of this 16th-century inn in 'Constable country'. The bar divides into two: a sitting area with carved beams, open brickwork, log fire and polished oak table, and a proper sitting room with deep sofas, wing chairs and grandfather clock. Fresh flowers and candles, fine prints and paintings, a few antique pieces and a dark-green décor add to the charm. The Angel fills early and its imaginative menus announce plenty of fresh fish (roast cod on tomato risotto, sardines with garlic mayonniase) plus game from the Denham estate; start with roast venison with red onion confit and juniper sauce, then plunge into iced dark chocolate bombe. Good rooms upstairs are reached via a small gallery above the restaurant – once a brewhouse. The whole place is a treat; on warm evenings tables are laid on the terrace at the back.

directions	On B1068 8 miles north of Colchester; off A12.
meals	12pm-2pm (5pm Sundays); 6.30pm-9.30pm (5.30pm Sundays). Main courses £9.95-£15.50.
rooms	6: 5 doubles, 1 twin £75-£85. Singles £60-£75.

Neil Bishop
The Angel,
Polstead Street, Stoke-by-Nayland,
Suffolk CO6 4SA
tel   01206 263245
web   www.horizoninns.co.uk

map: 11 entry: 396

The Ship
Levington

A world away from the busy A45 and Ipswich five miles west, The Ship is a 14th-century thatched beauty overlooking the River Orwell. This alone makes it a popular watering hole, the low-ceilinged bar and flower-festooned rear terrace filling quickly with yachting types, birdwatchers, regulars and townsfolk escaping to the country for lunch. Naturally, the bar emphasises a nautical theme, with pictures of barges, lifebuoys and a ship's wheel on the walls. Over the past year chef-patron Mark Johnson's imaginative cooking has made its successful mark, his chalkboard menus, changed twice a day, listing fresh fish and locally reared meats, notably venison from the nearby Suffolk Estate, as well as seasonal salads and local vegetables. Exemplary French cheeses come from the Rungis Market in Paris and superior real ales from East Anglian brewers Adnams and Greene King. Wonderful riverside walks await those who have had one glass too many – and those who haven't.

directions	A12/A14 to Woodbridge; follow signs for Levington.
meals	12-2pm (3pm Sun); 6.30-9.30pm. Main courses £7.50.
closed	Sunday evenings.

Stella & Mark Johnson
The Ship,
Levington,
Ipswich,
Suffolk IP10 0LQ
tel   01473 659573

map: 11 entry: 397

Crown & Castle
Orford

Ruth's sense of style has created one of the most distinctive bistro inns in the county out of a late-Victorian building and ex-Forte-hotel. The welcome is friendly to all, dogs included, the atmosphere relaxed, the food sublime, the bedrooms deeply comfortable, though just four have good views. The fire in the hall lures you in, there's Adnans bitter and great wines to drink at the bar, deep sofas urge you to stay. Floorboards clatter, quirky paintings amuse and the bar is as convivial as any. In the kitchen, Cromer crab, Orford wild sea bass and trout, local game and Gloucester Old Spot pork are splendidly taken care of. The cooking is robust – and it's quite impossible to resist warm marsala and polenta cake with poached pear and crème fraîche.

In summer a casual lunch on the terrace is heaven. The old Norman castle-keep stands proud across the road and you are minutes on foot from the river Alde, the comely village, the wild river marshes and Havergate Island's avocets.

directions	Leave A12 at Woodbridge; A1152 & B1084 to Orford.
meals	12pm-2pm; 7pm-9pm (9.30pm Saturdays). Main courses £10.50-£15.95.
rooms	18 twins/doubles £75-£135. Singles £60-£108.
closed	Sometimes in winter.

David & Ruth Watson
Crown & Castle,
Orford,
Suffolk IP12 2LJ
tel   01394 450205
web   www.crownandcastle.co.uk

map: 11 entry: 398

Suffolk

Crown Inn
Snape

A Suffolk gem. A well-preserved 15th-century inn with beams and brick floors only a stroll from the Maltings concert hall and a short drive from the Minsmere bird sanctuary. It claims to have the finest example anywhere of a double Suffolk settle, known as the 'old codgers'. Sadly, however, the old codgers have gone: this popular food pub attracts the gentrified Aldeburgh set who come for Diane Maylott's modern, brasserie-style food. Despite the foodie emphasis, there is a pubby atmosphere, and both the real ales and wines (11 by the glass) are supplied by Suffolk's most respected brewery, Adnams, who own the place. Key to The Crown's success is Diane's insistence on fresh, local produce, particularly fresh fish, game and organic vegetables. Standing timbers, beams, wonky walls and uneven floors continue upstairs to the attractively decorated bedrooms.

Suffolk

The Dolphin
Thorpeness

Thorpeness is a one-off, the turn-of-the-century brainchild of GS Ogilvie, who set out to create a holiday resort free of piers and promenades and entirely safe for children. The Dolphin, in the middle of the village, is a great little inn. There are two lively bars, open fires and wooden floors in the dining room and, outside, a terrace and lawn for barbecues and alfresco dinners. It's a paradise for families and excellent value for money. If you're staying here, you're spoiled for things to do: themed nights in the restaurant, tennis at the Country Club, a great golf course, an unspoilt sand and pebble beach, and a 64-acre lake, the Meare, which is never more than three-feet deep and was inspired by the creator of Peter Pan. The Dolphin has very good cottage-style bedrooms with old pine furniture, soft colours and spotless bathrooms.

directions	9 miles from Woodbridge on Snape cross-road. B1069 towards Snape Maltings (300yds)
meals	12pm-2pm; 7pm-9pm. Main courses £9.25-£13.50.
rooms	3 twins/doubles £70. Singles £60.
closed	Christmas Day; Boxing Day evening.

directions	On A12, 5 miles from Aldeburgh.
meals	12pm-2pm; 7pm-9pm. All day in summer. No food Sundays or Monday evenings. Main courses £4.75-£13.95.
rooms	3 doubles £75. Singles £55.
closed	3pm-6pm in winter.

Diane Maylott
Crown Inn,
Bridge Road,
Snape,
Suffolk IP17 1SL
tel   01728 688324

map: 11 entry: 399

Mr & Mrs J M Deredas
The Dolphin,
Peace Place,
Thorpeness, Aldeburgh,
Suffolk IP16 4NA
tel   01728 454994

map: 11 entry: 400

The Bell Inn
Walberswick

A tiny summer-soft, winter-bleak Suffolk fishing village – home in August to the International Crabbing Festival. Swim, sail, fish for crabs, paint, walk the beach to Dunwich. A 600-year-old inn, complete with ancient beams and flagstones, wooden settles and open fires. Time has also given it a few nooks and crannies in which to hide out with a pint of Oyster Stout. Sue is welcoming and attractive and has poured huge amounts of energy into making the Bell such a happy place. There's lots of hearty bar food and modern British in the restaurant: cream of pumpkin soup, flash-fried fillet of red snapper, bitter chocolate tart. The country-style bedrooms are on the small side but full of comforts and some have blissful views. Outside, soak up the sun in the big garden and look out on beach huts, dunes and the sea. It is also a perfect place for families, dogs and East Anglian architecture buffs.

directions	From A12, B1387 to Walberswick.
meals	12pm-2pm; 7pm-9pm (6pm Fridays, Saturdays & school holidays). Main courses £5.50-£10.
rooms	4 doubles, 1 twin, 1 family, £70-£130.
closed	3pm-6pm Monday-Friday.

Sue Ireland Cutting
The Bell Inn,
Ferry Road, Walberswick,
Southwold, Suffolk IP18 6TN

tel	01502 723109
web	www.blythweb.co.uk/bellinn

map: 11 entry: 401

Crown Inn
Southwold

The Crown has an eye for metropolitan sophistication. Ceilings are elegantly beamed, the walls of the big, laid-back bar are colour-washed and uncluttered – fitting for a town known as Kensington-on-Sea. The food comes as bar snacks in full modern-brasserie mode: gazpacho, grilled squid, country terrine. Fresh flowers sit on kitchen-style tables, there are newspapers to read, Adnams ales on handpump and fine wines to try. There's no pretentiousness and a fascinating mix of customers – suits, locals, trendies, grannies, families. A smaller, pubbier panelled back bar keeps hard-core traditionalists happy, and there's a smart, sunny, slightly more self-conscious restaurant. All in all, The Crown has succeeded admirably in being simultaneously a simple pub, a brasserie-wine bar, a restaurant with serious aspirations, and a comfortable place to stay the night.

directions	In centre of Southwold.
meals	12pm-2pm; 7pm-9.30pm; 6.30pm-10pm in summer. Main courses £10-£14; set menu £27.50.
rooms	13: 11 twins/doubles, 2 family, 1 suite, £110-£162.
closed	2.30pm-6pm

Michael Bartholomew
Crown Inn,
High Street,
Southwold,
Suffolk IP18 6DP

tel	01502 722275

map: 11 entry: 402

Suffolk

Randolph Hotel
Southwold

In taking over the tenancy of this late-Victorian Adnams' hotel and inn, the Williams realised a long-held dream. Michelle has filled the light, big bar with chairs and sofas in leather, wicker and fabric, while fresh cream walls contrast with aubergines and reds – a bold scheme that reaches into the dining room. The menu, admirably short, is of Glyn's devising, and strong on comfort food such as steak with crispy onions and chunky chips, toad-in-the-hole, game pudding with mustard mash. Order smoked salmon to start: later you may meet the people who smoked it at the bar. No end of folk drop by with braces of pheasant, rabbits, fresh fish – or to leave a flyer for the village notice board that stands in the Randolph's garden (immaculately maintained by Michelle's dad). Upstairs, the bedrooms are neat and comfortable, and exciting plans are afoot for them in 2004.

directions	From A12, A1095 to Southwold. Left along Wangford Road; signed.
meals	12pm-1.45pm; 6.30pm-8.45pm. Main courses £5-££16.75; set menu £13.50.
rooms	10: 7 doubles, 2 twins, 1 single. £70-£100; singles £50.

Glyn & Michelle Williams
Randolph Hotel,
Wangford Road,
Reydon, Southwold,
Suffolk IP18 6PZ
tel   01502 723603

map: 11 entry: 403

Suffolk

Queens Head
Bramfield

Chef-landlord Mark Corcoran is passionate about local and organic produce, and his daily-changing menus are a delight to read: rare-breed, Large Black pork from Elm House Farm near Diss, venison (served with redcurrant, port and orange sauce) from the Denham Estate, beef (braised in red wine) from the Stonehouse Organic Farm at West Harling. There are other treats: River Farm smoked Scottish salmon, mackerel with gooseberry sauce, lemon tart topped with Jersey cream. All this plenty is served in a high-raftered bar with dark timbered walls, scrubbed pine tables and a huge fireplace ablaze with logs in winter. The drinks at the only totally organic pub outside London are exemplary too: Adnams ales, cordials and apple juices, ciders and wines (eight by the glass). Make time for the pretty garden with bantams and bower – and Bramfield's thatched church with its unusual bell tower.

directions	2 miles N of A12 on A144 Halesworth road.
meals	12pm-2pm; 6.30pm-10pm; 7pm-9pm Sundays. Main courses £5.95-£14.95; set menu £16.95 (Sunday lunch).
closed	2.30-6.30pm; 3pm-7pm Sundays.

Mark & Amanda Corcoran
Queen's Head,
The Street, Bramfield,
Halesworth, Suffolk IP19 9HT
tel   01986 784214
web   www.queensheadbramfield.co.uk

map: 11 entry: 404

The King's Head
Laxfield

Known locally as the Low House because it lies in a dip below the churchyard, the 600-year-old thatched pub is one of Suffolk's treasures. Little has changed in the last 100 years and its four rooms creak with character – all narrow passageways and low ceilings. The simple parlour is dominated by a massive three-sided, high-backed settle in front of an open wood fire and there's no bar (far too new-fangled a concept for this place); instead, impeccable Adnams ales are served from barrels in the tap room and locals bang their empty glasses to summon the barman. In keeping with the timeless atmosphere, food is rustic, hearty and homemade, the short, daily-changing blackboard menu listing soup, sandwiches, hot dishes and nursery puddings. It's the sort of place where traditional folk music often starts up spontaneously, while summer brings Morris men and people arriving in horse and carriage. At the back, the secluded garden has its own bowling green.

directions	From Laxfield church, left down hill for 50yds. Left, then pub is on right.
meals	12pm-2pm; 7pm-9pm. No food Sun eve in winter. Main courses £5.50-£14.95.
closed	3pm-6pm (7pm Sundays).

George & Maureen Coleman
The King's Head,
Gorams Mill Lane,
Laxfield,
Suffolk IP13 8DW
tel   01986 798395

map: 11 entry: 405

St Peter's Hall
St Peter South Elmham

St Peter's is a one-off. John Murphy bought St Peter's Hall, a 13th-century moated manor, in 1996 – to brew beer using water from the site's 60-metre bore. Now St Peter's thrives, brewing and bottling its exemplary range of bitters, fruit ales and porters. From Friday to Sunday (and bank holidays) visitors venture across the moat into the medieval hall to eat and drink like kings. The lofty stone-flagged dining hall is filled with original Brussels tapestries, fine stone fireplaces and 17th- and 18th-century furnishings: sup at candlelit tables from French choir stalls or a bishop's chair. The main bar is small with a hatch. It's a tantalising setting in which to show off some tantalising beers, and there's food to match – local, seasonal, weekly-changing menus reveal a bang up-to-date British repertoire. There's Cromer crab and saffron tart, roast guinea fowl, chocolate fondant. A blissfully peaceful garden has tables overlooking the moat. And why not take the hour-long brewery tour, too.

directions	Off A144 3 miles south of Bungay.
meals	12pm-2.30pm; 7pm-9pm. Main courses £6.50-£12.
closed	Sunday evenings; Mondays (except Bank Holidays).

Stuart Cox
St Peter's Hall,
St Peter South Elmham, Bungay,
Suffolk NR35 1NQ
tel   01986 782322
web   www.stpetersbrewery.co.uk

map: 11 entry: 406

The White Horse Beer Festival

A cold and rainy Saturday morning in November was a drab start for a beer festival. But behind the heavy smoked glass doors of the White Horse (entry no. 266), where the fire was crackling and the beer taps were gleaming, things started to pick up. By 11am beer enthusiasts from all over the globe were propping up the bar. Grant, a Master Brewer from New England, described his annual pilgrimage to Parsons Green, the thought of the beers that weekend putting a gleam in his eyes. His passion for real ale started at home, where fresh smells of his mother's baking triggered an early interest in food, then wine and later beer.

Mark Dorber, owner of the White Horse and host to the two-day Beer Festival, is a self-taught beer connoisseur. With his cellars among the best kept in Europe, Mark is now sharing his knowledge with other enthusiasts through the Beer Academy he runs upstairs. Evening courses are about "ingredients, processes, history, beer styles, brewing and packaging technology and just about every other beer-related topic" – tastings, of course, are an integral part. To quote wine writer Oz Clarke at the opening: "The Beer Academy is an important initiative. Beer is about fun and sociability but, for the trade, it needs to be based on a foundation of knowledge. That is what the Beer Academy sets out to provide."

Feeling under-qualified – I know little about ale - I joined Mark and a few others for a beer tasting by the bar. As we munched hot bacon sandwiches, James, an engaging man who resurrects old ale recipes, proudly presented his own dark brews. Simonds Bitter (from 1880) brewed May 2003 slipped down easily as did the same beer brewed the year before, now with an added sharp tang. Then, as hot sausage nibbles arrived, James opened a bottle of old London Porter (recipe created 1850). The rich silky taste was new to me, but I knew I was privileged to be sipping this treacle-coloured ale created with such care by its proud owner.

By lunchtime, more crowds were gathering. Men old and young came with their mates, wives, girlfriends and dogs; some sat alone reading the papers. Women arrived in groups ready to taste some of the beers on the long list - Exmoor Beast, Lucifer and Kimberly's Rocking Rudolph and so on. Lower down the alcoholic scale were Smiles Holly Hop (5%), Cotleigh's Old Buzzard (4.8%) and Fuller's Jack Frost (4.5%). Harveys Imperial Stout (9.0%), Duvel Maredsons (10%) and Bass Museum's P2 Imperial Stout (10%) were all good contenders for what one friend described as "the kind of pint you'd want to drink before going up the aisle'".

For those with little knowledge of ales, the drinking was more a tasting lottery – like betting on a horse because you like its name rather than knowing much about it. But the expert tasters on hand were happy, as well-oiled experts often are, to share their tips. Hari, founder of Finland's beer society, was keen to point out that really good ale has the richest taste and the lowest alcohol content. And eyeing the cheerful crowd around me, I could only agree with his opinion that "beer is where the real people are". As Morris Dancers finally left their coveted spot by the bar to prance their stuff in the pouring rain, Hari was also right about something else – beer takes you to places you wouldn't normally go. That's precisely what it had done to me. The experience had been a delight and I felt grateful to Mark Dorber for bringing such fine and unusual beer, and the unusual culture that goes with it, to the very heart of London.

Rebecca Harris

Surrey

Inn @ West End
West End

The pub sign – Othello celebrating the virtues of drinking with an Englishman – might tempt you past the less than exciting exterior. Wine importer Gerry Price is drawing them in from all over Surrey. Stylishly revamped dining areas are light and modern with bright yellow walls, wooden floors and fine fabrics, and the homely bar has a wood-burning stove. The feeling is relaxed and friendly, handpumped ale comes from Fuller's and Courage, and Gerry's list of wines is huge. Monthly menus have modern British choices ranging from starters like smoked haddock kedgeree and warm salad of scallops with smoked bacon, to honey-roasted pork belly with apple and celeriac purée and thyme jus or turbot fillet with turmeric cream. Great lunchtime sandwiches, excellent value set-lunch menu, regular Saturday lunchtime wine-tasting sessions and popular wine dinners.

directions	On A322 towards Guildford, 2 miles from M3 junc. 3.
meals	12pm-2.30pm (3pm Sundays); 6pm-9.30pm (9pm Sundays). Main courses £7.95-£16; set menu £12.50-£16.50.

Gerry & Ann Price
Inn @ West End,
42 Guildford Road,
West End, Surrey GU24 9PW
tel   01276 858652
web   www.the-inn.co.uk

map: 5 entry: 407

Surrey

The Stag
Lower Eashing

Once through Eashing you'll come across a small bridge with a warning that heavy loads might lead to its demise. We trust this won't happen, as the pretty stone structure built by 13th-century monks forms an essential link to The Stag. With a lease dating back to 1771, this is an attractive, atmospheric place to stop off for some liquid refreshment and extremely good home cooking: pork with rosemary, mushroom risotto, banoffee pie. In spring and summer the garden, with teak-furnished terrace by the water, makes a languorous spot for quaffing Shepherd Neame Spitfire – or one of 15 wines by the glass. In winter, there are several cosily traditional rooms and two open fires; the weir outside the River Room provides a gurgling accompaniment. The friendly Stag likes children and dogs – the huge dog bowls at the entrance, belonging to residents Dotty and Bea, merely hint at their size.

directions	A3 south; 5 miles after Guildford, Eashing signed left at services. Left at garage; over bridge; on right.
meals	12pm-2.30pm (3pm Sundays); 6pm-9.30pm. Main courses £11.25-£17.50.
rooms	2: 1 double, 1 twin £50. Singles £40.

Marilyn Lackey
The Stag,
Lower Eashing,
Godalming,
Surrey GU7 2QG
tel   01483 421568

map: 5 entry: 408

Surrey

The Crown Inn
Chiddingfold

Another strong contender for the oldest hostelry in the country. Thirteenth-century bowed brick walls, warped weathered timbers, plaster ceilings and lattice windows... you could almost imagine yourself back in the dashing days of highwaymen. The bar's stained-glass leaded lights – for which Chiddingfold was once famous – tell of 'the Lion and the Unicorn's fight for the Crown', while the main bar holds the most enormous inglenook ever. It's hard to sit still in such a place: with a pint of Gobbledy Goose in hand, why not take a wander and a gander at the small glass case of coins that date back to 1558. This is better by far than any museum. There's simple food in the bar, and a panelled restaurant for more elaborate dishes; feast at one of the oldest trestle tables in the land, a 1285 butcher's block, still riddled with knife marks. Upstairs, wooden four-posters encourage deep sleep, while the resident ghost takes to relighting the restaurant candles at night.

directions	On A283 between Petworth & Haslemere.
meals	12pm-2.30pm; 6pm-9.30pm; 12pm-9pm weekends. Main courses £6.95-£18.95.
rooms	7: 5 doubles, 2 twins, £67-£110.

Clare Cunningham
The Crown Inn,
The Green,
Petworth Road, Chiddingfold,
Surrey GU8 4TX
tel   01428 682255

map: 5 entry: 409

Surrey

The Scarlett Arms
Walliswood

Peep in at the Scarlett Arms' windows to flickering candlelight – a sore temptation for any passer-by. Engagingly worn armchairs, an inglenook fireplace with glowing embers, original latched doors, flagstones, beams and a stack of roughly hewn logs: this is everyone's idea of the perfect country pub. The food is as country traditional as the décor: a new chef turns out proper British food from the freshest ingredients, with the emphasis on sausages and pies. Ruby velvet curtains in three cosy interconnecting rooms keep out winter chills, quirky antiques fill every corner: a reassuringly traditional setting in which to tuck into steak, kidney and Badger ale pie washed down with a pint of Thirsty Ferret. The pub's darts team, and the popular outdoor hog roasts, makes the place hum in summer – encouraged by benches and parasols on the front lawn.

directions	Walliswood 1.4 miles west off the A29 between Horsham and Dorking.
meals	12pm-2.15pm; 6.30pm-9.30pm. Main courses £7.95-£12.95.
closed	3pm-5.30pm.

Philip & Wendy Nisbet
The Scarlett Arms,
Walliswood, Ockley,
Surrey RH5 5RD
tel   01306 627243

map: 5 entry: 410

Surrey

The Plough
Coldharbour

The smell of woodsmoke wafting from the Plough's chimneys is impossible to resist, and the friendly greeting as you enter makes this another good reason to stop off for a pint. Nothing is too much trouble. Three open fires are kept smouldering from breakfast until closing-time, delicious dishes are cooked with fresh and local produce, even the chocolate fairy leaves gifts on the pillows of visiting guests. Landlady and ex-nurse Anne keeps her finger firmly on the kitchen pulse, while her husband Rick runs the pub's tiny micro-brewery with equal aplomb. With those wonderful home-brewed Crooked Furrow and Tallywacker, it's no wonder one local restored an antique lamp in exchange for two pints, and the doctor skied six miles to lunch one snowy winter… it must have been down Leith Hill. In seductive bedrooms, soft lighting and natural colours are a subtle backdrop to antique furniture and paintings.

directions	4 miles from Dorking.
meals	12pm-2.30pm; 6.30pm-9.30pm. Main courses £6.50-£10.95.
rooms	6: 5 doubles, 1 single. £65-£85; singles £55.

Richard & Anna Abrehart
The Plough,
Coldharbour,
Dorking,
Surrey RH5 6HD
tel 01306 711793

map: 5 entry: 411

Surrey

Stephan Langton
Abinger Common

Jonathan Coomb left the London restaurant scene in 2000 and arrived at the bottom of leafy Leith Hill, with a handful of cottages and a romantic old hammer pond for company. For years a favourite walkers' watering hole, this isolated country pub at the end of a very long lane is a perfect place for Jonathan's robust style of country cooking. In the kitchen, beyond the bare-boarded, log-warmed bar, he takes delivery of some first-class produce from local suppliers, bakes bread, rolls out pasta, whisks up ice cream. Walkers come here to devour bowls of hearty goulash soup, duck confit with puy lentils and Moroccan-style braised lamb, while evening additions may include such exotica as seared marlin niçoise and monkfish tagine with Merguez sausages and preserved lemons. Accompany these treats with a well-kept pint of Adnams, then head off to explore some of Surrey's finest walks.

directions	A25 from Dorking. 2 miles outside Westcott left; 2 miles; left, right at pond.
meals	12pm-3pm; 7pm-10pm. No food Sunday evenings. Main courses £9-£13.
closed	Mondays; 3pm-5pm.

Jonathan Coomb
Stephan Langton,
Friday Street,
Abinger Common,
Dorking, Surrey RH5 6JR
tel 01306 730775

map: 5 entry: 412

The King William IV
Mickleham

Open fires, fresh flowers, slab sandwiches and long views are a few of the reasons people make the steep, stepped climb – unless you're lucky enough to park in the lane. The old alehouse was originally built for Lord Beaverbrook's estate staff – a hilltop eyrie from which Chris and Jenny Grist have created a popular little pub, particularly in summer, when all and sundry spill into the terraced garden. There's a serving hatch to outside, a thoughtful touch for walkers with muddy boots. In winter it's super-snug, a place that just about squeezes in two bare-boarded bars. The real badgers have gone (see the photos on the walls) but their namesake ale remains on tap as well as ales from The Hogs Back Brewery. Equal attention is paid to food: chips are banned, but who cares, when huge homemade pies and proper bread and butter pudding are brought steaming to the table?

directions	From junc. 9 M25, A24 for Dorking. Just before Mickleham, pub on hill above Frascati restaurant.
meals	12pm-2pm; 7pm-9.30pm; 12pm-5pm Sundays. Main courses £6-£14.
closed	3pm-6pm Mondays-Saturday.

Chris & Jenny Grist
The King William IV,
Byttom Hill, Mickleham,
Dorking, Surrey RH5 6EL
tel   01372 372590
web   www.king-williamiv.com

map: 5 entry: 413

The Hare & Hounds
Lingfield

This whitewashed roadside pub may not look particularly beguiling but step inside and you'll know you've come to a special place. With proprietor-chef Fergus's collection of quirky objects filling every corner, the Hare & Hounds has an idiosyncratic feel. While the fireside burgundy sofa makes an ideal spot for perusing the tempting menu, the bustle of the bar can be surveyed from a throne-like chair, one of a pair: the other half lives at home with Fergus, which is fitting for the king of the kitchen. And there's a wooden elephant seat too. His specialities include Merguez sausages with saffron served with olive couscous and fennel, and fried salmon with sweet potato. Diners are as happy among the yuccas of the main bar as beneath the huge floral paintings (the work of Fergus's artist wife) in the lovely dining room. In summer nurse a pint of Flowers Original or Old Speckled Hen in the split-level, partly-decked garden.

directions	From A22 towards Lingfield Racecourse into Common Road.
meals	12pm-2.30pm (3.30pm Sundays); 7pm-10pm. Main courses £7.50-£14.95.
closed	Sunday evenings.

Fergus Greer
The Hare & Hounds,
Common Road,
Lingfield,
Surrey RH7 6BZ
tel   01342 832351

map: 5 entry: 414

The Stag
Balls Cross

The quintessential Sussex pub, worth, as Michelin would say, a detour. Under 16th-century beams by a log-fired inglenook, or in the garden in summer, riders, walkers and locals converse easily with the help of fine ales like Badgers and Harveys Sussex Bitter. Wholesome home-cooked food is another draw, and the lavish piles of crispy whitebait and pint-glass servings of pink prawns are particularly tempting. A sweet shop in a former life, this little inn is still a great place for children – in a set-aside room lively youngsters can romp undisturbed. There is also plenty for adults to do: The Stag has its own darts team, jazz nights outside in summer, carol singing in winter and visits from the travelling Mummers all year round. There's even a tethering post for those who have to trot home by horse.

The Lickfold Inn
Lickfold

The Lickfold's 15th-century bricks bulge in a riot of herringbone, as do the plump tweed cushions by the huge central inglenook. A fireside sofa with a selection of daily papers is another magnet for visitors: this is a wonderfully atmospheric place. The pub serves a popular, upmarket menu built around fresh local produce. Diners can relax downstairs in a cosy setting where fat cream candles, reflected in the latticed windows, give comfort and cheer. Upstairs, a more formal dining area with sumptuous silk curtains brings a contemporary twist to the pub's medieval framework. There's a super decked terrace at the back and a flower-filled garden for summer sipping. If you've eaten too much chocolate panettone pud, set off at a gentle pace to visit the child-friendly Weald and Downland Open Air Museum in nearby Singleton. There are more herringbones and beams there, too.

directions	2 miles from Petworth on Kirdford road.
meals	12pm-2pm; 7pm-9pm. No food Sunday evenings. Main courses £6.50-£10.50.
rooms	2: 1 double, 1 twin, sharing bathroom £60.
closed	3pm-6pm (7pm Sundays).

directions	Village off A272 between Midhurst & Petworth; through Lodsworth; on & pub at bottom of road on left.
meals	12-2.30pm; 7-9.30pm (9pm Sun). Main courses £8.50-£17.95.
closed	3.30pm-5.30pm Monday-Thursday.

Hamish Hiddleston
The Stag,
Balls Cross,
Petworth,
Sussex GU28 9JP
tel 01403 820241

map: 5 entry: 415

Tim Ashworth
The Lickfold Inn,
Lickfold,
Midhurst,
Sussex GU28 9EY
tel 01798 861285

map: 5 entry: 416

Sussex

Duke of Cumberland Arms
Henley Village

In spring The Duke looks divine, its brick and stone walls engulfed by flowering wisteria – and beyond is the terraced garden, with its babbling trout pools and Sussex Weald views. Latch doors lead to two tiny bars that creak with character – painted, panelled walls, low ceilings, ancient floors, pine tables with benches and log fires in the grate. Gas lamps, old indentures and stuffed animals and birds add to the atmosphere. Down a Young's Bitter or Hog's Back TEA drawn straight from the cask, or a glass of local cider. Landlord Gaston Duval's daily menu relies on fresh local produce, notably Sussex lamb and organic beef. There may be calves' liver with bacon, too, and cod in 'hatter' batter and, not surprisingly, trout from the pub's spring-fed pools. Book the private room for Sunday lunch and make a party of it – rib of beef is served as a joint to the table.

directions	From Fernhurst towards Midhurst; pass pub on right; next left to Henley Village; follow road, on right.
meals	12pm-2.30pm; 7pm-9.30pm. No food Sunday or Monday evenings. Main courses £8.95-£15.75.
closed	3pm-5pm (7pm Sundays).

Gaston & Christina Duval
Duke of Cumberland Arms,
Henley Village,
Fernhurst, Midhurst,
Sussex GU27 3HQ
tel   01428 652280

map: 5 entry: 417

Sussex

Keepers Arms
Trotton

A slice of Hungry Man's Hock in the kasbah? In this fabulous pub nothing seems impossible. Well-travelled owners Stephen and Jennifer Oxley have created a pub that buzzes with life. Spears adorning walls, a papier mâché zebra head by the bar, an African mask over the blackboard, gorgeous candelabra on the restaurant tables – all add colour, texture and fun. Choose your candlelit corner carefully: each one is evocative of a different continent or mood… and the huge squishy fireside sofas are the obvious refuge for Sunday lunchtime lounge lizards. Despite the exuberance, food and ales are taken seriously and are extremely good. On a menu packed with good hearty stuff you might find the best game pie in the land (venison, pheasant, partridge and wild duck) and a summer seafood platter that overflows with lobster, crab, giant crevettes and oysters. Book the corner kasbah if you can.

directions	On A272 between Midhurst & Petersfield.
meals	12pm-2pm; 7pm-9pm. Main courses £6.50-£14.
closed	Sunday evenings; Mondays; 2.30pm-6.30pm.

Steve & Jenny Oxley
Keepers Arms,
Trotton,
Midhurst,
Sussex GU31 5ER
tel   01730 813724

map: 4 entry: 418

Sussex

Halfway Bridge Inn
Halfway Bridge

The pub's 'thought for the day' roadside blackboard draws attention to an unprepossessing but fine pub. The Hawkins brothers, second generation publicans, have kept the original rustic wooden floors, plaster walls and open fireplaces, while homely touches such as a grandfather clock and china on old dressers create an easy, informal atmosphere. The food's good, too. In a warren of cosy corners, split levels and fireside seats, settle down to lemon-roasted chicken and basil risotto or duck confit with root vegetable mash. Refreshment includes local Hampshire and Sussex beers, and excellent cider from nearby Gospel Green. Old stables have recently been renovated into super rooms, where brass beds, wooden *bateaux lits* and natural fabrics sit well with old beams and brickwork. The sunny front garden with pergola sits well back from the road.

directions	On A272 halfway between Midhurst & Petworth.
meals	12pm-2pm (2.30pm weekends); 6pm-10pm. Main courses £7.95-£12.50.
rooms	8: 7 doubles, 1 twin £75-£80. Singles £45.
closed	3pm-6pm.

Simon & James Hawkins
Halfway Bridge Inn,
Halfway Bridge,
Midhurst, Sussex GU28 9BP
tel   01798 861281
web   www.thesussexpub.co.uk

map: 5 entry: 419

Sussex

The Hollist Arms
Lodsworth

There is something bucolic about gathering shitake mushrooms from Prickly Nut Wood. At the Hollist Arms it takes a local to know what dose of magic they need. Villager and proprietor George Bristow, once in recruitment, has recently rescued this lovely pub, injecting fresh enthusiasm among the staff and stuffing the menu with local and seasonal ingredients. Villagers prop up the – very long – bar for a good pint of King's Horsham Best or Young's, while comfortable sofas by a huge inglenook settle other dedicated drinkers in for the night. The smaller, more intimate rooms of this former smithy have been kept: one, a cosy claret-coloured private dining room, another a sweet snug with soft green armchairs, blazing fire and tables piled high with magazines and games. Children are welcome and there's a garden for summer. From the hand-cut, local-farm potato chips to the natural wall colours and pretty, feather-patterned curtains, this watering hole oozes magic.

directions	Halfway between Midhurst & Petworth.
meals	12pm-2pm; 7pm-9pm. Main courses £10-£12.
closed	3pm-6pm.

George Bristow
The Hollist Arms,
The Street,
Lodsworth, Petworth,
Sussex GU28 9BZ
tel   01798 861310

map: 5 entry: 420

The Three Horseshoes
Elsted

Low beams, latched doors, high-backed settles, deep cream, bowed walls, fresh flowers, cottage windows, big log fires and home-cooked food: all that you'd hope for, and more, from a Sussex pub. Built in 1540 as a drovers' ale house, it has no cellar, so staff pull ales from the barrel instead; the line of metal casks is clearly visible in the lower open-timbered bar, formerly a butcher's shop (still with the ceiling hooks). Local meat and game appear on a tempting country menu – braised lamb with apples and apricots, steak and kidney in Murphy's pie, pheasant breast in cider with shallots and prunes – and are served in snug little rooms. In the main dining room with its wood-burning stove you can't fail to notice the flock of chickens in china, pottery and wood – landlady Sue has a passion for poultry. In summer, her feathered friends cluck happily among the drinkers enjoying the golden pints outdoors. The South Downs views are fabulous.

directions	From Midhurst A272 for Petersfield; Elsted signed left in 5 miles.
meals	12pm-2pm; 7pm-9pm (8.30pm Sundays). Main courses £7.95-£14.95.

Sue Beavis & Michael Newton
The Three Horseshoes,
Elsted,
Midhurst,
Sussex GU29 0JY
tel   01730 825746

map: 4 entry: 421

White Horse Inn
Chilgrove

Charles Burton said he would one day buy this long, whitewashed inn, built in 1765 as a coaching stop on the difficult stage across the South Downs, and he did. Now it fusses over passing walkers, local diners and tourists for Goodwood and Chichester. The pull is both the celebrated cellar of 600 global wines, including some clarets of outstanding pedigree, and the great food. In the small, simple bar you can choose from eight wines by the glass or local Ballards Bitter, and tuck into Italian-style open sandwiches, fish soup, roast duck and dressed local Selsey crab. Emphasis is on the imaginative menu in the formal restaurant where you can dine in style on local fish (turbot and sea bass) and in-season game. Bedrooms are snazzy, with CD players, bathrobes and use of a private walled garden. Breakfast is a hamper of delicious goodies delivered to your room.

directions	On B2141 towards Petersfield; 6 miles north of Chichester.
meals	12pm-2pm; 6.30pm-10pm. Main courses £10.50-£16.
rooms	8 twins/doubles £95-£120. Singles £65-£95.
closed	Sunday evenings; Mondays in winter.

Charles Burton
White Horse Inn,
High Street, Chilgrove,
Chichester, Sussex PO18 9HX
tel   01243 535219
web   www.whitehorsechilgrove.co.uk

map: 4 entry: 422

Royal Oak
East Lavant

There's a cheerful, wine-bar feel to the Royal Oak but it's a country inn at heart, sitting in a dip in Pook Lane. Wax-jacketed young locals with children in tow come for the smart rusticity and the delightful staff. It's old (with the ghost of a landlord who came to a sticky end) and modern, with stripped floors, scrubbed tables, exposed brickwork, three fires, a dark leather sofa and racing pictures on the walls. Pop in for a glass of wine or a pint of Ballards, Badgers or Sussex Best drawn from the barrel. The dining area is huge, light and airy, with a conservatory, and you can overflow onto the front terrace, warmed by outdoor lamps on summer nights; you'll be facing a road but this one goes nowhere. Five chefs turn out excellent salmon and chorizo fishcakes, honey and clove-stuck roasted ham, fillet steak, lobster and crab – a satisfying mix of traditional and modern. Bedrooms are divided between a nearby barn and upstairs at the back: all have CD players and plasma screens, retro fans, brown leather chairs and big comfy beds; some even have a view. Breakfast is not to be missed – and you are brilliantly placed for Chichester Theatre and Goodwood.

directions	From Chichester, A286 for Midhurst. After 2 miles right for East Lavant. Over bridge; on left.
meals	12pm-2.30pm; 6pm-9pm. Main courses £8.50-£13.
rooms	5 doubles, 1 cottage for 4. £70-£100. Singles £60-£70.

Nick Sutherland
Royal Oak,
Pook Lane, East Lavant,
Sussex PO18 0AX

tel	01243 527434
web	www.sussexlive.co.uk/royaloakinn

map: 5 entry: 423

Horse & Groom
Chichester

Lamps, cosy corners, fresh flowers, a piano – the little 17th-century pub is like the cosiest family home. Michelle Martell explains that the glowing range in the flagstoned bar, used by visitors for roasting chestnuts, also delivers the family's Sunday roast. At new pine tables in the restaurant extension the food is appropriately 'home-from-home': Selsey crab, fresh fish (try the sea bass on samphire), rack of lamb with honey and rosemary jus, seasonal game. The Martell ploughman's continues the family theme, starring three cheeses from Gloucestershire that include one made by Michael's brother Charles: Stinking Bishop, a triumph of sense over smell. Wines are excellent, as are the handpumped beers. The stable block contains eleven comfortable bedrooms that overlook the garden where the home cricket team joins locals over barbecues in summer.

directions	On B2178, 2 miles NW of Chichester.
meals	12pm-2.15pm (2.30pm Sundays); 6.30pm-9.15pm. Main courses £7.25-£14.75.
rooms	11 twins/doubles from £60. Singles £40.
closed	3pm-6pm; Sun eve.

Michael Martell
Horse & Groom,
East Ashling, Chichester,
Sussex PO18 9AX
tel 01243 575339
web www.horseandgroomchichester.com

map: 4 entry: 424

The Spur
Slindon

Plonked right on the A29 it may not be pretty outside but it's a gem within, and has the loveliest garden where hens happily scratch and strut. Regulars from the flint village of Slindon prop up the bar – they have proclaimed the pub their "second home", and who can blame them? A good selection of ales on tap, a kitchen serving fantastic home-cooked food, a skittle alley to work off the excess, darts, pool and friendly dogs. In the deep terracotta bar with its 'double' log fire, portions are generous: you'll be hard-pushed to polish off the hugest half shoulder of lamb to ever appear on a plate. Beyond, in the elegant dining room, the à la carte menu is a memorable treat. A nearby farm sends pumpkins for the windowsills – an unusual choice of decoration, but one that works. Clive Smith and his wife Victoria are great hosts, and give you comfortable bedrooms upstairs for those who find it hard to leave.

directions	Beside A29 just outside Slindon; 10 miles east of Chichester.
meals	12pm-2pm; 7pm-9pm. Main courses £7.95-£14.95.
rooms	3 twins/doubles £65-£80. Singles £45-£70.
closed	3pm-6pm (7pm Sundays).

Clive & Victoria Smith
The Spur,
Slindon,
Chichester,
Sussex BN18 0NE
tel 01243 814216

map: 5 entry: 425

The Sportsman
Amberley

Paul Mahon's revamping of this little country pub has shifted the pace up a bit. In particular, his love of sleek, classic motor cars has spilled over, and summer brings the Goodwood Festival of Speed so the place becomes a focus for those who share his passion. Food is fresh and good: calves' liver and bacon, red lentil risotto with chargrilled aubergine and salsa, apple pie. And to go with that? Take a pint of well-kept ale to the pretty conservatory and watch wild geese take wing above the flooded wetlands. The decked terrace is an even better spot from which binocular-clad drinkers can watch birds compete for airspace with gliders from the nearby airfield. Overlooking Amberley Wild Brooks and Arun Valley, the Sportsman has some of the finest views in Sussex. There are good bedrooms for the weary, and a barn for visiting bikes – a thoughtful touch from a publican so devoted to classic cars.

directions	1 mile north of Arundel, off B2139. Follow brown signs to 'Sportsman'.
meals	12pm-2pm; 6.30pm-9pm (9.30pm Fridays & Saturdays). Main courses £8.50-£14.95.
rooms	5 twins/doubles £45-£80.
closed	3pm-6pm (7pm Sundays).

	Paul Mahon
	The Sportsman, Rackham Road, Crossgates, Amberley, Arundel, Sussex BN18 9NR
tel	01798 831787
web	www.amberleysportsman.co.uk

map: 5 entry: 426

The Fountain Inn
Ashurst

The 16th-century Inglenook Bar is a snug place to be on a cold and rainy night, as Paul McCartney and Wings thought when they made their Christmas video here. When the fireplace decides 'to blow' you're transported back centuries. In the flagstoned and candlelit bar, aromatic with woodsmoke from that wafting fire, be treated to wholesome food (steak and ale pie, fillet of bass with roasted peppers, nursery puds), along with a great selection of wines and real ales, including the seasonal 'Hoppy Christmas'. No need to bother with the wine list – just wander into the corridor where, on an ancient wonky wall, the bottles themselves are on display. Although the annual classic car and motorbike meeting attracts those from afar, The Fountain firmly remains a local pub. The community spirit comes into its own in September when locals bring their ripe apples along to be transformed into alcoholic nectar by the pub's cider press.

directions	On B2135, 4 miles north of Steyning.
meals	11.30am-2pm; 6pm-9.30pm. No food Sunday & Monday evenings. Main courses £7-£14.95.

	Craig Gillet
	The Fountain Inn, Ashurst, Henfield, Sussex BN44 3AP
tel	01403 710219

map: 5 entry: 427

Sussex

Sussex

Green Man
Partridge Green

William Thornton used to drive past this run-down boozer and dream of taking it over. It came on the market, he snapped it up, renovated with energy and redecorated with style – a challenging project, embarked upon by a single-minded individual with no previous experience of running a pub. Now William is behind the bar, busily overseeing a place full of cosy corners, prints on walls, big wooden tables and a woodburning stove. Even the pub garden reflects William's personal touch – wonderful Spanish-tiled plant holders on the walls, Bali furniture with simple parasols on the lawn, a herb garden. Against this vibrant backdrop good food is a big draw. William enthuses about the menu and not surprisingly; his love of Spain comes through in tapas dishes and olive oil and good bread on the table, though roast partridge with puy lentils and updated pub staples (say, fillet steak beefburger with hand-cut chips and onion bap) are big favourites too.

Royal Oak
Wineham

A rural survivor, the part-tiled, black-and-white-timbered cottage almost lost down a country road is six centuries old and has been refreshing locals for the last two. It is unspoilt in every way. In the charming bar and tiny rear room are brick and bare-boarded floors, a huge inglenook with winter log fires, sturdy, rustic furniture and low beams. Antique corkscrews, pottery jugs and mugs, sepia photographs and aged artefacts hang from beams and walls. Landlord Tim Peacock, who has been in charge for 35 years, draws Harveys Best and guest beers straight from the cask (no pumps) and, in keeping with ale house tradition, limits the menu to good, freshly-made sandwiches, generous ploughman's lunches, and hearty soups on chilly days. Blissfully free of music and electronic hubbub, the place also has traditional pub games. Picnic tables on the grass at the front overlook the peaceful road.

directions	On B2135 south of A272 & east of A24 junction.
meals	12pm-2pm (2.30pm Sundays); 7pm-9.30pm. Main courses £3.95-£17.95.
closed	Sunday evenings.

directions	Off A272 between Cowfold & Bolney.
meals	11am-2.30pm; 5.30pm-11pm. Main courses £2.25-£4.50.

William Thornton
Green Man,
Church Road, Partridge Green,
Horsham, Sussex RH13 8JT
tel   01403 710250
web   www.thegreenman.org

Tim Peacock
Royal Oak,
Wineham,
Henfield,
Sussex BN5 9AY
tel   01444 881252

map: 5 entry: 428

map: 5 entry: 429

The Jolly Sportsman
East Chiltington

Who would imagine, deep in the Sussex countryside, a little place with so much passion for its beers, food and wine? Brewery mats pinned above the bar demonstrate Bruce Wass's support of the micro-breweries that share his ideals, and his food has been described as "robust, savoury, skilled and unpretentious – a rare combination of attributes." In the stylish, pistachio-hued restaurant, with its seagrass floor, Venetian blinds and slabbed oak tables decorated with flowers and candles, visitors chatter away over plates piled high and irresistibly: game pâté with onion marmalade, mussel, cockle and saffron linguine, Cornish lobster with salad and potatoes, haunch of venison with port and juniper sauce. Puddings include spiced pear and almond tart, plates are filled with ripe French cheeses. Pull up chic chair in front of the bar's open fire and enjoy winter snifters from Bruce's impressive whisky collection (they include rare wee drams bought at auction) or a fine wine from a selected small grower. Outside, ancient trees give shade to rustic tables, and the idyllic garden has a play area for children. A team of talented enthusiasts run this pub; the Moroccan-tiled patio tables were even made by the pub's own 'washer-upper'.

directions	From Lewes A275; B2166 for East Chiltington.
meals	12pm-2pm (3pm Sun), 6pm-9.15pm (10pm Fri & Sat). Main courses £8.95-£15.85.
closed	Sun eve; Mondays; 2.30pm-6pm.

Bruce Wass
The Jolly Sportsman,
Chapel Lane, East Chiltington,
Sussex BN7 3BA

tel	01273 890400
web	www.thejollysportsman.com

map: 5 entry: 430

Sussex

The Rainbow Inn
Cooksbridge

This roadside pub is one for the foodies: limited ales but terrific food. The most intriguing part of this well-run place is the dining room's raised fireplace and its 'bookcase' door, beyond which lie the sleekest loos with the deepest basins. If you prefer traditional, the small bar with blazing hearth is clubbily-cosy – a good place in which to nurse a pint of Harveys and catch the murmur of diners in the bigger rooms beyond. Here smart suits and locals tuck into excellent seasonal food – cod and coriander fishcakes with tomato and gin coulis, chargrilled leg of lamb with ratatouille and garlic jus – to a backdrop of contemporary-country furnishings. Two charming little dining rooms, their walls decorated in huge checks, are for hire upstairs, but it's the bookcase door downstairs that wins the novelty prize. There's a pleasing garden with a decked terrace and views to the South Downs: a delicious spot to unwind in on lazy summer days.

directions	On A275 Lewes to Haywards Heath road.
meals	12pm-2pm; 7.30pm-11pm. Main courses £5-£7; set lunch £10.95 (weekdays).
closed	3.30pm-5.30pm; Christmas Day.

Sebastien Gorst
The Rainbow Inn,
Resting Oak Hill,
Cooksbridge, Lewes,
Sussex BN8 4SS
tel   01273 400334

map: 5 entry: 431

Sussex

The Giants Rest
Wilmington

Most East Sussex pubs are supporters of Harveys brewery in Lewes and this is no exception. Local produce is on the menu, too. Adrian's wife Rebecca is chef, and her wild rabbit and bacon pie, home-cooked ham with bubble-and-squeak and fruit crumbles are really popular. It's hardly old by rural standards, but the high ceilings, the black and cream Hedges & Butler wallpaper, the pine dressers, the ferns and the candlelight are the perfect backdrop for a plate of Victorian trifle. Menus for Burns Night or New Year are offered at normal prices as a 'thank you' to the regulars and served in front of a log fire. Furnishings include pews and pine tables at the long bar; games range from bar billiards to solitaire. Work up an appetite – or walk off that trifle – with an invigorating downland stroll to view the impressive Long Man figure carved into the chalk of the South Downs.

directions	On A27 just past Drusilla's roundabout.
meals	12pm-2pm; 7pm-9pm. Main courses £5.50-£11.
rooms	2: 1 double, 1 twin, sharing bathroom £40.
closed	3pm-6pm Monday-Friday in winter.

Adrian & Rebecca Hillman
The Giants Rest,
Wilmington,
Eastbourne,
Sussex BN26 5SQ
tel   01323 870207

map: 5 entry: 432

Sussex

Rose Cottage Inn
Alciston

In walking country close to the South Downs Way, this 17th-century, wisteria-clad cottage is on a quiet lane to nowhere. Run by the Lewis family since 1960, it's a bolthole for ramblers and locals looking for a decent pint. There are cosy bars, brimful with prints, bric-a-brac and farming implements, and neatly furnished with sturdy tables and cushioned pews. It's a lovely place to eat; the good food includes fish from Eastbourne, locally shot game and home-produced fruits and vegetables. Varied menus parade ploughman's lunches, homemade soups and daily specials like Firle pheasant braised with shallot and mushrooms in madeira. And to drink? A pint of Harveys Best, or local cider – most enjoyable out on the sunny front terrace on fine summer days. Jasper, the African grey parrot, puts in regular, and always surprising, lunchtime appearances at the bar.

directions	Off A27 midway between Lewes & Eastbourne.
meals	11.30am-3pm; 6.30pm-11pm. No food New Year's Day evening. Main courses £5.50-£13.50.
rooms	1 self-contained flat for 2, £50

Ian Lewis
Rose Cottage Inn,
Alciston,
Lewes,
Sussex BN26 6UW
tel   01323 870377

map: 5 entry: 433

Sussex

The Tiger Inn
East Dean

In the flickering candlelight of the old pub, where records go back nine centuries, landlord Nicholas Denyer explains why he sometimes has to say 'no': no mobile phones, no bookings, no credit cards. It's the size of this modest place – all low beams and ancient settles – that dictates the 'no's, and makes it such an unusual and delightful place to be – particularly after a breezy downland stroll. Beside an idyllic cottage-lined green in a fold of the South Downs, The Tiger Inn is a great supporter of the community: Harveys ales come from nearby Lewes, lamb and beef for casseroles and stews from the farm up the hill. Pheasant, rabbit, partridge and venison are local too – part of an ever-changing blackboard that offers 'home-cooked food when you can't be bothered to cook it yourself'. There are 35 varieties of the famous ploughman's lunch, including local sheep's cheeses and smoked meats from the Weald smokery.

directions	0.5 miles from A259 at East Dean, in village centre.
meals	12pm-2pm; 6.30pm-9pm; 6pm-8pm Sundays. Main courses £7.50-£9.95.
closed	3pm-6pm Monday-Friday.

Nicholas Denyer
The Tiger Inn,
The Green,
East Dean, Eastbourne,
Sussex BN20 0DA
tel   01323 423209

map: 5 entry: 434

The Lamb Inn
Wartling

In 12 months, landlord Rob and his chef wife Alison have transformed this little pub into a place known for great ales, excellent food and good cheer. There's a bar with a woodburner, a beamy no-smoking snug with chunky candles and fresh flowers, a dining room with enough space for comfy sofas around a log fire and no music. Alison's mum Norma had dog-walking and pruning the pub's roses on her original remit, but she was also the one who taught the lads in the kitchen how to prepare red bream with king scallops and breast of duck with madeira. A brilliant selection of cheeses, such as Cornish Yarg covered with nettles, will follow, and crème brulée – no wonder people are beating a path to The Lamb's door. Take a mental note of this secluded gem if you are planning a visit to nearby Herstmonceux Castle: the drive across the Pevensey Levels is worth it.

The Star Inn
Old Heathfield

Head for the church and the Star is next door. Built as an inn for pilgrims in the 14th century, with a rough, honey-stone façade, it has gained a few creepers over the centuries and its atmospheric interior has mellowed nicely. Low-beamed ceilings, wall settles and panelling, huge log-fuelled inglenook, rustic tables and chairs – it's cosy, candlelit and inviting in winter. The appeal in summer is the peaceful, award-winning garden, bright with flowers and characterful with hand-crafted furniture; the gorgeous view across the High Weald towards the South Downs was once painted by Turner. Popular bar food focuses on fresh fish from Billingsgate or, closer to home, Hastings and Pevensey. A chalkboard lists the daily-changing choice, perhaps large cock crabs, cod and chips or slow-cooked half shoulder of lamb. To drink, try Harveys Sussex Bitter from Lewes. Allow time to visit the impressive church with its fine early-English tower.

directions	A259 to Polegate & Pevensey; 1st exit for Wartling; on right after 3 miles.
meals	11.45am-2.15pm (12pm-2.30pm Sundays); 6.45pm-9pm. No food Sunday evenings. Main courses £6.95-£15.95.
closed	Sunday evenings.

directions	From A265, left onto B2096, then 2nd right.
meals	12pm-2.15pm; 7pm-9.30pm (9pm Sundays). Main courses £7.95-£15.95.
closed	3pm-5.30pm; 4pm-7pm Sundays.

Robert & Alison Farncombe
The Lamb Inn,
Wartling,
Hailsham,
Sussex BN27 1RY
tel   01323 832116

map: 5 entry: 435

Fiona Airey & Mike Chappell
The Star Inn,
Church Street, Old Heathfield,
Sussex TN21 9AH
tel   01435 863570
web   www.starinnoldheathfield.co.uk

map: 5 entry: 436

The Horse & Groom
Rushlake Green

An idyllic setting for a small, traditional, personally-run pub. Sue and Mike Chappel set out to attract people looking for more than a pint and a packet of crisps – they have succeeded admirably. The menu is simple but inviting with blackboards in the entrance listing fish such as local sea bass and lobster in summer, braised lamb fillets in rosemary and thyme, steak and kidney pudding, and game. Generosity is a strong point, seconds are willingly offered, and Sue insists that all meal prices include a healthy selection of fresh veg. Harveys, Shepherd Neame Masterbrew and seasonal guests are on handpump and they have half a dozen wines and champagne by the glass. Two small bars glow with horse brasses; the beamy dining room is a classic with its Windsor chairs, log fire and hunting trophies; the garden – handmade furniture and Weald views – is one of the nicest places for dining out in the area.

The Curlew
Bodiam

You could do a lot worse than round off a visit to Bodiam Castle with lunch at the old hop-pickers' ale house. Chef Andy Blyth took on the spruced-up, weatherboarded pub in 2001 and is turning out some delightful modern British cooking. Hops hangs from beams, framed watercolours line the walls, the woodburner glows, and Harveys Sussex Bitter is handpulled at the smart but homely bar. Classic and rare vintages dot the impressive list of wines (virtually every one available by the glass), while monthly menus and daily specials highlight light snacks of soups, salads and terrines. Main dishes include roast monkfish with red wine reduction and chive oil, and pork fillet with chorizo potatoes, black pudding tempura and calvados sauce. There may be caramelised vanilla panna cotta for pudding, and a board of English and French unpasteurised cheeses. Colour spills from tubs and borders in the lovely garden and on the teak-tabled terrace in summer.

directions	From Heathfield A265 for Burwash; B2096 for Battle. Right at Chapel Cross for Rushlake Green.
meals	12pm-2.15pm; 7pm-9.30pm (9pm Sundays). Main courses £7.95-£17.95.

directions	On B2244 Hawkhurst to Sedlescombe road; on the Bodiam crossroads.
meals	12pm-2pm; 6.45pm-9.30pm. Main courses £10-£14.95.
closed	Sunday evenings & Mondays.

Mike & Sue Chappel
The Horse & Groom,
Rushlake Green, Heathfield,
Sussex TN21 9QE
tel   01435 830320
web   www.thebestpubsinsussex.co.uk

Andy Blyth
The Curlew,
Junction Road, Bodiam,
Sussex TN32 5UY
tel   01580 861394
web   www.thecurlewatbodiam.co.uk

map: 5 entry: 437

map: 6 entry: 438

Best Beech Inn
Wadhurst

Roger Felstead has brilliantly transformed the once dilapidated 17th-century inn. The framework was always here – the rambling warren of rooms, the old beams, the open fires – but Roger has swept in with a fresh and modern broom. He's held onto the character, altered the décor and revolutionized the food; the Best Beech has become a chic and popular destination. Drinkers fill the cosy armchair-filled bar, imbibing Harveys Old and tucking into big bowls of chunky fries (mouthwateringly good); others study menus before claiming a table in the charming bistro or more formal restaurant. Food is a big draw, with local and seasonal supplies of beef, pheasant, wild mushrooms. Bedrooms upstairs are already comfortable and appealing, though Roger has further plans for them.

directions	From Wadhurst B2100 to Mark Cross.
meals	12pm-2pm; 7pm-9pm. No food Sunday evenings. Main courses £6-£10; set menu £12.95 & £14.95.
rooms	7 twins/doubles, 2 sharing bathroom £59.50-£79.50. Singles £45.

Roger & Jane Felstead
Best Beech Inn,
Mayfield Lane, Wadhurst,
Sussex TN5 6JH
tel   01892 784026
web www.bestbeechinn.co.uk

map: 5 entry: 439

The Coach & Horses
Danehill

With ale on tap from Harveys brewery in Lewes, fresh fish from Seaford and lamb from the fields opposite, the Coach and Horses is a very fine pub. The central bar is its throbbing hub; deep-terracotta walls, original wooden panelling and open fires encourage the gentle pleasures of mulled wine in winter-cosy rooms. During the rest of the year the big raised garden (with hedged-off play area) comes into its own; here you may spread yourselves on the new terrace under the boughs of the huge old maple. Whatever the weather, the wonderful food lures people from far and wide. In the stable block restaurant a changing seasonal menu from chef Chris places the emphasis on quality rather than quantity – in mussel and saffron risotto, slow-braised venison with beetroot and juniper berries, dark chocolate parfait. Harvey the golden retriever is a reminder that this rural pub is very much a local – particularly in its ales.

directions	Off A272 1 mile from Danehill towards Chelwood Gate.
meals	12pm-2pm; 7pm-9pm. Main courses £8.95-£13.50.
closed	3pm-6pm Monday-Friday; 4pm-6pm Saturdays (7pm Sundays).

Ian Philpots
The Coach & Horses,
School Lane,
Danehill, Haywards Hill,
Sussex RH17 7JF
tel   01825 740369

map: 5 entry: 440

Sussex

The Griffin Inn
Fletching

The sort of inn worth moving house to be near; comfortably imperfect because of the occasional touch of scruffiness. The Pullan family run it with gentle passion as a true local inn. Inside, six open fires, 500-year-old beams, oak panelling, red carpets. There's a club room for racing on Saturdays, two cricket teams play in summer and seven chefs turn out the best of modern British: ribollita soup; turbot, lobster and pea risotto; roasted wood pigeon. Bedrooms are full of country-inn elegance – wonky floors, lots of old furniture, rag-rolled walls, free-standing baths, huge shower heads, thick bathrobes – with those in the coach house the quietest. There's a great garden to loll in where jazz plays against the backdrop of a 10-mile view across Ashdown Forest… and they lay on a spit-roast barbecue in summer.

directions	From East Grinstead, A22 south; right at Nutley for Fletching. Straight on for 3 miles into village.
meals	12pm-2.30pm; 7pm-9.30pm. Main courses £8.50-£18.
rooms	8: 1 twin, 7 four-posters £70-£120. Singles £50-£70.

Nigel, Bridget & James Pullan
The Griffin Inn,
Fletching,
Uckfield,
Sussex TN22 3SS
tel   01825 722890

map: 5 entry: 441

Warwickshire

Fox & Hounds
Great Wolford

The gorgeous, honey-coloured pub has been trading since 1540. Recently taken on by Veronica and Paul, its blackboard is chalked up with some irresistible-sounding dishes, excellent Hook Norton ale and a long list of whiskies. Enjoy juicy figs with finely sliced Parma ham, grilled sea bass with langoustine sauce and parsley new potatoes, and fabulous puddings in the oak-panelled bar. Low beams are hung with bunches of dried hops, there are candlelit tables on flagstoned floors and old settles, a huge stone fireplace that crackles with logs in winter, an ancient bread oven and hunting prints on the walls. It couldn't be cosier, or more welcoming – a perfect country pub. Certainly a place to stay: there are three charming bedrooms under the eaves. There's also a good terrace for the summer.

directions	Off A3400 between Shipston-on-Stour & Long Compton.
meals	12pm-2pm; 6.30pm-9pm. No food Sunday evenings. Main courses £9-£17.
rooms	3: 2 double, 1 twin £70. Singles £45.
closed	Mondays.

Paul Tomlinson
Fox & Hounds,
Great Wolford, Moreton-in-Marsh,
Warwickshire CV36 5NQ
tel   01608 674220
web   www.thefoxandhoundsinn.com

map: 9 entry: 442

Warwickshire

White Bear
Shipston-on-Stour

It has long been a Warwickshire institution. You have two bars: the public one with its jukebox, telly and darts, and the posher lounge, with large stripped settles, rag-rolled walls and newspapers on sticks. George Kruszynskyj took the place over in 2000, and his cooking has put The Bear on the culinary map. The blackboard in the fresh, attractive restaurant chalks up traditional ham and eggs as well as modern British dishes like fillet of haddock with saffron potatoes and leek sauce, and braised lamb shank with cabbage. You can also eat in the lounge. There are four draught ales on handpump, nearly 30 wines. The food is a major pull, but The Bear remains first and foremost a vibrant local, with people from the town and surrounding villages drawn by the atmosphere – at its most exuberant on Sunday nights when visiting bands play.

directions	Off A3400 in centre of Shipston, 9 miles S of Stratford-upon-Avon.
meals	12pm-2pm (2.30pm Sundays); 6.30pm-9.30pm. No food Sunday evenings. Main courses £8-£12.50.
rooms	10: 4 double, 4 twin, 1 triple, 1 single £50. Singles £30.

George Kruszynskys
White Bear,
4 High Street, Shipston-on-Stour,
Warwickshire CV36 4AJ
tel   01608 661558
web   www.whitebearhotel.co.uk

map: 9 entry: 443

Warwickshire

The Castle Inn
Edgehill

A splendid site! Charles I raised his battle standard here, before the battle of Edge Hill, and the pub sits inside the crenellated, octagonal tower, built to commemorate the 100th anniversary of the battle. It opened as a pub in 1822, and later was bought by the Hook Norton Brewery. From the great big garden, spectacular views sweep down over the steep scarp to the plain below and away to the Malvern Hills. In the public bar are darts, pool, a fruit machine and carpeting that has seen better days; the octagonal walls of the lounge bar are decorated with all the Civil War paintings, maps and memorabilia you could wish for. Food is traditional English – soups and mixed grills, venison in red wine, beef and ale pie – to be washed down with perfect pints of Old Hooky, real cider and country wines. Malts are taken seriously, too. A smaller folly is linked to the inn by a wooden walkway; herein lie two good bedrooms and one four-poster suite.

directions	Off A422, 6 miles NW of Banbury.
meals	12pm-2pm (2.30pm Sundays); 6.30pm-9pm. Main courses £5.90-£7.60.
rooms	3 twins/doubles £57.50-£67.50.

John & Gill Blann
The Castle Inn,
Edgehill, Banbury,
Warwickshire OX15 6DJ
tel   01295 670255
web   www.thecastle-edgehill.co.uk

map: 9 entry: 444

Warwickshire

Howard Arms
Ilmington

The place buzzes with good-humoured babble as well-kept beer flows from the flagstoned bar. Logs crackle contentedly in a vast open fire; a menu hangs above; a dining room at the far end has great swathes of bold colour and some noble paintings. Gorgeous bedrooms are set discreetly apart, mixing period style and modern luxury; the double oozes old world charm, the twin is more folksy, the half-tester is almost a suite, full of antiques. The village is a surprise, too, tucked under a lone hill, with an unusual church and a long village green. Round off an idyllic walk amid buzzing bees and fragrant wild flowers with a meal here: how about seared scallops with lentils and coriander, beer, ale and mustard pie, British farmhouse cheeses served with homemade biscuits, Mrs G's toffee meringue? Fabulous food, good people, and Charlie the resident ghost who likes to move the table settings around at midnight.

directions	Off A3400 between Stratford-upon-Avon & Shipston-on-Stour; 2 miles NW of Shipston, 5 miles east of Chipping Campden.
meals	12pm-2pm (2.30pm Sundays); 7pm-9pm (9.30pm Fridays & Saturdays); 6.30pm-8.30pm Sundays. Main courses £9.50-£15.
rooms	3: 2 doubles, 1 twin £90-£105. Singles £57.
closed	Christmas day. 3pm-6pm daily.

	Robert & Gill Greenstock
	Howard Arms,
	Ilmington, Stratford-upon-Avon,
	Warwickshire CV36 4LT
tel	01608 682226
web	www.howardarms.com

map: 9 entry: 445

Four Alls
Welford-upon-Avon

'The king rules for all, the priest prays for all, the soldier fights for all, the citizen pays for all,' proclaim the ancient stained-glass windows at the Four Alls – good old-fashioned cynicism in a very up-to-date gastropub. This riverside pub next to the humpback bridge on the Avon is likely to become a Warwickshire institution. It has been done up inside and out for the second time in five years, and is unquestionably stylish: there are two dining areas, a bar and a large garden with a play area to keep children happy. The management is linked to the Kings Head in Aston Cantlow (see entry 449) and the chef is Michael Perry, who has cooked everywhere: in the Far East, on the Orient Express and at swanky London restaurants. So, good beers, wines and a menu full of surprises: perhaps green chicken curry with papaya, or fillet of beef with port sauce and celeriac purée.

directions	On B439 at Binton Bridge, between Stratford-upon-Avon & Bidford-on-Avon.
meals	12pm-2.30pm; 7pm-10.30pm (9.30pm Sundays). Main course bar £4.95-£15.95.

Andrew Richardson
Four Alls,
Binton Bridge,
Welford-upon-Avon,
Warwickshire CV37 8PW
tel   01789 750228

map: 9 entry: 446

The One Elm
Stratford-upon-Avon

Stratford has a reputation for great pubs and drama, and was the birthplace of the first ever Slug and Lettuce. In the narrow building that The Slug once occupied now stands The One Elm. Owned by Peach Pubs (of Warwick's Rose & Crown), it, too, is a cracker. It could hardly fail to be: the chefs trained at Raymond Blanc's Le Petit Blanc, Birmingham. The bar is light, airy and wooden-floored, and the décor modern and stylish, with leather sofas and bar stools that remind one of Giacometti sculptures. In the bar downstairs there are good beers and great wines; outside, an attractive, sheltered terrace; at the back, the restaurant, with a private, secluded mezzanine and a short but mouthwatering menu. There's a chargrill section, a risotto of the week, skate with mash, and a deli board that's available all day. The One Elm has a chic cosmopolitan feel and, being slightly off the tourist trail, is used by a local rather than an international crowd. The staff are friendly and serve you from breakfast right through until closing time.

directions	In town centre on corner of Guild Street & Shakespeare Street.
meals	12pm-10pm (9.30pm Sundays). Main courses £8.50-£13.

Victoria Moon
One Elm, 1 Guild Street,
Stratford-upon-Avon,
Warwickshire CV37 6QZ
tel   01789 404919
web   www.peachpubs.com

map: 9 entry: 447

The Crabmill
Preston Bagot

It is named not after the crustacean but after the crab apples that were pressed here. The lovely, rambling building once contained a cider press, and has been a pub for the last two centuries. Five years ago the Classic Country Pub group took it over and turned it into a busy gastro haven. Inside the sturdy A-frame building, designers have cleverly brought country casual and urban chic together. There's a wonky chimney piece to your left, and a steely bar with sand-blasted glass panels ahead: it's 'the Met Bar meets the Slaughtered Lamb'. At the back is a split-level lounge with mustard-yellow walls, wooden floors, deep armchairs, leather sofas and a landscaped garden that heads off into open countryside. To the right are three candlelit dining rooms divided by heavy beams and standing timbers; some call the Red Room the 'rude room', for its slightly risqué pictures. The food is justifiably popular, the Italian-influenced menu imaginative and colourful. Drool over sweet potato, red onion and goat's cheese crostini, fillet steak with onion and olive oil mash, or parmesan-crusted chicken breast stuffed with garlic, herbs and bacon — all washed down with a pint of Wadworth 6X or a glass of wine.

directions	From Henley-in-Arden on A4189 towards Claverdon.
meals	12pm-2.30pm; 12.30-3.30pm Sun; 6.30pm-9.30pm (10pm Sundays). Main courses £8.95-£14.95.
closed	Sunday evenings.

	Sarah Robinson
	The Crabmill,
	Preston Bagot, Claverdon,
	Warwickshire B95 5EE
tel	01926 843342
web	www.thecrabmill.biz

map: 9 entry: 448

Warwickshire

The King's Head
Aston Cantlow

It's rumoured the Bard's parents had their wedding reception at the King's Head: the pub has stood next to the parish church for 500 years and Mary Arden, Shakespeare's mother, lived down the road. (Her family home is now a museum.) One can imagine the scene at this long, low, creeper-fringed country inn with its flagged floors, low ceilings, small leaded windows and massive inglenook. Perhaps they even tucked into the famous Duck Supper, a house speciality. Other, more up-to-date delicacies join the menu today: venison bourguignon with stilton dumplings, salmon and spring onion fishcakes, Toulouse sausages, walnut pudding with toffee sauce. The delicious food draws diners from miles around, notably well-heeled Brummies. Regulars quaff pints of ale and good wines in the stylish bar with its newly lime-washed beams, old scrubbed pine tables, ancient settles and crackling logs. There's a pretty garden for summer; the village creaks with history and the walks start from the door.

directions	Off A46 at Aston Cantlow.
meals	12pm-2.30pm (3pm Sundays); 7pm-10pm (9pm Sundays). Main courses £9.95-£13.50.
closed	3pm-5.30pm Monday-Friday.

Andrew Richardson
The King's Head,
21 Bearley Road, Aston Cantlow,
Stratford-upon-Avon,
Warwickshire B95 6HY
tel   01789 488242

map: 9 entry: 449

Warwickshire

The Boot
Lapworth

The Boot was here long before the canal that runs past the back garden. With its exposed timbers, rug-strewn quarry floors, open fires and papers to peruse it marries old-fashioned charm with rustic chic. Eight years ago, under the guidance of Paul Salisbury and James Elliot, the down-at-heel boozer underwent a transformation and became one of the first gastropubs of the Midlands; it has been pulling them in ever since. People come from miles around for the buzz – the feel is still very much 'friendly local' – and to sample the fabulous food. Menus have a distinct touch of mediterranean and Pacific rim: savour roast lamb rump with baby onions and chorizo, or linguini arrabbiata, or seared squid with sweet chilli. Ingredients are as fresh as can be and seafood dishes are a speciality. Eat in the bars or in the white-beamed dining room upstairs, and in summer go alfresco: there's a lovely terrace to the side.

directions	Off M42 junc. 4 for Hockley Heath; Lapworth signed.
meals	12.15pm-2.30pm; 7pm-10pm (9pm Sundays). Main courses £8-£14; set lunch £15 & £19.50.

James Eliot
The Boot,
Old Warwick Road, Lapworth,
Warwickshire B94 6JU
tel   01564 782464
web   www.thebootatlapworth.co.uk

map: 9 entry: 450

Warwickshire

The Durham Ox
Shrewley

Nick Skelton, the showjumper, and his business partner Ross Sanders arrived two years ago, took on the ex head chef of the King of Jordan and the youngest Englishman ever to be awarded a Michelin star, and folk flocked. With fancy cars and fine steeds in the car- and horse-parks, it's obvious the Ox draws those with deep pockets. According to season, menus are 'classical' or 'contemporary': salmon and crab fishcakes with braised lettuce and coriander cream; Cornish lamb with olives, tomatoes and rosemary mash. The wines are fine, beers include Greene King Abbot Ale and Old Speckled Hen. The pub is a mix of traditional – it resembles a Warwickshire farmhouse on the outside – and modern, with its exposed timbers and rafters, solid wooden floors, bold colours, chunky furniture and exuberant flowers. The restaurant is particularly appealing, its huge windows filling the space with light.

directions	On edge of common in Shrewley.
meals	12pm-3pm; 5.30pm-10pm. All day at weekends. Main courses £4.50-£10; set menu £12 & £15.

Ross Sanders & Nick Skelton
The Durham Ox,
Shrewley Common, Shrewley,
Warwick, Warwickshire CV35 7AY
tel   01926 842283
web   www.durham-ox.com

map: 9 entry: 451

Warwickshire

The Case is Altered
Five Ways

No food, no musak and a Sopwith Camel propeller hanging from the ceiling. This is a marvellously old-fashioned pub. There's even a vintage bar billiards machine, operated by sixpences from behind the bar. In the main room are plain tables, leather-covered settles and walls covered in yellowing posters offering defunct beverages at a penny a pint. The lounge, open in the evenings, is cosier. Jackie does not open her arms to children or dogs: she regards pubs as places for adult conversation and liquid refreshment. Despite, or perhaps because of this, the pub has a great many devotees who travel some distance to enjoy the company and the expertly-kept beer. The bar is so small you can't help but join in the chat. The pub sign shows lawyers arguing but the name has nothing to do with the law. It used to be called, simply, The Case, and was so small that it was not eligible for a licence. So it was made larger, whisky was introduced, the name was changed, and everyone was happy. They've been that way ever since.

directions	Follow Rowington off A4177/A4141 junction, north of Warwick.
closed	2.30pm-6pm; 2pm-7pm Sundays.

Jackie Willacy
The Case is Altered,
Case Lane,
Five Ways, Hatton,
Warwickshire CV35 7JD
tel   01926 484206

map: 9 entry: 452

Rose & Crown
Warwick

Warwick has always been long on history – its castle is one of the finest in Europe – but was short on everything else. A surprise, then, to find one of its old pubs transformed into a vibrant gastro-pub-hotel. The brainchild of Victoria Moon and Lee Cash of Peach Pubs, the flagship Rose & Crown opens with bacon sandwiches for breakfast and stays open all day. You enter to a cheery, airy, wooden-floored front bar with red and white walls, big leather sofas, low tables and a crackling winter fire. To the back is the big and bustling eating area. Almost all of the staff trained at Raymond Blanc's Petit Blanc restaurants and the food has a reputation that people travel for. Served all day, the tapas-style portions of cheeses, hams, marinated anchovies and rustic breads slip down easily with a pint of Fuller's London Pride or a decent glass of wine. Hot dishes are modern British with a mediterranean touch, as in vegetable and goat's cheese parcel with tomato fondue and pesto dressing, and braised shank of lamb risotto. Bedrooms are understated and modern, most overlooking the market square, and there's a private room that can be booked for parties and meetings. It's young and fun.

directions	In Warwick centre in the Market Place.
meals	8am-9.30pm.
	Main course bar £8.50-£13.50.
rooms	5: 2 doubles, 3 twins £65-£75.

Victoria Moon
Rose & Crown,
30 Market Place, Warwick,
Warwickshire CV34 4SH
tel   01926 411117
web   www.peachpubs.com

map: 9 entry: 453

The Hollybush Inn
Priors Marston

Not many pubs have a cigar humidor and an oil painting of Ali G hanging in the bar. Down a quiet village lane the large, bright, idiosyncratic Hollybush Inn feels like a cross between a Soho bar and a traditional boozer. Seating in the flagged bar is in a series of alcoves stuffed with sofas and armchairs, or at tables in the large open area with walls of vibrant terracotta and exposed stone. A blazing log fire and a woodburner bring winter cheer. Tasty pies, scampi and steaks help soak up the good beers, wines and real ciders, while on Friday and Saturday evenings the chef dons his big white hat and delivers haute cuisine for the restaurant at the back: seared tuna fillet with roast butternut squash and rose dressing, perhaps. There are darts, TV, a friendly dog and a garden for the summer. It's a big rambling place and manages to squeeze in 10 comfortable bedrooms with no trouble at all.

The Inn at Farnborough
Farnborough

Turning a neglected inn into a pub-restaurant was an exciting prospect for chef Anthony and his wife Joanna. Their vision and dedication led to a change of name, a stylish revival and menus created daily from the best local suppliers. Three years on and it's all go. It's not just the food that is irresistible but the warm yellow walls, subtle lighting, open fires, rustic floors and fresh flowers. The food is gorgeous: turbot with saffron, mussel and chive beurre blanc or local pheasant with smoked bacon and calvados.... Or there's a good value lunchtime and early evening menu. Add fine wines by the glass, posh bar nibbles, Havana cigars, smiley staff and a fabulous landscaped garden... it would be hard to find a more civilised pub. There's even a private dining-room, with jaunty red walls, zebra-print chairs and a juke box.

directions	Off A361 just before Byfield, 12 miles from Banbury.
meals	12pm-2pm; 6.30pm-9pm. Main courses £6.95-£18.95.
rooms	10: 6 doubles, 1 twin, 3 singles. £45; singles £40.
closed	2pm-5.30pm; 3pm-6pm Saturdays; 3.30pm-7pm Sundays.

directions	From junction 11 on M40 follow signs for Banbury. At 3ird r'bout right onto A423 for Southam.
meals	12pm-3pm; 6pm-11pm. Main courses £8.95-£19.95; set menu £12.95.
closed	3pm-6pm Monday-Friday.

Richard Saunders
The Hollybush Inn,
Holly Bush Lane,
Priors Marston, Southam,
Warwickshire CV47 7RW

tel   01327 260934

map: 9 entry: 454

Anthony Robinson
The Inn at Farnborough,
Farnborough, Banbury,
Warwickshire OX17 1DZ

tel   01295 690615
web   www.innatfarnborough.co.uk

map: 9 entry: 455

Wiltshire

The Vine Tree
Norton

With a good collection of real ales and fine wines the old watermill is a watering hole in every sense. It may be hidden away but the faithful return – again and again. We would too, for the food and the beer. Roasted root vegetable and mango parcels, delicately spiced and served with a light curry sauce, can be devoured in seconds. There's wild mushroom risotto, too, and partridge, liver and fresh bream. Surroundings are cosy: deep red walls, candlelight and beams, a wood-burning stove. Treat yourselves to an intimate dinner in the miniscule upstairs room. In summer relax and gaze at the view from the terrace – a delicious spot with urns of flowers and a fountain – or watch the kids play in the big garden. This vine tree has a rich harvest for guests to reap – no wonder black lab Clementine looks content.

directions	M4 junc. 17; A429 for Cirencester. After 1.5 miles left for Norton. There, right; for Foxley. Follow road; pub on left.
meals	12pm-2pm (2.30pm Fri & Sat, 3pm Sun); 7pm-9.30pm (9.45pm Fri & Sat; 9pm Sun). Main courses £8.95-£15.
rooms	4 twins/doubles.

Charles Walker & Tiggi Wood
The Vine Tree,
Norton, Malmesbury,
Wiltshire SN16 0JP
tel   01666 837654
web   www.thevinetree.co.uk

map: 3 entry: 456

Wiltshire

The Red Lion
Lacock

The dashing Mr Darcy was sensible enough to stop here in the BBC's version of *Pride and Prejudice* – and how comforted he was by the inn's beamed embrace. It dates from the early 1700s and may well have been known to Jane Austen; big open fires, tankards hanging above the bar, rugs on flagstones, bare wooden floors – not a lot has changed. Sit down to fine home-cooked food among timber frames, old settles, a row of branding irons and Victorian birdcages – you may have to ask about the more bizarre farming tools on display. Climb the shallow tread of the stairs to small but excellent bedrooms done in a Georgian style. In summer, eat outside in the atmospheric courtyard garden with its country views. The National Trust village was built around the 13th-century abbey and lies on the old cloth route between London and Bristol. Fabulous walks from the pub; Lacock Abbey and the Fox Talbot Museum of Photography are just across the road.

directions	Off A350 between Chippenham & Melksham.
meals	12pm-2pm. Main courses £6-£13.
rooms	5 doubles, £75. Singles from £55.
closed	2.30pm-6pm.

Chris Chappell
The Red Lion,
1 High Street,
Lacock,
Wiltshire SN15 2LQ
tel   01249 730456

map: 3 entry: 457

The Pear Tree Inn
Whitley

More like a mellow farmhouse than a traditional inn, it perches unobtrusively behind well-tended gardens. Inside, too, the feel is almost of home. Here are flagstones, beams, exposed stone, old-fashioned latch doors, log fires – and a restful mix of tables, chairs, armchairs and cushioned window seats. The Pear Tree is a civilised spot where 25 wines are served by the glass, along with changing guest beers and speciality teas. Out at the back, the restaurant has a lofty, barn-like quality; cottagey furniture stands on jute matting, there's an intriguing montage of an old farm scythe painted white, and glasses sparkle by candlelight at night. The teak-furnished terrace and garden lie to one side. Restaurant menus announce stylish modern dishes based around well-sourced ingredients (fillet of beef with celeriac and stilton dauphinoise, Thai monkfish, warm pear and almond tart with rosemary ice cream) served by polite and cheerful staff. In the old barn are several fresh new bedrooms, with more upstairs in the pub.

directions	M4 junc .17; A350 for Melksham to Beanacre; right onto Westlands Lane; at T-junction left onto B3353; immed. right to Whitley; right again into Top Lane.
meals	12pm-2pm (2.30pm Sundays); 6.30pm-9pm (10pm Saturdays). Main courses £10.50-£18.
rooms	8 doubles £90.

Martin & Debbie Still
The Pear Tree Inn,
Top Lane,
Whitley,
Wiltshire SN12 8QX

tel   01225 709131

map: 3 entry: 458

The Tollgate Inn
Holt

All would pay the toll — were there one — to sample the delights of The Tollgate Inn. There's an exceptionally warm, relaxed and convivial atmosphere in both bar and lounge, with comfy sofas on rugged quarry tiles, log-burning stove and planked pine tables. Newspapers, magazines and homely touches encourage you to linger over a handpumped pint of Exmoor or a glass of chilled sauvignon. The two dining areas have distinct personalities. The smaller room off the bar downstairs has a traditional appeal, while upstairs, in the former chapel of the weavers who once worked below, is the restaurant with high rafters, a large open fire, the original chapel windows, country furniture and an eclectic décor. Chef Alexander Venables's pedigree shines through in dishes that make the most of top-quality local produce (suppliers are named with the menu) and daily fish from Brixham. Food is modern British: hearty game in winter, a nod to the Mediterranean in summer and an exemplary chocolate mousse. The bedrooms, overlooking either the paddock or the weavers' cottages on the village green, have character and all mod cons.

directions	On B3107 between Bradford on Avon & Melksham.
meals	12pm-2pm; 7pm-9pm. Main courses £10.75-£16.50; set menu £9.95.
rooms	4 twins/doubles £65-£85.
closed	Sunday evenings & Mondays.

Alison Ward–Baptiste
& Alexander Venables,
The Tollgate Inn, Ham Green,
Holt, Bradford on Avon,
Wiltshire BA14 6PX
tel   01225 782326
web   www.tollgateholt.co.uk

map: 3 entry: 459

The George & Dragon
Rowde

Ah, the George and Dragon... you fall in love at first sight. Behind the imposing black door hides a low-ceilinged bar room with a huge stone fireplace ablaze with logs in winter, its half-panelled walls painted plum and lined with old portraits. The antique clock ticks reassuringly in the background... this is almost like somebody's home. Furnishings are authentically period, there's lots of dark timber, bare boards in the dining room, carpets in the bar. The kitchen's chutneys and preserves are for sale, international bottled beers and organic ciders line the shelves and handpumped Wadworth, Butcombe and Milk Street are on the bar. Chef-patron Tim Withers has a passion for fish (even the fabrics have fish themes) and his seductive menus concentrate on fish delivered fresh from Cornwall — with the odd concession to meat eaters. Blackboards list the day's specials — perhaps skate with capers and black butter or fillet of turbot with Seville orange hollandaise — and puddings to diet for (as in brown sugar meringues with sinful amounts of Jersey cream). There's also an à la carte menu, and the wine list is 50-strong. Relax in the pleasant garden in summer, or wander along the dreamy Kennet & Avon Canal.

directions	On A342 2 miles west of Devizes.
meals	No food Sundays & Mondays. Main courses £7.50-£20.
closed	2pm-7pm; Monday lunchtimes.

Tim & Helen Withers
The George & Dragon,
High Street,
Rowde,
Wiltshire SN10 2PN
tel   01380 723053

map: 3 entry: 460

Wiltshire

The Linnet
Great Hinton

Back in 2001 young Jonathan Furby grasped the nettle and left the hothouse kitchen of a nearby gastropub to become chef-patron of his own. With enthusiasm, dedication and bags of talent he's brought this ailing pub to life. With a new kitchen and a dining room full of neatly laid flower-topped tables, the Linnet is now one of Wiltshire's jolliest pub-restaurants. Best of all, it's still the village pub with a happy atmosphere and loyal, beer-drinking locals. Bread, pasta and ice cream are homemade, a light lunch could be warm filled foccacia bread (smoked chicken and cheddar) or Thai seafood tagliatelle. Two- or three-course lunches are good value; expect some unusual combinations like grilled rib-eye steak with faggots and sage sauce. All is beautifully done and the staff are cheerful and informal.

directions	Off A361, 2 miles E of Trowbridge.
meals	12pm-2.30pm (3pm Sundays); 6.30-9.30pm; 7-9pm Sundays. Main courses £6.25-£16.50; set menu £10.25 & £12.50.
closed	Mondays.

Jonathan Furby
The Linnet,
Great Hinton,
Trowbridge,
Wiltshire BA14 6BU
tel 01380 870354

map: 3 entry: 461

Wiltshire

The Millstream
Marden

A modern bar-restaurant that opens all day and serves champagne by the glass: not perhaps what you'd expect in the Vale of Pewsey! A recent makeover of an old pub, The Millstream keeps bags of character and a range of handpumped ales. Mustard walls, pale beams, log-burners and open fires lend a fresh appeal to the open-plan space. There's a snug with a single table off to one end, and a non-smoking dining area at the other. This picks up the vibe from the bar, but is a gentler place to be, with its upholstered chairs and calming views over the lawn to the river. The daily, modern British menu uses local produce, much of it organic, and fish delivered from Looe; the wine list is long. Go for beef-filled pancakes with tomato and mozzarella, haddock with blackeye beans, and a pinenut and honey tart that comes with custard in winter, crème fraîche in summer. Staff in black aprons serve with smiles; on warm days you may sup on the terrace.

directions	On A302 5 miles from Devizes.
meals	12pm-2.30pm (3pm Fridays & Saturdays); 7pm-9.30pm; 12pm-5pm Sundays. Main courses £4-£15.
closed	Mondays.

Mrs Nicola Notton
The Millstream,
Marden,
Devizes,
Wiltshire SN10 3RH
tel 01380 848308

map: 4 entry: 462

Wiltshire

The Seven Stars
Bottlesford

Traditional English pub trappings but no ordinary pub. French waiting staff, masterminded by landlord-cum-chef Philippe Cheminade, greet you warmly. Fine Gallic wines accompany daily-changing dishes served in the bar areas as well as rooms designated for dining, and they deliver French classics – of course – with an emphasis on fresh fish and game. The food draws an appreciative crowd (book at weekends). Service is attentive, polite and professional: the continental mood suits the English setting beautifully. Should you wish to pop in just for a drink, the Seven Stars is as good a pub as you could hope to find, with Badger Best and Wadworth 6X on tap. Outside, a seven-acre slice of land borders a shallow stream; look across the Vale of Pewsey to the famous White Horse chalk man carved in the Downs.

directions	From Pewsey to Woodborough, then Bottlesford.
meals	12pm-2pm; 7pm-9.30pm. Main courses £8.75-£16.75; set menu £12.50 & £16 (Sundays).
closed	Sunday evenings & Mondays (except lunch on Bank Holidays).

Philippe & Kate Cheminade
The Seven Stars,
Bottlesford,
Pewsey,
Wiltshire SN9 6LU
tel   01672 851325

map: 4 entry: 463

Wiltshire

The Malet Arms
Newton Tony

Formerly a bakehouse for a long-lost manor, the old flintstone pub draws loyal locals, walkers and cyclists from miles around. Expect cracking real ales, robust country cooking and a cheerful welcome from Noel and Annie Cardew. In the low-beamed bar, cosy with rustic furnishings, blazing winter logs, old pictures and interesting bits and bobs, you sup a pint of Wadworth 6X drawn from wooden casks (a modern rarity!) or local Stonehenge Heelstone. Hearty food, listed on blackboards above the fireplaces, reflects the rural setting, with locally-shot game a winter favourite. Fill your boots with a rich stew of pheasant and pigeon in Guinness, a brace of roasted duck on braised puy lentils, or a big Malet Burger – 100% pure local beef glazed with blue cheese. In summer, knock a few boules about with the locals in the usually dry bed of the 'bourne' rivulet outside the door, or watch the pub cricket team on the playing field opposite.

directions	Off A338; 6 miles north of Salisbury.
meals	12pm-2.30pm; 6.30pm-10pm (7pm Sundays). Main courses £7.95-£14.

Noel & Annie Cardew
The Malet Arms,
Newton Tony,
Salisbury,
Wiltshire SP4 0HF
tel   01980 629279

map: 4 entry: 464

Wiltshire

Haunch of Venison
Salisbury

A tiny, ancient, city-centre pub with huge charm. It dates from 1320 when it was built as a church house for nearby St Thomas's. A trio of rooms, bustling with locals, businessmen and tourists in a music- and game-free atmosphere, radiate from a minuscule, pewter-topped bar. The rooms are affectionately known as the Horsebox, a tiny snug off the entrance lobby, the House of Commons, with its chequered stone floor and wooden panelling, beams and carved oak benches, and the House of Lords, the upper room, with its 600-year-old fireplace and small side window displaying a smoke-preserved, mummified hand holding a pack of 18th-century playing cards (spookily discovered in 1903). Amazingly, there are over 100 malt whiskies crammed behind the bar. Note, too, the rare set of antique taps for gravity-fed spirits.

directions	Opposite Poultry Cross, off Market Square.
meals	12pm-2.30pm; 6pm-10pm. No food Sunday evenings in winter. Main courses £7-£14.
closed	Christmas Day.

Anthony & Victoria Leroy
Haunch of Venison,
1-5 Minster Street,
Salisbury,
Wiltshire SP1 1TB
tel   01722 411313

map: 4 entry: 465

Wiltshire

The Forester Inn
Donhead St Andrew

Threatened with closure two years ago, the Forester is the hub of Donhead St Andrew. Now resplendent with new thatch, swish signs and landscaped garden, the 600-year-old inn has not lost its old character. Rustic walls, black beams and a log fire in the inglenook combine with fashionable terracotta walls, local art and planked floors. People come to eat and eat well, from a changing menu that's a cut above the norm. The new chef is introducing a classic-modern style in dishes such as pan-fried squid with chorizo, parsley, lemon and rocket, and chargrilled beef fillet with rösti, spinach and madeira sauce. And there are mussels, crabcakes, pasta, warm salads, soups and ciabatta sandwiches; good puddings, too. So far, five ales on tap, cider from Stowford Press and a decent list of wines with ten by the glass. Good views from the garden and the people are lovely... this is one to watch.

directions	A30 between Shaftesbury & Salisbury. Through Ludwell turning for Donhead on left after 2 miles.
meals	12pm-2pm; 7pm-9pm. No food Christmas Day. Main courses £7.95-£15.95.
closed	3pm-6pm.

Tony Lethbridge
The Forester Inn,
Lower Street,
Donhead St Andrew,
Wiltshire SP7 9EE
tel   01747 828038

map: 3 entry: 466

Wiltshire

The Compasses Inn
Lower Chicksgrove

In the middle of a village of thatched and timber-framed cottages, this old inn seems too good to be true. Its thatched roof is like a sombrero, shielding bedroom windows that peer sleepily over the lawn. Duck instinctively into the sudden darkness of the flagstoned bar and experience a wave of nostalgia as your eyes adjust to a long wooden room, its cosy booths divided by farmyard salvage, a cartwheel here, some horse tack there. At one end is a piano, the other a brick hearth. The pub crackles with Alan's enthusiasm – he's a great host. People come for the food, too: figs baked in red wine and topped with goat's cheese and chorizo; grilled fish from the south coast. Bedrooms have the same effortless charm and the sweet serenity of Wiltshire lies down the lane. Modest, ineffably pretty, great value.

directions	From Salisbury, A30; 3rd right after Fovant for L. Chicksgrove; 1st left down single track lane to village.
meals	12pm-3pm; 7pm-9pm. No food Sunday evenings. Main courses £4.95-£14.95.
rooms	4 doubles, £65. Singles £45.
closed	3pm-6pm; Mondays (except Bank Holidays when closed on Tuesdays).

	Alan Stoneham
	The Compasses Inn,
	Lower Chicksgrove, Tisbury,
	Wiltshire SP3 6NB
tel	01722 714318
web	www.thecompassesinn.com

map: 3 entry: 467

Wiltshire

The Beckford Arms
Fonthill Gifford

This substantial stone inn stands opposite magnificent Fonthill Park and near the site of eccentric 18th-century author William Beckford's attempt to build a "gothic dream palace" at Fonthill Abbey. An appropriate gothic theme runs through the inn's smartly rustic interior created by Karen, whose enthusiasm for unusual *objets d'art* is revealed in chunky candles and big bowls on huge plank tables, ornate mirrors and old paintings on warm terracotta walls. Order a pint of wonderful Timothy Taylor's Landlord, pick up the daily papers and bask like the resident cat before a blazing fire. Light lunches come in the form of ciabatta sandwiches – don't miss the Wiltshire ham and grain mustard – while seriously rumbling stomachs can be pacified with potato gnocchi with pesto and pecorino. Evening dishes include mixed seafood grill and chargrilled fillet steak with red wine and garlic sauce. There's a sun-trapping patio and a raised garden for dining out.

directions	Off B3089 between Hindon & Teffont Magna at Fonthill Bishop.
meals	12pm-2pm; 7pm-9pm. Main courses £8.50-£16.95.
rooms	5 twins/doubles £70-£85. Singles £40.

	Karen & Eddie Costello
	The Beckford Arms,
	Fonthill Gifford,
	Tisbury,
	Wiltshire SP3 6PX
tel	01747 870385

map: 3 entry: 468

Wiltshire

The Angel Inn
Hindon

The owners are new but chef Matthew Laughton still stars. Behind the Georgian exterior is a stylish bar area in earthy tones with wooden floors, chunky tables, deep leather sofas and a log fire. The more formal restaurant is softened by candles and fresh flowers. Modern British cooking draws folk from afar: watch the team at work in the glass-fronted kitchen. At lunch: fresh tagliatelle with smoked trout, fennel, cream and dill, an impressive cheese board from Neal's Yard Dairy. Cooking moves up a gear in the evenings, the daily-changing menu listing, say, crispy fish cakes with dill mayonnaise or braised pork belly and parsnip mash with black pudding and a sage and cider sauce. A teak-tabled courtyard and a gorgeous village at the door entice you out; good simple rooms (due for a revamp in 2004) may tempt you to stay.

directions	From A303, left 7 miles after main A36 Salisbury junction. Inn at crossroads in village.
meals	12pm-2.30pm; 7pm-9.30pm. Main courses £10.95-£16.50.
rooms	6 twins/doubles £76-£85. Singles £50.
closed	Sunday evenings.

Bradley Thurston
The Angel Inn,
High Street, Hindon,
Salisbury, Wiltshire SP3 6DJ
tel 01747 820696
web www.theangelathindon.co.uk

map: 3 entry: 469

Wiltshire

The Cross Keys
Lye's Green

Fraser Carruth and Wayne Carnegie put The Dove Inn at Corton on the foodie pub map; now they have taken on a new challenge. Their move to the old Wadworth-owned Cross Keys in tiny Lye's Green has already encouraged Dove regulars up the valley, and the convivial bar with its open log fire and rustic old tables is tailor-made for the quaffing of Wadworth ales. With its wooden floors and fresh flowers on big pine tables, the front dining area is slightly posher, as is the intimate dining room with log fire, green dresser and scrubbed oak tables bright with gleaming glasses and chunky candles. Three huge blackboards list the daily-changing menu. Find lunchtime baguettes and excellent 100% beef burgers, along with spicy bell-pepper soup, home-cooked ham and free-range eggs, fresh seafood salad (squid, crayfish, mussels and prawns), and rack of lamb with redcurrant sauce — all delicious. A landscaped garden is planned for summer 2004.

directions	Off A3098 east of Frome at Chapmanslade.
meals	12pm-2.30pm (bar snacks); 7pm-9.30pm (à la carte). Main courses £6.75-£14.

Fraser Carruth & Wayne Carnegie
The Cross Keys,
Lye's Green,
Corsley,
Wiltshire BA12 7PB
tel 01373 832406

map: 3 entry: 470

Wiltshire

George Hotel
Codford

By George! The old roadside inn has been given a new lease of life. Boyd Mackintosh and Joanne Fryer used to practise their art at the revered Howard's House in Teffont Evias. Here, Boyd delivers dishes from a compact modern menu that reeks of class: wild sea bass with lemon and chive beurre blanc, corn-fed chicken with mushroom risotto, foie gras ravioli and vanilla sauce. Joanne is a dab hand at front of house – and her influence is also stamped over the understatedly contemporary interiors. Floors are parquet, tiled or pale-carpeted, walls are warmly hued and the furniture is stylishly simple. The bar has a blond-wood counter, there are lush plants, eye-catching mirrors and a sitting room full of deep sofas. The vase of lilies on the bar adds a civilised touch, as do candles on tables; the winter fires are the icing on the cake. We haven't visited the new bedrooms, but they are likely to delight.

directions	Off A36 between Salisbury & Warminster.
meals	12pm-2pm; 7pm-9.30pm. Main courses £8.95-£16.95.
rooms	3 twins/doubles, 1 with separate bathroom, £65. Singles £45.
closed	Tuesdays.

Boyd Mackintosh
George Hotel,
High Street,
Codford, Warminster,
Wiltshire BA12 0NG
tel   01985 850270

map: 3 entry: 471

Worcestershire

Bell & Cross Inn
Holy Cross

Roger Narbett has few claims to fame apart from having been chef to the England football team, but over the last few years he has pushed this neglected old boozer and onetime butcher's shop into premier status. He does daily dinner specials, traditional Sunday roasts, regularly changing real ales (viz. Timothy Taylor's Landlord and Marston's Pedigree), and wines by the dozen. Holy Cross itself may not be too exciting but what you get here is a thoroughly spoiling pub with lots of small rooms and some very fine food. There are sandwiches and light bites, perhaps penne with poached salmon and rocket. Serious foodies will be unable to resist the daily-changing menu; to whet your appetite, seared scallops with black pudding and celeriac cream, or roast Angus châteaubriand with pancetta potatoes and truffled glazed veg. You may need to forego coffee, cheese and the papers and take some exercise to work off the pounds.

directions	Off A491 south-east of Hagley.
meals	12pm-2pm (2.30pm Sundays); 6.30pm-9pm (9.30pm Fri & Sat). Main courses £9.75-£15.95.
closed	3pm-6pm.

Roger & Jo Narbett
Bell & Cross Inn,
Holy Cross,
Clent, Stourbridge,
Worcestershire DY9 9QL
tel   01562 730319

map: 9 entry: 472

Worcestershire

The Crown & Sandys
Ombersley

Richard Everton owns the village store and delicatessen, is a wine merchant and has now taken over the old village pub. Keeping the flagstone floors, beams and settles he has cleverly created an airy, modern feel. You can eat and drink well in the large open-plan dining area or simply sip a pint in the garden which has a terrace and a fountain. If beer is your thing, try Wood's Shropshire Lad with classic French onion soup and a gruyère crouton, if not, choose from a number of house wines and champagnes by the glass. Rustic bread is delicious with a bowl of garlicky moules and chunky chips; beef fillet sizzles on a comforting bed of bubble-and-sqeak. You'll find classy bedrooms in the main house and more are to be added in the former stables where once coaching horses were watered on their way from Bristol to the Midlands.

directions	Off A449 between Kidderminster & Worcester.
meals	12pm-3pm; 6pm-10pm; 12pm-10pm weekends. Main courses £8.95-£16.95; set menu £16.95.
rooms	6: 5 doubles, 1 twin £65-£95.

Richard Everton & Rachael Compton
The Crown & Sandys,
Main Road, Ombersley,
Worcestershire WR9 0EW
tel   01905 620252
web   www.crownandsandys.co.uk

map: 9 entry: 473

Worcestershire

The Talbot
Knightwick

The bar may be a tad scruffy and the welcome variable, but all that is over-ridden by the Clift family's admirable dedication to all things self-sufficient. Hops for their micro-brewed beers are grown across the valley and organic produce for the menu comes from the farmers' market hosted here every second Sunday morning in the month. Their genuine commitment to using fresh food pulls a crowd, and the black pudding, raised pies, chemical-free vegetables and green salads are legendary; fresh fish comes from Cornwall and scallop beignets are wrapped in nori seaweed (not local, but delicious); the pot-roast lamb recipe comes from Alnwick Castle in Northumberland. The wild duck – drizzled with the meat juices and a little Grand Marnier and served over mashed potato – suggests somebody with a touch of genius is in the kitchen.

directions	From Worcester A44 for Leominster; 8 miles on, through Cotheridge & Broadwas; right on B4197; on left.
meals	12pm-2pm; 6.30pm-9.30pm; 7pm-9pm Sundays. Main courses £12-£17.
rooms	11: 9 doubles, 2 singles. £75; singles £40.
closed	Christmas Day evening.

Annie Clift
The Talbot,
Knightwick, Worcester,
Worcestershire WR6 5PH
tel   01886 821235
web   www.the-talbot.co.uk

map: 9 entry: 474

Worcestershire

Rose & Crown
Severn Stoke

Hidden down a lane deep in the Severn Valley, with a family-friendly garden at the front and the parish church behind, another outrageously pretty timber-framed pub. To a backdrop of 16th-century oak beams and open log fires, the young licensees show enthusiasm and brio. Lee, the chef, is self-taught (with a bit of help from his chef brother) and follows a long family tradition; Sian will give you a warm welcome in the bar where you can choose from a menu of baked ham, eggs and chips, chicken tikka skewers with Cajun mayonnaise, halibut with buttered spinach. On Friday's steak nights you can try ostrich, kangaroo and wild boar – but how will you choose between Pedigree, Bombardier and London Pride? This cheerful pub with its laid-back atmosphere and upbeat service has already caught the eye of the Little Pineapple Pub Company.

directions	M50 junc.1; A38 N to Severn Stoke; between Worcester & Tewkesbury.
meals	12pm-2.30pm; 6pm-9.30pm; 12-9pm Sundays. Main courses £9.25-£15.95.

Lee & Sian Finch
Rose & Crown,
Church Lane,
Severn Stoke, Worcester,
Worcestershire WR8 9JQ
tel   01905 371249

map: 9 entry: 475

Worcestershire

The White Lion
Upton-on-Severn

In the novel *Tom Jones* (hatched here in 1749) Henry Fielding spoke of a "house of exceedingly good repute". Its name lives on: food, service, bedrooms and real ales all continue in the same excellent vein. Upton appears at first sight to be a town of pubs, the High Street stretching down to the river and its busy waterfront, and the White Lion is a Georgian-fronted inn that fits easily into the good-to-know category. Comfortable bedrooms have their own bathrooms, the Pepperpot brasserie is justifiably popular and the selection of light meals and guest ales at the bar is well above the norm. Logs smoulder in the lounge's dog-grate in winter and for leisurely summer drinking there's a tidy rear patio – well away from the traffic that trundles slowly towards the only Severn crossing for miles around.

directions	M5 exit 8; M50 exit 1; A38 for Malvern & Worcester. Left onto B4104. Over bridge & left. On left after bend.
meals	12pm-2pm; 7pm-9pm. Main courses £7.95-£15.95; set menu £13.95 (Sunday lunch).
rooms	13 twins/doubles £92.50-£115. Singles £67.50.

Jon & Chris Lear
White Lion, 21 High Street,
Upton-on-Severn, Malvern,
Worcestershire WR8 0HJ
tel   01684 592551
web   www.whitelionhotel.biz

map: 9 entry: 476

Worcestershire

The Fleece
Bretforton

"No potato crisps to be sold in the bar." So ordered Lola Taplin when The Fleece was bequeathed to the National Trust after 500 years in her family. It's the sort of tradition that thrives in the Pewter Room where you can enjoy fresh local food, real ales from Uley and Weston's Old Rosie Herefordshire cider. Olde English hot-pots, cod in beer batter, faggots and mash and locally-culled rhubarb in pies and crumbles are what will tempt you. But there is so much more: summer festivals twirl with Morris dancers and asparagus auctions; the gorgeous original farmyard is intact and there's an adventure playground for children. The magpie black-and-white timbered building is as stuffed as a museum with some fabulous antiques, stone flagged floors, ancient beams and memorabilia. Leave the 21st century behind – by about half a millenium. Marvellous.

directions	B4035 from Evesham for Chipping Campden. In Bretforton bare right into village. Opp. church in square.
meals	12pm-2.30pm (4pm Sundays); 6.30pm-9pm. Main courses £5.95-£10.95.
closed	3pm-5.30pm in winter.

Nigel Smith
The Fleece,
The Cross, Bretforton, Evesham,
Worcestershire WR11 7JE
tel   01386 831173
web   www.thefleeceinn.co.uk

map: 9 entry: 477

Yorkshire

The Three Acres Inn
Roydhouse

Everything ticks over beautifully at the Three Acres. The bar is a work of art, brimful of bottles, pumps, flowers, with old fishing reels and tackle hanging picturesquely above. Seating is comfy pub style, the smart polished tables are craftsmen-made, and there's a large solid fuel stove to warm the central space. Separate areas around the bar have tables set for dining (white linen, shining glasses); one area specialises in seafood. The overall feel is roomy yet intimate, hugely inviting, too, with plants, flowers, mirrors, old prints and even a baby grand. A sizeable team runs The Three Acres, with all the food prepared on site, and their own delicatessen; the sandwiches are good – caramelised onions topped with blue cheese, for example. Well-kept beers on pump, scores of fine wines and over 50 whiskies. Bedrooms are excellent and in modern country-house style.

directions	5 miles south of Huddersfield on A629 between Emley, Shelley & Kirkburton.
meals	12pm-2pm; 6.45pm-9.45pm. Main courses £10.95-£15.95.
rooms	20: 13 doubles, 2 twins, 5 singles. £80-£120; singles £60.
closed	Xmas & New Year; 3pm-6.30pm.

Neil Truelove & Brian Orme
The Three Acres Inn,
Roydhouse, Shelley,
Huddersfield, Yorkshire HD8 8LR
tel   01484 602606
web   www.3acres.com

map: 14 entry: 478

The Old Bridge Inn
Ripponden

A Christmas-card image of a cobbled lane, an ancient packhorse bridge and a little low inn... this is the setting of The Old Bridge Inn. Family involvement over several decades has resulted in a thoroughly civilised, unspoilt little local; a friendly one, too. Three carpeted, oak-panelled, split-level rooms – suitably dimly lit – are furnished with a mix of old oak settles and rush-seated chairs. The small, terracotta-walled snug at the top is atmospheric; the bar has a lofty ceiling with exposed timbers and a huge fireplace with log-burning stove; the lower room is non-smoking and good for dining. The buffet lunches have been served for years and are as popular as ever, while the evening menu announces sound English cooking (country terrine with quince jelly, ragout of pheasant with chestnuts) with a modern slant. The bar is well-used by local folk who come for Timothy Taylor's Best and Black Sheep beers, and wines are good.

The Millbank
Millbank

Savour a pint and a rolling moorland view. The Millbank, clinging to the side of a steep hill and architect-designed, has a stripped-down interior that combines flagstones, simple church chairs and log fires with contemporary art and boldly painted walls. Its relaxed, cosmopolitan style is echoed in the food, prepared by chef-patron Glen Futter. Using fresh local produce Glen creates daily menus with, perhaps, a warm salad of spiced duck with truffle oil, salt cod with white beans, tomatoes and herbs, Holy Island lobster ravioli with asparagus, vermouth and tarragon, and calves' liver with mash, mushrooms and red wine. And then there are the spoiling puddings, the fine cheeses, the Yorkshire ales (Timothy Taylor's Landlord for one), 10 excellent wines by the glass, first-class snacks in the bar, and brilliant live jazz on Sunday evenings.

directions	Off A58 between Sowerby Bridge & Ripponden.
meals	12-2.30pm; 12.30-4.30pm Sun; 6-9.30pm (10pm Fri & Sat). No food Sunday evenings. Main courses £8.95-£14.95; set menu £10.95.
closed	3pm-5.30pm.

directions	4 miles from junc. 22 M62 in Ripponden village.
meals	12pm-2pm; 6.30pm-9.30pm. No food Saturday or Sunday eve. Main courses £6.50-£8.50.

Tim & Lindsay Eaton Walker
The Old Bridge Inn,
Priest Lane, Ripponden,
Sowerby Bridge, Yorkshire HX6 4DF
tel   01422 822595
web   www.porkpieclub.com

Glen Futter
The Millbank,
Millbank Road, Millbank,
Sowerby Bridge, Yorkshire HX6 3DY
tel   01422 825588
web   www.themillbank.com

map: 14 entry: 479

map: 14 entry: 480

Shibden Mill Inn
Shibden Mill

There's still a pubby feel to this rambling old inn – although a strong relationship with local suppliers has transformed the place into a first-class brasserie and restaurant. It may be known for its food but John Smiths, Theakstons and changing guest ales manage to keep real ale fans happy in front of an open fire. In summer, the valley setting beside the brook is a beautiful summer drinking spot. Unstuffy integrity lies behind it all, from the front-of-house warmth to Adrian's unpretentious approach in the kitchen. Backed by a judiciously chosen wine list, his back-to-basics style constructs dishes around simple but forthright flavour combinations. You can sample his take on the traditional – shepherd's pie tart with gravy and peas, aged fillet of beef on the bone – and the modern – warm red mullet and crayfish tails with saffron mayonnaise, or slow-roast pork shank with chorizo sausage, cabbage and potato. The hot cinder toffee soufflé with treacle sauce will make the sweet-toothed swoon. Dressing-gowns in the bedrooms, a video library in reception and superb treacle bread, jams and chutneys on sale for home consumption make this a high-class act.

directions	Off A58 Halifax to Leeds road near A6036 junction.
meals	12pm-2pm; 6pm-9.30pm; 12pm-7.30pm Sundays. Main courses £5.95-£14.50.
rooms	12 doubles £80-£115. Singles £65-£105.
closed	2.30pm-5.30pm Monday-Saturday.

Glen Pearson
Shibden Mill Inn,
Shibden Mill, Halifax,
Yorkshire HX3 7UL
tel   01422 365840
web   www.shibdenmillinn.com

map: 14 entry: 481

Travellers Rest
Sowerby

Caroline Lumley took over this old pub on the moors and started from scratch: she has worked wonders. The inn has kept its big fireplaces and cast-iron stoves, flagged bar, exposed stone walls and ancient beams, now sanded; Caroline has added atmospheric lighting, background sound, sofas, cushions and throws. It's a happy mix of traditional and contemporary and the result is a pub that appeals both to locals and diners from further afield. The pleasant dining room is two archways from the bar, with well-dressed tables and fine valley views. The blackboard menu highlights English dishes with a modern twist — tempura scampi with Caesar salad, homemade steakburger on foccacia bread with dill pickle — while in the stylish bar you'll find Timothy Taylor's on tap alongside champagne cocktails. From the terrace, stunning views over the Calderdale and the desolate moors.

directions	West of Sowerby Bridge on A672; 5 miles west of Halifax. Signed.
meals	12.30pm-2.30pm (3pm Sundays); 6-9.30pm (10pm Sat); 5-8pm Sun. Main courses £8.50-£16.
closed	Mondays & Tuesdays; Wednesday-Friday lunchtimes.

Caroline Lumley
Travellers Rest,
Steep Lane,
Sowerby, Halifax,
Yorkshire HX6 1PE
tel   01422 832124

map: 14 entry: 482

Whitelocks
Leeds

Fixtures and fittings have changed little since Victorian times — a remarkable achievement for a pub down an alleyway off bustling Briggate. The narrow bar is dominated by a tile-fronted counter with an original, marble-topped Luncheon Bar. Fine old button-backed leather banquettes come with panelled, mirrored dividers for intimacy, while copper-topped tables, stained glass and several grand mirrors add to the traditional mood. There is no piped music and the place is surprisingly quiet given its city centre position, though it fills up fast at peak times. Five handpulled ales, good wines and a mix of traditional and up-to-date dishes make this a real find. There's also a carpeted dining room with dark banquettes and upholstered chairs at linen-covered tables, and an open fire to add to the atmosphere. Tuck into hot filled baguettes, steak and potato pie and giant Yorkshire puddings.

directions	Next to Marks & Spencer in Central Leeds shopping area.
meals	12pm-2.30pm (2pm Sun). Restaurant: 5.30-7pm. Bar meals: 11-7pm (12-4pm Sun) . Main courses £3.45-£5.25.
closed	25-26 December; 1 January.

Nicholas James
Whitelocks,
Turks Head Yard,
Briggate, Leeds,
Yorkshire LS1 6HB
tel   0113 245 3950

map: 14 entry: 483

Yorkshire

The Three Hares
Bilbrough

Bilbrough's a pretty place, and The Three Hares reflects that. Though it looks traditional from outside, it has a freshly modern feel within. You'll find 18th-century beams and exposed brickwork, pale cream walls, dark patterned carpeting and contemporary art... It's appealing and individual. There's an atmosphere of quiet comfort here: log fires, sofas and a bar serving wine and hand pulled Yorkshire ales. Roast beef and horseradish mayonnaise sandwiches or salads and terrines are served in the bar. For those with bigger appetites, try the dining room for suet pudding with roast garlic and thyme, or duck with roast figs. Don't miss the super Yorkshire cheeses and homemade bread. In summer, eat and drink outside in the garden.

directions	A64 south-east of York; into Bilbrough, pub on main road in village.
meals	12pm-2pm; 7pm-9pm. Main courses £10.95-£17.
closed	3pm-7pm; Sunday evenings; Mondays.

Mr Mansford
The Three Hares,
Main Street, Bilbrough,
York, Yorkshire YO23 3PH
tel 01937 832128
web www.thethreehares.co.uk

map: 14 entry: 484

Yorkshire

The Blue Bell
York

Unlike most city pubs, the Blue Bell is exactly as it's always been. Its narrow brick frontage on Fossgate, not far from The Shambles and open-air market, is quite easy to miss, so look out for the sign above the pavement. Once you've found the old pub, step into the long corridor that runs through to the back. On the right, a little bar with red-tiled floor and high ceilings, wooden panelling, Edwardian stained-glass, a cast-iron, tiled fireplace, settle seating on two sides and iron-legged tables – one round, covered in copper, the other long, dressed in red formica, more Fifties than Edwardian. Ladies only used to be allowed into the narrow back lounge; now its cosy red carpet can be trod on by all. Original fireplaces, polished panelling dotted with interesting old pictures... the place is a visual delight, and there's a terrific range of cask beers and wines to boot – as well as a surprisingly sophisticated choice of tapas. Rumour has it the bar takes more money per square foot than any other public house in the country!

directions	In York city centre.
meals	12pm-8.30pm. Tapas dishes from £2.
closed	New Year's Day.

Jim Hardie
The Blue Bell,
53 Fossgate,
York,
Yorkshire YO1 9TF
tel 01904 654904

map: 14 entry: 485

Yorkshire

St Vincents Arms
Sutton-upon-Derwent

The St Vincent Arms is a great village local, unpretentious but with enough going for it to attract quaffers and scoffers alike. Through a small lobby you enter the public bar on the right. Humming with happy chat, this is the heart of the place, sporting a cheery coal fire, panelled walls lined with brass plates, warm red curtains and a tartan carpet. You have up to eight cask beers to choose from and no background music or electronic gadgetry – in spite of the old radiogram. To the left of the lobby is a smaller, snugger bar decorated in pale green with matching tartan carpet; this leads into a further room and the dining room, furnished with some fine old pieces of furniture. Food ranges from sandwiches or hot brie and bacon on ciabatta to diver-caught scallops in garlic butter, mussels (highly recommended), liver and bacon casserole, jam roly-poly... if you're not into ale there are several wines by the glass. The St Vincent Arms is a brilliantly run place, and the staff seem to enjoy themselves as much as the customers – a good sign.

directions	On B1228, 8 miles SE of York.
meals	12pm-2pm; 7pm-9.30pm. Main courses £7.50-£14.50.

Philip Hopwood
St Vincents Arms,
Main Street,
Sutton-upon-Derwent, York,
Yorkshire YO41 4BN
tel   01904 608349

map: 14 entry: 486

Yorkshire

The White Horse Inn (Nellie's)
Beverley

You could pass the White Horse by, its brick front and old pub sign do not stand out in busy Hengate. Inside it's more beguiling – step in and be transported back 200 years (the building itself is even older). Known as 'Nellie's', it's a wonderfully atmospheric little place; your eyes will take a while to become accustomed, so dim are the gas-lit passages. Very little has changed in these small rooms with their old quarry tiles, bare boards, smoke-stained walls and open fires. Furniture is a mix of high-backed settles, padded benches, simple chairs, marble-topped cast-iron tables, old pictures and a gas-lit pulley-controlled chandelier. Locals love the place – not least because of the sensible Yorkshire prices. Food is straightforward and good value: sandwiches, bangers and mash, steak and ale pie, spotted dick with custard. Charles Wesley preached in the back yard in the 18th century and the only concession to the modern age is the games room at the back with its juke box and darts.

directions	Off North Bar, close to St Mary's Church.
meals	11-3pm (5pm Fri & Sat; 4pm Sun). Main courses £3.95-£7.50.

Anna
The White Horse Inn (Nellie's),
22 Hengate, Beverley,
Yorkshire HU17 8BN
tel   01482 861973
web   www.nellies.co.uk

map: 15 entry: 487

Yorkshire

Stone Trough Inn
Kirkham Priory

A great find: traditionally pubby and welcoming, with excellent food. The bar is comfortable and cosy, with low beams, stone walls, a red patterned carpet and two log fires, sometimes fresh flowers, and separate areas for privacy. Much care goes into running this place, and it shows. Although the range of beers and wines is excellent – and the staff delightful – it's the food that people travel the extra mile for. Adam Richardson is a talented chef, dreaming up such treats as wild mushrooms with sherry, pigeon with black pudding and damson jus, monkfish with saffron cream sauce, syrup sponge pudding. You choose from two menus, one from the bar, the other from the restaurant. There's also a games room with pool, fruit machine, dominoes and TV. On warm days take your pint of Malton Golden Chance onto the front terrace that overlooks the gentle Derwent valley, then stroll down the hill to Kirkham Abbey.

directions	1.5 miles off A64, between York & Malton.
meals	12pm-2pm; 6.30pm-9.30pm. Main courses £7.25-£13.95.
closed	Mondays except Bank Holidays.

Adam & Sarah Richardson
Stone Trough Inn,
Kirkham Priory,
Yorkshire YO60 7JS
tel   01653 618713
web   www.stonetroughinn.co.uk

map: 14 entry: 488

Yorkshire

The Durham Ox
Crayke

It stands at the top of the Grand Old Duke of York's hill. In the lounge bar, bags of character… flagstones and warm terracotta walls, worn leather armchairs and settles, carved panelling and stone fireplaces. There are two more bars to either side, with lively locals downing Theakston, and a separate, yellow-walled dining room that draws all and sundry, including families. (The 'Early Bird' specials and Sunday roasts are particularly popular.) Chalkboards above the fire list the fruits of Michael Ibbotson's delicious country cooking: game hotpot with winter vegetables, roast pork loin stuffed with apricots and whisky marmalade, glazed pear and vanilla crème brulée. Priced bin-end bottles line the old dresser in the bar, there are lush gardens to lounge in, music twice a week, and smart bedrooms.

directions	A19 to Easingwold & Thirsk.
meals	12pm-2.30pm; 6pm-9.30pm (10pm Saturdays; 8.30pm Sundays). Main courses £8.95-£18.
rooms	Can sleep up to 15: 4 cottages & 1 flat for 4 (not self catering) £80-£160. Singles £60.
closed	3pm-6pm Monday-Thursday.

Michael Ibbotson
The Durham Ox,
West Way, Crayke,
Yorkshire YO61 4TE
tel   01347 821506
web   www.thedurhamox.com

map: 14 entry: 489

Yorkshire

Crown Inn
Great Ouseburn

The Tiller Girls began their prancing careers at this merry country pub. Memorabilia, bric-a-brac and old pictures coat every surface of the bars and dining rooms, cosy with their open fires, gleaming brasses, patterned carpets, candles and soft lights. Solid Yorkshire bonhomie is woven into the very fabric of the place. The food is generous and a good notch above the norm, whether you're here for the haddock with hand-cut chips in the bar, or for a set meal in the restaurant: crisp roast belly pork with apple sauce, fishcakes with dressed leaves, lobster Thermidor, warm chocolate brownie, Yorkshire farmhouse cheese. The wine list is compiled by an enthusiast, with 10 wines available by the glass, there's Hambleton Best Bitter and Black Sheep on handpump, and children enjoy the play area in the garden. Behind it all is Ian Gill, who shows all the signs of a man happy with his lot.

directions	On B6265 midway between Boroughbridge & Green Hammerton.
meals	5pm-9.30pm (from 12pm Saturdays); 12pm-9pm Sundays. Main courses £5.40-£22.
closed	Weekday lunchtimes.

Ian Gill
Crown Inn,
Great Ouseburn, York,
Yorkshire YO26 9RF
tel   01423 330430
web   www.the-crown-yorks.com

map: 14 entry: 490

Yorkshire

The General Tarleton
Ferrensby

The 18th-century coaching inn is masterminded by chef-patron John Topham who runs it with an easy charm. The rambling, low-beamed, nooked and crannied bar-brasserie mixes rough stone walls with red ones, there's country kitchen furniture and a big open fire. You have Black Sheep Bitter on handpump and 16 well-chosen wines by the glass. Brasserie-style dishes range from open sandwiches to interesting snacks and starters (oriental spice pork, noodle and sesame seed salad, tomato and goat's cheese tartlet) to Birstwith Angus steak and ale pudding. The very cosy dining room, formerly a granary, has a contemporary look – all white napery and cream-painted beams – with a menu to match. Bedrooms in the extension at the back have both style and comfort.

directions	From A1 junc. 48; A6055 for Knaresborough; by road in Ferrensby
meals	12pm-2.15pm; 6pm-9.15pm (8.30pm Sundays). Main courses £8.50-£15.50; set menu £29.50; set lunch (Sunday) £17.95.
rooms	14: 7 doubles, 6 twin, 1 four-poster £74.95-£84.90.

John Topham
The General Tarleton,
Boroughbridge Road, Ferrensby,
Knaresborough, Yorkshire HG5 0PZ
tel   01423 340284
web   www.generaltarleton.co.uk

map: 14 entry: 491

The Boar's Head
Ripley

When Sir and Lady Ingilby decided to reopen and revive the old pub, once known as the Star Inn, the attic at Ripley Castle (two minutes down the cobbles) was raided for furniture and the vicar came to bless the beer taps. You'll find them in Boris's Bar. Elegant fun is the net result and the place is run with panache. The sitting rooms and hall have crisp yellow Regency wallpaper, big old oils, roaring fires and gilt mirrors. The restaurant is a deep crimson, candlelit at night; you drink from blue glass. Games and newspapers, menus to drool over and a parasoled garden where you can sip long drinks. Up the staircase, past more ancestors, to smart bedrooms with floral fabrics, fresh flowers and rag-rolled bathrooms; those in the coachman's loft have pine panelling and the odd beam. Children and well-behaved dogs are welcome, and you have umbrellas and wellies for rainy days.

The Fleece
Addingham

A gorgeous old place run with flair and passion. The surroundings provide atmosphere, the friendly licensees add something special, and the food's good, too. Bags of character comes from big open fires, solid tables and old settles on flagged floors, beamed and boarded ceilings, exposed stone, white walls. It's a big space that at peak times gets busy, but in summer you can spill out onto tables on the paved terrace at the front and watch the world go by. Chris Monkman has brought a refreshing enthusiasm for fresh, local food with him: Wharfedale lamb, roast belly pork, fish and smoked fish. Even the children's menu is brilliant: home-battered fish, omelettes, one-minute steak, moules marinieres, grilled goat's cheese salad. Plenty of choice and it's all good value, with local cheeses playing a major role. Three of Yorkshire's best beers are always available, there's a thoughtful selection of wines, and a number of whiskies, too. A real find.

directions	From Harrogate, A61 north for 3 miles; left at r'bout, for Ripley.
meals	12pm-2.30pm (2pm in winter); 6.30pm-9.30pm. Main courses £8.95-£14.95; set menu £28-£30.
rooms	25: 4 doubles, 21 twins/doubles £120-£140. Singles £99-£120.

directions	2 miles north of Ilkley on A65-A650.
meals	12pm-2.15pm; 6pm-9.15pm (12pm-8pm Sundays). Main courses £6.75-£13

Sir Thomas Ingilby
The Boar's Head,
Ripley, Harrogate,
Yorkshire HG3 3AY
tel 01423 771888
web www.boarsheadripley.co.uk

Chris Monkman
The Fleece,
Main Street,
Addingham,
Yorkshire LS29 0LY
tel 01943 830491

map: 14 entry: 492

map: 14 entry: 493

The Angel
Hetton

The old drovers' inn remains staunchly, reassuringly traditional – but with a stylish restaurant and wines that have come, over the years, to rival the handpumped ales (Black Sheep Bitter, Tetleys, Timothy Taylor Landlord). There's even a 'cave' for private-party tastings. The building seethes nooks, crannies, beams and crackling fires, and the Watkinses have thought about every detail, from the antique furniture in the timbered rooms (one has a magnificent oak-panelled bar) to the fabrics and colour schemes. Enjoyable food ranges from filo 'moneybags' of seafood in lobster sauce – the fish comes fresh from Fleetwood and there's a fish night every Friday – to Yorkshire lamb and rosemary sausage with buttered spinach, crispy pancetta and juniper-scented red wine sauce. Or Goosnargh duck breast with braised red cabbage. Or wild mushroom risotto. The glorious up-hill-and-down-dale drive to get here is part of the charm, and it is best to book: the wettest night cannot deter the people of Yorkshire. It's a much-loved place, yet Denis and Juliet have not rested on their laurels. They recently converted a barn across the road into three delicious suites. So you can make as merry as you like, and stay.

directions	Off B6265, 6 miles north of Skipton.
meals	12pm-2pm; 6pm-9.30pm. Main courses £8.50-£14.50.
rooms	5: 2 studios, 3 suites £120-£170.
closed	Christmas Day; New's Years Day.

Denis Watkins
The Angel,
Hetton, Skipton,
Yorkshire BD23 6LT
tel   01756 730263
web   www.angelhetton.co.uk

map: 14 entry: 494

Tempest Arms
Elslack

A rambling 18th-century stone inn in rolling countryside, mid-way between Skipton and Colne. In the various areas of bar and lounge are exposed stone and old timber, prints and polished brass, three log fires and comfortable, cushioned seating. Drinkers may choose from up to four Yorkshire cask ales – Black Sheep, Theakstons Best, Timothy Taylor's – and several good wines by big or small glass. There's a fair mix of customers here, locals, walkers and – because it's close to urban north-east Lancashire – business folk. You can have light meals in the bar, and fancier dishes in the dining room, or swap between the two; they do exemplary club sandwiches, mushrooms in port and cream, crispy pork with thyme-roasted potatoes, sumptuous puddings, fine local cheeses. Staff are friendly and professional. In the bedroom wing are recently done-up rooms with hand-crafted furniture and spotless bathrooms.

directions	Off A56 between Skipton & Colne.
meals	12-2.30pm; 6-9pm (9.30pm Fridays & Saturdays; (12-8pm Sundays). Main courses £8.50-£13.95.
rooms	10 twins/doubles £74-£85. Singles £59.95.

Veronica Clarkson
Tempest Arms,
Elslack, Skipton,
Yorkshire BD23 3AY
tel   01282 842450
web   www.tempestarms.co.uk

map: 14 entry: 495

The Red Lion
Burnsall

Here is an inn for all ages, full of olde-worlde charm and fun. Even the ghost in the cellars has a sense of humour, turning off the beer taps from time to time. Elizabeth keeps a matriarchal eye on things while son-in-law Jim cooks seriously good food – roast calves' liver with pancetta, sage and celeriac purée, cod with tomato and courgette chutney. The result is a cosy place humming with locals. The sitting room, with sofas and wood-burning stove, has books for all, from guides to kids' adventure stories. Once a ferryman's inn, it was made redundant by the stone bridge that spans the shallow river whose gentle meander matches the pace of this sleepy village. Bedrooms above the inn are small but have bags of beamy character; rooms in the barn are larger.

directions	From Harrogate, A59 west to Bolton Bridge; B6160 to Burnsall. Next to bridge.
meals	12-2pm (3pm Sundays); 6pm-9pm; 6.30pm-9.30pm Sundays. Main courses £3.50-£15.95; set menu £28.98.
rooms	15: 4 doubles, 8 twins/doubles, 1 family £115. Singles from £57.50. Half-board from £85 p.p.

Elizabeth Grayshon
The Red Lion,
Burnsall, Skipton,
Yorkshire BD23 6BU
tel   01756 720204
web   www.redlion.co.uk

map: 14 entry: 496

The Falcon Inn
Arncliffe

Tucked into the top corner of Littondale, one of the most remote and unspoilt of Yorkshire's dales. Several generations of Millers have been licensees here and they have preserved an inn and a way of life almost lost. The fine bay-windowed and ivy-clad building looks more like a private house than a village local; expect few frills and old-fashioned hospitality. The entrance passageway leads to a small hallway at the foot of the stairs – there's a tiny bar counter facing you, a small, simple lounge, a log fire and sporting prints on the walls. A sunny back room looks out across the garden to open fells. Beer is served as it always has been, straight from the cask in a large jug, then dispensed into pint glasses at the bar. At lunchtime or early evening, walkers devour pie and peas, and plenty of them. If you stay overnight you get a set evening meal in the dining room overlooking the moorland green – and permission to fish on their stretch of river.

The White Lion Inn
Cray

For centuries the White Lion has stood high in the Pennines, serving local farmers and cattle drovers. And it still does, though walkers have taken the place of drovers. In the main bar there are deep, upholstered settles and dark, plain tables – just the place for homemade steak and mushroom pie and a pint of Pendle Witches Brew. At quiet times the crackle of the logs on the fire and the ticking of the clock are all you'll hear and the relaxed style of the owners permeates the whole place. Perfect. There are plenty of places for summer eating outside by the tumbling stream. Simple bedrooms with pine furniture (two that welcome dogs) are ideal for those wanting to linger and discover Wharfedale and its miles of footpaths, some of which pass right by the door. It's a peaceful spot, so sleep should be sound and a great breakfast the next morning will set you up for the day. The views are all you'd hope for, and more.

directions	Off B6160 16 miles N of Skipton.
meals	12pm-2pm.
	Snacks £2.50-£4.50.
rooms	4 twins/doubles, 2 sharing bathroom, £80.

directions	20 miles N of Skipton on B6160.
meals	12pm-2pm; 5.45pm-8.30pm.
	Main courses £7.95-£11.95.
rooms	8 twins/doubles £60-£70.
	Singles from £40.
closed	Christmas Day.

R Miller
The Falcon Inn,
Arncliffe, Grassington,
Yorkshire BD23 5QE
tel   01756 770205
web   www.thefalconinn.com

map: 14 entry: 497

Kevin & Debbie Roe
White Lion,
Cray, Skipton,
Yorkshire BD23 5JB
tel   01756 760262
web   www.whitelioncray.com

map: 14 entry: 498

The Blue Lion
East Witton

The Blue Lion has a big reputation locally; so big it followed our inspector round Yorkshire – "you must go there," everyone said. Paul and Helen came here several years ago, and have mixed the traditions of a country pub with the elegance of a country house. This is a bustling, happy place that serves superlative food (peppered duck breast with a port & blackberry sauce; pan-fried cod with seafood risotto; dark chocolate tart), and no one seems in a hurry to leave. Aproned staff, polished beer taps, stone-flagged floors, open fires, newspapers on poles, big settles, huge bunches of dried flowers hanging from beams, splashes of fresh flowers. The two restaurants have boarded floors and shuttered Georgian windows, two coal fires, gilt mirrors and candles everywhere. Bedrooms are comfortable rather than luxurious. East Witton has an interesting plague tale, Jervaulx Abbey is a mile away, there's tennis next door and a lush, enclosed garden at the back.

directions	From Leyburn, A6108 for 3 miles to East Witton.
meals	12pm-2pm; 7pm-9pm. Main courses £9-£18.
rooms	12: 9 doubles, 2 twins, 1 family £69-£89.

Paul & Helen Klein
The Blue Lion,
East Witton, Leyburn,
Yorkshire DL8 4SN
tel 01969 624273
web www.thebluelion.co.uk

map: 14 entry: 499

Sandpiper Inn
Leyburn

In 1999 former Roux scholar Jonathan Harrison swapped a slick city kitchen for an old stone pub in the Yorkshire Dales – lucky locals. In cosy alcoves beneath low black beams, locals and walkers put the world to rights over pints of Black Sheep and Theakston ale opposite chalkboards listing Jonathan's daily menus: fishcakes with chive and parsley sauce, club sandwiches, omelette Arnold Bennett. Cooking moves up a gear in the simple stylish dining room as in-season game, Wensleydale heifer beef and home-grown herbs and veg come into play. You'll need to loosen your belts before embarking upon roasted lobster and tomato soup, braised rabbit with wild mushrooms and thyme, and raspberry and almond tart with clotted cream. Malt whisky lovers will eye the 100 bottles behind the bar appreciatively. Two smart bedrooms await upstairs.

directions	From A1, A684 for Bedale; for 12 miles.
meals	12pm-2.30pm; 6.30pm-9pm (9.30pm Fri & Sat; 10pm in summer). Main courses £9.50-£16.
rooms	2 doubles, 1 cottage for 4 £60-£85. Singles £50-£75.
closed	3pm-6.30pm.

Jonathan & Michael Harrison
Sandpiper Inn,
Market Place,
Leyburn,
Yorkshire DL8 5AT
tel 01969 622206

map: 14 entry: 500

Yorkshire

Oak Tree Inn
Hutton Magna

A tiny cottage masquerading as a pub,
The Oak Tree has been snapped up by
Alastair and Claire Ross – happy to swap
London for the Dales. Alastair trained at
the Savoy and in three years he and
Claire have created a little gem. At the
end of a row of cottages the parking may
not be easy – but once over the
threshold you will cheerfully unwind.
The front bar has old wooden panelling
and whitewashed stone, and an attractive
medley of tables, chairs and pews,
newspapers, fresh flowers and open fire.
The dark green dining area at the back is
softly lit, its tables separated by pews –
all is delightful and informal. There's
plenty good food to be had in this part of
Yorkshire and The Oak Tree has already
made a niche for itself. Game appears
regularly on the menu in season and the
produce is as fresh as can be. The wine
list lengthens almost by the hour –
wherever will they store it all! – with a
choice of wines from the glass.

directions	Off A66, 8 miles west of Scotch Corner.
meals	12pm-2pm (bookings only); 6.30pm-9pm. Main courses £10-£14.50.
closed	Monday & Tuesday lunchtimes.

Alastair & Claire Ross
Oak Tree Inn,
Hutton Magna, Richmond,
Yorkshire DL11 7HH

| tel | 01833 627371 |
| web | www.elevation-it.co.uk/oaktree |

map: 14 entry: 501

Yorkshire

The Wheatsheaf inn
Egton

Unlike many pubs in this area, the
Wheatsheaf has shirked expansion and
held onto its character. It sits so
modestly back from the wide main street
you could pass it by – and miss a good
deal. The first entrance brings you into
the main room with bar, a restful room
with dark green walls, low beams and
comfy old settles, but the main treat here
is the locals' bar, dominated by its
wonderful Yorkshire range. This drinkers'
den takes 12 at a push and is hugely
popular with locals, walkers and
fishermen – and their dogs. A range of
cask ales ensures plenty of chatter, while
the restaurant dishes up hearty,
traditional food. The River Esk at the
foot of the steep hill is famous for fly-
fishing and so there is unsurprisingly,
fishing memorabilia on the walls, and a
few interesting angling pictures. Egton is
lovely – and worth a linger. The
Wheatsheaf's bedrooms are pleasing on
the eye and as comfortable as can be.

directions	Off A171; 6 miles west of Whitby.
meals	12pm-2pm; 6pm-9pm. No food Sunday evenings & Mondays. Main courses £8-£14.
rooms	4: 3 doubles, 1 family.
closed	Monday lunchtimes.

Nigel Pulling
The Wheatsheaf inn,
Egton,
Whitby,
Yorkshire YO21 1TZ

| tel | 01947 895271 |

map: 15 entry: 502

Yorkshire

The Birch Hall
Beck Hole

Two small bar rooms with a shop in between, unaltered for 70 years. Steep wooded hillsides and a stone bridge straddling the rushing river, and, inside, a fascinating glimpse of life before World War II. The Big Bar has been beautifully repapered but this is still a traditional lounge with a little open fire, dominoes, darts and service from a hatch; the benches and tables come from the station waiting room at Beck Hole. The shop (stacked with postcards, old-fashioned sweets, ice creams) has its original fittings, as does the Little Bar with its handpumps for three cask ales. The original 19th-century enamel sign hangs above the door. Food is appropriately simple and authentic: local pies, specially baked stotties or baps, homemade scones and delicious beer cake. On fine days negotiate the steep steps to the terraced garden that looks over the inn and across the valley. Parking is scarce so show patience and courtesy in this old-fashioned place.

directions	9 miles from Whitby on Pickering rd.
meals	11-3pm; 7.30-11pm (10.30pm Sun). All day in summer. Sandwiches & pies £1-£2.
closed	3pm-7.30pm August-April; Monday evenings in Winter.

Colin Jackson
The Birch Hall,
Beck Hole, Goathland,
Yorkshire YO22 5LE
tel 01947 896245
web www.beckhole.com

map: 15 entry: 503

Yorkshire

Moors Inn
Appleton le Moors

An ancient sign hangs from a long bracket. That's all there is to identify this unassuming inn but it is unexpectedly fresh and modern inside: white walls are unadorned, a few pictures and brasses on beams add colour, there's a charcoal-grey carpet, a stripped settle and a refreshing lack of clutter. Warmth and cosiness emanate from the big old Yorkshire range with open fire and built-in ovens at one end of the main room; there's a wood-fronted bar at the other, a number of thoughtfully designed seating areas and a small dining room. Expect hearty home-cooked food using their own or locally grown organic produce, well-kept beer and comfortable bedrooms. More unusual is the no-smoking policy (pool and darts room excepted). At the back, a large walled garden where residents can enjoy a creamy pint of Black Sheep and dreamy vale views. The village, with its wide main street and solid stone buildings, has a timeless feel... glorious walks start from the door.

directions	Off A170, 5 miles west of Pickering.
meals	12pm-3pm (Sundays); 7pm-11pm. Main courses £7.95-£13.90.
rooms	8 doubles/twins £50. Singles £30.
closed	Mondays.

Janet Frank
Moors Inn,
Appleton le Moors,
Kirkbymoorside,
Yorkshire YO62 6TF
tel 01751 417435

map: 14 entry: 504

The White Swan
Pickering

This place is full of surprises. There's a fantastic list of wines including over 50 fine clarets from St Emilion and breakfast inspired one traveller to write a poem, now framed. Victor gave up a job in the City to take over this old coaching inn from his parents; he and Marion have brought bags of flair. Through the front door a cosy, panelled tap room serving Black Sheep Best, and a lounge with burgundy walls and an open fire. The dining room is light and airy. Further on: a sitting room and handsome restaurant, with rich furnishings and blazing log fire. Bedrooms are attractively clutter-free, and the food is a real treat – chargrilled beef fillet with fresh herb pesto or braised lamb shank with butter bean stew. Close by are Rievaulx Abbey and the steam railway.

Appletree Inn
Marton

Melanie chooses the wines and TJ cooks. They are an unstoppable team and in three years have put the Appletree onto the Yorkshire foodie map. Locals pop in for sandwiches and a pint of Hambleton's. The food-conscious travel miles for breads and ice creams, chutneys and chocolates, butters and terrines – and that's just the shop. TJ's monthly menus promise crab cheesecake with tomatoes, orange-roasted turbot with braised fennel and pernod butter sauce, Marton lamb in puff pastry with tapenade, olives and rosemary, a delectable chocolate pyramid. Herbs from the garden, fruits from the orchard, farm-reared meats... here are intense flavours with modern British eclectism thrown in. The atmosphere is informal and comforting: a beamed bar with ruby walls, flickering candles and log fires, a farmhouse-style dining room, a miscellany of pre-dinner sofas in the lounge.

directions	From Thirsk, A170 to Pickering. At lights left; 1st right up Market Place. On left.
meals	12pm-2pm; 7pm-9pm. Main courses £8.95-£16.95.
rooms	12: 5 doubles, 5 twins/doubles, 2 suites from £120. Singles from £75.
closed	3pm-6pm; 4pm-7pm Sundays.

directions	2 miles from A170 between Kirkbymoorside & Pickering.
meals	12pm-2pm; 6.30-9.30. Sun 12-12.30; 7pm-9pm. Main courses £7-£16.50.
closed	Monday lunchtimes; Tuesdays.

Marion & Victor Buchanan
The White Swan,
Market Place, Pickering,
Yorkshire YO18 7AA
tel 01751 472288
web www.white-swan.co.uk

Trajan & Melanie Drew
Appletree Inn,
Marton, Pickering,
Yorkshire YO62 6RD
tel 01751 431457
web www.appletreeinn.co.uk

map: 15 entry: 505

map: 14 entry: 506

The Star Inn
Harome

You know you've 'hit the jackpot' as soon as you walk into The Star – it ticks over with such modest ease and calm authority. Andrew and Jacquie arrived in 1996, baby daughters Daisy and Tilly not long after, and the Michelin star in 2002. It's been a formidable turnaround given that the 14th-century inn had an 'iffy' local reputation when they took over, yet there's no arrogance; the brochure simply says: "He cooks, and she looks after you". And how! Andrew's food is rooted in Yorkshire tradition, refined with French flair and written in plain English on ever-changing menus: try fresh Whitby crab and plum tomato salad, tail fillet of beef with braised shin, baked ginger parkin, British cheeses. There's a bar with a log fire and a Sunday papers-and-pint feel (though drinks range from homemade schnapps to fizz by the glass to Scrumpy Jack). Bedrooms, rustically modern, are a stroll away; the largest has its own snooker table. There's also the Mousey Thompson bar, a roof mural, an organic deli and an enchanting loft in the eaves to which you may retreat for after-dinner coffee. Spill out into the fruit-treed garden for summer – bliss.

directions	From Thirsk, A170 for Scarboro'. Thru Helmsley; right, for Harome.
meals	11.30pm-2pm; 6.30pm-9.30pm. No food Sunday & Monday eve. Main courses (bar)£8.95-£16.95.
rooms	11: 6 doubles, 2 twins/doubles, 3 suites £110-£195.
closed	Monday lunchtimes.

Andrew & Jacquie Pern
The Star Inn,
Harome, Helmsley,
Yorkshire YO62 5JE
tel   01439 770397
web   www.thestaratharome.co.uk

map: 14 entry: 507

Yorkshire

The Abbey Inn
Byland Abbey

The monks of Ampleforth who built this farmhouse would surely approve of its current devotion to good food; whether they'd be as accepting of its devotion to luxury is another matter. The delightful inn overlooks the ruins of a 12th-century abbey (one American visitor asked the Nordlis when they were going to start on the renovation). Jane loves to see the look on people's faces as they enter the restaurant, a glorious flagstoned space that's lit by a skylight and full of Jacobean-style chairs and antique tables. Rambling, characterful bars have big fireplaces, oak and stripped deal tables, carved oak seats on polished boards. Food is British-based and interesting: venison with winter berry sauce or garlic-marinated rib-eye steak. Bedrooms are special with bathrobes, aromatherapy oils, fruit, homemade biscuits, a 'treasure chest' of wine.

directions	A1 junc. 49; A168 for Thirsk for 10 miles; A19. Left after 2 miles to Coxwold; left to Byland Abbey.
meals	12pm-2pm; 6.30pm-9pm. Main courses £6.95-£16.50.
rooms	3 twins/doubles £80-£135.
closed	Sunday evening; Monday lunchtime.

Jane & Martin Nordli
The Abbey Inn,
Byland Abbey, Thirsk,
Yorkshire YO61 4BD
tel 01347 868204
web www.bylandabbeyinn.com

map: 14 entry: 508

Yorkshire

The Wombwell Arms
Wass

Built as a grainstore for Byland Abbey, the Coles' 17th-century stone pub now hums with contented drinkers and is much loved by walkers and ramblers. Beams, flagged or tiled floors, stripped pine tables and watercolours add up to attractive dining rooms; in the bar area, logs burn in an open grate. Andy will pour you a perfect pint of Timothy Taylor's, or let you savour his wines. A huge blackboard displays the day's choice of wide-ranging, very good bar food. The menus are Sue's domain and bistro-ish in style; she ensures only fresh and mostly local produce is used. Filled ciabattas and hot sandwiches at lunch; award-winning steak pie, game casserole and lamb steak with port and redcurrant sauce at dinner. Upstairs are three pine-furnished, cottagey bedrooms.

directions	From A19 York to Thirsk road for Coxwold & Byland Abbey, then to Wass.
meals	12pm-2pm (2.30pm weekends); 6.30pm-9pm (9.30pm Saturdays). Main courses £8.45-£18; set menu £17-£20.
rooms	3 doubles £70. Singles £42.
closed	Sun evenings; Monday Oct-March.

Andy & Sue Cole
The Wombwell Arms,
Wass, Helmsley,
Yorkshire YO61 4BE
tel 01347 868280
web www.thewombwellarms.co.uk

map: 14 entry: 509

Yorkshire

Carpenter's Arms
Felixkirk

The Carpenter's Arms is cosy, unstuffy, endearingly eccentric. Oriental fans by the fire and other oddities are dotted around the heavily beamed interior, along with plants, pictures, books and antique carpentry tools. The long, panelled, barrel-fronted bar has three sections and bar stools, while tables in the several separate areas are cheerful with gingham. Beyond is the dining room, more formal with its white cloths, shining glassware and comfortable period dining chairs. A couple of Yorkshire beers are accompanied by some especially good wines by the glass and the menu is long: chunky fish soup with aioli, croutons and gruyere, honey-glazed breast of duck with stir-fry vegetables, crispy noodles and plum sauce, and simple hot dishes and baguettes at lunchtime. The enthusiastic young proprietors and staff add a bit of spice that makes a visit here great fun. The village on the edge of the moors has a floodlit church.

directions	From Thirsk A170 to Sutton Bank; first left for Felixkirk & Boltby. Pub 2 miles.
meals	12pm-2pm; 7pm-9pm. Main courses £7.25-£17.50.
closed	3pm-6.30pm (7pm Sun); Xmas Day; New Years Day evening; Jan 2-10.

Karen Bumby
Carpenter's Arms,
Felixkirk, Thirsk,
Yorkshire YO7 2DP
tel 01845 537639
web www.carpentersarmsfelixkirk.co.uk

map: 14 entry: 510

Yorkshire

Golden Lion
Osmotherley

There's never a dull moment at the old stone inn overlooking the village green and market cross. It bustles with booted walkers at lunchtime and hums with well-dressed diners at night. This thanks to the twin talents of Christie Connelly (barman-host extraordinaire) and Peter McCoy, legendary Yorkshire restaurateur. Get there early to bag a seat in the wood-panelled bar with pew bench seating, raised open fire and flickering evening candlelight. Nurse a pint of Timothy Taylor's Landlord or a first-class wine by the glass, as you choose from a refreshingly simple menu. Nothing is over-ambitious; the chef simply gives you fresh ingredients well put together and well presented. Start with fish soup or pâté with apricot relish, move on to chicken Kiev or calves' liver with onions and mash, finish with a calorific pudding. From beautiful Osmotherley on the flanks of the Cleveland Hills walkers head for the famous Coast to Coast Walk: don your hiking boots.

directions	Off A19 10 miles north of Thirsk.
meals	12pm-3.30pm; 6pm-10pm. Main courses £6.50-£13.95.

Christie Connelly
Golden Lion,
6 West End,
Osmotherley,
Yorkshire DL6 3AA
tel 01609 883526

map: 14 entry: 511

Yorkshire

Nag's Head
Pickhill

Sporting guests predominate at this popular country inn (three racecourses within 15 minutes drive; golf and shooting too). Beams, open fires and a display of ties distinguish the tap room, where Black Sheep is on handpump; head for the lounge bar or smart, book-lined dining room if you wish to eat. If the formula holds few surprises it's because that's what customers have come to expect, and the Boynton brothers have been here 30 years. That's not to damn with faint praise, only to acknowledge that good, unaffected cooking using fresh local produce can be better than high-risk experimentation under the guise of innovation. Tuck into locally smoked salmon, rack of English lamb, local game, cottage pie or poached cod and prawn mornay. It's not far from the A1 and the 16 newly done-up bedrooms are worth making the most of if you are here to explore this lovely area.

Yorkshire

Freemason's Arms
Nosterfield

The Freemason's whitewashed exterior may suggest an ordinary village pub but over the years an extraordinary assemblage of items has been added to the traditional décor: 1900s enamel advertisements, veteran agricultural implements, Union flags, miners' lamps, a piano, and beams littered with calling cards and old bank notes. It's a low-beamed place with inter-connecting rooms, some flagged floors, two open fires, pew seating, soft lighting, candlelight – traditional, unspoilt, cosy, fascinating. It's also a downright good pub, with at least four local cask ales on offer, and a blackboard to tantalise the hungry: partridge in rowan berry sauce, pink liver and onions with bacon. Kris Stephenson enjoys buying locally and dishes up fresh produce with flair. Eat in the bar, or at one of the bigger tables in the far room, perfect for dining. Just the spot after a day at the Ripon races.

directions	Pickhill off A1, west of Thirsk.
meals	12pm-2pm; 6pm-9.30pm. Main courses £7.95-£15; set menu £15.95 (lunch); £26 (dinner).
rooms	16: 5 twins, 10 doubles, 1 single. £60-£80; singles £45-£60.

directions	On B6267 for Masham, 2 miles off A1.
meals	12pm-2pm; 7pm-9pm. Main courses £8-£15.
closed	Mondays.

Edward & Raymond Boynton
Nag's Head,
Pickhill, Thirsk,
Yorkshire YO7 4JG
tel 01845 567391
web www.nagsheadpickhill.co.uk

map: 14 entry: 512

Kristian Stephenson
Freemason's Arms,
Nosterfield,
Ripon,
Yorkshire DL8 2QP
tel 01677 470548

map: 14 entry: 513

The Cock, 23 High Street, Broom, Bedfordshire, SG18 9NA 01767 31411
Remarkably unspoilt village boozer. Beers tapped from the cask in the original tap room —
there's a rarity! Plain pine-panelled rooms and a proper skittles room too.

Hare & Hounds, Old Warden, Bedfordshire, SG18 9HQ 01767 627225
Old village pub that's been given a gastropub overhaul within — loads of leather and funky
colours. Excellent food on short, seasonal produce-led menu.

The Swan Inn, Lower Green, Inkpen, Berkshire, RG17 9DX 01488 668326
Rambling 17th-century inn run by an organic beef farmer who supplies the kitchen and its
farm shop. Blackboard menu, excellent ales, pine-furnished rooms and great local walks.

Bel & the Dragon, Cookham, Marlow, Berkshire, SL6 9SQ 01628 521263
Black and white diminutive Tudor inn. Timbers, scrubbed wood panelling, lovely fires and
exposed brickwork. Behind, a great barn of vibrant pastel walls and an imaginative menu.

Hare & Hounds, Lambourn Woodlands, Berkshire, RG17 7SD 01488 71386
A handsome, brick roadside inn with an unusual mix of olde worlde timbers, light modern
bar and oriental-inspired food. Truly welcoming and very popular.

Land's End, Charvil, Twyford, Berkshire, RG10 0UE 01672 521225
Aptly named, tricky to find pub with a baronial theme. Leaded windows, latch doors,
dark sturdy furniture and a deep burgundy dining room.

White Lion, Hampton-in-Arden, Solihull, Birmingham, B95 5BY 01564 792623
Old pub with stripped pine, fresh flowers and fresh food. Good ales and wines and several
bedrooms, too.

The Beacon, Bilston Street, Sedgley, Birmingham, DY3 1JE 01902 883380
Fine pub with its own micro-brewery. Little's changed since WWII, with a fascinating period
piano bar and smoking lounge. The Victorian till is as ornate as they come. Sandwiches only.

The King's Head, 60 Victoria Street, Bristol, BS1 6DE 0117 927 7860
Classically Victorian inside, 1660 out. A charming period narrow bar and cosier, panelled
rear snug, splendid mirrored back bar, photos of old Bristol and gallons of Smiles.

The Merchants Arms, 5 Merchants Road, Bristol, BS8 4PZ 0117 904 0037
Honest and real, without a whiff of modern pretension, much loved by cultured locals.
Simple, friendly, Bath Ales-owned, with excellent beers and good snacks.

The Rising Sun, Little Hampden, Buckinghamshire, HP16 9PS 01494 488394
Walkers love this inn — the menu of delicious fresh goodies is enough to satisfy any hearty
appetite. A civilised dining pub in pretty countryside (but smokers not welcome).

Stag & Huntsmen, Hambleden, Buckinghamshire, RG9 6RP 01491 571227
The setting's the thing and the village is perfect. Bars are small and traditional, carpeted and lively; the dining room modern. Hearty food, excellent ale.

The White Hart, Pound Lane, Buckinghamshire, MK18 4LX 01280 847969
Thatched, timbered and latched — a deeply cosy village pub where locals in thick socks prop up the bar. Plans are afoot for a restaurant revamp under new owners.

The White Horse, Hedgerley, Buckinghamshire, SL2 3UY 01753 643225
Super local in easy reach of the M40 (J2). Swap the services for the flagstones, inglenook, beamed bar and perfect ploughman's lunch. Seven real ales are tapped from the barrel.

Chequers, Fingest, Marlow, Buckinghamshire, RG9 6QD 01491 638335
Chequers is renowned for its good food and attractive low-lit vaulted dining room. The garden with its pond is a fine spot for a summer tipple.

The Crown, Little Missenden, Buckinghamshire, HP7 0RD 01494 862571
An unspoilt brick cottage pub in a pretty village, run by the same family for 90 years. Excellent beers, good wines and sandwiches, a big garden and walking all around.

Full Moon, Hawridge Common, Buckinghamshire, HP5 2UH 01494 758959
The landlord claims this ancient inn used to be a brothel. Nothing so unsalubrious now, just yummy food (organic meat), good beers and bags of atmosphere.

Cambridge Blue, 85 Gwydir Street, Cambridge, CB1 2LG 01223 361382
Away from the centre, this simple local has a warm atmosphere and stacks of rowing paraphernalia. A wide choice of ales, among them Adnams and Nethergate — but no room for smokers.

White Pheasant, Fordham, Cambridgeshire, CB7 5LQ 01638 720414
Very welcoming dining pub with bare boards, wooden tables, crackling logs, blackboard menus of fresh fish and farmhouse cheeses. Handpumped Woodforde's Wherry and Hobson's Choice.

Tickell Arms, 1 North Road, Whittlesford, Cambridgeshire, CB2 4NZ 01223 833128
Unique gothic villa with a stunning garden and country-house charm. Try the local Milton ale. There's smart French cooking on the set lunch (good value) and dinner menus.

Black Horse, 14 Overend, Elton, Cambridgeshire, PE8 6RU 01832 280240
Rustic 17th-century spot overlooking the church and rolling parkland belonging to elegant Elton Hall (open). Log fires, antiques and old oak beams. Fishy blackboard menu.

Old Harkers Arms, Russell Street, Chester, Cheshire, CH1 5AL 01244 344525
A buzzy atmosphere and a great range of micro-brewery ales at this beautifully converted warehouse down by the canal. Run by Brunning & Price pubs — good modern pub food.

The Grosvenor Arms, Aldford, Cheshire, CH3 6HJ 01244 620228
Brunning & Price's flagship dining pub overlooking the Dee. Rugs on wooden floors,
a panelled library and a bright verdant conservatory. Interesting food – feedback please.

Bhurtpore Inn, Aston, Cheshire, CW5 8DQ 01270 780917
Indian artefacts decorate this unpretentious, idiosyncratic stone pub. Ten real ales, authentic
curries, interesting specials. B&B next door. Reports please.

Sutton Hall, Bullocks Lane, Sutton, Cheshire, SK11 0HE 01260 253211
Authentically 16th century: big fires, stained glass and flagstones. Decent handpumped ales,
lovely grounds with duck pond, gothic windows in the bedrooms.

Dusty Miller, Wrenbury, Cheshire, CW5 8HG 01270 780537
Hugely popular pub in a beautifully converted watermill beside the Shropshire Union Canal.
Local food is ever-present on the imaginative menus. Super alfresco areas.

The Blue Peter, Quay Road, Polperro, Cornwall, PL13 2QZ 01503 272743
Unspoilt little fishing pub built into the cliffside by Polperro's harbour. Dark and cosy wood-
floored bar with nautical artefacts, tip-top Cornish ales.

The Rashleigh, Polkerris, Cornwall, PL24 2TL 01726 813991
A pub on the beach in a tiny cove! The old coastguard station is cosy in winter, unbeatable
in summer; down a pint of real ale and watch the sun set across St Austell bay.

The Royal Oak, Lostwithiel, Cornwall, PL22 0AG 01208 872552
Supposedly linked to nearby Restormel Castle by a smugglers' tunnel, a homely, 13th-
century pub known for its Cornish-brewed ales and Mrs Hine's homecooked food.

The Rising Sun, The Square, St Mawes, Cornwall, TR2 5DT 01326 270233
Delightful harbour views from the sunny terrace at St Austell Brewery's flagship inn-hotel.
Smartly decorated, lively bar, conservatory restaurant and eight rooms.

The White Hart, Churchtown, Ludgvan, Cornwall, TR20 8EY 01736 740574
Granite stone 14th-century pub with ochre-coloured walls, low beams and real ale from
the cask. Come for intimate boxed seating areas and log-burning fires.

Victoria Inn, Perranuthnoe, Cornwall, TR20 9NP 01736 710309
An exciting new set-up, with imaginative takes on fresh Cornish seafood every day. Beers
from Sharps and Greene King, and inexpensive house wines. Modest, modern bedrooms.

The Pheasant Inn, Casterton, Cumbria, LA6 2RX 01524 271230
18th-century inn overlooking Casterton's green and nearby fells of the Lune Valley. Great
base for walking (10 smart rooms) and a popular eating venue. Reports please.

The Sun Inn, Dent, Cumbria, LA10 5QL 015396 25208
Dent is an unspoilt Dales village of cobbles and cottages. After an invigorating walk pile into the Sun for log fires and pints of Dent beers, brewed up the valley.

The Bay Horse Hotel, Canal Foot, Ulverston, Cumbria, LA12 9EL 01229 583972
More of a restaurant with rooms, Robert Lyon's old pub sits on the shore of the Leven estuary with magnificent views across Morecambe Bay. Sublime bar food at lunchtimes only.

The Pheasant, Bassenthwaite Lake, Cumbria, CA13 9YE 017687 76234
The snug at the Pheasant is wonderful, a reminder of past times: it was a busy coaching inn, now it's a hotel with pristine rooms. Jennings on tap, good bar food, glorious gardens.

The Watermill, Ings, Cumbria, LA8 9PY 015398 21309 015398 21309
The draw of this converted old wood mill, in prime walking country near Windermere, is the mind-boggling range of 16 real ales, heady farm ciders and 50 malt whiskies.

Old Crown, Shardlow, Derbyshire, DE72 2HL 01332 792392
A fine pub for beer and cider drinkers on the banks of the Trent. Three house ales, up to seven guest beers and plenty of real ciders in the summer. Reasonable pub food.

The Bear Inn, Alderwasley, Derbyshire, DE56 2RD 01629 822585
Sturdy, hugely atmospheric stone pub in the middle of nowhere. A delightful place, with nooks and crannies, heavy black beams and roaring fires; good bedrooms too.

The Red Lion, Litton, Derbyshire, SK17 8QU 01298 871458
Pretty, stone pub overlooking the village green, complete with stocks. 'Free from brewery' declares the pub sign, backed up by Jennings, Barnsley Bitter and Black Sheep within.

Waltzing Weasel, Birch Vale, Derbyshire, SK22 1BT 01663 743402
A real local with a good atmosphere (and a devoted ale-swigging crew at the bar), helped by a roasting fire and simple bar décor. Bedrooms, though old-fashioned, are fine.

Eyre Arms, Hassop, Derbyshire, DE45 1NS 01629 640390
Traditional pub covered by Virginia creeper, close to Hassop Hall and good walks. Beams, log fires, lamplight, ancient knick-knacks and country cooking that's great value.

Chequers Inn, Froggatt Edge, Derbyshire, S32 3ZJ 01433 630231
A former row of 16th-century cottages with a raised garden in an idyllic alpine-like setting. Country prints and pine, wooden floors, modern bistro-style food, good bedrooms.

The London Inn, Molland, Devon, EX36 3NG 01769 550269
Cracking village local in the Exmoor foothills full of locals, dogs, hunters and shooters. Few frills in rambling flagstoned rooms – hearty food and great beer. Reports please.

Tuckers Arms, Dalwood, Devon, EX13 7EG 01404 881342
Postcard-pretty thatched pub in the tranquil Axe valley. Originally a manor house, parts date back 700 years; old stone floors, beams aplenty, big log fires, enjoyable food.

The Cherub, 13 Higher Street, Dartmouth, Devon, TQ6 9RB 01803 832571
Dartmouth's oldest building (1380) creaks with age: a magnificent timbered house with an overhanging beamed façade. Good ales in tiny bar with inglenook; pub food in restaurant.

The Tower, Slapton, Devon, TQ7 2PN 01548 580216
An atmospheric 14th-century inn with new owners. Past reputation of good fresh food and ale in rambling, low-beamed, log-fired bars. Reports please.

The Warren House Inn, Postbridge, Devon, PL20 6TA 01822 880208
High on Dartmoor, this austere whitewashed pub is a welcome sight for drivers and walkers crossing the moor. Hearty bar food and a peat fire that has burnt continuously since 1845.

The Sloop Inn, Bantham, Devon, TQ7 3AJ 01548 560489
A 16th-century smugglers' pub smack on the coastal path in the glorious South Hams and a stroll from the beach – the perfect stop-off for fresh fish and a pint of Palmers IPA.

The Mill Brook Inn, South Pool, Devon, TQ7 2RW 01548 531581
Arrive by boat (high tide) at this 400-year-old village pub on the Salcombe estuary. Cosy bars, cracking crab sandwiches, Bass from the barrel and a tiny streamside terrace.

The Manor Inn, Lower Ashton, Devon, EX6 7QL 01647 252304
Small, traditional Teign Valley local overlooking field and valley. Crackling log fires in cosy bars, honest grub, local cider and excellent west country ales.

Beer Engine, Newton St Cryres, Devon, EX5 5AX 01392 851282
Devon's oldest brewery sits behind the glass downstairs in this former railway hotel. Great steaks and Sunday lunches washed down with Piston Bitter and Sleeper Heavy, BBQs in summer.

Northmore Arms, Wonson, Devon, EX20 2JA 01647 231428
A treasure buried down tiny lanes on the edge of Dartmoor. Wonderfully unspoilt, simple beamed rooms, homemade food, great beer, exceptional walking. Open all day.

Pig's Nose, East Prawle, Devon, TQ7 2BY 01548 511209
Devon's most southerly pub overlooking the village green and Lannacombe Bay. Three homely rooms, sofas, fires, cask ales and homemade food. Live music in hall next door.

The Anchor Inn, Seatown, Dorset, DT6 6JU 01297 489215
A cracking coastal path watering hole below Golden Cap. The big sun terrace and gardens overlook a pebbly beach. Open fires, pints of Palmers and crab sandwiches. New landlord.

The Brace of Pheasants, Plush, Dorset, DT2 7RQ 01300 348357
In rolling downland, one of Dorset's prettiest pubs – two thatched cottages tucked away in a rural hamlet. A fine summer garden and great walkers' pitstop. Reports please.

The Langton Arms, Tarrant Monkton, Dorset, DT11 8RX 01258 830225
Five micro-brewery ales and a bistro-style menu draw locals and walkers to this rose-and-creeper-clad, 17th-century village pub. Meat from owners' farm.

The Marquis of Lorne, Nettlecombe, Dorset, DT6 3SY 01308 485236
Isolated inn with gardens (good for kids) at the base of Eggardon Hill. Worth the trip down tortuous lanes for log fires, Palmers ales, lovely food and valley views across Powerstock.

The West Bay, Station Road, West Bay, Dorset, DT6 4EW 01308 422157
Opposite the beach in this busy coastal village, the West Bay is fast winning a name for superb fresh fish and locally-landed crab. Cosy carpeted bar; lovely Palmers ale.

Lord Crewe Arms, Blanchland, Durham, DH8 9SP 01434 675251
Here lie the remains of Blanchland's 12th-century abbey lodge set in cloistered gardens. One of England's finest inns, replete with grand fireplaces and a vaulted crypt bar.

The Mole Trap, Tawney Common, Essex, CM16 7PU 01992 522394
The single-track drive through miles of gloriously unspoilt countryside is the 'wow' of this very rural pub. Excellent beers (Ridley, Couch Vale, Fullers London Pride).

Peldon Rose, Mersea Road, Peldon, Essex, CO5 7QJ 01206 735248
A 14th-century smugglers' inn rescued from decay. Wonky walls, head-cracking beams and huge fires – wonderful. Fine wines, scrummy food and stylish, simple bedrooms.

The Whalebone, Fringringhoe, Essex, CO5 7BG 01206 729307
Visit Vivian Steed's convivial village local for valley views from a glorious garden (Shakespeare plays in summer). Come for pints of Ridley's, fresh food, great walks.

Blue Boar, Silver Street, Maldon, Essex, CM9 4QE 01621 855888
Old coaching inn, now a hotel, with a smart but pubby bar. Its own micro-brewery churns out Farmers Ale, Blue Boar Bitter and Hotel Porter stout, all tapped from the cask.

The Bull Inn, Hinton, Dyrham, Gloucestershire, SN14 8HG 0117 937 2332
Fine 16th-century stone pub set back from a deep-cut Cotswold lane. Enticing with tiny windows, low beams, open fires and an inventive menu. Sunny south-facing terrace.

The Baker's Arms, Broad Campden, Gloucestershire, GL55 6UR 01386 840515
Traditional Cotswold pub that serves home-cooked food and a good selection of well-kept beers. Good walking all around and a welcome for children.

The Horse & Groom, Upper Oddington, Gloucestershire, GL56 0XH 01451 830584
Set in a tranquil Cotswold village near Stow, a bright, airy pub popular for its food.
Comfy bedrooms and a full wine list. For sale as we went to press – reports please.

Queen's Head Inn, Stow on the Wold, Gloucestershire, GL54 1AB 01451 830563
A traditional pub overlooking the market square of this beautiful Cotswold town. A favourite
among race goers and locals. Good beer and good simple pub food.

The Falcon Inn, Painswick, Gloucestershire, GL6 6UN 01452 814222
Handsome old inn on the Cotswold Way with a colourful history, panelled bars, fires,
local ales and interesting menus. The world's oldest bowling green is in the garden.

The Old Fleece, Rooksmoor, Gloucestershire, GL5 3NB 01453 872582
A fine, mullion-windowed Cotswold stone roadhouse. Mammoth sandwiches all day;
real ales and ciders; a dozen wines by the glass and over 50 eclectic menu items.

Yew Tree Inn, Clifford Mesne, Gloucestershire, GL18 1JS 01531 820719
Seriously ambitious diner in the back of beyond. Tons of fresh local produce dished out in
rather un-pubby dining rooms. Do check opening times. Comfortable bedrooms.

Rose & Crown, Redmarley D'Abitot, Gloucestershire, GL19 3NB 01531 650234
Truly handsome 18th-century spot by the A417 outside Ledbury. The new licensees are truly
pub people and love their food; the county deserves more of their ilk.

Eight Bells, Chipping Campden, Gloucestershire, GL55 6JG 01386 840371
A 14th-century treasure by the church of eight bells. Daily menus are based on local
produce. Hook Norton, guest ales and good-value wines. Worth booking.

Eagle & Child, Stow-on-the-Wold, Gloucestershire, GL54 1BN 01451 830670
Part of the Royal Hotel which dates back to 947, this is a cracking pub serving Hook Norton
beers in a rustic setting. But both were up for sale late 2003. Reports, please.

The Mayfly, Testcombe, Hampshire, SO20 6AX 01264 860283
Unrivalled tranquil river scenes draw summer crowds to this beamed old farmhouse on the
banks of the swiftly-flowing Test. Comfortable bar, pubby food and splendid decked terrace.

The Fleur de Lys, Pilley, Hampshire, SO41 5QB 01590 672158
History is as much of a pull as a good pint at this thatched pub. Deeply traditional, serving
hearty food in beamed bars. Roaring fires, lovely garden, forest walks from the door.

The East End Arms, East End, Hampshire, SO41 5SY 01590 626223
Unpretentious pub hidden down narrow New Forest lanes. Everything a real pub should be –
plain locals' bar, carpeted lounge bar with open fire, real ale and country cooking.

The Hawkley Inn, Hawkley, Petersfield, Hampshire, GU33 6NE 01730 827205
This honest, no-frills inn has a fine reputation for its collection of ales and robust, unpretentious food. A chatty mix of locals and walkers from the Hangers Way Path.

The Trooper Inn, Alton Road, Froxfield, Hampshire, GU32 1BD 01730 827293
Rustic and remote downland inn with laid-back atmosphere of candlelit, wood-floored bars, cracking real ale and solidly good, monthly-changing menus. Snazzy ensuite rooms.

The Oak Inn, Bank, Hampshire, SO43 7FE 023 8028 2350
New Forest walks from this friendly, low-beamed 18th-century pub. Walkers, cyclists and locals pour in. Ale tapped from the cask, hearty homemade food.

The Jolly Sailor, Bursledon, Hampshire, SO31 8DN 023 8040 5557
Reached via 45 steps or by boat, this former shipbuilder's house overlooks the river Hamble. Watch all things nautical from the terrace.

Five Bells, Nether Wallop, Hampshire, SO20 8HA 01264 781572
Set at the heart of a pretty thatched village, a typical small-community pub with locals' bar up front and small, convivial restaurant behind. An interesting menu.

Selborne Arms, Selborne, Hampshire, GU34 3JR 01420 511247
In charming village, handy for the climb up Zig-Zag path to the Selborne Hill viewpoint (NT). Winter fires, hoppy beams and hearty pub food that cranks up a gear in the evening.

Hampshire Arms, Crondall, Hampshire, GU10 5QU 01252 850418
Refurbishment of the village pub was almost complete as we went to press. The food, under chef Paul Morgan, should be good. Reports please.

The Verzons, Trumpet, Herefordshire, HR8 2PZ 01531 670381
Fine views of the Malverns from the bedrooms. Sandwiches and Butty Bach in the bar, or feast on roast turbot, local lamb and Gressingham duck with complementary wine. Splash out!

Sun Inn, Winforton, Herefordshire, HR3 6EA 01544 327677
Just on the Hereford side of the border, a little roadhouse that's happy just the way it is. The blooming summer garden, with boules and crazy golf, is great for families.

The Cottage of Content, Carey, Herefordshire, HR2 6NG 01432 840242
Gloriously hidden down by the river, with farmhouse tables, beams and settles. Wye Valley beers, cider, perry and wines score more highly than the slightly bland cooking.

The Boot, Orleton, Herefordshire, SY8 4HN 01568 780228
Half-timbered village inn beloved of locals with orchard garden, horse-brasses, big fire. Real ales and cider matched by traditional pub roasts, grills, curries and casseroles.

Carpenter's Arms, Walterstone, Herefordshire, HR2 0DX 01873 890353
Two-room cottage-pub with fabulous views up to Hay Bluff. Unaltered log-fired hob and bread oven; 6X from the drum; flagons of cider and perry; good food. Be spoiled rotten.

Hope & Anchor, Ross-on-Wye, Herefordshire, HR9 7BU 01989 563003
A divine spot on Ross's Wye riverbank (though not at spring tide!). Family room, garden with BBQ and occasional jazz. Good guest ales, less adventurous wines.

Kilverts, Hay-on-Wye, Herefordshire, HR3 5AG 01497 821042
Trendy town-centre inn with a sense of fun, olde-worlde-style bar and brassy new wave bedrooms. Easy atmosphere, but varying service.

The Holly Bush, Potters Crouch, Hertfordshire, AL2 3NN 01727 851792
An immaculate, 18th-century country pub elegantly furnished with antiques and big oak tables candlelit at night. Fabulous Fuller's ales, straightforward food, nice garden.

The George & Dragon, Watton at Stone, Hertfordshire, SG14 3JA 01920 830285
Greene King pub with IPA and Old Speckled Hen on tap and champagne/wine specials by the glass. Bit faded around the edges, but food is its thing with blackboards everywhere.

The Jolly Waggoner, Ardeley, Hertfordshire, SG2 7AH 01438 861350
Pretty rural pub with pink walls, bare floorboards, blazing fires and lots of knick-knacks. Blackboards list popular bar specials and there's a cottagey restaurant next door.

Chequers, Fowlmere, Hertfordshire, SG8 7SR 01763 208369
Much-cared-for village pub that makes more of its associations with pilots from WWII than its Samuel Pepys link. Scrumptious Irish cheeses go down well with a glass of Adnams.

Red Lion, Freshwater, Isle of Wight, PO40 9BP 01983 297171
A short stroll from the tidal river Yar and a handy stop-off for local Goddards ale and special food. Sofas, flagstones and fires in the open-plan bar; very civilised.

The Gate Inn, Boyden Gate, Kent, CT3 4EB 01227 860498
A charming rural local, run for years by a landlord who resists change. Two small, well-worn bars, log fires, Shepherd Neame tapped from the cask, and simple, hearty food.

Harrow, Ightham Common, Kent, TN15 9EB 01732 885912
A rustic country pub from the outside, subtle rural chic inside; the whole place oozes gentrified prosperity. Stonkingly good food rolls out of the kitchen.

Rock Inn, Hoath Corner, Tonbridge, Kent, TN8 7BS 01892 870296
A timeless, tile-hung brick cottage in a glorious location. Scuffed and delightfully laid-back, the perfect walker's stop for a pint of Larkins and a satisfyingly thick sandwich.

The Greyhound, Leigh, Kent, TN11 8LZ 01892 870275
Hard to find down winding country lanes but worth it. Beautifully cared-for traditional interior and homely local fare. Adnams, Kings and Barnes Sussex on handpump.

The Cartford Hotel, Little Eccleston, Lancashire, PR3 0YP 01995 670166
Whitewashed old former farmhouse beside a toll bridge over the River Wyre. Beer-lovers haven: Hart ales (Ice Maiden, Dishie Debby) brewed on site. Much character and good pub food.

Spread Eagle, Sawley, Lancashire, BB7 4NH 01200 441202
A 17th-century inn on the banks of the Ribble. A serious pub-restaurant; soup and sandwiches only in the bar. Great for a riverside drink in summer.

Water Witch, Aldcliffe Road, Lancaster, Lancashire, LA1 1SU 01524 63828
Bustling former stable block on the canal towpath, a stroll from the town centre. Go for beer (eight on tap) and their famous cheeses and cold meat boards. More reports, please.

Fox & Goose, Illston on the Hill, Leicestershire, LE7 9EG 0116 259 6340
A good old-fashioned local. No food; the only animals in this shrine to country pursuits are stuffed or on the walls. Excellent beers in a charming rural setting.

The Berkeley Arms, Wymondham, Leicestershire, LE14 2AG 01572 787587
We've heard great things about the food at this rustic village inn. Scrubbed pine and dried flowers create an easy informality. Feedback on the food, please.

Chequers, Gedney Dyke, Lincolnshire, PE12 0AJ 01406 362666
Popular dining pub at the mouth of The Wash, specialising in fish dishes and intriguing meats such as crocodile (not locally sourced...). Recently given a facelift – reports please.

Black Horse Inn, Grimsthorpe, Lincolnshire, PE10 0LY 01778 591247
This large coaching inn has re-established its reputation as a hotspot for both posh nosh (unusually good) and bar food. Great wine list available. Reports welcome.

Leagate Inn, Leagate Road, Coningsby, Lincolnshire, LN4 4RS 01526 342370
A friendly old inn, one of the last Fen Guide Houses, providing refuge for travellers crossing the treacherous marshlands before they were drained. Have a meal, stay the night.

The Crown, 223 Grove Road, Hackney, London, E3 5SN 020 8981 9998
Singh and Boultons' second organic pub follows the same fabulous formula. Impeccable produce, 50 organic wines, food that zings, a lively atmosphere and a hello for dogs.

The Salusbury, 50–52 Salusbury Road, London, NW6 6NN 020 7328 3286
Lively gastropub with a deli on the side. Red walls are covered with seminal jazz album sleeves. Delicious mainly Italian food and a lengthy wine list.

The Perseverance, 63 Lamb's Conduit Street, London, WC1 2NB 020 7405 8278
Former rough Irish inn reinvented as a gastropub with an individual feel – colourful flock
wallpaper, wooden floors. Sophisticated daily menus and tapas at lunch.

The Abbey Road, 63 Abbey Road, St John's Wood, London, NW8 0AE 020 7328 6626
Fresh, aqua-walled gastropub serving northern Italian and mediterranean food. Tables outside
in summer in this pretty if busy road, just yards from the Beatles' zebra crossing.

The Grapes, 76 Narrow Street, Limehouse, London, E14 8PB 020 7987 4396
A little gem overlooking the Thames in the heart of the docklands. Come for well-kept
Adnams, unbeatable fish 'n' chips downstairs (more fish up), chess, draughts, views.

The Highgate, 79 Highgate Road, Kentish Town, London, NW5 1TL 020 7485 8442
Set in a refurbished Victorian carpet factory, a modish bar famed for its wines and food
(great Sunday lunches). Leather sofas, huge windows, a cool but friendly feel.

Lord Palmerston, 33 Dartmouth Park Hill, London, NW5 1HU 020 7485 1578
Bustling gastropub stripped down to bare boards and wooden tables, with food that's quite
something (Moroccan touches; great steaks) and good wine and beer. Garden for summer.

The Flask, 77 Highgate West Hill, London, N6 6BU 020 8348 7346
A Highgate landmark; Dick Turpin hid in the cellars. Cosy corners in a cavernous inside;
an outside that's mobbed in summer. It still serves good beer and wine, and great pub food.

William IV, 786 Harrow Road, London, NW10 5JX 020 8969 5944
There's excellent food and wine in the elegant and sedate restaurant – and a laid-back bar
with sofas, fires and music. Also a garden for summer at the back.

The Pelican, 22 Waterford Road, Fulham, London, SW6 2DR 020 7792 3073
Leather sofas, palm fronds, cane blinds… a civilised place where Fulhamites and shoppers
meet over fresh nibbles with wine and the best value steaks in town.

Fox & Hounds, 29 Passmore Street, Chelsea, London, SW1W 8HR 020 7730 6367
Lovely unpretentious boozer, all the cosier for being decked out in hunting red. Be entertained
by the 'Wicked Wit' blackboards from a corner pew as you tuck into doorstep sandwiches.

Cittie of York, 22 High Holborn, London, WC1V 6BS 020 7242 7670
Atmospheric vaulted Victorian chamber with confessional-type booths, huge wine vats and
coal-burning stove. Legal types drop by for pub fare, Sam Smiths beer and trendy nachos.

Spaniards Inn, Spaniards Road, Hampstead, London, NW3 7JJ 020 8731 6571
A legendary hangout with a history. Oak-panelled snugs, open fires and delightful garden
with aviary (packed in summer). Ciabattas, risottos, Sunday roasts, smiley staff.

WORTH A VISIT

The Northgate, 113 Southgate Road, Islington, London, N1 3JS 020 7359 7392
Gastro bar with a terrific reputation for fish (menu changes daily). Loll on couches and
admire the art; take a wine onto the terrace, heated for late summer drinking. A joy.

Viaduct Tavern, 126 Newgate Street, St Paul's, London, EC1A 7AA 020 7600 1863
The only unaltered gin palace in London, wonderfully lavish and famous for its triptych oil
painting of four Viaduct statues. Join the city lunchtime throng for good beer and bar food.

Anglesea Arms, 15 Selwood Terrace, Chelsea, London, SW7 3QG 020 7373 7960
Splendid Regency pub, dark floral wallpaper, heavy velvet curtains and scrubbed tables:
wonderfully cosy. Comfortingly English food downstairs, hot chocolate, Adnams ales.

The Latchmere, 503 Battersea Park Road, London, SW11 3BW 020 7223 3549
A pub and a theatre rolled into one. Spruced up high-ceilinged bar, leather sofas, warm fire,
bags of smoky atmosphere and a mini-theatre to watch new comic talent.

Prince of Wales, 48 Cleaver Square, Kennington, London, SE11 4EA 020 7735 9916
Once a gangland boozer, now an intimate little place serving good Spitfire to students and
yuppies. Packed in summer when locals gather in the lovely square to play boules.

The Cow, 89 Westbourne Park Rd, Ladbroke Grove, London, W2 5QH 020 7221 5400
A restaurant in disguise, but Tom Conran has done it very well. Superb fish and crustacea:
you can eat up or down. Laid-back staff serve a laid-back crowd – and it's friendly.

The Archery Tavern, 4 Bathurst Street, Bayswater, London, W2 2SD 020 7402 4916
Everyone loves this place, once the haunt of the London Toxophilite Society. The Hyde Park
stables are in the mews behind, so ponies clop by. Excellent beers on tap, simple food.

Approach Tavern, 47 Approach Road, Bethnell Green, London, E2 9LY 020 8980 2321
The embodiment of fashionable East London: half trendy music pub, half soignée eaterie.
The fittings are traditional but the vibe is young and cosmopolitan. Crazy!

The Warrington Hotel, 93 Warrington Crescent, London, W9 1EH 020 7286 2929
Cavernous, splendid, Victorian. Good beers, 22 wines by the glass and Thai food, too.
The bar has a huge arched ceiling and a magnificent staircase. Good for celeb spotting.

The Well, 180 St John Street, Clerkenwell, London, EC1 020 7251 9363
A great relaxed atmosphere; book ahead if you want to eat. The food is modern British, the
décor understated (except downstairs where back-lit fish tanks provide the only illumination).

Fat Cat, 49 West End Street, Norwich, Norfolk, NR2 4NA 01603 624364
Victorian corner pub and beer drinkers heaven. 25 real ales with some on handpump, others
tapped from cask. The owners proudly keep this a traditional and simple drinking pub.

George & Dragon Hotel, Cley-next-the-Sea, Norfolk, NR25 7RN 01263 740652
Norfolk Naturalists' Trust was formed at this recently-refurbished Edwardian inn overlooking
windswept saltmarshes. A haven for twitchers and walkers for its Woodforde's ales.

White Horse Hotel, 4 High Street, Blakeney, Norfolk, NR25 7AL 01263 740054
What a spot for this 17th-century coaching inn, just up from the quay in the narrow High
Street. A pleasant bar serving great food and plenty of fish. Attractive bedrooms, too.

The Chequers Inn, Griston Road, Thompson, Norfolk, IP24 1PX 01953 483360
Splendid, long, low, thatched 14th-century inn loved for its peaceful air and unspoilt charm.
Wonky timbers and open fires in low-ceilinged rooms, local walks and pub grub.

Earle Arms, The Street, Heydon, Norfolk, NR11 6AD 01263 587376
Unspoilt 17th-century pub hidden away in a timeless estate village. Classic lobby with longcase
clock and two cosy old-fashioned parlours with open fires. Cottage garden for summer.

The Windmill, Badby, Northamptonshire, NN11 3AN 01327 702363
Thatched 17th-century inn with hotel extension close to Althorp Park and Sulgrave Manor.
Warmly decorated flagstoned bar has log fires, cask ales and traditional/modern menu.

The Red Lion, East Haddon, Northamptonshire, NN6 8BU 01604 770223
A posh country inn that serves traditional food with a continental twist, and sweets from
the trolley. Two dining rooms, five bedrooms, four ales and an impressive wine list.

The Queens Head, Bulwick, Northamptonshire, NN17 3DY 01780 450272
Super 17th-century stone inn opposite the parish church. Expect flag floors, real fires,
an unpretentious mood and changing real ales. New owners – reports please.

Snooty Fox, Lowick, Northamptonshire, NN14 3BS 01832 733434
New man Clive Dixon has introduced a rotisserie and grill menu in the restaurant of this
impressive stone built pub; smart bar and classy snacks, too. More feedback please.

The Star Inn, Netherton, Northumberland, NE65 7HD 01669 630238
Timeless gem lost in remote countryside north of Rothbury. Little has changed in 70 years –
simple 'living room', excellent Castle Eden ale; no food. Ring for opening times.

Dipton Mill, Dipton Mill Road, Hexham, Northumberland, NE46 1YA 01434 606577
Single intimate, panelled, low-ceilinged bar and blazing fires. Warming soups, pies,
ploughman's with lovely local cheeses, home-brewed ales. Walled garden with mill stream.

Anglers Arms, Longframlington, Northumberland, NE65 8AX 01665 570655
Fishing memorabilia crams the bar at this big, traditional old inn overlooking the river
Coquet, with super riverside garden. Unusual retired Pullman carriage serves as restaurant.

The Ship, Holy Island, Northumberland, TD15 2SJ 01289 389311
Rustic bare boards and beamed bars – a spotless little pub that sits in a terrace of cottages on a fascinating tidal island. Hadrian and Border ales and good seafood.

Allenheads Inn, Allenheads, Northumberland, NE47 9HJ 01434 685200
In one of England's highest villages, a fascinating 18th-century pub with a thousand artefacts: sup and browse. Simple pub food, great walks.

Three Horse Shoes, Walkeringham, Nottinghamshire, DN10 4HR 01427 890859
Visit this flower-festooned local to catch a glimpse of John's hanging baskets, 10,000 bedding plants and Japanese garden. Soups, steaks and pies, real ales, cheery staff.

Black Horse, Caythorpe, Nottinghamshire, HG14 7ED 0115 966 3520
A tiny, carpeted bar where Sharron Andrews sells beer brewed on the premises and the fish menu is so popular that booking is essential. Dick Turpin once hid in the gents, apparently.

Robin Hood, Elkesley, Nottinghamshire, DN22 8AJ 01777 83859
A far better pitstop than the roadside 'restaurants' on offer: take the Elkesley turning off the A1 for a decent ploughman's or a lamb confit with mint pesto, garlic and thyme sauce.

The Five Horseshoes, Maidensgrove, Oxfordshire, RG9 6EX 01491 641282
A super pub with magnificent views. The garden's a wonderful place to drink in the Oxfordshire beauty and spot the wheeling resident red kites. New ownership – reports please.

The Lamb, Buckland, Oxfordshire, SN7 8QN 01367 870484
This little pub turns out wonderful, if slightly expensive, grub. The fresh seasonal menu is a treat as are the homemade jams and chutneys for sale by the front door.

The Fish, Sutton Courtenay, Oxfordshire, OX14 4NQ 01235 848242
Fresh Cornish fish and seafood is the focus of Mike Gaffney's pub-restaurant in this quiet Thames-side village where George Orwell is buried. Excellent value set lunch menu.

Bishop Blaize, Sibford Gower, Oxfordshire, OX15 5RQ 01295 780323
Views over three counties from the gardens of this 17th-century pub, once the epicentre of the local wool trade. Squeeze into an inglenook seat for homely food and good ales.

Wykham Arms, Sibford Gower, Oxfordshire, OX15 5RX 01295 788808
Stylishly modernised thatch pub with a sunny terrace, wooded garden and welcome for families. Noel Coward lived opposite, Gordon Ramsay landed his first job here. Reports on food, please.

Lamb Inn, Shipton-under-Wychwood, Witney, Oxfordshire, OX7 6DQ 01367 870484
A gorgeously done-up pub with contemporary furnishings, huge flowers and log fires. Good wines and beers, special food. Unusual bedrooms each have a global theme.

WORTH A VISIT

Hand & Shears, Church Hanborough, Oxfordshire, OX29 8AB 01993 883337
Sister pub of the White Hart in Wytham, a civilised boozer with a wide range of food.
Sink into wing chairs by a cosy, flower-crowned fireplace to read the papers.

Three Horseshoes, 78 Corn Street, Witney, Oxfordshire, OX28 6BS 01993 703086
A romantic's treasure – low candlelight, open brickwork and a tantalising menu. A cosy place
for winter warmers on a chilly night.

Unicorn, Kingswood Common, Oxfordshire RG9 5LX 01491 628452
A recent makeover sees floorboards stripped and leather chesterfield-style seating installed.
The dining area is more characterful and the food is 'modern pub'.

King's Head, Wootton, Woodstock, Oxfordshire, OX20 1DX 01993 811340
Come for homemade bread with lunchtime soups and a modern British menu at dinner –
all freshly prepared. Hook Norton ales and cosy beamed bars, too.

The Black Bull, Market Overton, Rutland, LE15 7PW 01572 767677
A cheery thatched pub in a village that was once the stomping ground of Sir Isaac Newton.
It has a thriving local trade and specialises in fresh fish and continental dishes.

George & Dragon, Much Wenlock, Shropshire, TF13 6AA 01952 727312
High street paradise for ale aficionados in timbered 18th-century setting with coal fires and
a warm feel. Competent pub food from a long-standing kitchen crew.

The Royal Oak, Cardington, Shropshire, SY6 7JZ 01694 771266
At the foot of Caer Caradoc, a 500-year-old pub loved by muddy-booted ramblers – with
a dependable range of real ales, cider and inexpensive daily specials from local suppliers.

The Plough, Wistanstow, Shropshire, SY7 8DG 01588 673251
A friendly Shropshire Lad with well-above-average pub food: steak and ale pie, venison
casserole, Sunday roasts. Woods Brewery lives next door.

Three Tuns, Salop Street, Bishops Castle, Shropshire, SY9 5BW 01588 638797
Home to John Robert's micro-brewery and beer museum, with a delightfully cluttered
interior. Hearty soups, organic bread, local sausages, and the best ale from across the yard.

The Lime Kiln, Porth y Waen, Oswestry, Shropshire, SY10 8LX 01691 831550
Changed hands in early 2004 after our visit. We loved the food, the service and the corner
table by the fire reserved exclusively for locals. Reports please.

The Notley Arms Inn, Monksilver, Somerset, TA4 4JB 01984 656217
A village pub deep in the Brendon Hills with a reputation for homemade food served in cheery
rooms. The people who made this a 'must visit' pub have moved on – feedback please.

Carpenter's Arms, Stanton Wick, Somerset, BS39 4BX 01761 490202
Rambling, rose-clad stone inn overlooking the Chew Valley. Civilised beamed bar with cosy fires and rustic furnishings. Modern pub food and peaceful, pine-furnished bedrooms.

The Horse & Groom, East Woodlands, Somerset, BA11 5LY 01373 462802
Delightfully rustic 17th-century pub on the edge of peaceful woodlands by the Longleat estate. Tip-top ale from the barrel, homecooked food – perfect after a long country walk.

Stags Head, Pounds Head, Somerset, BA9 8DG 01963 440393
New licensees have made a promising start serving local real ales, organic cider and good fresh food. Lovely country interior. Reports, please.

Fleur de Lys, High Street, Norton-St Philip, Somerset, BA2 7AG 01373 834333
More locals than ever flock to this lively, atmospheric pub since the architecturally magnificent George (opposite) lost its pubbiness. Wadsworth ales and good value food.

Black Lion Inn, Butterton, Staffordshire, ST13 7SP 01538 304232
In a secluded village on the edge of the Manifold Valley, this old cottage-like stone inn dishes up robust pub food by open fires, with splendid Peak District views.

Yew Tree, Cauldon, Staffordshire, ST10 3EJ 01538 308348
A museum of a pub that refuses to modernise. Tuppence to play the old Polyphon, nowt for shove-ha'penny or skittles. Baps or pies for under £1; cask Burton Bridge for under two.

De la Pole Arms, Wingfield, Diss, Suffolk, IP21 5RA 01379 384545
Tricky to find this lovingly restored 16th-century pub (follow signs to Wingfield College). Noted for fresh fish. Due to be sold: reports on the new regime, please.

The Cornwallis, Rectory Road, Brome, Suffolk, IP23 8AJ 01379 870326
Down a tree-lined drive in 20 acres, this stylish hotel, restaurant and bar is not as intimidating as it first seems. Relaxing beamed bar, modern bar food and St Peter's remarkable beers.

Harbour Inn, Blackshore Quay, Southwold, Suffolk, IP18 6TA   01502 722781
Cracking ale from Adnams Brewery up the road, fresh cod 'n' chips and harbour views at this rustic old waterside pub. Super panelled front bar full of nautical bric-à-brac.

Ramsholt Arms, Ramsholt, Woodbridge, Suffolk, IP12 3AB 01394 411229
Idyllic – on the shore of the river Deben. Sup a pint of Nethergate on the terrace, listen to the calls of the curlew. Cosy fires, game in season and great fish and chips.

The Angel, Market Place, Lavenham, Suffolk, CO10 9QZ 01787 247388
A delightful ancient inn overlooking Lavenham's market place and famous timbered guildhall. Dining area has huge inglenook fireplace. East Anglian ales and daily-changing menus.

Butt & Oyster, Pin Mill, Suffolk, IP9 1JW 01787 280245
Impossibly charming riverside pub with old settles, tiled floors and fine views across the Orwell. Arrive early if you want one of the window seats.

Punch Bowl Inn, Oakwood Hill, Dorking, Surrey, RH5 5PU 01306 627249
15th-century charm: a roaring inglenook, scrubbed tables and uneven flagged floors.
The tile-hung pub is in superb walking country. Summer BBQs and Badger beers.

The White Cross, Water Lane, Richmond, Surrey, TW9 1TJ 020 8940 6844
Real fires in cosy bars and huge windows overlooking the Thames – what views! Enjoy a
pint or three on the terrace, hugely popular in summer. Bar food is swiftly served.

Old School House, Stane Street, Ockley, Surrey, RH5 5TH 01306 627430
Some of the best fish and seafood here at Bill Bryson's former boys' boarding school.
Expect fresh Selsey crab and Loch Fyne oysters alongside Gales beers.

The Fox Goes Free, Charlton, Chichester, Sussex, PO18 0HU 01243 811464
An extremely pretty pub round the corner from Goodwood. Cosy timbered rooms, a wide range
of bar food and a large garden looking over miles of countryside – a splendid sight at harvest time.

The King's Arms, Fenhurst, Sussex, GU27 3HA 01428 652005
Chef-landlord Michael Hirst's impressive modern cooking is the star attraction at this
beamed 17th-century pub. Great real ales and a walled garden.

Six Bells, Chiddingly, Hailsham, Sussex, BN8 6HE 01825 872227
Gary Glitter, Led Zeppelin and Leo Sayer have played in this quirky little boozer renowned
for its music. Logs fires, atmosphere and great value food.

The Cricketer's Arms, Berwick, Lewes, Sussex, BN26 5RE 01323 870469
Charming quarry-tiled bars with blazing fires – a 500-year-old brick-and-flint cottage tucked
below the South Downs. Harveys from the barrel and a great garden.

Star & Garter, East Dean, Chichester, Sussex, PO18 0JG 01243 811318
Inn with a gorgeous new refurb (old brick, stripped pine) in the pretty village of East Dean.
Delicious daily specials, teak tables in the garden, serene bedrooms.

The Bell, Alderminster, Warwickshire, CV37 8NY 01789 450414
Cheerful bar and bistro in converted coaching inn. Fresh food on daily chalkboards, in bar
rooms or restaurant, and popular musical suppers. Conservatory and garden with valley views.

Fox & Goose, Armscote, Warwickshire, CV37 8DD 01608 682293
Beams, flags and Farrow & Ball… renowned for super seasonal food and stylish rooms but
Sue Gray is selling up to weave her magic elsewhere. Will this stay the same?

The Bell, Tanworth-in-Arden, Warwickshire, B94 5AL 01564 742212
The local on the green in pretty Tanworth has had a smart refurb – and has a growing
reputation for freshly-produced food. Re-opened Feb 2004. Reports please.

The Angel Inn, Upton Scudamore, Wiltshire, BA12 0AG 01985 213225
Classy gastropub in a sleepy Wiltshire village. A relaxed and unpretentious atmosphere,
stylish décor and fresh food on daily menus. Super bedrooms and summer dining terrace.

The Angel, High Street, Heytesbury, Wiltshire, BA12 0ED 01985 840330
Big changes afoot at this 17th-century village inn with chef Antony Worrall-Thompson planning to wave his wand – new bar, bistro-style eating area. Should be good.

The Neeld Arms, The Street, Grittleton, Wiltshire, SN14 6AP 01249 782470
True country boozer with friendly locals, two glowing inglenooks, fresh, tasty food, good beers and drinkable wines. Four-poster beds upstairs, breakfast feasts.

The Three Crowns, Brinkworth, Wiltshire, SN15 5AF 01666 510366
Intimate, old-style bars and a huge no-smoking conservatory. Real ale, good wine, a garden with views and a large, surprising menu contribute to a winning formula.

The Horseshoe, Ebbesbourne Wake, Wiltshire, SP5 5JF 01722 780474
The unspoilt, rural charm of Ebbesbourne Wake is here in abundance: climbing roses in the garden, beams and open fire, cask ale and honest, fresh local food.

The Bell, The Square, Ramsbury, Wiltshire, SN8 2PE 01672 520230
On the square of this quaint market town, a handsome, bay-windowed, whitewashed 17th-century inn with a sympathetic makeover… a woodburner in the small bar and a stylish dining room.

The Bath Arms, Crockerton, Wiltshire, BA12 8AJ 01985 212262
Dean Carr escaped the heat of top London kitchens to become chef-patron at this rambling old inn. Worth a look for interesting short menus and local beers. Reports please.

Fountain Inn, Tenbury Wells, Worcestershire, WR15 8TB 01584 810701
Majestic half-timbered roadside inn. Much talk of the famous shark tank in the bar, less so of the fairly average food. Bedrooms in modern extension.

The Chequers, Cutnall Green, Worcestershire, WR9 0PJ 01229 851292
Second pub (see Stourbridge) for the ex-England soccer chef. Again, good beers, wines and service, imaginative cooking and a friendly atmosphere. More reports, please.

Hadley Bowling Green Inn, Hadley Heath, Worcestershire, WR9 0AR 01905 620252
Recently acquired by the owners of the Crown & Sandys in nearby Ombersley. Expect a similar style here: real ales, global wine list and promising food.

The Crab & Lobster, Asenby, Yorkshire, YO7 3QL 01845 577286
Rambling, characterful pub-restaurant. A bohemian, whacky interior and ceilings that are a riot of memorabilia provide the backdrop for excellent seafood. Amazing rooms in Crab Manor.

The Fox & Hounds, Sinnington, Yorkshire, YO62 6SQ 01751 431577
Old coaching inn in a sleepy backwater below the North York Moors. Come for homely panelled bars with open fires, well-presented modern pub food and cottagey rooms.

The Plough Inn, Fadmoor, Yorkshire, YO62 7HY 01751 431515
Yorkshire ales and real fires draw walkers to this elegant little local on the edge of the moors. Colourful menus, locally-sourced food and good wines draw the rest.

The White Swan, Middleham, Yorkshire, DL8 4PE 01969 622093
A refurbished Tudor coaching inn that sits proudly in Middleham's cobbled square. Popular
with the racing set for generous helpings, local ales and well-chosen wines. Good B&B.

Black Sheep Brewery, Masham, Yorkshire, HG4 4EN 01765 689227
Follow a fascinating tour of Theakston's high-flying brewery with a perfect pint of Riggwelter
or a hearty meal in the informal bar-bistro: try shank of lamb with Square Ale sauce.

Fox & Hounds, Carthorpe, Yorkshire, DL8 2LG 01845 567433
Slip off the hectic A1 for peace and nourishment at this pristine village pub. Come for
traditional interiors, delicious wines and fresh food with a fishy slant.

The Laurel, New Road, Robin Hood's Bay, Yorkshire, YO22 4SE 01947 880400
A super little pub in an unspoilt fishing village with views out to sea. Few frills other than
a roaring fire, tip-top Theakston ales and good sandwiches.

Charles Bathurst Inn, Arkengarthdale, Yorkshire, DL11 6EN 01748 884567
Retreat after a bracing walk to the Codys' wonderful inn tucked high above Swaledale.
Rustic pine-furnished interiors; hearty dishes of local produce. You can stay the night too.

Galphay Arms, Galphay, Ripon, Yorkshire, HG4 3NJ 01765 650133
Run-down village local now transformed. Understated, stylish country décor; fresh, simple
food using local produce; great wines and Yorkshire ales. Reports please.

Blacksmith's Arms, Lastingham, Yorkshire, YO62 6TL 01751 417247
New owners at this 17th-century stone pub in a beautiful village on the edge of the North
Yorkshire Moors. Theakston ales, hearty food, super walking. Check opening times.

Golden Lion, Duke Street, Settle, Yorkshire, BD24 9DU 01729 822203
With a grand staircase, big stone fireplace and dark panelling, this old coaching inn on Settle's
fine 17th-century market place oozes character. Thwaites beers, traditional pub food.

The Greyhound, Saxton, Yorkshire, LS24 9PY 01937 557202
Unchanging 13th-century stone inn next to Saxton's church. Packed with ornaments, plates
and brasses in three cosy rooms with blazing winter fires. Sam Smiths from the cask.

The Kingfisher, Biggin, Yorkshire, LS25 6HJ 01977 682344
Low beams, cream and half-timbered walls, stone flagged floors throughout intimate bars,
real ales, fresh fish and local game.

The Bull, Broughton, Skipton, Yorkshire, BD23 3AE 01756 792065
A characterful old inn, a sheltered terrace overlooking Broughton Park, great pub food and
run by the owners of Shibden Mill, Shibden (see entry). Reports welcome.

Photography by David Norton Photography, Alamy Images

wales

Anglesey

Olde Bulls Head Inn
Beaumaris

The ancient inn was a favourite of Samuel Johnson and Charles Dickens, in whose memory the sumptuous bedrooms are named. Now it attracts drinkers and foodies like bees to a honey pot. In the rambling, snug-alcoved bar are draught Bass and beef 'sarnies'. In the brasserie in the old stables, are chicken Caesar salad and gnocchi with leeks and gruyère cheese, and 10 wines by the glass. Downstairs lurk ancient weaponry and the old ducking stool; upstairs, a hammer-beamed restaurant, boldly remodelled in colours that defy its age. Welsh dishes are designed around seafood from the Menai Straits and as much beef, lamb and game as the chefs can find on the island. The results are Welsh black beef with Conwy mustard sauce, lamb noisettes with thyme risotto and port sauce, sea bass in lemon juice and herbs with Anglesey salt from the fabulous marine Zoo at Llanfairpwll (if you want the full name you'll have to ask the train to stop at the station!).

directions	Castle Street is main street in Beaumaris.
meals	12pm-2pm; 6pm-9pm (Brasserie). À la carte restaurant: 7pm-9.30pm (not Sundays). Main courses £6-£12; set menu £30.
rooms	13: 6 doubles, 4 twins, 2 suites, 1 four-poster £92-£140. Singles £67-£110.

David Robertson
Olde Bulls Head Inn,
Castle Street,
Beaumaris,
Anglesey LL58 8AP

tel	01248 810329

map: 12 entry: 514

Anglesey

Ship Inn
Red Wharf Bay

Red Wharf Bay was a busy fishing port 200 years ago and the boatmen still walk across from the estuary with their catch. Inside the Ship, fires roar in several fireplaces and bars share nautical bits and bobs. There are Toby jugs and hunting scenes and huge blackboards where the 'daily specials' change almost by the hour. At night, the upstairs restaurant proffers Welsh seafood based on the best the boats have brought in: there may be crab ravioli with mango and coriander salsa, or sea bass with Thai-scented sauce. But the old Ship Inn is so much more – a family-friendly public house where, for 30 years, regulars and visitors have been tucking into brechdanau, pysgod, prydau plant and pwdin (sandwiches, fish, children's meals and desserts). Ales are handpumped and perfect, house wines are decent. These lovely people are as proud of their hospitality as they are of their language – and the vast bay views from the front terrace are deeply inspiring.

directions	Off B5025, north of Pentraeth.
meals	12pm-2.30pm; 6pm-9.30pm; 12pm-9pm Sundays. Main courses £7-£13.50.

Andrew Kenneally
Ship Inn,
Red Wharf Bay,
Anglesey LL75 8RJ

tel   01248 852568

map: 12 entry: 515

Carmarthenshire

Y Polyn
Nantgaredig

Freddie Burns has lived in nearby Capel Dewi for years; now she's taken on the pub at Nantgareddig. It sits by a fork in the roads – one takes you to Aberglasney, the other to the National Botanic Garden of Wales. The energetic Freddie has converted the old public bar into the 'Green Room' – it's posh, but you'll still find a decent pint of Brains bitter – and has brought in a chef who knows his Pembrokeshire onions. Heading an ambitious kitchen, he brings skill and finesse to the cooking. Be won over by his parsnip consommé with tortellini of duck confit, poached and roasted rump of Welsh salt marsh lamb, and apple crumble soufflé with apple-pie ice cream. Fixed-price lunch and dinner menus are served in a dining room of character: open fire, bare brickwork and a laid-back, jazzy mood. So, only just a pub – but undoubtedly a boon to the area. And you can ramble through the woods or fish on Freddie's private stretch of the River Towy.

directions	Off junction of B4300 & B4310 between A48 & A40 east of Carmarthen.
meals	12pm-2pm; 6pm-9pm. Main courses £8.50; dinner £17.50.

Fredena Burns
Y Polyn,
Nantgaredig,
Carmarthenshire

tel   01267 290000

map: 7 entry: 516

Carmarthenshire

The Brunant Arms
Caio

The Vale of Cothi is a place of mystery and legend – the final resting place of John Harries, one of Wales's wizards. The pub has a less back-of-beyond feel. Justin and Jane say they do "good pub food" and what you get is marinated salmon with basil, lemon grass and pepper noodles – and boy do they do it well. Walkers drop by for a ploughman's or a baked potato with chilli in the lounge bar where Ystwyth ale is on tap. With high-winged settles, a log fire in the grate, books and bagatelle, it's a snug, carpeted corner away from the TV, darts and pool of the public bar. Diners return for beef, beer and rosemary cobbler, all-vegetable Grandma Guy's Cawl with cheese and bread, and superb venison steak with cranberry Cumberland sauce. Explore the Cambrian mountains by pony and stay: bedrooms are old-fashioned and none the worse for that. Just don't expect a very early morning wake-up call.

The Naked Snail & Head Salad
Pen y Dropp

Jasper and Toby were derivatives dealers in the City until their doctors warned them off a life of bubbly and smoked mussels. But they had made some money, bought a pub chain, sold 63 of them and tarted this one up with the proceeds. It is a stupendous achievement. A moving walkway glides you to the bar, automatically – and astonishingly – dispenses a glass of bubbly and then moves you into the back. There's an authentic Bedouin tent in here, where you may recline and try the North African goats' cheese tapas, with a light drizzle of palm oil. Then to the dining-room, entirely mirrored – riveting. Toby has recently honed his culinary skills in the library but has a deft touch, especially with the puddings. Try his sliver of kumquat on a duvet of roast pine needles…exquisite. But don't be misled into thinking that this is just a smart place for the wax-jackets. The regulars still love the place. Indeed, they are both to be found in the Bedouin tent every night after the others have gone, enjoying clouds of hookah smoke.

directions	Signed from A482 midway between Lampeter & Llanwrda.
meals	12pm-2pm; 6.30pm-9pm. Main courses (bar) £3.95.
rooms	4: 2 doubles. 1 twin, 1 single sharing bath, £45.

directions	Follow the golden snails from the Severn Bridge.
meals	Allah Carte served all day.

Justin & Jane Jacobi
The Brunant Arms,
Caio,
Llanwrda,
Carmarthenshire SA19 8PF
tel   01558 650483

Jasper Etwas & Toby
The Naked Snail & Head Salad,
Pen y Dropp,
Llan Cebab,
Carmarthenshire SA1B T0F
tel   0101 0100010

map: 8 entry: 517

map: 0 entry: 518

Harbourmaster Hotel
Aberaeron

Like a butterfly from a chrysalis, an old spit-and-sawdust pub has metamorphosed into a smart hotel with bar and restaurant. The accolades that have followed are entirely justified: Glyn and Menna Heulyn's dedication to all that is best about Wales shines forth. Among the jolly Georgian frontages on the bay, the Harbourmaster is an unmissable blue. Inside you find a space that's cosy but cool: soft shades, a curving bar, an open fire, solid blocked-oak tables. In the restaurant, daily menus are studded with the best local produce: Carmarthen ham, Sir gar butter, Talybont jams, free-range eggs, organic leaves, oceans of fish. The young chef is a dab hand at chargrilled Welsh Black beef with square-cut chips and watercress sauce, perfect grilled trout, raspberry and yogurt bavarois and passionfruit coulis. Then up the listed spiral stair to bedrooms with harbour views and cosy minimalism where you have all you need, from powerful showers to CDs. Come for lobster boats at lunch, twinkling harbour lights at dinner, real ale, well-chosen wines and dazzling service. Splendid coastal walks are at the door, there are dolphins in the bay and beaches a short drive away.

directions	Between Aberystwyth & Cardigan off A487.
meals	12pm-2pm; 6-30pm-9pm. Main courses £9.50-£16.50.
rooms	7: 5 doubles, 2 singles £85-£105. Singles £55.
closed	Sun evenings; Monday lunchtimes.

	Glyn & Menna Heulyn Harbourmaster Hotel, Pen Cei, Aberaeron, Ceredigion SA46 0BA
tel	01545 570755
web	www.harbour-master.com

map: 7 entry: 519

Conwy

Kinmel Arms
St George

One of those places that local growers take pride in supplying and diners flock to. It's for the sheer pride that Lynn and Tim take in what goes on the plate – Conwy Bay seafood and top quality meats, simple local food that is fresh and beautifully cooked. When they took over just two years ago, it was a run-down, barred and bolted pub; now it sports open-plan bars, a comfy dining room and a conservatory that looks down over the village. Plenty of real ales and wines by the glass are an added bonus when tucking into chicken Caesar salad with freshly-baked rolls, "boat-sinking battered cod" with tartare sauce, or a signature dish of Welsh Black beef with caramelised leeks that has earned the kitchen more than a little notoriety.

directions	A55 for Conwy. After Bodelwyddan exit, next exit, forSt George. Left at junc.; follow road up for 200yds.
meals	12pm-2pm; 6.30pm-9pm. Main courses £2.95-£16.95; set menu £14.95 Tues & Thurs.
rooms	4 suites, full board. Call for prices.
closed	3.30pm-6.30pm; Mondays except Bank Holidays; Sunday evenings.

Tim & Lynn Cunnah-Watson
Kinmel Arms,
The Village, St George,
Abergele, Conwy LL22 9BP
tel 01745 832207
web www.thekinmelarms.co.uk

map: 12 entry: 520

Conwy

The Queen's Head
Glanwydden

The old wheelwright's cottage has gone up in the world. It now has low beams, polished tables, walls strewn with old maps and a roaring fire in the bar. The food is good, the portions generous and you can see the cooks at work through the open hatch. This is home-cooked pub food with a modern twist that in summer might be fresh Conwy crab and Great Orme lobster. No need to stand on ceremony; in the lounge you eat on a first-come, first-served basis. Try your Welsh lamb cutlets and lavender and port sauce with a pint of Burton ale, then go to the buffet to collect your pudding: chocolate nut fudge pie, black cherry cheesecake, bara brith bread-and-butter pudding. Robert and Sally Cureton have been here for years, nurturing a country local that puts those of Llandudno to shame. No need to go home: there's a cottage for two in the grounds and it's exquisite.

directions	From A55; A470; right at 3rd r'bout for Penrhyn Bay; 2nd right to Glanwydden after 1.5 miles.
meals	12pm-2pm; 6pm-9pm; 12pm-9pm Sundays. Main courses £8.25-£14.50.
rooms	1 cottage for 2 £100-£125.

Robert & Sally Cureton
Queen's Head,
Glanwydden, Llandudno Junction,
Conwy LL31 9JP
tel 01492 546570
web www.queensheadglanwydden.co.uk

map: 12 entry: 521

Denbighshire

The Boat
Erbistock, Wrexham

An old riverside favourite that draws crowds in summer. Spruced up but not without traditional charm, this original 17th-century pub has open fires, stone floors, bare brick walls, heavy oak beams and a bright conservatory of marble-topped tables and metal-and-wicker chairs. The view from its picture windows is of lines of picnic benches on the Dee river bank. Fresh open and closed sandwiches by day yield, in the evening, to white onion and tarragon soup, trout with pine nuts and lemon butter, and pan-fried chicken breast with caramelised onions – the stuff of 'mod-Brit' pub food. Wine choices, though limited, are global; there is a regularly changing choice of real ales and Addlestone's Cloudy cider on handpump. Cheery, youthful staff whizz around at quite a pace; perhaps they've also selected the 'background' music – and its volume!

directions	From Wrexham A483 for Chirk; A359 to Erbistock.
meals	12pm-2.30pm; 6.30pm-9pm (9.30pm Fridays & Saturdays). Main courses £5-£8; set menu £25 (2 courses for 2 people). Call for winter food offers.
closed	Sunday evenings in winter.

Andrew Coke
The Boat,
Erbistock, Wrexham,
Denbighshire LL13 0DL
tel   01978 780666
web   www.theboatinn.co.uk

map: 8 entry: 522

Glamorgan

The Blue Anchor
East Aberthaw

Inglenooks and open log fires, stories of smugglers and derring-do – it's rich in atmosphere. Inside is a warm warren of little rooms and doorways less than five feet high. The Colemans have cheerfully nurtured this 700-year-old place for almost half a century. Dine in winter on pheasant from their local shoot; in summer on sewin from Swansea Bay and salads from the vegetable garden. You can pop in for a sandwich at any time and a pint of well-kept Boddingtons – or dip into the chef's selection of regional cheeses at almost giveaway prices. Under the eaves of a classic thatched roof, the restaurant delivers steamed Penclawdd cockles from the Gower, spinach and cream cheese mousse, fillet of turbot in tomato and prawn bisque, beef Wellington, Sunday roasts (do book). It's pubby, good looking and wonderful at doing what it knows best.

directions	2 miles west of Cardiff Airport just off B4265.
meals	12pm-2pm (2.30pm Sundays); 6-8pm (bar); 7-9.30pm (restaurant). Main courses £6.50-£8.50.

Jeremy Coleman
The Blue Anchor,
East Aberthaw,
Glamorgan CF62 3DD
tel   01446 750329
web   www.blueanchoraberthaw.com

map: 2 entry: 523

Gwynedd

Penhelig Arms Hotel
Aberdyfi

You may fall in love with the Penhelig and wake up in the dead of night wishing you were there. The magnificent Dyfi estuary can inspire awe in the fiercest storm or lie like a millpond under the full moon. It's a place to share with someone special, such is the hospitality and kindness shown by the Hughes family and their staff. In front is the tiniest harbour, whence you can still set sail for Anglesey, while along the quay come the fishermen, butchers, bakers and various smallholders who deliver their daily produce to Jane's kitchen. Her seemingly inexhaustible menus are up-dated at every session to reflect what's wettest and freshest that day. At white-clothed tables you may feast on mediterranean fish soup, plaice with a buttery prawn velouté sauce, chargrilled leg of Welsh lamb steak with roast vegetables, panna cotta with fresh fruit. Soup and sandwiches are the staples of the pub bar, extra-cosy with its central log fire; on sunnier days they'll serve you at your chosen spot astride the harbour wall. Robert is in charge "of the ales and wines only" – but all are impeccably chosen and in the right spirit. And the bedrooms have sea views.

directions	From Dolgellau, A470 for Porthmadog; A493 to Aberdyfi.
meals	12pm-2pm; 7pm-9pm. Main courses £2.75-£22.
rooms	14: 4 twins/doubles, 9 doubles £70-£92. Singles £42.

Robert & Sally Hughes
Penhelig Arms Hotel,
Aberdyfi,
Gwynedd LL35 0LT
tel   01654 767215
web   www.penheligarms.com

map: 7 entry: 524

Bell at Skenfrith
Skenfrith

Hedonism is 'in' at this swish gastropub in a 17th-century coaching inn on the banks of the River Monnow. Follow remote country lanes to a blissful village setting, with a ruined Norman castle and an ancient humpback bridge. The inside is smartly done but informal, and run with warmth – Janet treats staff like members of the family. Expect the best of everything: coffee comes from a proper cappuccino machine, food is mostly organic, there's Freeminer Bitter and the wine is superb. There's even an organic menu for kids (Mash Bang Wallop etc). Bedrooms, all different, are luxurious, with Farrow & Ball colours and beds dressed in cotton piqué and Welsh wool; there are homemade biscuits, Molton Brown goodies, even a hi-tech console by the bed so you can listen to music in your bath. After an energetic day out on the river or hills tuck into braised pheasant in a cabbage, baby onion and potato cocotte in the candlelit restaurant. Polish it off with tarte tatin and toast the occasion with a glass of perry. Then flop into one of the big sofas next to a blazing fire.

directions	From Monmouth B4233 to Rockfield; B4347 for 5 miles; right on B4521 for Ross. Pub 1 mile.
meals	12-2.30pm; 7-9.30pm (9pm Sun). Main courses £11.90-£17.60.
rooms	8: 5 doubles, 1 twin/double, 2 twins £90-£150. Singles £70-£110.
closed	Mondays November-March; 2 weeks end January/early February.

William & Janet Hutchings
Bell at Skenfrith,
Skenfrith, Abergavenny,
Monmouthshire NP7 8UH
tel   01600 750235
web   www.skenfrith.co.uk

map: 8 entry: 525

Monmouthshire

The Clytha Arms
Clytha

The lovely country inn with its palatine frontage stands on the old coaching route into border country. You may sit outside in fine weather and enjoy cockles, crab sandwiches or a ploughman's that promises three local cheeses. In the kitchen is Andrew Canning, the local genius who rustles up hake fish cakes with spiced tomato salsa at a moment's notice. The monthly à la carte menu has blue cheese and port soufflé, John Dory with prawns and capers, prune and armagnac ice cream. Wines, local beers and Herefordshire ciders are excellent too, and there's homemade perry for the bibulously curious. Solid furniture, log fires, draughts and darts in the bar – it's the sort of place where younger members of the family serve in jeans and nobody minds a bit.

directions	6 miles east of Abergavenny off old Abergavenny to Raglan road.
meals	12.30pm-2.15pm; 7pm-9.30pm. No food Sun evenings & Mondays. Main courses £5.25-£10; set menu £17.95.
rooms	4 twins/doubles £70-£90. Singles £50-£70.
closed	Monday lunchtimes.

Andrew & Sarah Canning
The Clytha Arms,
Clytha, Abergavenny,
Monmouthshire NP7 9BW
tel 01873 840206
web www.clytha-arms.com

map: 8 entry: 526

Monmouthshire

The Trekkers
The Narth

High on a wooded escarpment between the Wye and the Usk valleys, this isolated log cabin attracts few passers-by. Yet its amazing position acts as a magnet to walkers, twitchers and pub historians. (Digest the pamphlets and guides as you cradle your pint.) The Wye Valley Brewery supplies its own Summer Ale while the kitchen produces hearty ploughmans, pungent curries and uses local butchers' meats, all in quantities to satisfy the heartiest fresh-air-sharpened appetites. Looking out over wild woodland, the pine-clad bar has a central brick fireplace around which, at weekends, you will almost certainly have to hunt for a space. (Larger parties should call Susan in advance for a cooked-to-order meal.) There's one rough-and-ready, self-contained sleeping unit with breakfast provisions laid on, perfect for walkers – or you can camp nearby, disturbed only by the odd screech owl.

directions	Signed to the north of B4293 between Trellech & Monmouth.
meals	12pm-2pm; 6pm-9pm. Main courses £8-£10.
rooms	1 twin, from £40.
closed	Mon-Wed except Bank Holidays.

Susan & Peter Fowler
The Trekkers,
The Narth,
Trellech, Monmouth,
Monmouthshire NP25 4QG
tel 01600 860367

map: 8 entry: 527

Monmouthshire

Monmouthshire

Black Bear
Bettws Newydd

The first thing you see is the bar with a band of regulars enjoying their Timothy Taylor's. Beyond the glowing fire (patron-chef Molyneux drove off in mid-interview to get more coal!) is a dining room that hints at passion for the Sport of Kings. At the lower end are more dining tables in what looks like a 1930s tea room, but the Black Bear actually dates from the 16th-century and some original features remain. Stephen Molyneux uses produce in season, Usk salmon, pheasant, venison and duck, for example. And there's avocado with hot seafood, beef fillet with stilton, Welsh lamb rack with minted cream sauce, and – heaven on a plate for some – Baileys Irish Cream cheesecake. Whatever comes out of the kitchen will be unusual, unpredictable and very good. Why not stay? Bedrooms are modest and quiet, and you will feast on local farm bacon and free-range eggs in the morning.

Raglan Arms
Llandenny

Two reasons to stop here – the castle and the pub. The Raglan Arms has had new life breathed into by Ian and Carol's successful makeover and now effortlessly combines its function of village local and excellent place to eat. A sense of anticipation mounts as you read the daily-changing blackboards from the plush leather sofas arranged around the log fire. You won't be disappointed... risotto of wild mushrooms and herbs, heaps of fresh fish and shellfish, excellent local pork and leek sausages with mash, char-grilled chicken, Caesar salad. Cheeses come from the best local suppliers, as does the meat. There's a conservatory restaurant, too, where you can try wild boar with black-and-white puddings and Dijon sauce and salmon fillet with leeks and brie. Good real ales that change regularly and very fairly priced wines from a short but global list are the icing on the cake. Well worth the small detour to get here.

directions	On B4595 2 miles north of Usk.
meals	12pm-2pm; 6pm-9pm. Main courses £6-£12.
rooms	7: 3 doubles, 2 twins, 2 family £50-£65. Singles £25.
closed	Monday lunchtimes.

directions	In the centre of Llandenny.
meals	12pm-2pm; 7pm-9pm. Must book: only 12 tables. Main courses £7.75-£14.80.
closed	Sunday evenings; Mondays except Bank Holidays.

Stephen Molyneux
Black Bear,
Bettws Newydd,
Usk,
Monmouthshire NP15 1JN

tel 01873 880701

map: 8 entry: 528

Ian & Carol Black
Raglan Arms,
Llandenny,
Monmouthshire NP15 1DL

tel 01291 690800

map: 8 entry: 529

Monmouthshire

The Greyhound Inn
Llantrissant

Nick and Helen's business relies on their total commitment to running a residential country inn properly. It takes a little finding on the back roads out of Usk but anyone will point you in the right direction: look for massive summer flower baskets and a pine and 'collectables' shop. Separate bedrooms are in the former stable block (treble-glazed against the dual carriageway hum) with its own pretty garden and trout pond. Linked bars with open fires ooze with pine and there's a huge menu – prawn and chilli coriander fishcakes, smoked Welsh venison with junipers and orange, sirloin steak with port and stilton sauce, spinach and wild mushroom canelloni. Freshly caught Usk salmon or trout is a firm and succulent favourite. Quaff up to half a dozen real ales, classic bottled ciders and wines of the month at giveaway prices. Staff couldn't be friendlier, and there's lots of spoiling for both families and dogs.

directions	Off A449. From Usk centre follow signs to Llantrissant for 2.5 miles.
meals	12pm-2.15pm; 6pm-10.30pm. Main courses £6.70-£13.60.
rooms	10: 2 doubles £70, 6 twins, 2 family, £70. Singles £51.

Nick Davies
The Greyhound Inn,
Llantrissant, Usk,
Monmouthshire NP15 1LE
tel 01291 672505/673447
web www.greyhound-inn.com

map: 8 entry: 530

Pembrokeshire

Cresselly Arms
Cresswell Quay

The day we called, trainer Peter Bowen's Cresswell Quay had just won his fourth race of the season and there was an air or euphoria. We were treated to beer that was that much better than we had any right to ask and the horse was paying! The walls of this old pub are hung with wisteria; you can sit at tables outside and gaze out onto the estuary and tranquil woods. Inside, meet Mrs Cole pouring real ale from a plastic jug. When asked how long this place had been in the family, she riposted "donkeys' years". There's no truck with modern innovation here. You down well-kept pints surrounded by memorabilia of a more sober age: cast-iron grate, red-and-black tiled floors, coal-fired Aga in the parlour. And, of course, pictures ancient and new of famous nags. The local talk (and occasionally TV) will be of horses and history. When the tide is up, you can get here by boat… you won't be late for lunch – there isn't any. Take home instead a jar of the famous lemon curd.

directions	Off A4075 between A40 & A477.
meals	No food served.
closed	3pm-5pm Mon-Fri (7pm Sun).

Maurice & Janet Cole
Cresselly Arms,
Cresswell Quay,
Pembroke,
Pembrokeshire SA68 0TE
tel 01646 651210

map: 7 entry: 531

The Old Point House Inn
Angle

So close to the sea, they're cut off at spring tide! The little old flagstoned inn, part-built with shipwreck timbers, was originally a bakehouse for ships' biscuits. Doug was a fisherman on this coast for years and son Lee is an accomplished cook. Expect to find the best homemade Milford cod fishcakes around, served with piles of chips, alongside John Dory fillets in modern mediterranean style. In fine weather, sit outside and devour vast prawn sandwiches. Inside, to one side, is a dining area; to the other, a place where the farmers and fishermen meet over pints of Felinfoel and cider. Wallcharts show the navigation channels to get sailors home in the morning and there are three perfectly acceptable bedrooms for the rest of you. The jetty and lifeboat post are rare and special survivors and, as the walk around Angle Point literally passes the door, you'd be a spoilsport not to call in.

The George's
Haverfordwest

Nothing in Pembrokeshire can hold a candle to John and Lesley's café, pub and diner. Up on the hillside overlooking castle and town, its walled, award-winning garden has stupendous views. The old brewhouse is much as it always was, only funkier, and now you can buy all sorts of eco-friendly items – hemp bags, leather sandals and candles. There is an inexhaustible supply of coffee along with real ales and splendid wines. The honest, wholesome cooking is based almost entirely on local produce, including organic vegetables from the Lewis's own farm. Look out for Cardigan Bay crab cakes with toasted pine nuts; fillets of sewin in a lime and fennel butter; pasta with wild mushroom sauce; 'raw food energy salad'. John and Lesley can claim a real food menu that really stands out from the crowd.

directions	From Pembroke follow signs for Angle. There, from Lifeboat Trust in village, cross beach to pub.
meals	12pm-2.30pm; 6.30pm-9pm. Main courses £6.50-£20.
rooms	3 twins/doubles £50. Singles £25.
closed	Tuesdays November-March.

directions	Follow signs for town centre & then St Thomas Green. Left into Hill St; left opp. cinema into Market St.
meals	11.45am-5pm (9.45pm Fri & Sat). Main courses £5.50-£9.50.
closed	Sundays.

Doug, Carol & Lee Smith
The Old Point House Inn,
Angle,
Pembroke,
Pembrokeshire SA71 5AS

tel   01646 641205

map: 7 entry: 532

John Glasby & Lesley Lewis
The George's,
24 Market Street,
Haverfordwest,
Pembrokeshire SA61 1NH

tel   01437 766683

map: 7 entry: 533

Pembrokeshire

The Druidstone
Broad Haven

Extraordinary, perched high above a sandy beach looking northwest towards the sweep of Cardigan Bay. This is an inn with rooms and the sort of place where everyone feels part of the family. Few drop by just for a drink: there's no pub sign and the cellar bar operates as a member's club, sometimes late into the night. Terrific food, happily roaming children and unruly pets are all part of the scene, and a landlord brimming with bonhomie. Barring two roof-top suites, bedrooms are pretty basic but most share views that are little short of sensational; the same can be said of the massive cooked breakfasts, which include homemade breads and marmalades. Developed around a Victorian stone mansion by the Bell family over the last 30 years, several cottages are sprinkled over the estate. Druidstone has become an institution, and you'd be crazy not to try it out for yourself.

directions	Off B4341, 6 miles W of Haverfordwest.
meals	12.30pm-2.30pm; 7pm-9.30pm. Main courses £6-£8.
rooms	11 twins/doubles £70-£116. Singles from £35.
closed	Midweek Nov, Jan & Feb.

Rod & Jane Bell
The Druidstone,
Broad Haven, Haverfordwest,
Pembrokeshire SA62 3NE

tel   01437 781221
web   www.druidstone.co.uk

map: 7 entry: 534

Pembrokeshire

The Wolfe Inn
Wolfscastle

We salute Gianni di Lorenzo, Pembroke's honorary Welshman – a shining light in good inn-keeping and a leader in promoting local produce for an ever-enthusiastic following. The pub, too, is a delight, its hub the locals' bar which leads back into separate dining rooms (all different) and a conservatory, prettily candlelit at night. Pride of place goes to the chilled cabinet of Italian desserts to which the British have so willingly become addicted: authentic tiramisu and the booziest gâteaux. When there is nobody else to hand, the landlord himself will rustle you up a meal; anything you like, from the famous Wolfe pâté to slow-cooked Welsh lamb shank and Pembrokeshire seafood – possibly lobster and fillets of plaice in a light breadcrumb crust. There's baked avocado with crabmeat and pasta with Italian green pesto. As well as real ale and cider you have some remarkable collector's wines – from Italy, naturally.

directions	Between Fishguard & Haverfordwest on A40.
meals	12pm-2pm; 6.30pm-9pm. Main courses £4.95-£12.95; set menu £15.
rooms	3: 2 twins, 1 double £60-£70. Singles £45.

Gianni di Lorenzo
The Wolfe Inn,
Wolfscastle, Haverfordwest,
Pembrokeshire SA62 5LS

tel   01437 741662
web   www.thewolfe.info

map: 7 entry: 535

Pembrokeshire

Pendre Inn
Cilgerran

Brooding beside the River Teifi, this small village with its medieval castle is an historian's dream. So is the white 14th-century stone inn, whose frontage appears about to be uprooted by the gnarled ash that almost blocks its tiny entrance. Just about as tiny inside, with a single bar on two levels, lovely old worn stone flags, oak beams and log-burning inglenook. City-slickers will blanch (with envy) at the price of a pint of Tomos Watkin, or Thatchers cloudy cider, and good sirloin steak with all the trimmings comes for well under a tenner. And there is more: the dining room on the other side is romantic, candlelit and cluttered with collectables; here, you can quietly tackle dishes that could feed a small family. Typically liver, bacon and onions might come with a stroganoff sauce or a whale-sized piece of Milford Haven haddock with as many chips as the kitchen can muster. 'As old as old can be', almost, and well worth the detour.

directions	Off A478 from Cardigan south.
meals	12pm-2pm; 6pm-8.30pm. Main courses £4.50-£7.95.
closed	3pm-6pm; Tuesdays; Sun evening.

Carol & Colin Dark
Pendre Inn,
High Street,
Cilgerran, Cardigan,
Pembrokeshire SA43 2SL

tel 01239 614223

map: 7 entry: 536

Powys

The Bear Hotel
Crickhowell

Viewed from the square of this small market town, the 16th-century frontage of the old coaching inn looks modest. Behind the cobbles and the summer flowers, it is a warren of surprises and mild eccentricity – bars and brasserie at the front, nooks and crannies carved at the back behind which is the family- and dog-friendly garden. The beamy lounge has parquet, plush seating and a mighty fire; settle in and savour their good beers, wines, whiskies and ports. There are two dining areas where at night you can feast on line-caught Usk salmon, Brecon venison and locally grown seasonal salads, vegetables and regional farmhouse cheeses. Homemade ice creams, mousses and puddings are equally sumptuous. We've never seen the place empty; the bedrooms around the courtyard are usually full. Octogenarian Mrs Hindmarsh is firmly in charge of an operation that rarely comes off the rails.

directions	On A40 between Abergavenny & Brecon.
meals	12pm-2pm; 6pm-10pm. No food Sundays. Main courses £6-£10.
rooms	35 twins/doubles, £70. Singles £55.

Judy Hindmarsh
The Bear Hotel,
High Street, Crickhowell,
Powys NP8 1BW

tel 01873 810408
web www.bearhotel.co.uk

map: 8 entry: 537

Powys

Nantyffin Cider Mill
Crickhowell

On the other side of the road, the River Usk pours down the valley. Diners pour in here for a sight of menus that feature the owners' home-grown produce from nearby Llangynidr at the foot of the Beacons. A cider press from the pub's previous life – it stretches back 350 years – occupies the middle of the main dining room; but you are more likely to eat in one of the two rather more intimate bars, choosing from blackboard daily specials or a bargain fixed-price Drover menu. The cooking is generally of high quality without perhaps setting the world on fire (depending on who is in the kitchen), although Black Mountain smoked salmon and ravioli of locally smoked chicken with leeks and bacon are delicious. There is plenty of fairly-priced traditional pub food to be taken with beers from Brains and Tomos Watkin, Old Rosie cider and a global wine list that features some interesting choices by the glass. Do check their somewhat erratic winter opening hours.

directions	1 mile outside Crickhowell on the A40 to Brecon.
meals	12pm-2.30pm; 6.30pm-10pm. Main courses £7.50-£16.
closed	3pm-6pm.

Glyn Bridgeman
Nantyffin Cider Mill,
Brecon Road, Crickhowell,
Powys NP8 1SG

tel 01873 810775
web www.cidermill.co.uk

map: 8 entry: 538

Powys

The Farmer's Arms
Cwmdu

This cracking place takes some beating, with Barney the dobermann in residence by the log stove, and the regulars propping up the bar. Filled with farm folk on Saturdays, there's no escaping the infectious laughter that fills the place. Commendable meals emanating from an open kitchen are a tribute to the produce from the farms and fisheries that dot this corner of The Beacons. Real ales and ciders are local too, and the careful choice of a handful of good quality wines is sensibly priced. Eat royally from the single menu either in the flagstoned bar hung with dried hops, or in the fancier dining room beyond, where vintage photographs and informal table settings add to a warm atmosphere. If tempted to make a night of it, the two bedrooms echo the simple pleasures of country living. Ideal for pony-trekkers and walkers in love with the Black Mountains.

directions	On A40, right onto A479; after 3 miles on right in centre of village.
meals	12pm-2pm; 7pm-10.30pm. Main courses £6-£15.
rooms	2 twins/doubles from £35. Singles from £20.
closed	Mondays; 3pm-6.30pm; 4-6.30pm Saturdays (7pm Sundays).

Andrew & Sue Lawrence
The Farmer's Arms,
Cwmdu, Crickhowell,
Powys NP8 1RU

tel 01874 730464
web www.thefarmersarms.com

map: 8 entry: 539

Usk Inn
Talybont-on-Usk

A few years ago, you may not even have noticed this old village inn; the village itself is barely discernible. But the Taylors took it on after years as hotel keepers and Michael installed himself in the kitchen. He has transformed the cooking and reinforced the emphasis on real ale, while the wine-of-the-month selection reveals a mix of passion and real knowledge. There's always soup and a sandwich and the daily-changing blackboard menus bring together the best ingredients from the Beacons and Usk Valley (the river is literally yards away). Michael has a light touch, too: faggots and peas come under the heading 'It must be Wales'- so don't ask what 'Burger It' means. Welsh Cawls, shank of Brecon lamb and salmon with chargrilled asparagus and butter sauce are filling and delicious. From Talybont you can follow trails along the Brecon Canal or up into the hills by Tor-y-Foel.

directions	Off A40 6 miles east of Brecon.
meals	12pm-3pm; 6.30pm-9pm. Main courses £7.95-£13.95.
rooms	11: 7 doubles, 3 twins, 1 single £70-£100.
closed	Christmas.

Michael & Barbara Taylor
Usk Inn,
Station Road, Talybont-on-Usk,
Brecon, Powys LD3 7JE
tel 01874 676251
web www.uskinn.co.uk

map: 8 entry: 540

The White Swan
Llanfrynach

The front resembles the row of cottages the pub once was. Its cavernous interior has been recently remodelled and its central bar is a split-level zone, making bar staff appear unnaturally tall as they serve Brains Bitter and other fine ales or wines. Make the most of the open fire, while you consider the Specials Board; it majors in fish so there are seared scallops with spicy salsa, and baked sea bass with chilli and basil, as well as chilli-chicken bruschetta with mediterranean veg, or strips of beef with wild mushroom risotto. The restaurant menu includes Hereford beef, Brecon lamb, local pheasant; the cheeses are Welsh, and the digestive biscuits homemade. There are farmhouse tables, leather sofas, big woodburners, and a trellised patio at the back – gorgeous in summer. You're spoilt for walks here, so stride off into the Brecon Beacons – or potter along the towpath of the Monmouthshire & Brecon canal.

directions	Signed from A40 3 miles east of Brecon on Crickhowell road.
meals	12pm-2pm; 12.30pm-3pm Sundays; 7pm-9.30pm (9pm Sundays). Main courses £10.45-14.95.
closed	Mondays & Tuesdays.

Stephen Way
The White Swan,
Llanfrynach, Brecon,
Powys LD3 7BZ
tel 01874 665276
web www.the-white-swan.com

map: 8 entry: 541

Powys

The Felin Fach Griffin
Brecon

Add a dash of London to a liberal dose of the Brecon Beacons and you have The Felin Fach Griffin. This bold venture mixes the buzz of a smart city bistro with the easy-going pace of good old country living and it's proving very popular. Full of casual elegance, the ground floor fans out from the bar into several eating and sitting areas with stripped pine and old oak furniture. Make for three giant leather sofas round the open fire, sit back and settle in. A Dutch chef stars in the kitchen, producing local smoked salmon, wild mushroom tagliatelli and braised ox cheeks with mash at smartly-laid tables, or opt for the rustic charm of the chatty backroom bar. Charles hosts with aplomb – he is young and ambitious, as are smiley staff who genuinely seem to be enjoying themselves. Bedrooms are in modern Scandinavian style with a few designer touches and breakfast is served round one table in the morning room; make your own toast on the Aga, as you like it, and enjoy the papers.

directions	On A470, 3.5 miles north of Brecon.
meals	12.30pm-2.30pm; 7pm-9.30pm. Main courses £11.50-£15.50.
rooms	7 twins/doubles £92-£115. Singles £67.50.

Charles Inkin
The Felin Fach Griffin,
Felin Fach,
Brecon, Powys LD3 0UB
tel 01874 620111
web www.eatdrinksleep.ltd.uk

map: 8 entry: 542

Powys

Castle Coaching Inn
Trecastle

For centuries it was a welcome stop for weary coachmen and their charges. The suitably-named Mr Porter is now in charge, and well qualified for the task. The pleasantly informal tiled bar has shiny pine tables, a log fire and a bow window overlooking the road; the old-fashioned, carpeted dining area is up a few steps. In the bar there are hot filled baguettes of bacon, mushrooms and melted cheese; in the dining room, perhaps pork hock with prune, apricot and orange sauce, 'subtly citrus' mousse and luxury ice creams. Greene King and Old Speckled Hen rival guest ales that change with unerring regularity and the house wines come at kind prices. Ask for a bedroom with bags of space if here with the family, many have sweeping valley views. Try to take a ride on the Brecon Mountain Railway; this is one of Wales' many areas of great beauty.

directions	10 miles west of Brecon on A40.
meals	12-2.30pm; 6-9pm (7pm Sundays). Main courses £7.95-£15.
rooms	8: 5 doubles, 1twin, 2 family £60-£100. Singles £45.
closed	Monday lunchtimes October-April.

John Porter
Castle Coaching Inn,
Trecastle,
Powys LD3 8UH
tel 01874 636354
web www.castle-coaching-inn.co.uk

map: 8 entry: 543

The Harp
Old Radnor

Landlord Erfyl meets and greets you like a mate, and sure as eggs you soon become one: it is the kind of place where you'd feel it's almost an insult to lock the bedroom door. Being so small – with arguably the tiniest bar counter in the county – it needs to be booked ahead, at least for Thursday's steak and fish nights. Enjoy a pint of Timothy Taylor's with a peppered Herefordshire rump steak, trout fillet with parmesan and basil cream, or maybe casserole of pork with apples and cider. The interior is spick-and-span: 14th-century slate flooring in the bar; tongue-and-groove in a tiny room that seats a dozen diners; crannies crammed with memorabilia. Village life remains unchanged: you can overlook the Radnor Forest from here at will, but don't expect much action until after sunset. Don't, either though, dream of driving anywhere else when there's a comfortable bed and a good breakfast to look forward to.

The Talkhouse
Pontdolgoch

From the outside it looks like a nice, neat pub. Which is exactly what it used to be. Today it serves a raft of bottled beers and over 70 'niche boutique' wines. The Garratt brothers have a winning formula in their 17th-century drovers' rest – exotic rooms, attentive service, marvellous food. The bar has beams, log fire and sumptuous sofas; the claret-and-cream dining room has French windows that open to the garden in summer, and you can dine outside. Bedrooms are rich and relaxing: one with a 1920s bathroom decorated in Moustier tiles, another with a corona over the bed and a shower of glass, stainless steel and African slate. Classical, seasonal cooking – the lightest sweet potato and butternut soup, the most delicately cooked Welsh lamb – is a treat, the daily-changing menu uses the finest local produce. Breakfasts come with fresh orange juice and homemade jam. A small, perfect find in the rolling wilderness of mid-Wales.

directions	From Kington A44; after 3 miles left for Old Radnor.
meals	12pm-2pm (weekends); 7pm-9pm. Main courses £8.75-£10.50.
rooms	5 doubles, 1 sharing bath, £58. Singles £35.
closed	Mondays.

directions	On A470 1 mile west of Caersws & 5 miles from Newtown.
meals	12pm-2pm; 7pm-9pm. Main courses £11-£15.95.
rooms	3 doubles £95. Singles £70.
closed	Sunday evenings & Mondays.

Erfyl & Heather Price
The Harp,
Old Radnor,
Powys LD8 2RH

tel 01544 350655

Stephen Garratt
The Talkhouse,
Pontdolgoch, Caersws,
Powys SY17 5JE

tel 01686 688919
web www.talkhouse.co.uk

map: 8 entry: 544

map: 8 entry: 545

Powys

The Lion
Berriew

A haven for country walkers as well as guests at local shoots and the history buffs who flock to Clive of India's former seat at nearby Powis (sic) Castle, this is just as a village pub should be, now thriving under the hands-on approach of its new licensees. The carpeted lounge bar remains very much the focal point for baguettes or a ploughman's with a pint of guest ale – perhaps Spitfire from Shepherd Neame – and there is a chalk-board of daily specials inspired by the best of the day's shopping which might mean Welsh lamb shoulder with mint gravy or salmon fillet with dill hollandaise. The black-and-white timbered restaurant mirrors the pub's striking exterior and is filled with landlord Tim Woodward's evocative photography of the area. Bedrooms are less chintzy than they used to be and more keenly priced – and all the better for both. The village setting next to the church makes up for any minor shortcomings.

directions	Off A483 from Welshpool.
meals	12pm-2pm; 7pm-9pm. Main courses £7.50-£15.
rooms	7: 5 doubles, 1 family, 1 twin £80. Singles £55.
closed	2.30pm-6pm; 3-7pm Sundays.

Tim Woodward
The Lion,
Berriew,
Welshpool,
Powys SY21 8PQ
tel   01686 640452

map: 8 entry: 546

WORTH A VISIT

Groes, Ty'n y Groes, Conwy, LL32 8TN 01492 650545
A 500-year-old drovers' inn much extended to include smart bedrooms and extra dining.
Real ale, a conservatory and gardens. Notable for its fabulous views over the Conwy Valley.

West Arms, Llanarmon Dyffryn Ceiriog, Denbighshire, LL20 7LD 01691 600665
Trout streams border the garden of this civilised 17th-century inn at the head of the fabulous
Ceiriog Valley. Modern Welsh dining. Worth staying after an all-day hike.

Plough Inn, The Roe, St Asaph, Denbighshire, LL17 0LU 01745 585080
North Wales's best example of gastropubbery. Real ale bar; wine shop; fresh fish and steaks
waiting on crushed ice to be cooked to order; art deco bistro. Gets busy.

The Corn Mill, Dee Lane, Llangollen, Denbighshire, LL20 8PN 01978 869555
Spectacular three-storey conversion of a derelict mill, with popluar summer terraces
teetering on the south bank of the Dee. Massive choice of real ales, wines and daily dishes.

Plough & Harrow, Monknash, Glamorgan, CF71 7QQ 01656 890209
Not the prettiest, but an enthusiast's pub – real ales from the cask and up to 300 bottles
of rare beers and ciders. Plenty of Guinness in the beef pie and logs on the fire.

Pelican in her Piety, Ewenny Road, Ogmore-by-Sea, Glamorgan, CF32 0QP 01656 880049
Fine views of the castle ruins across Ogmore river basin. Extraordinary interior of bare brick
and garish purple hue; at least six real ales and oriental twists to the traditional menu.

The George, Penmaenpool, Gwynedd, LL40 1YD 01341 422525
One of Wales's finest views across the Mawddah estuary towards Snowdonia. Family-friendly
basement and bedrooms in the former railway station (more hotel-like with new owners).

Pen-y-Gwryd Inn, Nant Gwynant, Gwynedd, LL55 4NT 01286 870211
Snowdonia's ex-mountain rescue HQ and training base for the 1953 Everest expedition.
See their boots in the bar; dine by candlelight; stay the night. A treasure.

Beaufort Arms, High Street, Raglan, Monmouthshire, NP15 2DY 01291 690412
Classic posting house by the gateway to the Brecons. Decent accommodation and meals;
warm atmosphere and log fires; real ales.

The Bridge Inn, The Back, Chepstow, Monmouthshire, NP16 5EZ 01291 625622
17th-century inn full of character, official start of Offa's Dyke path across cast-iron road bridge.
Unstuffy locals' bar with food to match: restaurant unashamedly 'grillroom', with unspoilt river views.

Hunter's Moon Inn, Llangattock, Monmouthshire, NP7 8RR 01873 821499
A classic – a 13th-century inn with bedrooms often booked by shooting and walking parties.
Be sure to arm yourself with good directions. Reports on new ownership, please.

Plantagenet House, Quay Hill, Tenby, Pembrokeshire, SA70 7BX 01834 842350
Local produce takes centre stage at this cavernous pub/bistro with its unique 12th-century
Flemish chimney. Own-recipe sausages, Tenby Bay crab and St David's cheeses.

Swan Inn, Little Haven, Pembrokeshire, SA62 3UL 01437 781256
Highly traditional pub on the coastal path by one of the coast's prettiest inlets. Welsh cawl
and sandwiches for lunch. Book for dinners and check eccentric winter opening hours.

Stackpole Inn, Stackpole, Pembrokeshire, SA71 5DF 01646 672324
Former village store and post office of this hamlet on the fringe of spectacular National Trust coastline. Great choice of fresh local dishes in whopping portions.

Griffin Inn, Llsywen, Powys, LD3 0UR 01874 754241
Old coaching inn with plenty of local trade, Brains beers and passable bedrooms. Fresh fish from Newlyn, salmon from the Wye and lamb from the Beacons.

Red Lion, Llanfihangel–nant–Melan, Powys, LD8 2TN 01544 350220
Family-owned and run, there's a caring attitude, comfy accommodation and some bright ideas in the kitchen. New ownership – reports please.

Brickys, Chirbury Road, Montgomery, Powys, SY15 6QQ 01686 668177
A new crew puts food first in a restaurant-bar that keeps its pubby feel. Steak-and-onion baguettes, baked trout, Welsh borders cheeses, a good pint and a pot of peppermint tea.

WHAT'S IN THE BACK OF THE BOOK?

Best for Real Ale • Best Breweries on site • Best unspoilt pubs • Best for Locally sourced/Organic produce • Best for Fish • Best for Cheese • Best Waterside pubs • Best Pubs with views • Best Winter pubs • Best Summer pubs

What is Alastair Sawday Publishing?

www.specialplacestostay.com

Fragile Earth series

Six Days

Book order form

Report form

Quick reference indices
50% or more of local produce used & a significant percentage organic • Pub & loo access for wheelchair users • Dogs welcome in some areas of pub • No piped music • Live music • Family room

Index by pub name

Index by town

How to use this book

Explanation of symbols

BEST FOR...

BEST FOR REAL ALE
- Shepherds Arms, Ennerdale Bridge, Cumbria • 75
- Bridge Inn, Topsham, Devon • 116
- The Swan, Little Totham, Essex • 141
- The Ostrich, Newland, Gloucestershire • 170
- Royal Oak, Fritham, Hampshire • 180
- White Horse, Parsons Green, London SW6 • 266
- The Victoria, Beeston, Nottinghamshire • 320
- Turf Tavern, Oxford, Oxfordshire • 346
- Halfway House, Pitney, Somerset • 374
- The Crown, Churchill, Somerset • 383

PUBS WITH OWN BREWERIES ON SITE
- Old Crown, Hesket Newmarket, Cumbria
  (Hesket Newmarket Brewery) • 71
- Queens Head, Tirril, Cumbria (Tirril Brewery) • 73
- Drunken Duck Inn, Barngates, Cumbria
  (Barngates Brewery) • 79
- Flower Pots Inn, Cheriton, Hampshire
  (Cheriton Brewhouse) • 184
- Swan on the Green, West Peckham, Kent
  (Swan Brewery) • 207
- Church Inn, Uppermill, Manchester
  (Saddleworth Brewery) • 225
- Bell Inn, East Langton, Leicestershire
  (Langton Brewery) • 234
- Greenwich Union, Greenwich, London SE7
  (Meantime Brewery) • 284
- Baltic Fleet, Liverpool, Merseyside (Wapping Brewery) • 287
- Grainstore Brewery, Oakham, Rutland • 348
- Exeter Arms, Barrowden, Rutland (Blencowe Brewery) • 353
- Old Cannon Brewery, Bury St Edmunds, Suffolk • 389
- St Peter's Hall, St Peter South Elmham, Suffolk
  (St Peter's Brewery) • 406
- Plough Inn, Coldharbour, Surrey (Leith Hill Brewery) • 411
- The Talbot, Knightwick, Worcestershire
  (Teme Valley Brewery) • 474

BEST FOR...

BEST FOR...

BEST FOR FISH

BEST FOR CHEESE

BEST FOR...

BEST WATERSIDE PUBS
- Shipwrights Arms Helford, Cornwall • 58
- Pandora Inn, Mylor Bridge, Cornwall • 60
- The Ship, Noss Mayo, Devon • 104
- Ferry Boat Inn, Dittisham, Devon • 107
- Ship Inn, Wandsworth, London SW18 • 268
- White Horse, Brancaster Staithe, Norfolk • 299
- Old Ship, Seahouses, Northumberland • 309
- Boat Inn, Erbistock, Wrexham • 522
- Penhelig Arms, Aberdyfi, Gwynedd • 524
- Cresselly Arms, Cresswell Quay, Pembrokeshire • 531
- Trout at Tadpole Bridge, Buckland Marsh, Oxfordshire • 341

BEST PUBS FOR VIEWS
- Mole & Chicken, Easington, Buckinghamshire • 32
- Pheasant Inn, Higher Burwardsley, Cheshire • 49
- Halzephron Inn, Gunwalloe, Cornwall • 56
- Brackenrigg Inn, Ullswater, Cumbria • 74
- Drunken Duck, Barngates, Cumbria • 79
- Chequers, Woolsthorpe by Belvoir, Lincolnshire • 242
- White Horse, Brancaster Staithe, Norfolk • 299
- King William VI, Mickleham, Surrey • 413
- The Sportsman, Amberley, West Sussex • 426
- Griffin Inn, Fletching, East Sussex • 441
- The Castle, Edgehill, Warwickshire • 444
- The Millbank, Millbank, West Yorkshire • 480

BEST FOR...

BEST WINTER PUBS – REAL FIRES
- Mason's Arms, Cartmel Fell, Cumbria • 86
- Old Gate Inn, Brassington, Derbyshire • 96
- The Harrow, Steep, Hampshire • 182
- Three Chimneys, Biddenden, Kent • 211
- Falkland Arms, Great Tew, Oxfordshire • 344
- Royal Oak, Luxborough, Somerset • 367
- Halfway House, Pitney, Somerset • 374
- Kings Head, Laxfield, Suffolk • 405
- Lickfold Inn, Lickfold, West Sussex • 416
- Blue Lion, East Witton, North Yorkshire • 499

BEST SUMMER GARDENS
- Royal Oak, Bovingdon Green, Buckinghamshire • 34
- Shipwright Arms, Helford, Cornwall • 58
- Shave Cross Inn, Marshwood, Dorset • 124
- Riverside Inn, Aymestrey, Herefordshire • 189
- The Dove, Dargate, Kent • 220
- The Crown, Old Dalby, Leicestershire • 236
- Lamb Inn, Burford, Oxfordshire • 340
- Hundred House, Norton, Shropshire • 361
- The Stag, Eashing, Surrey • 408
- Star Inn, Old Heathfield, East Sussex • 436

WHAT IS ALASTAIR SAWDAY PUBLISHING?

These books owe their style and mood to Alastair's miscellaneous career and his interest in the community and the environment

To publish good books is not just a matter of publishing well. The effort needs something more. How shall we continue to publish, with integrity and flair, the best books of their kind?

One solution is to make the company as 'human' as possible. Thus we encourage spontaneity and sensitivity, creativity and whimsy. Each of the 30 or so individuals who work here is allowed to be himself or, more commonly, herself. Somehow it shows, as each book takes on something of the personality of the people involved.

We have dogs in the office; it is hard to be pompous with a dog demanding a tickle. They are stress-relievers, too; staff are more likely to be found stroking a dog than kicking a computer.

We try to be alive to the big issues, too. So we have a Green Team that pushes us to reduce our ecological footprint (we are already Carbon Neutral). We do the strangest things: we put recycled vegetable oil in our diesel car and have experimented with electric bikes. We ponder ethical matters, with a separate Team to raise and debate tricky questions, and have our own charitable trust, operated by staff. Our annual 'away' session was devoted to the question of how to run an ethical business.

This year we are launching a Fine Breakfast scheme among our UK owners, to celebrate and encourage the use of local and organic food. And we are looking for ways of encouraging environmental initiatives among our owners.

Lastly, we have our own set of environmental books, under the imprint Fragile Earth Books. The Little Earth Book is in its fourth edition. The other books, radical and provocative, are The Little Food Book and The Little Money Book.

All these initiatives are intended, among other things, to give us extra spark, an added dash of interest – qualities that, we hope, show in our books. We will battle to avoid becoming dull, witless, sclerotic, devoid of soul and just another publishing company.

So the pubs you find in here are a dazzling mixture of the smart and the engagingly scruffy, the authentic and the unusual – just like the B&Bs and hotels in our other books. I hope they bring you moments of deep pleasure.

WWW.SPECIALPLACESTOSTAY.COM

Britain

France

Ireland

Italy

Portugal

Spain

Morocco

India

and, soon, Ski

all in one place!

On the unfathomable and often unnavigable sea of online accommodation pages, those who have discovered **www.specialplacestostay.com** have found it to be an island of reliability. Not only will you find a database full of trustworthy, up-to-date information about all the Special Places to Stay across Europe, but also:

- Links to the web sites of all of the places in the series

- Colourful, clickable, interactive maps to help you find the right place

- The opportunity to make most bookings by e-mail – even if you don't have e-mail yourself

- Online purchasing of our books, securely and cheaply

- Regular, exclusive special offers on books

- The latest news about future editions and future titles

- Notices about special offers, late availability and anything else our owners think you'll be interested in.

The site is constantly evolving and is frequently updated with news and special features that won't appear anywhere else but in our window on the worldwide web.

Russell Wilkinson, Web Producer
website@specialplacestostay.com

If you'd like to receive news and updates about our books by e-mail, visit the site and at the bottom of every page you can add yourself to our address book.

FRAGILE EARTH SERIES

The Little Earth Book
Now in its fourth edition
and as engrossing and
provocative as ever,
it continues to highlight
the perilously fragile
state of our planet.
£6.99

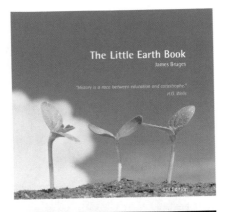

The Little Food Book
Makes for a wonderfully
stimulating read — one that
may change your
attitude to the
food choices you
make daily.
£6.99

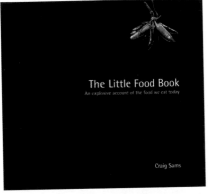

The Little Money Book
Could make you look
at everything financial —
from your bank statements
to the coins in your pocket —
in a whole new way.
£6.99

This fascinating series has been praised by politicians,
academics, environmentalists, civil servants — and 'general'
readers. It has come as a blast of fresh air, blowing away
confusion and incomprehension.

www.fragile-earth.com

SIX DAYS

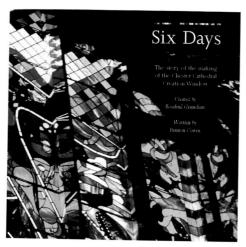

Celebrating the triumph of creativity over adversity

The inspiring and moving story of the making of the stained glass Creation window at Chester Cathedral by a woman battling with Parkinson's disease.

"Within a few seconds, the tears were running down my cheeks. The window was one of the most beautiful things I had ever seen. It is a tour-de-force, playing with light like no other window ..."

Anthropologist Hugh Brody

In 1983, Ros Grimshaw, a distinguished designer, artist and creator of stained-glass windows, was diagnosed with Parkinson's disease. Refusing to allow her illness to prevent her from working, Ros became even more adept at her craft, and in 2000 won the commission to design and make the Creation Stained Glass Window for Chester Cathedral.

Six Days traces the evolution of the window from the first sketches to its final, glorious completion as a rare and wonderful tribute to Life itself: for each of the six 'days' of creation recounted in Genesis, there is a scene below that is relevant to the world of today and tomorrow.

Extracts from Ros's diary capture the personal struggle involved. Superb photography captures the luminescence of the stunning stained glass, while the story weaves together essays, poems, and moving contributions from Ros's partner, Patrick Costeloe.

Available from Alastair Sawday Publishing £12.99

ORDER FORM UK

All these books are available in major bookshops or you may order them direct. **Post and packaging are FREE within the UK.**

		Price	No. copies
French Bed & Breakfast	Edition 8	£15.99	
French Hotels, Châteaux & Inns	Edition 3	£13.99	
French Holiday Homes	Edition 2	£11.99	
Paris Hotels	Edition 4	£9.99	
British Bed & Breakfast	Edition 8	£14.99	
British Hotels, Inns & Other Places	Edition 5	£13.99	
Bed & Breakfast for Garden Lovers	Edition 2	£14.99	
British Holiday Homes	Edition 1	£9.99	
Pubs & Inns of England & Wales	Edition 1	£13.99	
London	Edition 1	£9.99	
Ireland	Edition 4	£12.99	
Spain	Edition 5	£13.99	
Portugal	Edition 2	£8.99	
Italy	Edition 3	£12.99	
Europe with courses & activities	Edition 1	£12.99	
India	Edition 1	£10.99	
Morocco	Edition 1	£10.99	
The Little Earth Book	Edition 4	£6.99	
The Little Food Book	Edition 1	£6.99	
The Little Money Book	Edition 1	£6.99	
Six Days		£12.99	

Please make cheques payable to Alastair Sawday Publishing

Total £ _____

Please send cheques to: ASP, The Home Farm Stables, Barrow Gurney, Bristol BS48 3RW. For credit card orders call 01275 464891 or order directly from our web site www.specialplacestostay.com

Title _____ First name _____ Surname _____

Address _____

Postcode _____ Tel _____

If you would prefer not to receive information about special offers on our books, please tick here ☐

REPORT FORM

Comments on existing entries and new discoveries · If you have any comments on entries in this guide, please let us have them. If you have a favourite house, hotel, inn or other new discovery, please let us know about it.

Existing Entry:

Name of pub _____

Entry no: _____

Date of visit: _____

New recommendation:

Name of property: _____

Address: _____

_____

Postcode: _____

Tel: _____

Comments: _____

_____

_____

_____

Your name: _____

Address: _____

_____

_____

Postcode: _____

Tel: _____

Please send the completed form to:

Alastair Sawday Publishing,
The Home Farm Stables, Barrow Gurney, Bristol BS48 3RW
or go to www.specialplacestostay.com and click on 'contact'.

Pubs 1   Thank you.

QUICK REFERENCE INDICES

QUICK REFERENCE INDICES

QUICK REFERENCE INDICES

QUICK REFERENCE INDICES

INDEX - PUB

INDEX - PUB

INDEX - PUB

INDEX - PUB

INDEX - PUB

INDEX - TOWN

INDEX - TOWN

INDEX - TOWN

INDEX - TOWN

HOW TO USE THIS BOOK

sample entry

Hampshire

The Star Inn
East Tytherley

Come for comfort and good food to this 16th-century inn overlooking Tytherley's cricket pitch. In summer the front terrace is festooned with flowers, replete with big brollies and chessboard; in winter, there's a pew by the fire in the modernised bar. Although food is the main attraction, Paul and Sarah have kept the village pub atmosphere, with Ringwood Best on tap and a nice little skittle alley. Tuesdays and Saturdays in summer see The Star filled with thirsty cricketers. Eat in the bar or in the restaurant; the menu is modern British. Choose from old favourites like steak, kidney and Guinness pie and freshly battered cod and chips, or something more elaborate, such as exquisitely presented seared scallops with smoked salmon kedgeree, or beef fillet with potato rösti, foie gras and madeira jus. There are also sandwiches and filled jacket potatoes, and comfortable bedrooms in a building by the cricket pitch.

❶	directions	Off B3084 north of Romsey.
❷	meals	12pm-2pm; 7pm-9pm. Main courses £7-£17.
❸	rooms	3 twin/doubles £70. Singles £50.
❹	closed	Mondays except Bank Holidays; 26 December.

Paul & Sarah Bingham
The Star Inn,
East Tytherley, Romsey,
Hampshire SO51 0LW
tel 01794 340225
web www.starinn-uk.com

❺ 🕭 🕭 🕭 🕭 🕭 🕭 🕭 🕭

❻ map: 4 entry: 177

explanations

❶ **directions**
Use as a guide; the owner can give more details.

❷ **meals**
Approx. cost of a main course in restaurant or bar.

❸ **room price**
For two people sharing a room; single occupancy rate when it applies.

❹ **closed**
Assume normal pub hours (12pm-3pm; 6pm-11pm) unless stated otherwise.

❺ **symbols**
see the last page of the book for full explanation.

❻ **Map & entry numbers**
Map number; entry number.